Spectacle of Grief

Civil War America

Peter S. Carmichael, Caroline E. Janney, and Aaron Sheehan-Dean, editors

This landmark series interprets broadly the history and culture of the Civil War era through the long nineteenth century and beyond. Drawing on diverse approaches and methods, the series publishes historical works that explore all aspects of the war, biographies of leading commanders, and tactical and campaign studies, along with select editions of primary sources. Together, these books shed new light on an era that remains central to our understanding of American and world history.

Spectacle of Grief

*Public Funerals and Memory
in the Civil War Era*

SARAH J. PURCELL

The University of North Carolina Press
Chapel Hill

This book was published with the assistance of the Anniversary Fund of the University of North Carolina Press.

© 2022 Sarah J. Purcell
All rights reserved
Set in Minion Pro by Westchester Publishing Services
Manufactured in the United States of America

The University of North Carolina Press has been a member of the Green Press Initiative since 2003.

Library of Congress Cataloging-in-Publication Data
Names: Purcell, Sarah J., author.
Title: Spectacle of grief : public funerals and memory in the Civil War era / Sarah J. Purcell.
Other titles: Civil War America (Series)
Description: Chapel Hill : University of North Carolina Press, 2022. | Series: Civil War America | Includes bibliographical references and index.
Identifiers: LCCN 2021049358 | ISBN 9781469668321 (cloth ; alk. paper) | ISBN 9781469668338 (pbk. ; alk. paper) | ISBN 9781469668345 (ebook)
Subjects: LCSH: Funeral rites and ceremonies—United States—History—19th century. | Death—Social aspects—United States—History—19th century. | Collective memory—United States. | United States—History—19th century. | United States—History—Civil War, 1861-1865—Public opinion.
Classification: LCC GT3203 .P87 2022 |
    DDC 393/.93097309034—dc23/eng/20211022
LC record available at https://lccn.loc.gov/2021049358

Cover illustration: Detail of Joseph Becker, "The Late Senator Sumner. Ceremonies in the Capitol—Colored People of Washington, Headed by Frederick Douglass, Viewing the Remains," *Frank Leslie's Illustrated Magazine*, March 28, 1874. Courtesy of the Library of Congress Prints and Photographs Division.

Portions of this book were previously published in a different form. Chapter 1 includes material from "All That Remains of Henry Clay: Political Funerals and the Tour of Henry Clay's Corpse," *Commonplace: the Journal of Early American Life*, http://commonplace.online/article/remains-of-henry-clay/.

To my family and to my students

Contents

Illustrations and Maps

Maps

Acknowledgments

I extend thanks to everyone I have talked to for more than a decade who managed not to look too distressed when they asked, "So, what's your book about?" and I answered, "Funerals." So many people have aided me in researching and writing this book that a true accounting of my thanks would fill volumes. If I am able to convey even a shred of the gratitude that I feel, it will be remarkable. If I forget to mention someone, please forgive me. It has taken almost an army of people to get me to the finish line of this project.

I have been blessed to have been a faculty member at Grinnell College during the entire duration of this project, and the institution and its people have given me measureless support at every turn. Funds from the Committee for the Support for Faculty Scholarship, the Furbush Faculty Fellowship, the L. F. Parker Endowed Chair in History, and other sources supported my research and writing time. My colleagues in the history department give me strength every day not only to raise my level of teaching but to continue being an engaged scholar and friend. Grinnell College Libraries staff and librarians hold me up and nurture my scholarship. Special thanks must go to Richard Fyffe (gone way too soon), Mark Christel, Chris Jones, Catherine Rod, Julia Bauder, Allison Haack, Kevin Engle, Liz Rodrigues, Rebecca Ciota, Katie Dunn, Sharon Clayton, Leslie Gardner, Kim Gilbert, Karla Harter, Betty Santema, Amy Babb Brown, Micki Behounek, and Chelsea Soderblom. Other amazing Grinnell College colleagues who deserve acknowledgment include Susan Ferrari, Laura Nelson-Lof, Lisa Mulholland, and De Dudley.

Kathy Kamp spent years convincing me I could try GIS technology; then, when she founded Grinnell's Data Analysis and Social Inquiry lab, she launched a thousand research ships, the maps in this book among them. For additional help with mapping, Emily Hackman and I would like to thank Justin Erickson, Leif Brottem, Eric Carter, Sarah Sanders, Bonnie Brooks, all the folks at the first Institute for Liberal Arts Digital Scholarship (ILIADs) conference, Katie Walden, and Jeremy Atack (for generously sharing railroad shape files before they were public). For help in formatting the final maps, we also thank Stephanie Peterson for her skill and friendly help with Adobe Illustrator.

At UNC Press, I have received expert editorial advice and patience from the editorial director, Mark Simpson-Vos, and I thank the very able assistant editors Dominique Moore and María García. Immense thanks go to series editors Aaron Sheehan-Dean and Carline Janney, each of whom in different ways had great influence on this project and my ability to complete it. I also thank the anonymous readers for UNC Press, whose insights made this a richer and more significant work.

I benefited greatly from trips to and fellowships from archives and libraries all around the country. In its early stages, the research for this book was spurred by month-long fellowships at the Newberry Library and the American Antiquarian Society, both (in their own ways) models of scholarly community and support. I would especially like to thank Paul Erickson, Caroline Sloat, Philip Lampi, and Georgia Barnhill for guidance and help at AAS. B. J. Gooch, the special collections librarian at Transylvania University, was also very encouraging in early stages of my research and provided guidance about Henry Clay. At the Massachusetts Historical Society, Conrad Wright and Kate Viens offered direction and encouragements. Thanks also to librarians and archivists at the Virginia Historical Society, the College of William and Mary, the Library of Virginia, the New York Public Library, the Monroe County (NY) Public Library Special Collections, the Peabody Institute Library Archives (Peabody, MA), the Phillips Library at the Peabody Essex Museum, Washington and Lee University, Rice University, the University of Kentucky, the Library of Congress, the National Archives, the Army Medical Museum, the National Library of Medicine, Old Dominion University, the Historical Society of Pennsylvania, the American Philosophical Society, Harvard University, Brown University, the Abraham Lincoln Presidential Museum and Library, and the University of Texas at Austin.

Other scholarly colleagues have encouraged this work, organized panels where I tried out ideas, and provided intellectual support. A faculty-student summer fellowship for the Society for the Historians of the Early American Republic (SHEAR) Mellon seminar got me started on initial ideas for this project and provided research time in Philadelphia. Friends and colleagues from SHEAR have watched this work develop for well over a decade and cheered me on; I have special gratitude for Rosemarie Zagarri, Martha King, Patrick O'Neil, Steve Bullock, Catherine Denial, and John Brooke. Thanks also go to Volker Depkat, Megan Kate Nelson, Michael McDonnell, Fitzhugh Brundage, Clare Corbould, Frances Clark, Laura Free, Catherine Kelley, and Marvin Bergman for being so collegial and inspiring.

Students are at the center of my life, and without them this project would have been so much poorer. Over the many years I worked on this book, I was blessed to be able to conduct related independent, collaborative research with a slew of talented Grinnell College students, most of them as part of Grinnell's Mentored Advanced Project (MAP) program. Many summer MAP students provided intellectual community, research help, and good spirits. They have gone on to be successful lawyers, CPAs, museum professionals, journalists, ministers, musicians, businesspeople, librarians, data scientists, parents, and a few historians in their own right, but I have never forgotten the support and insight of any one of them, and they have a special place in my heart forever. First and foremost I must thank Emily Hackman, who is the cocreator of the maps in this book, for her creativity, calm intelligence, and drive. Other MAP students who provided assistance with parts of this book and who deserve eternal thanks are Sam Jones, Katy Alexander, Amy Drake, Becky Bessinger Bobba, Holly Lutwitze Rapp, Sean Warlick, Justin Erickson, Katharine Dean, Jon Richardson, Tom Elliott, Ethan Drutchas, Amanda Borson, Sara Lowenburg, Christian Snow, Evan Ma, Eric Mistry, Connor Schake, Hayes Gardner, Irene Bruce, Peter Bautz, Joey Kathan, Liz Sawka, Anthony Fitzpatrick, Sam Nakahira, Liz Stepp, Abby Doudna, Katie Orsund, Charun Upara, and Vince Reilly. All the students who have taken my U.S. Civil War and Reconstruction courses at Grinnell (and even earlier at Central Michigan University) let me try out ideas on them and have given me great inspiration, and I thank them.

In addition to the greatest students, I am beyond blessed to have the most wonderful friends who constantly support my work and my career as a historian and teacher. To all my friends who talked over this book on endless occasions, took me out to dinner, and provided places to stay when I was giving talks and traveling on research trips, I say, "Thanks, and keep it up!" Worthy of special appreciations are Dave Iaia, Sarah Leavitt, Jay Chervenak, Marie Myers, Ed Rafferty, Laura Prieto, Rich Canedo, Susie and Bill Hansley, Chrissy Cortina, David and Evelyn Krache Morris, Tom and Yancy Ackerman, Gary and Martha Anderson, Ed Senn, Elizabeth Prevost, Mike Guenther, Vance Byrd, and Ida Casey. Al Lacson's friendship and "accountability lunches" fueled me, especially during long summers. Laura Prieto has been my close friend and academic inspiration for almost thirty years, and without her crucial push in the summer of 2019, I would not have finished this book. Also key to the completion of this book was the newer (but essential) friendship and writing partnership of John Garrison, whose dedication and own scholarly accomplishments raise my horizons. I also thank Elaine Marzluff, Laureen VanWyk, Joyce Stern, Laura Sinnett, and all my "potluck" and church friends for their friendship, laughter, and constant support.

My family makes me who I am, and I rely on their love for every part of life. Scholarship is no different. No one could be more fortunate than I am in having a family who provides support in all the ups and downs of scholarly life. Before his death in 2020, my father, Ed Purcell, talked over every idea in this book with me, reading draft upon draft and giving me the same kind of affirming analysis and emotional balm that has sustained me all my life. He was simply the best, and my mourning for him will be eternal. My mother, Mary Purcell, gave constant love and care, as she has my whole life. My dear husband, Hugh Sheridan, whom I married not long before I started this project, sustains me with his love and support every single day. He has also given me additional great joy in my stepdaughter, Frances Beavers, and son-in-law, Brian Beavers, and the two best grandkids, Avery and Evelyn Beavers. When it is time for my own death and funeral, I know that I will rest easy, having lived a full and meaningful life because of my family.

Introduction

Frank Leslie's Illustrated Newspaper portrayed national mourning with a particular emphasis on Black grief in its extensive coverage of the March 13, 1874, public funeral for Sen. Charles Sumner, who had died of a heart attack on March 11. The cover of the issue featured a full-page visual tribute by *Frank Leslie's* head cartoonist Matt Morgan that aptly expressed the scale of the public mourning for Sumner that had filled the pages of newspapers and magazines for the two days prior. The cartoon showed a mourning female allegorical figure of Columbia placing a laurel wreath on Sumner's shrouded coffin, while a group of Black men and boys weep and pray reverently at its head, and overhead an angel descends bearing a banner reading "Equal Rights to All!" Instead of depicting Sumner as a foe of President Grant and radical Republicanism, as *Frank Leslie's* had so frequently done during its support of the Liberal Republican movement in the 1872 presidential election, the popular periodical now highlighted Sumner's long-term advocacy for Black rights and equality and posed him as the subject of national mourning—the nation personified as a woman crying over his remains. The same issue of *Frank Leslie's* contained a smaller amount of coverage of the funeral of former president Millard Fillmore, who died the same week, but it was Sumner who received the most extensive coverage as the true subject of national grief.[1] It was Sumner, after all, who was the fourth person to lie in state in the rotunda of the U.S. Capitol building as Fillmore was more quietly buried in Buffalo, New York.

Other news coverage of Sumner's public funerals, especially his tributes in Washington, D.C., included the national grief mixed with special Black mourning for the dead senator that the *Frank Leslie's* cover so literally depicted. The Chicago *Inter-Ocean* newspaper headlined its coverage of Sumner's D.C. funeral "A Nation's Honor" and stressed how the proceedings were characterized by "a general sorrow and a universal sense of the national loss in every circle and among all classes." But the paper also especially noted the presence of Black mourners and reported, as did other papers, that Sumner's body was transported from his home to the U.S. Capitol in a procession headed by "a great assemblage of colored men, headed by Fred. Douglass."[2] The Associated Press dispatch about Sumner's D.C. funeral noted that Frederick Douglass and P. B. S. Pinchback (at the time waiting in vain to see whether he would ever be seated as the Senate's first Black member) headed the procession,

CHARLES SUMNER.

"Charles Sumner" by Matt Morgan, cartoon from *Frank Leslie's Illustrated Newspaper*, March 28, 1874. Library of Congress, Prints and Photographs Division, LC-USZ62-139439.

and also reported that thousands of Black men and women viewed Sumner's body as it lay in state. The Associated Press noted that Black observers packed the outside steps of the Capitol during Sumner's congressional funeral, since they were mostly "excluded" from the gallery that would have allowed them to personally observe the service in honor of "their departed friend." Charles Sumner, vilified for decades by proslavery southerners, was now even mourned by some former Confederates like Rep. Lucius Q. Lamar of Mississippi, who eulogized him inside the Capitol that day.[3]

As part of the extended ritual of national mourning, on March 17, prominent African American leaders in Washington, D.C., gathered at the Sumner School (renamed Sumner Memorial Hall) to add honors to the dead senator on the day he was buried in Massachusetts. Frederick Douglass eulogized Charles Sumner, and he also emphasized that Sumner's death was both a national calamity worthy of "extraordinary tokens of sorrow" and a special cause of Black grief. Douglass argued that Sumner was "dear to every colored man's heart" because he believed "simply that each individual man belongs to himself." Sumner had been willing to sacrifice himself for the cause of antislavery before and during the Civil War, and "he opposed every step towards reconstruction without a full, clear, complete recognition of the rights of the colored man." Invoking emancipationist Civil War memory and declaring himself "not one of the forgetting and forgiving kind," Douglass expressed no surprise that Sumner's public mourning was so much greater than "narrow" funeral rituals for President Fillmore because Sumner's antislavery and pro-equality work constituted a more important legacy for the nation than did Fillmore's proslavery capitulation. Douglass emphasized in his eulogy for Sumner that taking part in public mourning for Senator Sumner was an important civic act for Black Americans: "We do well to be here this evening; these meetings do us credit, which no other meetings have ever done us." It may have been an exaggeration, in honor of Sumner, to say that "no other meetings" of Black D.C. citizens had ever honored them so much, but in the exaggeration Douglass expressed that taking part in national rituals of collective public mourning for a great man who had fought so hard for Black freedom and political equality could be a powerful way to take part in the American nation itself.[4] Frederick Douglass, like many other people who took part in "universal" public mourning, used the occasion to advocate for a particular vision of racial justice, politics, and Civil War memory.

Public funerals, as cultural practices of collective mourning, helped to define American national identities in the second half of the nineteenth century, and they provide a lens for examining anew debates over competing strands of Civil War memory. Public funerals for major figures like Sumner—both Northern and Southern—formed an important aspect of the public memory of the Civil War, creating an opportunity for commemorative rituals that enabled many different Americans to argue about their own opinions of and relationships to the American nation itself. Funerals encompassed and connected a wide range of ritual mourning practices stretching far past simple burial ceremonies. Public funerals—and the press coverage, eulogies, material culture, monument-building efforts, and reverence for bodily remains that went with them—put mourning at the center of what Nina Silber has called "the imagined reconstitution of the nation" during and after the U.S. Civil War.[5]

Silber has called on historians to focus on "the imagined reconstitution of the nation" as a way to move forward from the decades-long debate about the trajectory of Civil War memory and its meaning, and this study of public funerals takes inspiration from her urging. Scholars of Civil War memory have taken off from Silber's earlier pathbreaking work and work by David Blight to explore how Civil War memory framed regional, racial, and individual identities between 1861 and 1913. Generally, historians have emphasized the contests between different strands of Civil War memory (reconciliationist, white supremacist, Lost Cause, emancipationist, Union Cause), but they disagree about which strand dominated the national discussion at any particular time during and after Reconstruction. Did reconciliation overtake simple reunion as a theme in Civil War memory by the 1880s? Was emancipationist public memory silenced by white supremacy by the turn of the twentieth century? Did the Union Cause or the Lost Cause persist more robustly for the long term? Silber suggested in 2016 that studying, instead, how competing memories of the Civil War all contributed to "the imagined reconstitution of the nation" could move us past just asking whether "reunion," "reunification," "healing," or "justice" alone dominated postwar memory.[6]

This book takes up Silber's call and uses public funerals as a lens to examine just how competing memories helped different individuals and groups of Americans contribute to their own versions of the "imagined" American nation by participating in commemorative rituals for significant figures related to the American Civil War. The process began in the run-up to the Civil War when the massive funerals for Sen. Henry Clay in 1852 amplified previous public mourning traditions in the United States as Clay's death heightened anxiety about the possible fracture of the union. Then, public funerals during the Civil War contributed to belligerent versions of Union and Confederate national identities fueled by vengeful mourning. After the war, public mourning rituals for figures as different as Robert E. Lee and Charles Sumner continued to provide cultural battlegrounds over how the war ought to be remembered, and their funerals provided opportunities to praise the accomplishments of dead heroes while trying to "reconstitute" the American nation in ways compatible with rival political interests. Mourning rituals seemed consensual, but they often showcased contesting ideas about the dead and what they stood for. Public funerals show how the "imagined reconstitution of the nation" often contained, for example, sectional competition *and* ideas of reconciliation right alongside one another. At the turn of the twentieth century, new kinds of public heroes like Frederick Douglass and Varina "Winnie" Davis became the subjects of public grief, and their funerals proved that conflicting national identities were still being imagined alongside competing ideas of Civil War reconciliation and resistance.[7]

Public funerals provide an especially good opportunity to examine the imaginative process of contested American national identities. In a classical tradition stretching back to Pericles, the forms of mourning for great public figures emphasized, by their nature, unity and consensus. Community mourning—funeral processions, eulogies, and burial services—were designed to emphasize the positive virtues of the deceased public figures, and, as political theorist David McIvor reminds us, the "most prominent voices" in public mourning were often officials who sought to use memories of the past to "reinforce common or binding traditions within the polity."[8] Public mourning hyperbolized positive qualities of the dead and exaggerated unity among mourners. Praising a dead hero was exactly the kind of occasion that was designed to prompt a community to reflect on memories of the past and to decide on some version of agreed-upon meaning—in this case, the meaning of the Civil War past. But, actually, public funerals show that in the context of Civil War memory, those meanings were always contested. The notions of "consensus" that leaders invoked in public funerals were fractious, and dissenters used public funerals as a chance to advocate for alternative visions of the past. Rival, seemingly mutually exclusive, themes of Civil War memory commonly coexisted and conflicted in public funerals that bore all the trappings of consensus building.

This book examines public funerals and mourning rituals for nine prominent figures related to the Civil War—starting with Henry Clay and ending with Frederick Douglass and Winnie Davis—to show how American identities were built out of *competing* and sometimes *opposite* ways of thinking and being. The already-contested nationalism imbued in Clay's funeral splintered during the war and then continued to be expressed in fractured forms after the war as both the Lost Cause and the Union Cause contributed to the "imagined reconstitution of the nation." For example, participants in public mourning valorized both white supremacy and Black liberation and used funerals as moments of public visibility to attach themselves to very different visions of what the United States stood for. Frederick Douglass, for example, advanced a particular version of Black progress when he praised the deceased Charles Sumner for his work to liberate Black Americans and praised the power of Black mourners themselves.

This book is about both memory and mourning. Public mourning is a form and an aspect of public memory that was important in particular ways during the very special circumstances of nineteenth-century America. By showing how public mourning contributed to "the imagined reconstitution of the nation," my work contributes to the overall debate about Civil War memory, but it is not wholly contained within that debate. Public funerals relied on deep traditions and simultaneously constantly introduced innovation and change in this period because people shaped public mourning to their own current political and ideological needs. Very different people engaged in the ritual practices of mourning: draping their homes in black cloth, marching in processions, publishing cartoons, giving and listening to speeches about the virtues of the dead, producing and purchasing images of dead heroes to hang in their homes, raising funds to build funerary monuments, bringing flowers to coffins and graves, writing and reading thousands upon thousands of newspaper articles that telegraphed their grief to a wider community of participants.

Engaging in these processes helped create an imagined community of American national belonging, but even as it did, not everyone agreed on what that community meant or what it should look like. American national identities were forged out of the desire for unity alongside the reality of division and contest. Public funerals followed general patterns but developed different mixtures of rituals and ideas in particular cases, as elaborate rites of mourning contained public eulogies and rituals that attributed nationalistic values to the deceased. Americans projected often conflicting ideas about the nation onto famous figures whom they mourned, and they explored their divisions and commonalities in public mourning as a form of collective memory and their imagined community of grief.[9] Collective memory has been recognized by historians and sociologists as one of the most important factors in national identity formation, and this book charts how public funerals played a specific role in the memory process.[10]

The book also contributes to the larger conversation on the meaning of death in U.S. history, especially by providing a bridge between scholarship that examines the period of the American Revolution and early Republic and scholarship that focuses on the Civil War and Reconstruction era. Thomas J. Brown reminds us that scholars in these two fields often work in too much isolation from one another.[11] My work shows how Americans who mourned public figures in the nineteenth century did so using forms, rituals, and symbols that began in the era of the American Revolution.[12] Civil War era and postwar eulogies, processions, visual culture, and news coverage of funerals often echoed public culture from pre–Civil War America, but they used new technologies and injected new political meanings with a modern twist.

Civil War America was not the only time or place in which public funerals played an important role in culture and politics, but public mourning rituals did play a particular role in shaping late nineteenth-century U.S. society. Public mourning took on special importance because the scale of death in this period was enormous; the U.S. Civil War was, as J. David Hacker has so effectively put it, "the nation's most destructive war by a wide margin."[13] A number of other scholars, most notably Drew Gilpin Faust, Mark S. Schantz,

Caroline Janney, John R. Neff, and William Blair, have recently established ways that the culture of death in Civil War America contributed to politics and national identity.[14] *Spectacle of Grief* furthers that discussion by turning the analytical focus onto specific ritualized funerals. Many of the meanings of death in personal or family life were politicized when writ large in the civic rituals of public funerals. Americans engaged their bodies and their minds in politicized mourning as they cried and read about their heroes, gazed on bodily remains and the material culture of mourning, listened to songs and sermons, and engaged in public discourse.

Funerals have been taken seriously for some time as an object of cultural, social, and political history in a number of contexts. Historians of Europe, Latin America, and China have charted the ways that state funerals have often helped to consolidate monarchies and/or state power from the thirteenth century until today.[15] Other historians have analyzed Indigenous and vernacular funeral traditions in early America, the material culture of cemeteries, and the growth of commercialized funeral directing at the turn of the twentieth century.[16] Scholars of anthropology and religion have plumbed the ritual and liturgical meanings created by funeral rituals in many times, places, and cultures.[17] Cultural historian Thomas W. Laqueur has argued that the treatment of and meanings assigned to human remains have much to tell us about how "the dead make social worlds" for the living.[18]

This book, while drawing on these previous areas of scholarship, focuses more on how public funerals functioned as politicized rituals in the very specific context of the United States in the second half of the nineteenth century. Public mourning brought together political anxiety, racialized politics, Civil War memory, and material culture to give a whole variety of Americans the tools to imagine where they fit into a fractured and reconstituted nation.

These public funerals have not been taken seriously enough as a group by historians. Although all of the individuals discussed in this book are quite important to American politics, warfare, and public life, their funerals and the public mourning in their honor receive spotty treatment by their biographers. Although some of the individual funerals to be examined in the chapters, such as those for Elmer Ellsworth and Robert E. Lee, have received brief discussion in larger works, and a few, like George Peabody's funeral, form the topic for scholarly articles, no existing work considers deeply enough how the funerals relate, as a historical phenomenon, to Civil War era political and social issues.[19] Even biographies of individuals who had large and important funerals, like Henry Clay, treat them lightly, if at all.[20]

Generally, American public funerals, as a specific lens onto issues surrounding the U.S. Civil War, have not been studied enough. Important works that deal with the funerals of Abraham Lincoln, Jefferson Davis, and Ulysses S.

Grant provide key scholarly context for this work, but the focus on presidential funerals has, perhaps, blinded us a bit to the many other important public funerals that defined American politics and society.[21] The point of this project is to look beyond presidential funerals to see how commemorations of the deaths of other political leaders, social reformers, and activists were all important to American culture and national identities.

The trajectory of my argument in this book follows the path of the particular funeral case studies; the details of the public funerals themselves reveal how the rival versions of Civil War memory competed for attention behind a facade of consensual national ritual. Each chapter uses public funerals for particular figures as a lens onto the ways that disparate Americans asserted their versions of American national identity: the fragile identity of a fracturing union, rival versions of wartime Union and Confederate identities based in bellicose mourning, and, after the Civil War, a search for ways that public mourning could reunify and reconcile the nation, whose fictitious bonds were still always contested. Public funerals show how, even during cultural rituals that were meant to be the most universal, Americans often imagined their nation in contradictory terms.

Chapter 1 explains how Henry Clay's huge public funerals in 1852 both built upon the past and created a new scale, and new forms, of public mourning that would echo through the rest of the nineteenth century—setting the pattern for public mourning that would be so important as an expression of Civil War and post–Civil War civic identity. The outpouring of public grief as Clay's remains went on an extensive tour gave mourners the opportunity to imagine national unity, even as they battled over what American national identity meant and expressed anxieties over an imperiled union and deep disagreements over abolition and slavery.

Chapter 2 argues that both Union and Confederate mourners picked up on these forms of public grief to impel the fight and imagine their rival wartime identities as the war pitted them against one another. Public funerals during the Civil War, especially monumental public mourning rituals for Elmer Ellsworth (1861) and Thomas J. "Stonewall" Jackson (1863), reinforced opposing Union and Confederate national identities. But public funerals also—even as they reinforced competing values—demonstrated the common cultural and political power of collective mourning. Public tears valorized dead, manly, white heroes; moved Americans and Confederates to fight one another; and also created common sets of rituals that could strengthen rival political identities.

Chapter 3 examines how, after the war and during Reconstruction, public funerals for the transatlantic philanthropist George Peabody (1869–70) and Confederate general Robert E. Lee (1870) created powerful scenes of reunification—both sectional and Anglo-American. Both men's public funerals—Peabody's in England and New England and Lee's in Virginia—promoted visions of national reunion that favored Confederate forgiveness. Funeral rituals showed that many former Confederates wanted to rejoin the American nation on pro-Southern terms and that many Northerners let them. As always, not everyone agreed, and some resisted the pro-Confederate themes in national grief, but it was also clear in these public funerals that some versions of U.S. national identity could make room for the nascent Lost Cause.

In chapter 4, public funerals for Charles Sumner (1874) and Joseph Johnston (1891) show the complex relationships between Civil War memory and forgetting, reconciliation and sectional grievances. To promote reconciliation, Sumner and Johnston each wanted to silence some aspects of Civil War memory near the time of their deaths, but public mourning for them proved that no major figure could control either his own mourning or Civil War memory itself as sectional memories persisted. Both emancipationist memory and the Lost Cause helped shape the "imagined reconstitution of the nation"; even national identity found no consensus in reconciliation.

Chapter 5 examines innovations in public grief, as public funerals for Frederick Douglass (1895) and Winnie Davis (1898) showed how the ritual forms of public mourning could stretch to include new subjects of public grief: a Black man and a white Southern woman. Douglass's and Davis's funerals also demonstrated contested versions of the national reconciliation that characterized overall Civil War memory at the turn of the twentieth century. Public mourning for Douglass evidenced the vigor of emancipationist memory in the face of intensifying Jim Crow segregation, but his funerals also prompted white supremacist backlash. Winnie Davis, in contrast, personified whiteness and the Lost Cause, but her large public funeral also showed how vitriolic Lost Cause ideas could sometimes coexist with visions of national reconciliation.

Public funerals were an important part of American culture in the nineteenth century, and they especially shaped national memory in the era of the U.S. Civil War. Walking alongside processions of mourners, peering over their shoulders to read newspaper articles about the dead, listening to eulogies, and gazing upon grave markers will allow us to see some of the most important ways that Americans expressed values that were important to them and how they imagined and contested their relationships to one another. Public grief was an important political language that was available to many different Americans, who shaped it to their own needs.

Chapter 1

The Death of Compromise

Henry Clay's Funeral

On the evening of July 8, 1852, a "beautiful and affecting scene" greeted the U.S. mail boat *Benjamin Franklin* as it steamed down the Ohio River past the town of Rising Sun, Indiana.[1] The citizens of Rising Sun gathered to pay their respects to Sen. Henry Clay, whose corpse rested in an elaborate coffin on board, and they enacted a pageant of mourning intended to show how the states in the union themselves mourned the dead senator. At Rising Sun, "about 200 ladies stood upon the quay, of whom thirty were arrayed in a snowy white, draped with funereal black," wearing black veils and holding banners representing the states.[2] The thirty-first young woman, representing Clay's home state of Kentucky, "was dressed in deep mourning."[3]

The women "waved their handkerchiefs and small flags, which they had purposely made for the occasion," while men and boys "stood a short distance off with their heads uncovered."[4] One of the party aboard the boat noted that the beautiful patriotism of the scene reflected "a large amount of credit upon the young ladies of Rising Sun."[5] The symbolic mourning of the women—their allegorical embodiment of the states and homemade patriotic emblems— resembled previous female participation in Clay's Whig Party political campaigning, but this time the Whig hero, Henry Clay, was not on a campaign swing; he was on his way to be buried.[6] The citizens of Rising Sun expressed their patriotism and their politics not at a rally but at a funeral ritual.

The *Benjamin Franklin* had been specially chartered to carry the senator's remains from Cincinnati to Louisville, where they would be transferred to a train for the last leg of their circuitous, ten-day journey from Washington, D.C., to burial in Lexington, Kentucky. The boat was draped in black cloth, and a large black canopy was stretched over the deck to protect the remains held within "a metallic burial case, exquisitely ornamented with suitable drapery and placed inside a mahogany coffin." The metal burial case, a Fisk's patent coffin, was intended to preserve Clay's remains with its hermetic seal. The *Cincinnati Daily Gazette* reported that the coffin "was thus the most prominent object seen from shore, presenting, as it moved down the Ohio, the grandest and most solemn pageant ever borne on its bosom."[7] The congressional committee that accompanied Clay's remains and dignitaries from several cities that had already hosted the senator's corpse to great public fanfare sat beside the coffin on board the *Benjamin Franklin* and acknowledged the women at Rising Sun as they expressed their public regard for "the genius and services of the great man departed."[8]

This moment of public mourning—rural men and women gathering to create a tribute to honor politician Henry Clay in 1852—might seem like a strange place to begin a book that centers on how public funerals intervened in the memory of the U.S. Civil War to create American national identity. But any consideration of politicized Civil War funerals must start with Henry Clay. Clay's immense public funerals bridged the rituals of the eighteenth century and the Civil War era and cemented the close relationship between public mourning and contests over how to define the nation and the union. The public mourning rituals for Clay in 1852 set the pattern that would make public funerals a key tool in the politicization of Civil War memory for the rest of the nineteenth century. Just as we could never understand the Civil War and Reconstruction without any reference to antebellum context and conflict, we will not be able to understand how the funerals for figures like Robert E. Lee or Charles Sumner intervened in key debates about Civil War memory without first understanding how Henry Clay's funeral related to the breakdown of the union.

The public mourning for Clay connected the mid-nineteenth century to an eighteenth-century culture of mourning great men that had been an important part of U.S. national identity since the Revolutionary War. In 1799, George Washington, for example, had been mourned all over the nation and in mock funerals, funeral sermons, and print culture, although his actual remains were interred relatively quietly at Mount Vernon.[9] In 1831, Washington's family moved his body to a new tomb on the estate, in part because it attracted so many nationalist visitors.[10]

Henry Clay's public funerals echoed many of the nationalist themes in mourning for George Washington, but they took place on a scale never before seen and involved the widespread veneration of his remains, which traveled through much of the nation. Clay's public mourning altered previous American ritual tradition and amplified the power of the public funeral to communicate a broad cultural and political message. Technology, transportation, print media, material culture, and even consumer goods all amplified the tradition of national mourning and gave it new power—suddenly in 1852.

This new-scale outpouring of public grief took place in a particular political context and as part of the crisis of the 1850s. The sudden amplification of funeral rituals in honor of Clay did not happen only because technology and travel made such a funeral celebration possible—it happened because mourning Clay met a societal need for an outlet for political anxiety and debate. In mourning Clay, the Great Compromiser, Americans expressed concern about the possible death of compromise itself. Political rivals—Democrats and Whigs, abolitionists and proslavery forces—battled over how best to remember Clay or whether he was worthy of the huge spectacle at all because his funeral rituals provided a very public outlet to battle over the nature of the union. Arguing over the propriety of Henry Clay's funeral was a way to argue over the sturdiness of the American nation itself. Supposedly universal mourning actually provided opportunities for contests over clashing visions of American national identity and politics.

Clay's funerals set the pattern that would repeat time and again over the next five decades: mourning a great man (or perhaps, later, even a great woman) provided a safe but high-stakes way to claim a part of national memory and a place in the American nation itself. Henry Clay's mourning established the ritual context for many of the most important contests that would mark battles over Civil War memory in decades to come: slavery, race, region, section, compromise, union, and the meaning of national identity. Also contained in the 1852 funeral rituals are many instructive details and questions about how funerals could function to preserve national memory: Who got to claim a role in the national dialogue by playing a key role in the mourning ritual, and how? How could Americans as far apart as San Francisco and Boston, New Orleans and Indianapolis grieve together and imagine themselves as part of a national community of mourners?

The travels of Henry Clay's remains foreshadowed Civil War corpses traveling before burial, and most of all, the funerals for Clay presaged the funerals for the assassinated Civil War president, Abraham Lincoln. The tour of Clay's remains, and the celebration of the man both during and after, set the form and precedent for Lincoln's even longer and larger funerals in 1865. Yet scholars really have not taken enough notice of Clay's funerals or of how important they were as a model for Lincoln and for the American tradition of public mourning more generally.[11] Once the union was fractured and the Civil War resulted, the occasions for such ritualized funerals would multiply. But for a time in 1852, the looming crisis over the strength of the union focused especially on public grief for Henry Clay, the politician whose brokered compromises had held the union together for decades, for better or for worse.

Mourning for Henry Clay provided an opportunity for ritualizing national unity, but reactions to Clay's death did not establish consensus. His funeral became a contest over how to express grief for the failing union itself. The funeral rites also demonstrated that the Whig Party was shaky. Clay had created the Compromise of 1850 as a way to preserve national unity, but public and political support for the Compromise was patchy, and its constituent parts, especially the Fugitive Slave Act, quickly became wedges that exacerbated threats of disunion. The Compromise could not even be passed as an omnibus bill, as Clay wished, because it was too controversial as a whole.[12] Even as hundreds of thousands of Americans followed Clay's funerals and the tour of his remains in person and in the press, they sometimes disagreed about the meaning of the unprecedented national grief. Rival visions of national identity came to be defined as Clay's funerals allowed Americans to argue about the nature of union and compromise, while simultaneously agreeing about other aspects of national grief. The forms of mourning—processions, eulogies, material culture—seemed unifying, but Whigs and Democrats, abolitionists and proslavery advocates would ultimately bitterly contest what they should be said to stand for.

Henry Clay and Public Grief

Public mourning for Henry Clay started immediately upon his death. When Clay died of tuberculosis on June 29, 1852, President Fillmore closed all executive offices, and the U.S. Senate immediately took action to prepare an elaborate Washington funeral and to send six senators to accompany Clay's remains to Lexington, where he wished to be buried.[13] The funeral subcommittee included both Whigs and Democrats who represented a wide geographic base from New Jersey to Texas.[14] Very quickly, the usual congressional funeral arrangements for a deceased senator ballooned into something new.

On June 30, Whig and Democratic senators and congressmen rose in the Senate chamber to eulogize Clay, and their words were reprinted in newspapers in every region of the country for weeks to come.[15] Senate chaplain Clement Moore Butler declaimed at Clay's Washington, D.C., funeral on July 1 that it was futile to talk of "*Burying* Henry Clay!" since the people might as well "bury the records of your country's history—bury the hearts of the living millions—bury the mountains, the rivers, the lakes, and the spreading lands from sea to sea, with which his name is inseparably associated, and even then you would not bury HENRY CLAY."[16]

But seemingly the whole nation turned its attention to doing just that, and by the time Clay's body reached Lexington, Kentucky, on July 10, his burial service was the culminating event in a ten-day festival of mourning. Clay's remains had traversed many of the expansive rivers and lands that he embodied in the imagination of the Senate chaplain. Henry Clay's remains traveled a long, meandering path from D.C. through Maryland, Delaware, Pennsylvania, New Jersey, New York, and Ohio to Kentucky, stopping in major cities along the way so that elaborate funeral rituals could be enacted. Clay's remains did not travel through the entire United States, but they did cover a lot of ground, and press coverage amplified the impact.

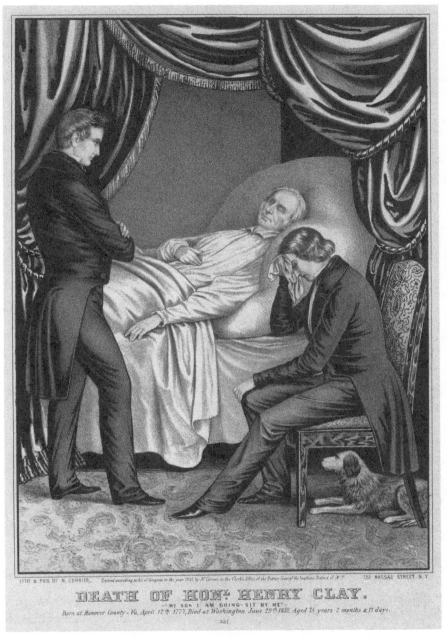

"Death of Honl. Henry Clay" engraving by Currier and Ives, 1852. Library of Congress, Prints and Photographs Division, LC-DIG-pga-08567.

Public grief had played an important role in American political culture since the eighteenth century, but Clay's funerals marked a turning point toward a more modern form of ritualized mourning that combined an interest in his body with an extensive apparatus of popular culture and publicity.[17] Newspaper circulation, for instance, had increased radically since the time of George Washington's death in 1799.[18] In the years preceding Clay's death, notable public funerals had been held for Rep. John Quincy Adams and Sen. John C. Calhoun, but neither was remotely as large as Clay's. The scale and reach of public grieving, combined with the chance for the great numbers of people to view Clay's remains, were new.

The public mourning for Henry Clay was measurably larger, even, than Zachary Taylor's recent presidential funeral. When Taylor died in office in 1850, he was first given a large funeral in Washington, D.C. Taylor's remains traveled via rail and steamboat to Louisville, Kentucky, but without enormous publicity and with a minimum of public celebration along the way. Taylor did receive a second large funeral when he was buried in the family cemetery at Louisville, but the public mourning in 1850 paled by comparison to what took place when Clay died in 1852.[19] Close to 100,000 people saw Taylor's funeral in Washington, D.C., and tens of thousands more witnessed his burial in Kentucky, but the public did not attend his body in between. Clay's body, which had not been embalmed, traveled a longer route from Washington to Kentucky accompanied by huge rituals at every stop along the way—and public mourning for him continued for months after his burial, extending the national discussion about the meaning of his death.

Lavish press attention to Clay's death and the progress of his remains through the countryside allowed a more spontaneous outpouring of public grief among the rising political uncertainty of 1852. As the *Benjamin Franklin* moved down the Ohio River bearing the senator's remains, its bell was "answered by every boat they met," and people gathered by the river to pay their respects.[20] One newspaper correspondent on board observed that "clustered together and dotting the banks, men, women, and children gathered in silent awe, as the boat glided along," and he reported that at Lawrenceburg, Indiana, "there assembled a large number of its citizens who bowed in sorrow . . . and saluted it as it passed by firing minute guns."[21]

People could only synchronize their gathering on the riverbanks to the passage of Clay's remains because the speed of print culture and communication made it possible. Americans in 1852 appreciated, to some extent, that they were living in an age of technological advancement that was changing their festive culture and making it possible for them to coordinate this kind of response that enabled them to share grief. Some mourners who took part in the elaborate rituals in honor of Clay explicitly noted how modern technology had changed the scale and enhanced the simultaneity of the national culture in honor of the dead since George Washington's day. One New Jersey newspaper expressed amazement that bells and minute guns could sound for Clay in Trenton, Baltimore, and "throughout the country" at the exact moment that Clay's Washington funeral began. He commented, "It is only since the use of the magnetic telegraph became common, that the whole of our extensive country can thus unite, at one time, in those mournful solemnities by which the living manifest respect and sorrow at the burial of illustrious men."[22]

Even though, or maybe because, Americans could communicate better and more quickly, their politics were far from consensual. The unanimity of the American populace had been fractured over the decades since 1800 by openly partisan politics, sectionalism, and conflicts over slavery. Elizabeth Varon reminds us that "both the Whig and Democratic parties had emerged from the debates of 1850 and 1851 battered and divided."[23] Clay died during the same week that the Whig Party convention nearly tore itself apart over the nomination contest between Millard Fillmore and Winfield Scott.[24]

Henry Clay's funeral created national identity by allowing for imaginative rituals of common mourning in a country that was increasingly threatened by slavery and sectional conflict; the Compromise of 1850 was creating more problems than it had solved. Even when both Whig and Democratic newspaper editors around the country agreed about the necessity of mourning Clay as a public hero, they also sometimes allowed party conflict and even presidential campaigning for the fall 1852 election to accompany his funeral coverage. Mourning for Clay became a way to express political anxieties over the longevity of American union as the transsectional Whig Party, which he had helped to found, fractured. Henry Clay died, and the Whig Party would soon follow him to the grave.

Clay was the perfect focus for this kind of seemingly unifying, yet very political funeral procession because he embodied both union and conflict, and he had been the subject of political pageantry as politics and popular culture developed alongside one another in the early nineteenth century. His long career in national politics spanned almost fifty years: he was first elected to the U.S. Senate in 1806 and subsequently served in the House of Representatives, as Speaker of the House, and secretary of state. Upon his death, Clay was best known as a four-time-unsuccessful presidential candidate and senator; he served several terms in the senate from 1831 until his death in 1852.

Henry Clay had spent his political career trying to transcend region. Clay, known as "Harry of the West," started his career as a western Democratic-Republican and built his reputation as a War Hawk advocate of the War of 1812. In the 1820s, Clay, who was also a slaveholder, fused northern, western, and southern interests as the architect of economic development in the American

System. He helped to hold together disparate northerners and southerners in the Whig Party through the 1830s and 1840s. Clay was dubbed "the Great Compromiser" for his role in orchestrating both the Missouri Compromise in 1820 and the Compromise of 1850, and even his political enemies respected his parliamentary acumen. When Sen. Henry S. Foote accused Clay of forsaking southern interests in the Compromise of 1850, Clay responded on the floor of the Senate: "I know no South, no North, no East, no West, to which I owe my allegiance. . . . My allegiance is to this Union and to my own state."[25] This ability to embody both regional interests and national union during his long career enhanced his appeal as a symbol, even after death, at a time when that union started to seem truly imperiled by political and sectional strife.

Henry Clay's Body

Henry Clay's dead body concentrated public attention on his ideas of union and compromise, even as it (and they) threatened to decay. The close public attention paid to Clay's body throughout the public mourning in his honor is one of the aspects of his public funerals that would most influence political ritual and Civil War memory in decades to come.

Anthropologist Katherine Verdery reminds us that "dead bodies have enjoyed political life the world over and since far back in time," but Henry Clay's body played a specific, unique role at a perilous moment in U.S. history.[26] The dead bodies of saintly and holy persons, especially men, had played a role in several centuries of Western European Christian religious tradition, and their relics had served as objects of devotion that occupied a central role in sacred spaces such as cathedrals.[27] Clay's remains functioned as civic relics as a fascinated and reverent public looked upon and read about his body. The tour of Clay's body, as a relic, anticipated the same kind of treatment that would be given to Abraham Lincoln after his assassination more than a decade later, and Clay's body symbolized an imperiled union that anticipated the one that had to be reassembled after civil war.[28]

The symbolic appeal of Clay's remains was enhanced by the attention contemporaries had paid to his physical being in the decades before his death and to his bodily presence in mid-nineteenth-century popular culture. While he was alive, Clay's physical body attracted considerable comment, and it formed part of his political appeal. Contemporaries noted that Clay possessed a social and physical "magnetism" that helped him to achieve compromises, even when opponents wanted to hate him. He lived in the public eye, and for most of the century "his bodily strength seemed inexhaustible."[29] Clay's phys-

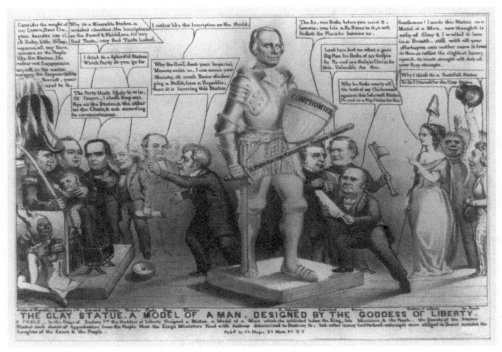

John L. Magee, "The Clay Statue. A Model of a Man. Designed by the Goddess of Liberty," cartoon, 1850. Library of Congress, Prints and Photographs Division, LC-USZ62-1424.

ical form was familiar to Americans, since he was a frequent presence in engravings and political cartoons that were newly popular in the first half of the nineteenth century. As the Whig presidential candidate in 1844, Clay was one of the first politicians whose portrait was sold in elaborate, fine-quality steel engravings meant to be framed and hung on parlor walls.[30] Portrait engravings of Clay were popular from the 1840s onward, and he was well known as a physical role model.

For his entire career, Clay had taken pains to use his body—his height, deep voice, and talent for elegant gesture—to his advantage as a speaker, whether in the courtroom or the halls of Congress.[31] An 1845 phrenology manual that related the talents of great public figures to their cranial measurements declared Clay to be the greatest bodily specimen among politicians because of his large head and good organ placement.[32] An 1849 oratorical manual for boys declared Clay the "highest exemplification of masculine charms" and described his "impressive" body and face in exquisite detail.[33] S. G. Brown eulogized Clay at Dartmouth College by reminding students that Clay's oratorical skill depended on "the glance of the eye, the motion of the hand, the firm or yielding position of the body. . . . His form seemed to dilate to a superhuman height, rising, as one said of him on a certain occasion, 'forty feet high' in . . . remonstrance."[34]

This idea that Clay's body was especially suited to the causes he believed in, and especially to the cause of compromise itself, took root in popular culture. John L. Magee published a lithographed political cartoon in 1850, "The Clay Statue. A Model of a Man," which represented Clay as a larger-than-life physical monument to "Compromise," created by the goddess of liberty. In the lithograph, the goddess of liberty tells the foes of Compromise that they must admire Clay as "a Model of a Man . . . though it is only of Clay . . . with all your efforts, you can neither move it from its Base, or inflict the slightest Injury upon it. its innate strenght [sic] will defy all your Puny attempts." The followers of Liberty cheer behind her: "Why I think it's a Beautifull Statue," and "So do I! Hurrah! for the Clay Statue."[35] Unlike a statue, however, his frame was mortal. Clay's body stood for compromise, so what would happen when it passed away and decayed?

It was a notable contradiction that Clay could still be conceived of as a strong, physical symbol, since the public was well aware, by 1851, of his failing health. Clay had been fighting severe illness since at least 1850, and he had visited Cuba and several southern American hot springs seeking relief from the respiratory symptoms that were probably early signs of the tuberculosis that would eventually kill him.[36] Clay submitted a letter of resignation from the U.S. Senate in December 1851, but it was not set to take effect until the following September, and in the meantime the press allowed the public to pursue an interest in his failing health and its effects on his once-great physical form.[37]

Because his body had been so revered, some observers were troubled by seeing him in a sickly state. The Washington correspondent of the *Charleston Mercury* wrote that Clay seemed "to possess so unbounded a vitality . . . that the tidings [of death], come when they might, would give a shock, and excite surprise."[38] In January 1852, Frederick Douglass printed an article in his abolitionist newspaper noting that the "eminent politician is rapidly sinking into the grave. He is greatly emaciated and his cough is incessant and severe."[39]

Clay's condition worsened through the year, and public attention remained fastened on his weakened body. Stories of his failing health were mixed not only with political news but also with popular culture. The *Daily Alabama Journal* reported at the beginning of June that "Henry Clay is dying" and urged "a nation's Faith, and Hope, and Memory" to rally around the memory of him as a great American hero.[40] In keeping with cultural practices of the "good death," Clay was sure to get his affairs in order and to communicate his burial wishes to his family, and the public also prepared themselves for his eventual passing.[41] All the public attention to Clay's body, both during his political life and during his failing health, took on a new and intensified form after he died on June 29, 1852.

The Tour of Clay's Remains

The tour of Henry Clay's remains across more than 1,200 miles of the United States with many stops for funeral pageants constituted the most innovative part of the public mourning in his honor. On June 30, the day after Clay died, the Senate held a solemn funeral for him in its chambers, similar to the ceremony held four years earlier for John Quincy Adams in the House chamber.[42] But, immediately after, Clay's body began to receive much greater attention than had been previously accorded to any deceased statesman. After the Senate ceremony, Clay's body became the first ever to lie in state in the U.S. Capitol rotunda, and a large number of people assembled to view the body. The *New York Weekly Tribune* reported that "the capacious Rotunda was altogether unable to contain the vast multitude assembled, and the porticos and public grounds were occupied by those anxious to get in to have the last opportunity to see all that remains of Henry Clay."[43]

Senate chaplain Butler eulogized Clay by imagining how Americans would be unified by grief. He said, "In many cities banners droop, bells toll, cannons boom, funereal draperies wave. . . . In crowded streets and on sounding wharfs, upon steamboats and upon cars, in fields and in workshops, in homes, in schools, millions of men, women, and children have their thoughts fixed upon this scene" as the nation's leaders mourned Henry Clay.[44] As a longtime advocate of commerce and internal improvements, Clay probably would have delighted in Moore's image of busy Americans pausing in workshops and fields, on steamboats and railroads, to commemorate him.

Moore's eulogy could have served as a ritual template for the next ten days, as millions of Americans had the chance to memorialize Clay in person and millions more followed the progress of his remains in the press. The same rail cars, steamboats, and city streets that Moore imagined actually provided the means for Clay's body to travel through a large part of the northern United States with greater speed than anyone could have imagined even twenty years earlier. Transportation improvements had formed a cornerstone of Clay's nationalist economic program since just after the War of 1812, and although the entirety of his grand federal vision had never been implemented (and had been the subject of serious political battles), the journey of Clay's corpse over rail, land, and water testified to the eventual success of his vision (albeit concentrated in the North and upper South).[45] As Americans gathered together at many points along the route to catch a glimpse of one of the specially

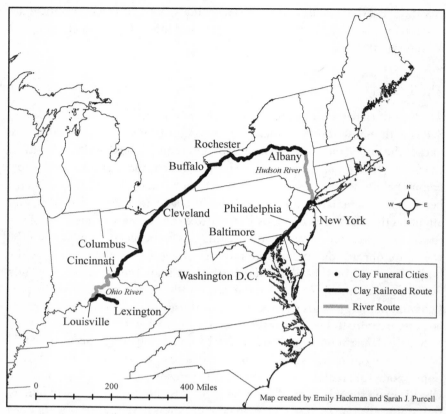

Henry Clay funeral route, 1852. Data from IPUMS, National Historical Geographic Information System; Jeremy Atack, "Historical Geographic Information Systems (GIS) Database of U.S. Railroads for 1852 (May 2016); University of Nebraska, Railroads and the Making of Modern America," http://railroads.unl.edu/resources/; National Weather Service, Geographic Information Services. Map by Sarah J. Purcell and Emily Hackman.

decorated rail cars bearing Clay's coffin or one of the steamboats or ferries that carried him across lakes and rivers, they saw both the immediate progress of his bodily remains and the grand progress of his early political vision.[46] This did not mean that everyone in the country supported Clay's nationalist vision, but it acquired symbolic power, nevertheless, during his funeral.

Clay's 1,200-mile funeral procession was both a ritual of mourning and a huge spectacle. Following the Senate funeral on June 30, citizens from Washington, D.C., and all the surrounding towns gathered in the streets to watch a gilded hearse transport Clay's remains to the railroad depot. The elaborately decorated coffin, along with the six designated congressional representatives, Clay's son and chief heir Thomas, and other dignitaries, departed at 4:00 P.M. on a special train to Baltimore. Lucretia Clay, Henry's wife, had been kept in Lexington during his decline by her own poor health. Baltimore officials met Clay's body early in the morning hours of July 1, and a procession through the city followed at noon. The *Baltimore Weekly Sun* declared that all businesses closed and offered this description: "The city presented a gloomy and mournful aspect. . . . The bells of all the churches, engine houses and other places were tolled . . . the sidewalks completely jammed up with men, women and children, all eager to take a last look at the remains of the great American statesman." Clay lay in repose on a specially constructed catafalque in the rotunda of the Exchange Building until the next day, as thousands of people filed by to see his face, which was exposed through a glass window in his special airtight metal coffin.[47]

On July 2, the delegation left Baltimore with Clay's body on another train, and in rural Maryland it was viewed by "crowds of the people of the country who had congregated to see the train pass."[48] Later the same day, Clay arrived in Wilmington, Delaware, where his coffin was again unloaded and placed in repose at City Hall. The plate covering his face was again removed, as "an immense concourse of citizens, male and female, passed through the lines and took a last look at the features of the deceased."[49]

The funeral party then accompanied Clay's body on a train to Philadelphia, where they arrived at 9:00 P.M. Clay's remains were paraded for two hours through Philadelphia in a torchlit procession in which forty-one fire companies, important participants in the city's culture of civic rituals and parades, carried the 3,000 torches. The procession ended at the "sacred edifice" of Independence Hall, which "was brilliantly lit up with bonfires, and [where] thousands of ladies had congregated inside its walls to witness the passage of the procession." Clay's coffin was placed on a cenotaph in the center of Independence Hall, and crowds of people flocked to see it through the night.[50] The Philadelphia rituals for Clay—tied to Independence Hall and falling two days before Independence Day—served to remind the public of a narrative of national unity, drawn from the glory of the Revolutionary past, that might act as a salve against disunion.

The next morning, July 3, Clay's remains departed Philadelphia on the steamer *Trenton* on the Delaware and Raritan Canal to Trenton, New Jersey, where the coffin was placed on another train. The *Baltimore Sun* reported that "at every town in going through New Jersey there were imposing and affecting demonstrations."[51] As the train traveled through New Jersey, it stopped at Princeton, New Brunswick, Elizabethtown, and Rahway, where town committees had erected temporary triumphal arches over the tracks and where crowds gathered to see the train, even though they were not allowed to glimpse the coffin, which was stowed safely in a special freight car.[52] The coffin was removed from the train at Jersey City and marched slowly through the streets. At the Jersey City ferry landing, where the delegation departed for New York, "a large concourse of people assembled" under a sign expressing "our love for the remains."[53]

When Clay's ferryboat arrived at Castle Garden in New York City on the afternoon of July 3, thousands of people were on hand to greet it, and "an immense military and civic procession was then formed, which escorted the remains to the City Hall" in an open hearse. New York City, long a hotbed of support for Clay and home of the Whig Clay Festival Association, tried to outdo all the previous cities in the lavish honors it paid to him. The procession accompanying Clay's remains through New York streets lasted more than three hours as hotels, stores, theaters, public buildings, and streets "were literally shrouded in mourning."[54] As the remains passed through the city's streets, one reporter claimed that "the exhibition of feeling is universal. . . . It is wider, more sincere and profound, than has marked the loss of any American patriot."[55] New Yorkers paid respects to Clay as he lay in state at City Hall overnight, although visitors were unable to gaze upon his face, as the face plate was not removed from his coffin because of the hot weather and "in order to preserve the lineaments of the great man perfect, for the gratification of his family and nearest friends, when the body shall reach its final resting-place in Kentucky."[56] All day on July 4, "great numbers of citizens" continued to file past the coffin, which was displayed with huge floral tributes and a sign reading "A Nation Mourns Its Loss."[57] Since Independence Day fell on Sunday, clergy all over town preached sermons that wove together a commemoration of the national holiday and a eulogy for Clay.[58]

Clay's funeral delegation departed New York City on the morning of July 5 to travel up the Hudson River aboard the steamer *Santa Claus* headed for Albany. Residents of Poughkeepsie used small boats to approach the steamer and deposited floral arrangements on the deck of the *Santa Claus*.[59] The steamer paused at Newburgh so local officials could board to pay their respects.[60] At Albany, Clay's coffin was accompanied by fire companies bearing torches to the New York state capitol, where guards attended the body overnight.[61] The next morning, Clay was placed aboard a special car on the New York and Erie Railroad. He traveled west through Schenectady, Utica, Rome, Syracuse, and Rochester to Buffalo, where he was loaded directly onto the Erie steamer *Buckeye State*, which carried him overnight to Ohio.[62]

On the morning of July 7, Clay's remains arrived in Cleveland and then moved via rail through Columbus to Cincinnati, arriving on July 8. In Cincinnati, "a large procession of military, Free Masons, Odd Fellows, Firemen

Henry Clay's funeral procession in Lexington, Kentucky. Daguerreotype.
Henry Clay Memorial Association Papers, University of Kentucky Archives.

and citizens, conducted the remains through a portion of the city" for more than an hour as over 10,000 people gathered outside heavily draped public buildings.[63] After the procession through Cincinnati, Clay's remains were placed aboard the *Benjamin Franklin* for the ceremonial trip down the Ohio River. On July 9, his body made its final journey via rail from Louisville through Frankfort to Lexington.[64]

Lexingtonians held a massive series of ceremonies commemorating Clay as an esteemed national politician and hometown hero, and newspapers reported that "the citizens vied with each other in ministering to the comfort of the thousands of strangers present, in opening their houses and appropriating what they had to the public."[65] Henry Clay's final funeral on July 10, 1852, was the largest ceremonial occasion ever witnessed in Lexington, Kentucky, up until that time. When the correspondent from the *Frankfort Commonwealth* arrived in town at 6:00 A.M., he "found the streets already thronged with strangers and citizens, while every road leading to the city poured in a continual stream of carriages, horseman [*sic*] and pedestrians." He wrote that "the number of people assembled at Lexington, was greater than ever was seen in her streets before." Clay's son James wrote to his wife, Sarah: "I have never seen in Lexington, any thing like the number of people." Estimates from observers ranged between 30,000 and 100,000 in attendance. Lexington's businesses closed, and black crepe, banners, and portraits of the dead senator adorned streets and houses all over town.[66]

Lexington mourners did not get a chance to view Clay's remains directly. Popular writer Henry Burchstead Skinner visited Clay's estate, Ashland, on the morning of the Lexington funeral, and the undertaker told him that "the metallic burial case had proved defective, and that as the body had become decomposed . . . it was thought not best to expose the face even to the family."[67] The failure of the Fisk's metallic coffin to preserve Clay's remains was a disappointment, especially given that the coffin manufacturer had built a national advertising campaign tied to Clay's funeral. Even though Clay's face could not be shown, a huge crowd still pressed to get close to the coffin. When the undertaker moved the coffin for the burial ceremony, "the pressure of the crowd around the bier was so great as to render it almost impossible to place the coffin in the hearse."[68]

After an Episcopal service at Ashland, a grand and solemn procession of local, state, and federal government officials and dignitaries accompanied Clay's remains to the beautiful Lexington Cemetery recently constructed at the western edge of town. The people of Lexington and visitors followed on foot for hours as church bells tolled and mourners lined the procession route. The reporter claimed the procession "was the most imposing demonstration of sorrow we ever saw. . . . The carriages in it passed two abreast, and by far the greater portion of its length was occupied by persons on foot marching . . . its length must have been from a mile and a quarter to a mile and a half long."[69] When Clay was interred on a hillside at Lexington Cemetery, according to his wishes "by the side of his friends and relatives," the long, ten-day funeral procession from Washington, D.C., finally came to an end.[70] The "torrents of public sorrow" (as one paper put it) would continue in other cities for weeks after, but not in the presence of Clay's bodily remains.[71]

Imagined Community, Real Community, National Identity

By providing people an opportunity to imagine collective participation in a national ritual, the tour of Clay's remains contributed to a national identity—the kind that was forged by public celebration linked to patriotic reverence for heroic politicians. The tour bore out the prediction by the *New York Daily Times* upon first reporting Clay's demise that "his death will be celebrated throughout the length and breadth of the land, with heartfelt grief."[72] The

Charleston Courier noted that "such evidences of national sorrow have not been witnessed since the death of WASHINGTON."[73] Clay's fellow senator from Kentucky, Joseph R. Underwood, the chair of the committee that accompanied Clay's remains, alluded to the similarity between Clay's journey and another kind of spectacle familiar to Americans—triumphal tours of living politicians and heroes. Underwood remarked upon arrival in Lexington: "Our journey since we left Washington has been a continued procession. . . . Every where the people have pressed forward to manifest their feelings towards the illustrious dead. . . . Delegations from cities, towns, and village have waited on us. . . . It has been no triumphal procession in honor of a living man, stimulated by hopes of a reward. . . . It has been the voluntary tribute of a free and grateful people to the glorious dead."[74]

Like the nationwide tour of the Marquis de Lafayette in 1824 and 1825, for example, celebrating Clay's remains was meant to remind U.S. citizens of their unity.[75] The pageantry of the tour dramatized national unity when entire communities joined in ritual together, an effect that was magnified by press coverage. Clay's tour also contained elements of campaign tours and the tours of successful candidates such as those conducted by Presidents James Monroe and Andrew Jackson.[76] But this time, the politician on tour was a corpse, and public mourning replaced the campaign swing.

Paying the costs of the ritual mourning also emphasized the shared nature of the national grief for Clay. Henry Clay's elaborate D.C. funeral, the tour of his remains, and his burial at Lexington were extremely expensive, and the costs were shared by Congress, municipalities, private and political clubs, individual citizens, and business donations. The Senate and the House of Representatives paid $16,651.26 for expenses related to Clay's Washington, D.C., funeral and the tour of this remains.[77] This huge amount (equal to almost $500,000 in current dollars) eclipsed the $4,861 that Congress had spent on John Quincy Adams's funeral in 1848, the only ceremony that came close to Clay's in size, or the $3,088.09 spent on the funeral of sitting president William Henry Harrison in 1841.[78] Congress did, on a regular basis, pay funeral and burial expenses for its own members who died in office, but the costs usually were in the hundreds of dollars, not in the tens of thousands it took to mount Clay's huge funeral.[79] The Clay appropriation included money for decorations, mourning clothes, horses, preparation of the body, the hearse, copies of Clay eulogies, and portrait engravings that could be distributed to the public. It also included hotel and baggage expenses for the congressional committee that accompanied Clay to Lexington.

Although Congress paid a large amount for Clay's funeral and tour, the congressional payments covered just a portion of the overall cost of the events. The train costs, the cost of the elaborate coffin, and all the ceremonies outside Washington, D.C., were paid for by locals and by donations.[80] When Clay was celebrated in cities along the route of his tour, the costs to individual municipalities were considerable. For the most part, towns and cities viewed their contributions as a chance to celebrate Clay and to demonstrate their patriotism; there were few complaints about cost. But in New York, some city officials faced criticism over the expenditures—perhaps a measure of the enormity of the costs and the level of political friction in that city. The *Herald* and the *Daily Times* feuded in print weeks after Clay passed through the city about whether some of the lavish payments approved by New York City authorities were proper—or perhaps constituted excessive payments to Whig political cronies.[81]

In this case, the newspapers themselves became part of the political feud and part of the mourning. Readers, accustomed to interacting with their newspapers, expected that papers would not only report on the funeral pageantry but become part of the ritual.[82] For instance, the editors at the *New York Daily Times* had to answer reader complaints that the paper was not edging its columns in black to honor Clay: "The sole reason why the *Times* was not dressed in mourning . . . was because the mammoth cylinder press upon which it is worked will not permit any such variation from the usual style of typography."[83] Newspapers had played a large role in collective mourning for George Washington and in the national tours of Jackson, Monroe, and Lafayette. But the growth of the American press by 1852 meant that its reach was far wider than it had been in the 1810s and 1820s. The United States had the highest per capita newspaper circulation in the world in the 1850s.[84]

News coverage of the tour of Henry Clay's remains reached far beyond the route where his body actually traveled, helping disparate Americans to imagine themselves as part of the national community of mourning. Newspapers in every region updated readers daily on the progress of Clay's body and detailed the military processions, decor, flags flown at half mast, tolling bells, and the number and character of the crowds of people attending. The extensive press coverage and the widespread publication of Clay eulogies and tributes saturated print culture and helped to connect Americans in an "imagined community" of mourners for Henry Clay.[85]

The community of mourners was not purely imaginary, however, and a vast number of Americans mourned Clay in person. A significant portion of the U.S. population could have seen Clay's extended funeral procession. Consider a map tracing the path of Clay's remains along rail lines, waterways, and through cities, and then add to it information from the 1850 U.S. Census.[86] The population of the counties through which the remains traveled was almost 3.5 million, or 15 percent of the total U.S. population in 1850. If we allow that some people may have traveled to see the body and add a twenty-mile buffer to those counties, the total increases to almost 6 million, or roughly 26 percent of the population in 1850. Obviously, not every single person in this area viewed the funeral cortege, but even so, Clay's trip through some of the most densely populated areas in the United States meant that a significant number of people saw the funerals or knew someone who did.

Funeral celebrations for Clay became part of the fabric of civic culture throughout the nation in 1852. Many of those who had not had an opportunity to see Clay's body, or who lived in southern or western states where the corpse did not travel, also were able to participate in the national rituals of mourning. Of course, many of them had followed in the press the progress of Clay's body and the rituals surrounding it. But tens of thousands more Americans, many of them in locations far flung from the in-person funeral ceremonies, participated in civic ceremonies in his honor. Many cities and towns around the country held observances in Clay's honor—sometimes more than one. These celebrations ranged in size, sometimes featuring parades and mock funeral processions, but always including a eulogy or sermon given by a prominent local politician or minister. Starting on July 4, as Clay's body was still traveling to be buried, and stretching until the end of 1852, many municipalities gave their citizens opportunities to gather for a Clay commemoration. Residents of cities, towns, farms, and mining camps in Florida, California, Louisiana, New Hampshire, Illinois, and many other states—in all regions of the country—had a chance to participate in mourning rituals for Clay.[87]

The press coverage, eulogies, and continuing funeral celebrations effectively spread the mourning experienced by those who directly saw Clay's remains to a much wider population. Whether turning out to see Clay's body in person, marching in a parade in his honor, or reading newspaper articles and books about him, citizens connected themselves to the national culture of grief. Millions of Americans participated in some form of mourning for Clay.

Material Culture, Popular Culture, and Mourning

In some ways, this public mourning for Henry Clay, probably the most widespread in U.S. history up to that point, is not as surprising as twenty-first-century Americans might think. Mark Schantz has argued, "Death was intimately familiar to early nineteenth-century Americans. . . . The very pervasiveness of death in antebellum America trained up an entire generation to see it not as something to be avoided, but as the inevitable destiny of humanity." Elaborate expressions of grief, both familial and national, held great fascination by the 1850s. In consolation literature, postmortem photographs, keepsakes fashioned out of hair, and mourning dress, "Americans celebrated the deaths of the old, the young, and those cut down in their primes." When

Henry Clay's son Henry Clay Jr. was killed during the Mexican War at the Battle of Buena Vista in 1847, the Clay family experienced the mixture of personal and public grief—hundreds of condolence letters, commercialized engravings of Lieutenant Clay's death, and public encomiums—that would explode again in 1852 upon the father's demise.[88]

What is astounding, however, was the way that mourning rituals for the elder Henry Clay drew together new and old death traditions and made him the object of a new scale of public attention. Technology and political instability threw increased attention onto Clay and made possible a scale and variety of mourning never before available. The newly vibrant consumer culture, especially evident in American cities, also made it possible for some of the traditions of family mourning that involved material culture—pictures of the deceased, mourning clothing, somber home decor—to spread on an unprecedented public scale. Clay's funerals exemplified the mourning culture that was available to all middle-class and wealthy Americans and simultaneously enshrined him as the most exceptional case of a publicly mourned great man.

The public mourning for Henry Clay was created at the crossroads of politics, material culture, visual culture, and commerce. Focusing on specific aspects of the material and commercialized culture in his funerals will show this process at work. Some material objects drew on long traditions of public mourning, while others mixed old-fashioned inspirations with newer, market-oriented commodities. Many aspects of the antebellum culture of death were associated with material objects that showed changing ideals of class and gentility; the rural cemetery movement especially showed that even nature and the process of burial itself might be used in the service of creating American gentility.[89] For example, the Lexington Cemetery, where Clay was interred, had been opened in 1850 when a civic committee hired landscape architect Julius Adams to improve a "beautiful woodland" on the edge of town to provide burials in a Gothic, parklike setting.[90]

Some genteel objects used in Clay's funerals resonated with historic notions of opulent splendor. For example, newspaper descriptions of the hearses that carried Clay's remains in several major cities emphasized the close association between material culture, refinement, and proper respect for him as a revered hero. Newspapers praised the "superb hearse" used in Washington, D.C., to bear Clay's remains through the city.[91] A correspondent for the Columbus, Ohio, newspaper noted that "the funeral car was a beautiful specimen of art."[92] The hearse was covered in black cloth, rimmed with silver stars and lace and topped with four "gilded representation[s] of a torch." The platform that bore the coffin "six feet from the ground" was also covered in black and edged with black silk tassels. The spectacle was enhanced further by the livery: "The car was spanned by a semi-circular frame-work, festooned with entwined black and white bright relief to the dark black ground. . . . The car was drawn by six white horses, each attended by a groom clad in white."[93] The Boston *Daily Atlas* called it "a gorgeous funeral car, constructed for the occasion," and noted that it was "attended by six grooms, who were young white men suitably attired."[94] The grandiose hearse depicted national grief in visual terms that relied on a vocabulary of eagles, stars, and columns that had been popular forms of American iconography since the eighteenth century, and the use of sumptuous fabric, gold, and other decorative elements went back centuries beyond that.[95] Even a hearse could function as a symbol of longed-for national unity.

Similarly, the press lavished attention on the floral arrangements that many citizens presented at Clay's funerals. Flowers, as mourning objects and when used as gifts, in the mid-nineteenth century carried a strong association with sentimentality, and newspapers reported on floral arrangements calculated to evoke emotional reactions. While flowers had long been used at funerals, elaborate displays associated with specific meanings linked to an increasingly familiar "language of flowers" were even more popular by the 1850s.[96] Clay's funeral celebrations displayed floral sentiments on a national stage. In Philadelphia, for example, a wreath featuring the "night blooming cereus" was placed on his coffin, and the newspapers noted that the flowers opened their blooms as Clay's corpse reached Independence Hall in "apparently unconscious sympathy" and then "drooped and died" when the corpse was removed.[97] This kind of floral tribute—interpreted by the public to be pregnant with meaning—would continue to be a mainstay of all public funerals for the rest of the century.

During Clay's long funeral procession, flowers often drew special attention in the press. Flowers were strewn on his coffin as it was floated on the Hudson River, chief among them "a beautiful wreath made from the 'immortelle' (or life everlasting flower) brought from France, and presented by Mrs. Ann S. Stephens, the Poetess, with a request that it might be placed on the tomb of Henry Clay in Kentucky. . . . It is bright yellow, while a cross of dark brown of the same flower is worked in it. It is admired by all as a fit emblem of the memory of Henry Clay, which will live forever in the hearts of his countrymen."[98] Immortelles gained their association with life beyond death because they retain their color and form after they have dried and therefore seem to remain alive forever. Kara Marler-Kennedy has argued that their nostalgic use at funerals (and by poets) associated national sorrow with a rejection of modernity and change.[99] Stephens's wreath was placed on Clay's coffin when it was interred in Lexington and left intact when the body was reinterred in 1857.[100] In this case, her wreath was probably not intended as an outright rejection of modernity but as a symbol of national grief that would stay in the crypt, unchanging for years to come. Flowers, as material culture, communicated emotion and symbolized traditional mourning culture tied to mid-nineteenth-century sentimentality.

The material culture of death was an integral part of the visual spectacle of Clay's funerals, and material culture would continue to influence the ways that funerals made public memory for decades to come. Market commodities, especially as they contributed to rituals like Clay's funeral, helped to define American nationhood in a manner that fit with the political principles of the Whig Party.[101] Public mourning for Clay fused old and new in a commercialized context, as did failing Whig Party politics. The visual spectacle of mourning showed how old traditions of public mourning, such as funeral processions and flowers, could be changed by market-oriented, modern material culture. Americans could take pride in the process, but the process was not without strain.

Remembering Clay's face in visual form, especially as technology allowed for reproduction of Clay images, became a key way to extend the reverence inspired by his funeral commemorations long after he was interred. Portraits of Clay, which had become important Whig political souvenirs during his lifetime, became souvenirs of national mourning after his death. Several artists capitalized on public interest in Clay during the widespread mourning and offered portraits for sale in the same pages of the newspapers that reported on funeral ceremonies. The photographer Marcus A. Root advertised to New Yorkers he would "publish soon a fine Print of his Daguerreotype, which Mr. Clay himself pronounced the best ever taken," and advised the public they could view the daguerreotype at his gallery on Broadway.[102] Horace Greeley advertised that his commemorative biography of Clay featured an "accurate steel portrait," which would help the public to remember "the great Commoner."[103] Clay portraits were both souvenirs and essential parts of the mourning process. For public use during Clay's official Washington funeral, Congress commissioned 21,000 copies of two different Clay portraits from engraver Henry Benner and commissioned a third portrait from W. H. Dougal.[104]

Clay portraits blurred the distinction between public and private mourning—as they could be used as part of the national visual spectacle and also displayed in homes for personal use. Artists, both distinguished and ordinary, felt compelled to commemorate Clay in visual form in works that also blurred the lines between high and low, commercial and commemorative. Italian painter Giuseppe Fagnani presented his Clay portrait to the nation, and Congress placed it in the Library of Congress, providing the seed for the subsequent national collection of portraits of each Speaker of the House.[105] Amateur artists also felt compelled to exhibit their portraits of the great man: the Ladies' Department at the 1852 Indiana State Fair featured a "tastefully wrought monument to Henry Clay" produced in shellwork by an unnamed woman artist, and the 1858 California State Fair exhibited a painted Clay portrait.[106] Within just a few years, Clay portrait busts had become popular decor in public buildings and homes, and art critic Clarence Cook remarked sarcastically that he knew an Italian artist who occupied "his robust life in the dolorous occupation of making eternal casts of Daniel Webster and Henry Clay."[107] The mourning for Henry Clay was so massive that it had become clichéd. Whig commercialism and Clay's image survived, but neither the party nor the man did.

Politics and Mourning

The extraordinary public mourning for Clay and the tour of his remains raise several important questions. It is clear that Clay's funeral and public mourning were enormous and elaborate, and they reached deeply into commercial culture. But why? Why was Henry Clay's funeral so much larger than any that had come before, certainly the largest public funeral for any American but George Washington? Why was he the first to lie in state in the Capitol rotunda? Why did he capture the imagination of the entire country like never before? Did the public mourning mean that all Americans ought to agree with Clay?

The *Newark Daily Advertiser* claimed that "the extraordinary homage to this great statesman is readily accounted for, as it was the direct result of his open and generous temper and commanding abilities."[108] Undoubtedly, that is true—to an extent. Clay's political talents, his long career, and his personal magnetism probably accounted for some of the wide public acclaim. Certainly, as we have seen, technology also changed just at the right moment to ensure that transportation, communication, and manufacturing played a role. But reputation and technology alone cannot explain why Clay's funeral eclipsed others so completely.

The answer lies in the politics of the 1850s. The Compromise of 1850, brokered by Clay and Stephen Douglas, had admitted the territories won in the Mexican-American War to the union, but not without considerable cost. The Fugitive Slave Act and its aggressive enforcement in northern territory threatened to worsen sectional conflict over slavery as slave catchers clashed with vigilance committees trying to protect the personal liberty of Black fugitives such as Shadrach Minkins and William and Ellen Craft.[109] Partisan conflict between Whigs and Democrats was not solved, but rather worsened, by the Compromise. In fact, the Whig Party itself, as a coalition between Northerners and Southerners, was increasingly imperiled by internal regional rifts.

The huge outpouring of grief for Clay in 1852 and the identification of Clay with a supposedly impartial version of national identity founded on unity came at a moment of anxiety over the fragility of union itself. Clay's former vice presidential running mate Theodore Freylinghuysen claimed in his eulogy of Clay that "no man in the nation was so well qualified to harmonize the distracting elements of discord. . . . He would speak of Slavery to the South, and of forbearance and conciliation to the North, as no other could."[110] The writer and Alabama socialite Octavia Le Vert declared that without Henry Clay, no "human can save the Republic."[111] Now with Clay gone, who would be ready to harmonize the nation upon the next violent clash over slavery?

The mourning for Henry Clay evinced a great desire to hearken back to an era of compromise and the possibility of national unity, and it came at the very moment when actual compromise was weakening the national union. Many of those who participated in Clay's funerals and public mourning desired to see him as a symbol of unity, even as they worried that his death would hasten the death of compromise itself. One *New York Daily Times* correspondent wrote that Clay's death and funeral in Washington, D.C., had provided a time of quiet unity "amid the hot contention of political strife."[112] The aldermen of New Orleans resolved just after his death that "while the Union lasts, the name of Henry Clay shall be hallowed," and they wished that "this may be for all time."[113] Many of those who favored the American nation as it stood in 1852 wanted to remember Clay as a national and universal symbol of unity. One correspondent for the *Christian Recorder* claimed that as he watched Americans "from North to South, from East to West" mourn for Clay, "I felt proud of my country—proud of the great American heart."[114]

Not everyone wanted to preserve the union as it was in 1852, but Clay was actively mourned by Americans of many political persuasions. The *Daily Picayune* noted just before Clay passed away that "every generous and feeling heart in the community, without distinction of party," would gather to honor him.[115] One Democratic Kentucky newspaper wrote: "Though thrice in his long life, he officiated as a Pacificator and negotiator of compromises, he was never guilty of the folly or bad taste, of uniting in the demagogical outcry that the Union was in danger. . . . Far from it, he invariably asserted that, ours was the strongest government on earth, and that he would like to see the guilty wretch who sought its dissolution."[116] Clay was celebrated in counties that in 1852 were strongly Whig but also in many that voted majority Democrat and even majority Free Soil.[117]

Still, Clay's mourning rituals were sometimes entangled with partisan politics. Both Whigs and Democrats took the opportunity to mourn him as a way to show their commitment to national unity, but they sometimes did so in partisan ways that emphasized their particular versions of American national identity and their own political programs. Whigs and Democrats, therefore, also accused one another of using Clay—supposedly transformed by his death from a Whig partisan into an impartial symbol for the ages—for crass political purposes. Mourning for Clay allowed both Whigs and Democrats simultaneously to claim the mantle of impartial national spirit and to engage in partisan battle. This important aspect of mourning—seizing the opportunity for partisan or ideological advantage while posing it as nonpartisan—would become a durable part of public funerals right up to the present.

In 1852, Whigs often took the lead in memorializing Clay. Whig political organizations mobilized to plan the Clay funeral commemorations in most major cities. In New York City, the Clay Festival Association, a club of Whigs who had celebrated Clay's birthday as a city holiday, took the lead in planning his funeral ceremonies.[118] During the torchlit funeral procession in Philadelphia, Whig associations from various wards in the city "carried banners trimmed with crape, and lanterns with mottoes, honoring the lamented dead."[119] In Hoboken, Cincinnati, and Louisville, Whig committees were the lead organizers of Clay's funeral processions.[120] Most of these Whig associations and clubs, however, worked with Democratic mourners to put on civic ceremonies that were impartial.

But Whig newspapers were not always as quiet on partisan matters in relation to Clay's funeral. Several Whig editors did try to juxtapose stories about the funeral procession with coverage of Whig conventions and with positive stories about Whig presidential politics. The *New York Daily Times* and many other papers took great care to mention how General Winfield Scott, the Whig candidate for president, stood close to Clay's hearse in the funeral procession through the streets of Washington, D.C., on June 30. He wore a "suit of black," which contrasted with other army and navy officers who processed around him in full uniform.[121] This association between Scott and Clay mattered especially because Clay had shown little interest in or support for Scott's candidacy as the pro- and antislavery factions inside the party battled openly.[122] Clay had claimed that President Fillmore's "signal success and ability" had the best hope of holding together the Whig Party, and he had publicly implored Fillmore to run for a second term.[123] It took fifty-three rounds of balloting for Winfield Scott to be nominated as the Whig candidate over Fillmore and Daniel Webster.[124]

Mourning Henry Clay in a conspicuous manner allowed Whig politicians to claim his mantle and to share in some of the public acclaim for his great patriotism—even as the party failed. The Alabama state Whig convention in Montgomery, for example, was held on September 1, the same day as the city's second funeral for Clay.[125] In Springfield, Illinois, many of the men who were gathering for the state Whig convention attended the civic funeral for Clay organized by Abraham Lincoln the day before the convention began.[126]

The presidential race was not the only contest influenced by Clay's death, which had both a real and a symbolic effect on the Whigs' balance of power. Within days of his demise, conflict arose over who would fill his vacant Senate seat. Recently elected Democratic Kentucky governor Lazarus Powell clashed with the Whig-dominated Kentucky legislature over the proper allocation of the seat. The legislature chose Whig Archibald Dixon to succeed Clay, but Governor Powell announced he intended to appoint proslavery Democrat James Guthrie to the seat.[127] A struggle ensued over who had the right to fill the vacancy, but Dixon won the seat after Guthrie declined Powell's offer.[128]

Many Democrats also mourned Henry Clay, perhaps hoping to gain in political capital or at least being unwilling to cede the patriotic mourning completely to the Whigs. To match the coverage of Winfield Scott's mourning in the Whig papers, Democratic editors countered with their own Clay panegyrics. Democratic papers lauded two Clay eulogies delivered by Democratic presidential candidate Franklin Pierce: one delivered at a nonpartisan meeting in Concord, New Hampshire, and one to Boston's Society of the Cincinnati.[129]

Several noted Democratic Party clubs also contributed showy displays to Clay funeral commemorations. The *New York Daily Times* noted that Tammany Hall, the Democratic headquarters in New York City, was "clad in widow's weeds" during the July 20 funeral procession for Clay and that the Democratic club displayed a bust of Clay draped in black on an outdoor balcony. The *Times*, itself more sympathetic to the Whigs, noted sarcastically that it was certainly the first time Tammany Hall had ever praised Clay.[130]

The Granite Club, organized as a prominent gathering of San Francisco Democrats, passed memorial resolutions expressing "profoundest regret" at Clay's death during its very first meeting, even though the city's Whig clubs took the lead in planning the funeral observance in that city.[131] The cartmen of New York City participated in that city's July 20 parade for Clay, identifying public grief as a way to participate in civic culture with "their fellow citizens" to assert their political presence among the city's workingmen—most of whom identified with the Democratic Party.[132] Even one nativist political club got in on the act. The "Native American" Pennsylvania state convention, meeting in Harrisburg on the day after Clay's congressional funeral, passed a resolution "deploring the death of Hon. Henry Clay" alongside resolutions proposing to tax all "foreigners landing on our shores" $250 and one calling for a law to prohibit the immigration of "convicts or felons."[133]

Some observers hoped that signs of public mourning by Clay's political enemies meant that his death could provide a chance for the suspension of political hostilities. Several editors hoped that the public mourning for Clay would "soften" the political struggle leading into the presidential election.[134]

Harriet Beecher Stowe commented that she hoped the mourning for Clay would cause the public to reflect on religious devotion and "would moderate the fury of political strife . . . that the heat and dust and noise of this great tournament might cease for a moment."[135] But that hope was not to be fulfilled, as some Whigs and Democrats began to use Clay's funerals as a chance to batter one another anew.

Whigs and Democrats each accused the other of using mourning for Clay for vulgar political gain. The *Rochester Daily Advertiser*, a New York Democratic paper, wrote, "We regret to notice that a few of the Whig papers are attempting to make political capital, or at least to indulge their political spleen at the circumstance that many prominent Democrats and Democratic presses are speaking in laudatory strains of the life and services of HENRY CLAY. . . . We are willing, on such an occasion as this, to drop the curtain of oblivion, and to remember only that in the character of the distinguished patriot, which we can admire and approve."[136] The same editor later accused Whigs of shedding "crocodile tears" over Clay, when they had not sufficiently supported him since the Compromise of 1850.[137] The editors of the Democratic *Kentucky New Era* made sure to note that Clay had no monopoly on patriotism: "That Mr. Clay was patriotic in all that he did, no man can doubt. . . . Still, he made no extraordinary profession to exclusive patriotism. . . . He loved his country as well as other men, but no better; nor did he arrogate to himself the condition of a monopolist of the exclusive patriotism of the Republic."[138] This critique of Whigs who tried to make Clay into a demigod verged on a criticism of Clay himself.

Some Southern Democrats went even further—using the occasion of Clay's funeral to flog the Whigs—even as they still tried to praise Henry Clay, the man. The *Richmond Examiner* praised Clay's political skill and oratory, noting the "sincere and grave sorrow in the bosom of very many citizens" upon hearing of his death. But, the paper continued, all his "perfect Whig" policies had failed: "Dust and ashes are all that he leaves in the world. . . . Clay's Compromise died at its birth."[139] The Democratic *Louisville Daily Times* wrote that the Democratic Party "respected Mr. Clay's memory" but then used Democratic mourning to denounce the Whigs for exploiting Clay's death: "We despise any attempt, come from what source it may, to make political capital out of a nation's mourning. . . . Whatever good it may do Gen. Scott, let him have it."[140]

In the end, the outpouring of grief for Henry Clay did not do much political good for Scott or the Whig Party. Scott's candidacy was hamstrung by arguments within the party over slavery and the effects of the Compromise of 1850, and he lost the election badly, receiving only 35 percent of the vote in the lower South.[141] Although slavery troubled the Democratic Party, too,

Pierce won the popular vote and overwhelmed Scott in the Electoral College by a vote of 254 to 42.[142]

Democrats had successfully integrated mourning for Clay into their campaign season. Although a few Democrats had critiqued Clay's Whig policies and ideas, none of them rejected mourning for him. Whigs and Democrats might disagree about how to mourn Clay and whether it was acceptable for their enemies to make political points out of celebrating him, but they did not reject the public's duty to mourn him as a great man.

Slavery, Race, and Death

Many abolitionists, in contrast, outright rejected public grief for Henry Clay. Many of them protested his funerals and the version of U.S. nationhood they celebrated. Clay's nation preserved slavery, and that was unacceptable to abolitionists. When the *Pennsylvania Freeman* first reported that Clay was sick and "sinking into the grave" in January 1852, the paper also noted, "We wish there was some ground to hope that, before his departure to another world, he might repent in dust and ashes of his heartless and unprincipled course on the question of slavery." Instead of using his great talents to "elevate and ennoble the race . . . his life has been mostly spent in a vain effort to 'split the difference' between Right and Wrong and to reconcile slavery in practice, with freedom in the abstract."[143] Clay himself was a slaveholder and colonizationist, and his compromise efforts had held together a union grounded in the institution of slavery. Abolitionists rejected mourning for Clay just as they rejected the national identity founded on reverence for men like him—the politicians who built and supported a slaveholding republic.

The abolitionist rejection of public mourning for Henry Clay was, in some sense, a preliminary front in what would become the battle over emancipationist memory of the Civil War. No one in 1852 knew that the Civil War or the end of the institution of slavery was coming; this is not an argument that abolitionists saw into the future or that Clay magically embodied a fight that took place after he was dead. But the abolitionist resistance to mourning him—in the face of huge national pomp and patriotic ritual that were creating an American national identity that valorized compromise—was a precursor to similar, later contests over Civil War memory. Resistance to instilling national memory in an idealized version of Henry Clay—who enslaved people and compromised to protect the institution—set the scene for resistance to triumphalist national Civil War memory that crowded out slavery and Black people.[144] Abolitionists, most notably Frederick Douglass, argued that Clay was not worthy of admiration by a public who ignored the suffering of enslaved people.

As far as the abolitionist press was concerned, the national unity created by mourning for Henry Clay came at the cost of compromising with slavery and the abuse of Black people. As the *National Era* contended a few months before Clay's death: "Mr. Clay's idolaters may worship him as much as they please, but there are some of us who have no faith in his divinity, and deny his claim to speak in behalf of the whole American People."[145] Antislavery activists envisioned a different kind of nation—one founded on true freedom and equality between the races rather than on the worship of great political compromise with slaveholders.

As might be surmised by the outpouring of grief at Clay's death, abolitionists faced an uphill battle in 1852 in their critique of him. Most public eulogists avoided talking about Clay's views on slavery, but Abraham Lincoln, who eulogized Clay in Springfield, Illinois, on July 6, praised him as a longtime supporter of gradual emancipation.[146] Many general press reports tried to link Clay to progressive ideas about slavery, since he held moderate antislavery views and was president of the American Colonization Society.

Some reports of Clay's funerals attempted to communicate how good Clay was to individual, obedient Black people by stressing the loyalty of the people he enslaved. Some newspapers even included faithful slaves in the list of family members who survived him, striking a note of paternalism in which enslaved people were considered part of the family. Other papers noted that Clay was attended at his death only by his son and by his loyal body servant. They noted that "Thornton, Mr. Clay's body servant received from the hands of his master his free papers, but never left him, even after death, until the corpse was placed in the tomb."[147] The language was remarkably similar to reports of Henry Clay's loyal dog, which refused to leave his side, even after Clay's death.

Some observers took great pains to note the participation of the people Clay enslaved in mourning rituals for their dead master. The *Weekly Herald* reported to its New York readers that at Clay's home in Lexington, "The domestics and all of the family are in deep lamentations."[148] When he visited Ashland on the day of Clay's funeral in Lexington, Henry Burchstead Skinner observed that the enslaved were "wearing the mourning badge upon their holiday garments."[149] The enslaved people may have been loyal or felt a connection to the family, but their participation in the mourning cannot be judged as voluntary, and press reports on their loyalty had no concern for their individual opinions. Rather, the image of the loyal enslaved person was used to link Clay to a benevolent view of the institution itself much as nostalgic images of loyal slaves would be deployed to shore up white supremacy during Reconstruction.[150]

The message of racial solidarity in Clay funeral commemorations transcended Black and white. West Coast newspapers similarly emphasized the participation of Chinese people in Clay's funeral pageantry in California to provide a boost to the vision of the unanimity of national grief in a directly political way. Eighteen fifty-two was a contentious year for Chinese immigrants in California, which had only just become a state as a result of the Compromise of 1850. Twenty thousand Chinese workers arrived in the state in 1852 and faced severe opposition, exemplified by Governor John Bigler, who worked to "check the tide of Asiatic immigration" and who expressed considerable racial hatred against them.[151] Yet when city leaders planned a parade in honor of Henry Clay to be held on August 10 in San Francisco, they invited two different Chinese associations to participate.

Norman Asing, the Chinese community leader and businessman who openly opposed Governor Bigler's exclusionist policies, received one invitation.[152] Perhaps Chinese residents decided to participate as a way to prove they were, in Asing's words, "lover[s] of free institutions" as much as white government officials were.[153] When the "grand funeral procession" took place, newspapers noted that "some 500 Chinese traders and merchants appeared in the procession, and conducted themselves with the utmost propriety."[154] Although they came at it from drastically different points of view, the Chinese merchants and the press each claimed that Chinese participation bore witness to the solidarity of community mourning for Henry Clay.

Images of loyal enslaved people and Chinese traders reverencing Clay notwithstanding, abolitionists refuted the otherwise unanimous praise for him at every chance they got. The Boston Free Soil newspaper wrote that "no incense can be burnt upon the altar of his memory by a single sincere lover of truth and the right."[155] A letter to the editor in the Cleveland Plain Dealer raged: "We acknowledge his genius and talents, his eloquence, his statesmanship, but Missouri, black with the curse of slavery sends a groan back to his grave, re-echoed and repeated by his own slaves in bondage. . . . his death has not effaced their wrongs."[156] A Canadian abolitionist newspaper called Clay the "dead . . . embodiment of pro-slavery."[157]

Beyond being undeserved, several abolitionists felt that the mourning rituals for Henry Clay outright mocked the notion of American liberty and even the American people themselves. A writer for the Pennsylvania Freeman expressed disgust that the papers "are filled" with stories about honors paid to Clay and asked whether if Clay had devoted "his life to the cause of emancipation, would the American people have shed tears over his remains or covered his bier with flowers?" The writer posited that the outpouring of grief for Clay showed how the public "applaud and glorify themselves for their guilty connivance at the great crime in the perpetration of which he was so conspicuous."[158]

Frederick Douglass published a letter from a "Brooklyn Correspondent" that noted that "half the world" was caught up in mourning Clay, but that "no crape [descends] from my arm, and no tears fall from my eyes, and no sorrow penetrates deep my bosom." The correspondent deplored the "vast amount of fuss and ado the whites make about their leading men . . . while they equally underrate the merits of the black men" among them.[159]

Abolitionists did not want the union preserved if it meant preserving slavery, and so they declined to take part in the public grief for the Great Compromiser, urging true lovers of liberty to boycott the funeral rites. The *Liberator*, the nation's most prominent abolitionist paper, reported that Providence, Rhode Island, abolitionist Samuel W. Wheeler hung a sign in his shop window during Clay's funeral procession that read: "Humanity hath no tears or sorrow to manifest for the death of slaveholders, and other oppressors of the human race."[160] Abolitionist William C. Nell reported to the *Liberator* that the "colored citizens" of Rochester, New York, held an anticolonization meeting at the Ford Street Baptist Church on August 9, at which they voted that "the conduct of certain colored men, by participating in the funeral pageant of Henry Clay, in this city, evinces either a lack of self-respect—or a most lamentable state of ignorance, and is deserving the severest reprobation and censure."[161] Mourning for Clay, for the men of color in Rochester, became by its nature a proslavery act. Douglass concurred, noting in his paper that among those eulogizing Clay in upstate New York were prominent Whig clergy who supported slavery and slave catchers.[162]

Douglass and other abolitionists noted with outrage how Clay's mourning coincided with Independence Day celebrations. A Missouri Free-Soiler, using the pseudonym "Gibbon," wrote bitterly of the Clay eulogies delivered in Jefferson, Missouri, on July 4 in a letter to the *Cleveland Plain Dealer*. "Gibbon" noted that, despite all the plaudits to his greatness, slavery would be Clay's real legacy: "Laud him as you will, posterity and all just men will pronounce that he deserves the fate of a gigantic sinner, gliding to the grave amid clanking chains, riveted with his own hand, and a heart filled with bitterness towards political rivals. . . . We do not assail him; he has entered the untried realm of the eternal future, where he meets alike the naked spirit of his fellow sinners, and his unshackled bondman. Peace to his ashes. God be merciful to his soul, but let his sins be remembered."[163] The idea that Clay should be remembered as a "gigantic sinner" with the sound of "clanking chain" instead of the roar of a grateful crowd flew in the face of public mourning for Clay.

The *Plain Dealer* may have been directly invoking Frederick Douglass by referencing the sounds of a "clanking chain" rebuking Clay. The clanking chain was a trope in what became Douglass's most famous oration, "What, to the Slave, Is the Fourth of July?" delivered just days earlier on July 5, 1852, in Rochester, New York. And Douglass's speech took place in the middle of Henry Clay's funerals—a fact of which he was well aware.

Douglass condemned Clay's hypocrisy, and Douglass's Fourth of July speech, one of the most important orations in American history, was influenced by public mourning for Clay. Previous scholars seem to have missed how Douglass's oration related directly to Clay's funeral and public mourning. None of the major works on Douglass's speech mentions Clay's influence on Douglass, even though he wrote and delivered the oration as Clay was being mourned and just before Clay's body passed through Rochester.[164]

Douglass confronted the meaning of Clay's death as he wrote and delivered his antislavery address on July 5 in Rochester. On July 1, Douglass had published a very dark eulogy for Clay in his newspaper, noting that Black people and abolitionists would not be able to join in mourning Clay because they had "vastly more reason to condemn, than to applaud his character; to rejoice, than to mourn his death." Douglass wrote in the eulogy that even "with the *Declaration of Independence*' sounding in his ears, from childhood to old age," Henry Clay did nothing to advance the cause of freedom, but was rather a slaveholder and "a man-stealer! Having done more than any other man in this country to make slavery perpetual."[165] With the newspapers full of praise for Clay, Douglass's Fourth of July speech similarly denounced the founders, calling them "brave" and "great men" who nonetheless denied the true meaning of their own Declaration of Independence. Douglass denounced the Compromise of 1850 and the Fugitive Slave Act, which he said "nationalized" slavery "in its most horrible and revolting form" by commanding "all good citizens" to become the hunters of men.[166] On July 6, one day after Douglass's speech, the celebrated corpse of Henry Clay, architect of the Compromise, passed through Rochester to great public acclaim. Douglass's scorching Fourth of July speech, known as perhaps the most significant denunciation of American proslavery hypocrisy up to that point, drew directly from the tone of his Henry Clay eulogies and happened against a backdrop of public mourning for the great white politician, whose greatness Douglass questioned.

The only hope that Douglass and other abolitionists harbored for the rehabilitation of Clay's memory was the prospect that his will might provide for freeing the people he had enslaved.[167] When Clay's will was read at the beginning of August, however, abolitionists were disappointed. Clay's will freed very few of the enslaved, and those who were freed were to be let go extremely gradually, in keeping with his colonizationist views. Clay bequeathed people he owned who were born before 1850 as property to his family and provided that "children of his slaves born after January 1, 1850, are to be liberated and sent to Liberia," men at age twenty-eight and women at twenty-five. The *National Era* observed that this quite conservative arrangement did not show "the generosity of character for which his friends gave him credit."[168] By 1853, abolitionist papers noted bitterly to their readers that Clay's executors were selling Ashland, his Lexington estate, along with "a number of Slaves and thorough bred Horses."[169] Clay's son James, who purchased Ashland after the will was executed, became a speculator in the internal slave trade within a few years.[170]

Abolitionists rejected the national festival of mourning for Clay because he represented compromise, and they were ready to see compromise with slavery and slaveholders die. Clay's Whig coalition and his own status as a slaveholder held out no hope for him as a symbol of racial equality. Frederick Douglass noted in his newspaper, without sorrow, that "the Compromisers are passing away to their final account."[171] For antislavery activists, compromise came at too great a cost to the enslaved, and it belonged in the grave with Henry Clay.

The Death of Compromise

The political controversy around Clay's mourning—the election-year squabbling between Whigs and Democrats as the Whig Party was weakened by regional tensions and the objections to Clay by abolitionists—made it clear that unity was not absolute and could not be taken for granted. Although arguments over Clay's mourning helped to create different versions of American national identity, the large-scale pageantry and mourning were not enough to guarantee national unity. Divisions over mourning for Clay served as an example of the kind of rifts over slavery and the role of racism in American society that would carry forward into the Civil War and after. The national mourning for Henry Clay represented an innovation in American public funerals, but the national sentiments it created were not strong enough to counter the rising tide of disunion over the following decade.

Many who had taken part in the outpouring of public mourning for Henry Clay worried that his passing also marked the death of sectional compromise—or at least his version of sectional compromise, one that stressed unanimity of opinion centered around patriotism. Clay's obituary in the *National Era* stated that he had been so powerful because of what he represented to "the masses." The paper continued that "Clay represented the Principles of Compromise and Nationality" but tried to reassure its readers that "the spirit of Compromise has not departed with Clay."[172] Members of the Board of Assistant Aldermen in New York City resolved that their sorrow for Clay deepened because he would no longer be devoted to "reconciling sectional animosities, and to vindicating and preserving that glorious Union in whose service he has so long and so faithfully labored."[173] At one of the Montgomery, Alabama, funerals for Clay in September 1852, the eulogist, former Alabama congressman Henry W. Hilliard, praised the "breadth and nationality of his views," reminding Montgomery's citizens that "Mr. Clay's cast of character was American—distinctly American."[174]

A varied set of public men eulogized Clay as the greatest champion of the union, and many eulogies expressed concern that Clay's absence might make possible the failure of the United States. On the floor of Congress, Whigs and Democrats alike praised Clay for his ability, in the words of Pennsylvania representative James Cooper, to spot severe threats to "the integrity of the Union," and "he has always been the first to note danger, as well as to suggest ways of averting it." John J. Crittenden, whose own family would be split by the Civil War and who would continue to argue for union and compromise into the 1860s, eulogized Clay in Louisville in 1852 for his talent at compromise in 1850, "when the foundation of the Union trembled under the fierce sectional agitation."[175] Clay was lionized as union's greatest champion, which begged the question of what would happen now that he was gone.

Clay continued to serve as a symbol of union and compromise, even in uncertain times, in the decades after his death. To many, Clay's memory was part of the national political fabric. As the *Farmer's Cabinet* newspaper noted, "His physical frame will decay, but his great history will never be forgotten."[176] Sarah Bischoff Paulus has argued persuasively that eulogies for Clay continued to influence political debates, even as compromise became increasingly impossible in the decade before the Civil War. Similarly, visual commemorations that linked Clay to ideas of compromise and union, such as envelopes bearing his portrait, remained popular even after 1861.[177]

To help preserve his everlasting memory, a national memorial to Clay, only one of several statues in his honor, was constructed in Lexington Cemetery, and he was permanently interred in the crypt beneath it in 1857.[178] The monumental column, more than 100 feet high with a statue of Clay in an orator's pose atop it, served as a draw to those interested in his compromise politics as soon as it was finished. Visitors could peer through the iron gates at the base of the monument to glimpse Clay's marble sarcophagus, "ornamented with gathered rods and bonds emblematic of union."[179] But, ironically, Clay's monument towers over a funerary landscape marked not by compromise and union but by national division. The other prominent memorials in Lexington Cemetery are the Lexington Confederate Soldier Monument, the Ladies' Confederate Monument, and the grave site of Confederate cavalry general John Hunt Morgan.[180]

In 1852, the innovative tour of Clay's remains that ended at Lexington Cemetery offered more Americans than ever the chance to personally encounter the subject of their ritualized grief. But the political controversy around Clay's mourning and the loss of his political talents also made it clear that unity was not absolute and could not be taken for granted. In fact, Henry Clay's public funerals set precedents not for continued rituals of compromise and union but for the many ritualized funerals that would result from the Civil War once the union was fractured.

Chapter 2

The Death of Union and the Martyrdom of Elmer Ellsworth and Stonewall Jackson

On May 24, 1861, an unnamed correspondent from the *New York Herald*, along with Sen. Henry Wilson, the incoming chair of the Senate Military Affairs Committee, visited President Abraham Lincoln in the White House. They found the president in a state of extreme agitation and overcome by emotion.

They approached Lincoln, but the president called out, "Excuse me . . . for I cannot talk."

They were about to ask if Lincoln had a throat ailment, when, as the correspondent wrote, "to our surprise, the President burst into tears, and concealed his face in his handkerchief. . . . He walked up and down the room for some moments, and we stepped aside in silence, not a little moved at such an unusual spectacle, in such a man, in such a place."[1]

After "composing himself somewhat," Lincoln explained that his outburst was due to the news of the violent death, early that morning, of his friend and former law student, Col. Elmer Ellsworth. The Union army officer had led the men of his famous Fire Zouave unit across the Potomac to occupy the Confederate city of Alexandria, Virginia. Ellsworth removed from the roof of the Marshall House hotel a Confederate flag, hoisted by innkeeper James W. Jackson as an intentional provocation to Unionists in Washington across the river. As Ellsworth descended the Marshall House staircase, Jackson stepped forward and killed him with a blast from a shotgun. Instantly, Cpl. Francis Brownell shot Jackson with his service musket rifle and then ran through Jackson's body with the attached bayonet.

Lincoln continued to explain his grief to his two visitors: "I will [make] no apology, gentlemen . . . for my weakness; but I knew poor Ellsworth well, and held him in great regard. . . . Just as you entered the room, Captain Cox left me, after giving me the painful details of Ellsworth's unfortunate death. . . . The event was so unexpected and the recital so touching, that it quite unmanned me." The president continued talking about Ellsworth in a "tremulous voice," regretting that he was killed "not by the fortunes of war, but by the hands of an assassin."[2]

Two years later, during the last week of May 1863, a similar scene unfolded when Confederate Brig. Gen. William Nelson Pendleton went to consult with his commander, Robert E. Lee, who was planning a new invasion of Union territory. Page found Lee crying; he was in an emotional mood and wanted to discuss religion. The topic was not entirely surprising, since, before they were fellow officers, Pendleton had served as Lee's priest at the Episcopal parish in Lexington, Virginia. But this conversation was not an ordinary theological discussion; rather, it was prompted by Lee's deep grief. Pendleton later told his wife that Lee brought up "the great question of religion" because he was "deeply concerned for the spiritual welfare of the soldiers." Lee broke into tears, and Pendleton realized that Lee was pondering religion because he was thinking about the recent death of Lt. Gen. Thomas J. "Stonewall" Jackson. Page wrote to his wife that he and Lee "wept a good deal as we talked of Jackson."[3] The tears shed by Robert E. Lee as he contemplated the death of Stonewall Jackson, his most talented subordinate, mixed sorrow with concern for the souls of his men. But Lee was also pondering the fate of the Confederacy.

The president's tears and the Confederate general's tears, as personal emotions and as signs of sorrowful memory, defined grief as a significant component in rival forms of nationalism during the U.S. Civil War. The "unusual spectacle" of crying by both the president and the general aroused sympathy and action. Their tears signified personal and national sorrow for the deaths of two brave officers—Elmer E. Ellsworth and Stonewall Jackson—whose deaths helped to establish the martial sacrifice of strong, white men as bedrock values of both American and Confederate nationalism. Heroic wartime death occupied a central place in public culture and the popular imagination and helped to justify the war itself. The public funerals that followed provided the opportunity for rival versions of national identity to be ritualized.

Mourning for the dead heroes of the Civil War—in both regions—became part of U.S. nationalism and Confederate nationalism. Even as they were diametrically opposed as national symbols, Elmer Ellsworth and Stonewall Jackson as symbols drew from the same kind of military memory during the war and propelled both sides of the conflict as both men received huge public funerals. Of course, their deaths were exceeded by hundreds of thousands more, and citizens lacked the resources to mourn even every officer's death with equal pageantry. Some dead officers stood out and demanded more attention. As important martyrs for each side, Ellsworth and Jackson set important patterns in how their nations commemorated death as part of national identity and Civil War memory—even as the war still raged.

Public funerals for Elmer Ellsworth and Stonewall Jackson demonstrated the power of collective mourning, even as they helped to create opposing national identities. The funerals for these heroes—who embodied a mix of nineteenth-century ideals of restrained and martial manhood—prefigured many of the contests over Civil War memory for decades to come.[4] By participating in public funerals for Ellsworth and Jackson, people not only mourned their heroes but also created ties between themselves and reinforced sectional divides, displaying in their very public grief that they were supporting what it meant to be American or to be Confederate. Public mourning rituals were similar, even as their meanings were diametrically opposed.

The tears of President Lincoln and of General Robert E. Lee would join the private tears of millions of Americans to fix sorrow at the heart of national identity, and public funerals would teach Americans how to imagine their own versions of America into being as they remembered the sacrifice of war. Public funerals were important during the Civil War, even though they grew more difficult to pull off as the conflict intensified, and they helped set the standard for much of the mourning and memory that would follow the war.

The Death of Ellsworth

Elmer Ellsworth's epic public funerals made him a martyr to the Union Cause and shored up Union support in the first months of the Civil War. Ellsworth was a good candidate to become the first major Union martyr of the Civil War because he was already quite famous in both the North and the South when he perished in Alexandria in 1861. This fact, combined with his friendship with Abraham Lincoln, helped him to achieve posthumous glory. Ellsworth was a dashing young man of twenty-four from upstate New York, who had a long-standing interest in military matters but who lacked the wealth and connections in his youth to receive a commission to West Point.[5] He studied military drill on his own while working in business in the Midwest, and he achieved wide notice in 1859 when he organized the National Guard Cadets of Chicago into a Zouave unit and took them on a highly publicized tour to display their colorful uniforms and their polished military discipline.[6] The visual appeal of military drill and especially flashy uniforms added to the Zouaves' popularity, and they inspired a fashion craze for items that matched their style.[7] Zouave units imitated French Algerian military costume and wore stylish blue jackets with red bloomers and an elaborate sash belt, sometimes accompanied by a fez. Alice Fahs writes that Ellsworth's Zouaves embodied "the glittering, dazzling, show-uniform side of the military," and their popularity made Ellsworth into a national celebrity.[8] Ellsworth's acclaim drew the attention of Abraham Lincoln, who admired his Zouave drill.

In 1860, Ellsworth left the National Guard Cadets to return to Springfield, Illinois, and study law under Lincoln and William Herndon, and he became a faithful Lincoln political organizer in that year's presidential campaign. In early 1861, Ellsworth could not win a clerkship or a high command position, despite Lincoln's support, because of political wrangling with Secretary of War

Simon Cameron. Instead, he went to New York City and organized a new unit, the Eleventh New York, dubbed "Ellsworth's Fire Zouaves," because it was made up of New York City firemen, a group with a notorious reputation for heroic, rowdy toughness.[9] At the very beginning of the Civil War, Ellsworth's Zouaves were enlisted into federal service. They were one of the first volunteer companies to arrive in Washington; they first headquartered in the U.S. Capitol building and then camped across from the Navy Yard.[10] On May 24, 1861, the day after Virginia seceded from the union, the unit was dispatched from Washington, D.C., to occupy Alexandria, Virginia, in order to secure the approaches to the capital city.

The man Ellsworth encountered in Alexandria in the early hours of May 24, James W. Jackson, was an almost equally colorful figure, if less well known on the national scene. He also possessed qualities that would help elevate him to mythic status after death: he was a tall, tough man from Fairfax County, Virginia, who had marched with the state militia on John Brown at Harpers Ferry. He was a vocal proslavery, anti-Lincoln man and an early supporter of secession.[11] He was known as something of a hothead.[12]

By 1861, Jackson was the innkeeper of the Marshall House hotel in Alexandria, and during the run-up to the war, he exhibited his support for the secessionist cause by flying a huge Confederate national flag above his establishment. He meant the flag as a visual insult; it was clearly visible across the Potomac in Washington, D.C., and newspapers there took notice in the days leading up to Ellsworth's expedition to Alexandria.[13] Jackson contended that he was merely showing his political commitment to the new Confederacy, and he declared (in what some later thought was prophetic fashion) that if anyone tried to remove the flag, "There would be two dead men about when that flag came down."[14]

That is exactly what happened on May 24, 1861. Colonel Ellsworth and the Fire Zouaves captured Alexandria without much resistance in a military action of little excitement. What followed, however, became much more important. As Ellsworth led some of his men to capture the Alexandria telegraph office, he noticed the Confederate flag flying over the Marshall House, and he told his companions: "Boys, we must have that down before we return."[15]

Ellsworth entered the hotel with a few men and climbed unopposed to the roof, where he cut down the banner. As Ellsworth came down the stairway with the flag in his hands, he met James Jackson, who confronted the Union officer and shot him dead. Almost simultaneously, Cpl. Francis E. Brownell (who was later awarded the Medal of Honor for his actions) shot Jackson and impaled him on his bayonet. At the end of the exchange, the young Union colonel lay dead, bleeding on the Confederate flag. Jackson, the flag's owner, lay dead as well, pinned to the floor by a Union bayonet.

The ritualized public mourning that followed the events of May 24 in Alexandria, and the subsequent cultural adoration of both Ellsworth and Jackson, elevated their clash into something much larger than the specifics would seem to warrant. The public worshipped or reviled Ellsworth and Jackson, according to their Union or Confederate loyalties, and claimed each man had died for a "cause." Ellsworth's massive funeral commemorations helped to fuel the conflict between Union and Confederacy just as the war was starting in earnest and helped to define white, male sacrifice as a national goal worth fighting for in and of itself. After Ellsworth and Jackson battled to the death in a hotel stairway in Alexandria, Virginia, the ritualized public mourning that followed turned them into the first two martyrs of the Civil War, one for the Union and one for the Confederacy. The rituals of mourning for these martyrs showed how reverence for military heroes, one of the bedrock unifying elements of American national identity in the early nineteenth century, helped at the beginning of the Civil War to drive a wedge between the North and the South.[16]

Funerals and "Sorrowing Spectators"

When the furor at the Marshall House died down on May 24, Ellsworth's body was wrapped in the flag and borne to the Navy Yard, where it was embalmed and visited by "hundreds of sorrowing spectators," including President and Mrs. Lincoln, before being taken back to the capital. Lincoln talked to Corporal Brownell, who narrated the Marshall House incident for the president and showed him the bloody Confederate flag he still held as he guarded Ellsworth's body at the Navy Yard.[17]

Lincoln arranged for Ellsworth's remains to lie in state at the White House, where they were viewed by thousands before a formal funeral in the East Room.[18] A special correspondent to the *Philadelphia Inquirer* wrote that a mass of "citizens and soldiers" passed by Ellsworth's coffin before Lincoln and his cabinet surrounded it for the funeral ceremony. The paper described the scene to an eager public: "During the [funeral] obsequies President LINCOLN sat, with his head leaning upon his hand, silent and seemingly very sorrowful."[19]

After the funeral in Washington, D.C., Ellsworth's remains received continued national attention and more public funerals on their way to burial near his home in Mechanicville, New York. National attention was focused on Ellsworth's mourning rituals, although it was extraordinarily unusual for a fairly low-ranking officer, or anyone other than a president, to be given a White House funeral.[20] Alfred Waud, a sketch artist for the New York *Illustrated News*, did a pencil drawing of the funeral that shows a mournful, if opulent, scene. President Lincoln, Gen. Winfield Scott, Secretary of State William

Alfred Waud, "Funeral Service over Col. Ellsworth at the White House East Room," 1861. Library of Congress, Prints and Photographs Division, LC-USZ62-4283.

Henry Seward, and other military and government officials surround the casket, which is draped with a huge American flag and bouquets of white lilies. Mrs. Lincoln and the other two ladies in the scene hold white handkerchiefs to their faces, presumably to wipe away tears. Ellsworth's remains are the center of attention, and his coffin is highlighted by its location within black draping beneath an ornate crystal chandelier. Rev. Smith Pyne, who conducted the ceremony, is depicted with arms open—captured seemingly mid-invocation.[21]

After the White House funeral, Ellsworth's body was paraded down Pennsylvania Avenue, which was lined with mourners. The *Philadelphia Inquirer* reported that "Zouave BROWNELL, who killed JACKSON, was a great centre of attraction as he walked in line his eyes still red with weeping. . . . He carried the Secession banner bathed with ELLSWORTH's blood."[22] The bloodstained Confederate flag and Ellsworth's body parading down Pennsylvania Avenue became symbols of Union martyrdom. The newspapers emphasized scenes of manly sentimentality—the weeping president and the red-eyed fellow soldier. These inspired melancholy and also touched a vein of sympathy designed to move the reader to action. By taking part, in print, in Ellsworth's funeral, readers were supposed to react by defending the nation.

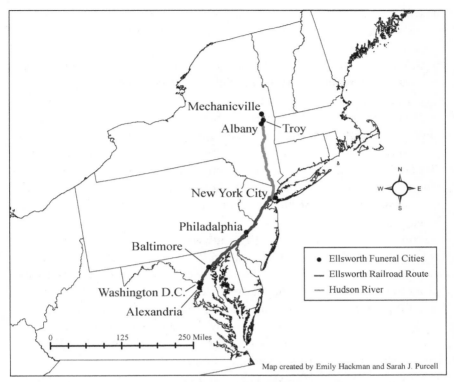

Col. Elmer Ellsworth funeral route, 1861. Data from IPUMS, National Historical
Geographic Information System; Jeremy Atack, "Historical Geographic Information
Systems (GIS) Database of U.S. Railroads for 1861 (May 2016); University of Nebraska,
Railroads and the Making of Modern America," http://railroads.unl.edu/resources/;
National Weather Service, Geographic Information Services. Map by Sarah J. Purcell
and Emily Hackman.

Ellsworth's remains traveled for burial in a set of rituals that resembled
Henry Clay's nine years earlier. A specially shrouded train transported the
remains to Philadelphia, where they were transferred to another train headed
for New York City via Jersey City.[23] In New York City, Ellsworth lay in state at
City Hall and was visited by thousands more people, who by this time had
been captivated by coverage of his death in the Northern newspapers. Newspapers emphasized the scale and sincerity of public mourning for Ellsworth
in New York City—the viewing was held in City Hall rather than at the Astor
House as originally planned because the hotel proved too small to hold the
number of mourners who turned out to see Ellsworth's remains.[24] Ellsworth's
parents received visitors at the Astor House, where, just one month earlier,
W. H. Wickham, president of the New York City Fire Department, had

presented Ellsworth and the Fire Zouaves with their regimental colors in a ceremony designed to praise the "gallant band" and inspire them to fight.[25]

Even in a city that saw frequent public ceremony and that had turned out for similar funerals of Henry Clay and others, the scale and seeming national importance of public mourning for Ellsworth were noteworthy. As one paper claimed: "The Colonel's death was a national calamity, and his burial was a national solemnity. . . . The coffin was borne through the street[s] laden with flowers, and all along the route of march many eyes were in tears."[26] The *New York Times* claimed that at least 10,000 people viewed Ellsworth's remains at City Hall and that thousands more were turned away when there was not enough time to admit them and when police worried about crowd control.[27] Another observer felt the New York crowds were so large that they "almost defied computation."[28]

From New York City, Ellsworth's body was taken by the steamboat *Francis Skiddy* to Albany, where it again lay in state inside the hall of the State Assembly and was viewed by additional "vast numbers" of mourners.[29] Cities across the North flew their flags at half-staff to honor Ellsworth.[30] After Albany, his parents conducted Ellsworth's remains to his hometown of Mechanicville, New York, where he was buried with additional military ritual, every detail of which the papers recounted for a wide readership. The *New York Times* correspondent pronounced it a "simple but deeply impressive" burial ceremony that would please even city dwellers who were tired of "pomp" but felt a "deep current of genuine sorrow" for Ellsworth's burial.[31]

In addition to daily newspaper coverage, all the illustrated news weeklies, popular sources of news and entertainment around the country, featured Ellsworth and his funeral prominently. *Frank Leslie's Illustrated Newspaper* published a large pictorial on Ellsworth's funeral ceremonies accompanied by a biography praising his virtuous life and death.[32] *Harper's Weekly* featured portraits of Ellsworth and Brownell, images of the Zouaves in camp, and large pictures of the Marshall House and the Ellsworth and Jackson death scene alongside descriptions of the funeral proceedings.[33] The *New York Illustrated News* also ran an engraving of the Marshall House scene, portraits of Ellsworth, and images of the Fire Zouaves in action.[34]

Confederates also paid attention to the incident, and James Jackson, the Southern martyr killed by Ellsworth's aide, also received a public funeral and attracted press attention immediately after his death. The Southern press was less far-reaching than Northern publications, and Jackson's funeral was less elaborate than Ellsworth's, but reaction to Jackson's death was nevertheless widespread and notable in the South. Alexandria mercantile clerk Henry B. Whittington wrote in his diary on the night of the invasion of Alexandria that "when it was announced that Ellsworth . . . had been killed whilst endeavoring to carry off a Confederate flag from the 'Marshall House' . . . a general expression of joy was manifested by our most quiet citizens at this result." Whittington pledged that "death of the brave and patriotic Jackson" and his stand for the Confederate flag "will long be remembered by our people."[35] James W. Jackson seemed destined to match Elmer Ellsworth in future memory—each a hero, and each a villain.[36]

This process of converting sacrifice instantly into significant war memory helped to make commemoration an important part of both American and Confederate national identity. Both Elmer Ellsworth and James W. Jackson were transformed, even as they were being buried, into figures meant to motivate military and political action. Ellsworth, as a Union martyr, became the subject of poetry, *tableaux vivant*, sheet music, quick biographies, commemorative stationery and envelopes, portraits, busts, and dozens of newspaper articles from Philadelphia to Madison to San Francisco.[37] In all of these various cultural forms, Jackson was depicted as a villain and was branded as Ellsworth's "assassin." In the Southern press, by contrast, Jackson was represented as a martyr who died heroically defending the Confederate flag from Ellsworth and his "villains," who brutally shot Jackson and "mangled" his dead body, as the *Macon Daily Telegraph* put it.[38] Both men became subjects of elegy and mourning poetry.[39]

Martyrs and Relics

The spectacle of mourning for Elmer Ellsworth and James Jackson, as martyrs, contributed to the formation of national identity for both Americans and Confederates at a key moment, just as the Civil War was beginning. Their altercation took place less than a month after the attack on Fort Sumter and just as both sides were mobilizing for war. In the first months of war, mobilization took many forms: calls for enlistments, political organizing, gathering resources, and also motivating both soldiers and civilians to support violence. Reverence for early martyrs, respect for their relics, and loud praise for their sacrifices played an important part in defining the war causes for each side and in supporting that mobilization process.[40] The cultural veneration of martyrs mattered in concrete ways as the war began.

Part of the power of Ellsworth's martyrdom, as with religious and military martyrs of the past, issued from the veneration of his physical remains. The ritual display of the martyr's remains worked to cement the allegiance of the faithful.[41] Nineteenth-century Americans were accustomed to the regular display of corpses in both family and political contexts, but here at the beginning of the war, visual contact with Ellsworth's remains became an important means of communicating the larger meaning of sacrifice in the Union Civil War cause.

During the public funeral processions, Ellsworth's body and the Confederate flag stained with his blood were treated as a martyr's relics, and descriptions of his corpse in the press helped to bolster the connection between manliness, sacrifice, and patriotic death. In New York City, as mourners paid their respects, Ellsworth's body was displayed with symbolic flower arrangements, a large American flag, and the Confederate flag he had removed from Jackson's roof "sprinkled here and there with his blood."[42] The *Philadelphia Inquirer* called the "rebel flag stained with his blood" a "trophy of his glory."[43] One of Ellsworth's Zouaves wrote to the *Inquirer* a few days later that the flag "stained with his blood" had been "purified by this contact from the baseness of its former meaning," and its treatment in Ellsworth's funerals seemed to indicate that the public looked to his blood to consecrate a meaning for the war.[44]

Ellsworth's body became the object of Union patriotic fascination, and his public funerals invited scrutiny of his remains. The physical attributes of Ellsworth's body during his lifetime had already been an object of popular comment during his prewar tour with the Chicago Zouaves, and the public expressed fascination with how death had affected this famous specimen of vigorous manhood. Lincoln's secretary (and future secretary of state) John Hay wrote in the July 1861 *Atlantic Monthly* magazine that before the war Ellsworth had possessed a strong body comparable to a well-muscled "antique sculpture," which created a manly ideal: "What would have killed an ordinary man did not injure Ellsworth. His iron frame seemed incapable of dissolution or waste."[45]

The greatness of Ellsworth's physique elevated the greatness of its sacrifice. One Ohio newspaper commented that the public was distraught at his death because "as a military man, he was accomplished, cool and brave, and all eyes were turned to him in hope and confidence in this great struggle."[46] All "eyes" remained focused on him after death, only now he would have to lead through the inspiration of his martyrdom instead of by his military talent.

Both Ellsworth's manly ideal and his body's treatment as a relic contributed to public fascination with just how death affected his physical being. Large numbers of Americans wanted to "view the features" of their dead hero.[47] Thomas Holmes, who embalmed Ellsworth, built a lucrative wartime business in part upon his reputation for preserving Ellsworth's corpse.[48] Newspaper articles about Ellsworth's funerals often commented on his appearance and reported that mourners were keen to catch a glimpse of the martyr's flesh, even though embalming had not perfectly preserved the remains. The *Philadelphia Inquirer*'s special correspondent assured his readers that, although a ghastly corpse, Ellsworth looked "natural, even beautiful, in his slumber of death. . . . He appeared like one who might unite great firmness with great judgment; like one who might strike a foe to the earth, but who would be as gentle as a woman in attending the couch of the wounded after the battle was over."[49] The final act before Ellsworth was buried in Mechanicville, New York, was to uncover his face to allow the hometown mourners a look.[50]

The press claimed that this visual contact with the martyred Ellsworth would play a special role in his power to motivate the coming fight. Newspapers stressed that "many persons, especially soldiers, have taken a farewell look at him."[51] That "farewell look" was meant to mix melancholy with inspiration. The Springfield Illinois State Journal asked of Ellsworth's surviving Zouaves: "Do our New York Firemen need a visible evidence of the manner of the death of him who mustered and trained them and led them out for this war? We are sure they do not need it, and yet we beg them to cherish sacredly the traitors' flag that is filled with his blood, and let the South learn to tremble and grow pale at the sight of the crimson folds when they go to battle with the war cry of REMEMBER ELLSWORTH!"[52] The Zouaves (and really all Northern readers) were told to call upon their visual memory—of Ellsworth's face, of his strong manly body, of his wasted corpse, and of his blood on the captured Confederate flag—in order to fire their lust for vengeance against the South.

Public mourning extended into popular culture as the same visual memory helped to fuel the popularity of Ellsworth engravings, cartes de visite, and lithographed covers of sheet-music funeral marches. Within weeks of the incident, printmakers and publishers had rushed to press with visuals— depicting both the death scene and portraits of the major actors. In one popular example, Currier and Ives depicted the Marshall House scene in a print that elevated Ellsworth to monumental proportions, showing an exaggerated scene of his tragic death clutching the Confederate flag.[53] In the image Ellsworth, notable in life for his short stature, towers over landlord Jackson, who is significantly clad in plain, civilian clothes as he takes murderous aim at the Union hero. The dripping blood, often reddened in hand-colored editions, also highlighted the drama, as it was depicted flowing from Ellsworth directly onto the flag in his hands. Corporal Brownell takes aim at Jackson simultaneously to avenge his commander, albeit in a manner demonstrating the artist's unfamiliarity with firearms.

Gazing on Ellsworth's image could act as an extension of gazing on his remains—both acts used his body as a form of Union patriotic inspiration. All told, more than eighty different Ellsworth visuals were sold all over the North in 1861 and 1862.[54]

Pictures of Ellsworth were meant to motivate sympathy and action, urging anti-Confederate revenge. One New York ballad sheet displayed a portrait

"Death of Col. Ellsworth after hauling down the rebel flag," engraving by Currier and Ives, 1861. Library of Congress, Prints and Photographs Division, LC-DIG-pga-08555.

"Remember Ellsworth!" Envelope featuring the colonel standing on a Confederate flag, c. 1861. Library of Congress, Prints and Photographs Division, LC-DIG-ppmsca-35582.

of Ellsworth as it warned, "The Southern land shall rue the day, When he became the assassin's prey."[55] The *Newark Daily Advertiser* invoked the memory of the Revolution when seeking to explain why Ellsworth's memory could be so powerful to motivate action. Ellsworth was "handsome in person, one who knew no fear, and courted danger. . . . The historian loves such characters as Col. Ellsworth. Their portraits adorn his pages like pictures of an illustrated work. . . . Such are those of the men of Lexington, and of Bunker Hill. . . . Forever hallowed in our memories may they be! They are the battle cries of our republic."[56]

Civilians and soldiers could purchase a variety of commemorative envelopes that featured pictures of Ellsworth with slogans such "Remember Ellsworth" juxtaposed against "To the End of the Rebellion."[57] Dozens of versions of such envelopes were imprinted with military portraits of Ellsworth and scenes of his death match with Jackson. Others showed lively Zouaves standing guard or leaping into action, moved by the memory of Ellsworth's sacrifice. At least two different envelopes depicted Ellsworth in pantheons of heroes alongside portraits of presidents, including Washington and Lincoln, visual material that emphasized a deliberately political message about the meaning of Ellsworth's death.[58] President Lincoln had declared that war was necessary to preserve union (and many Northerners who were not radical, antislavery

Republicans thought of union as the heart of the cause), and such talk of vengeance meant that union could only be restored through blood.

Public grief for Ellsworth directly connected the Civil War to the public memory of the Revolutionary War, seen as a glorious inspiration for American nationalism. Ellsworth was frequently compared to Joseph Warren, the revered martyr of the Battle of Bunker Hill, whose memory impelled Americans to fight in the Revolutionary War and since 1775 had helped to define American national identity.[59] James McPherson and others have commented that both Union and Confederate patriots saw in the American Revolution the justification of their political ideals, but the heritage of the Revolution influenced more than just ideas about the constitutionality of secession or the general patriotism of either side.[60] Comparing Elmer Ellsworth to Joseph Warren both linked him to nationalism and demanded that men rise to the nation's defense to avenge the martyr's sacrifice. The imaginative process of forming a nation out of martyred memory was very similar.

An edition of Ellsworth's infantry drill manual, written before the war during his tour with the National Guard Cadets, was now republished for Civil War soldiers with a biography of its author appended. The brief biography told its soldier readers that Ellsworth's "memory will be revered, his name respected, and long after the rebellion shall have become a matter of history, his death will be regarded as a martyrdom, and his name will be enrolled upon the list of our country's patriots, by the side of Warren and others who fell among the first in the Revolution in defense of their country."[61]

The idea behind linking Ellsworth's sacrifice to the memory of the Revolutionary War and to Joseph Warren was to inspire public action in defense of the Union. Ellsworth, like Warren, must move men to fight. The editor of the New Jersey *Atlantic Democrat* claimed, "The death of Col. Ellsworth will mark an era in the history of this war, and his name will hereafter stand by the side of Warren, and others who fell among the first in the Revolution in defense of their country. . . . The effect of his murder will be to intensify the war feeling in the North, and to furnish a battle-cry in future conflicts!"[62] A Sandusky, Ohio, paper added that Ellsworth's name would be "enrolled by the side of that of Warren and the other braves who died upon the altar of Human Liberty" because he became a "sacrifice, that in his wicked death the cause might be sealed and the people be aroused to avenge his blood.—And truly they will do it."[63]

George William Curtis, writing in his "Lounger" column in *Harper's Weekly*, amplified the idea that Ellsworth would follow in Warren's footsteps as a useful symbol and inspiration for military action to protect the nation. Curtis wrote in the first issue of *Harper's Weekly* after Ellsworth was buried, "As Warren died in the beginning of the struggle to obtain constitutional liberty, so dies Ellsworth at the opening of the war to maintain and perpetuate it." He took great pains to emphasize that even though Ellsworth's "military genius" would be missed, "his death also helps fuel the good cause." Readers could also see how, as with Warren's death in the Revolution, Ellsworth's death should prove to others now enlisting in the cause that their own potential deaths would be worth something: "Remembering him, brave men will be braver, and the strong arm strike more strongly. . . . War has many terrible aspects; but it also develops grand and noble qualities."[64] The idea that Ellsworth must be avenged combined the terrifying notion of vengeance with the "noble" quality of heroism.

Soldiers responded to the calls for vengeance. A volunteer soldier wrote in a letter to the *Philadelphia Inquirer*, "The news of the brutal murder of Col. ELLSWORTH has, of course, cast a universal gloom over our camp; but depend upon it, the foul outrage shall be avenged. . . . The gallant and noble soldier has fallen in a noble and a holy cause, and we shall see to it that his wicked assassination is properly rewarded."[65]

Ellsworth played the dual role: representing Union military ideals and serving as a devotional object that could inspire others to adopt those same ideals.[66] Some people took the inspiration literally. For example, Charles E. Abbey carried a soldier's New Testament with Ellsworth's carte de visite pasted into the front cover.[67] In this Bible, Ellsworth's photo literally resembled a saintly icon—which mixed religious consolation with patriotic inspiration. New Yorker George Templeton Strong wrote in his diary that Ellsworth "could hardly have done such service as his assassin has rendered the country. . . . His murder will stir the fire in every northern state."[68]

The public mourning for Ellsworth was consciously meant to motivate direct action in the war. Melissa Bellanta has argued that in nineteenth-century Australia sentimentalized mourning culture "actively sought to mediate between representation and practice; to produce bodily responses in audiences, such as tears in the eyes or lumps in the throat."[69] Ellsworth's death played the same function for Americans and upped the ante by additionally motivating men to offer the sacrifice of their own bodies in the war. The press noted that as soon as news of Ellsworth's death reached New York, "regret at his loss" was "mingled with a general feeling that his death must be avenged," and many outlets called for vengeance for Ellsworth.[70] A Madison, Wisconsin, newspaper wrote under the headline "Vengeance! Vengeance!!" that "the blood of Col. Ellsworth will be atoned not only by the blood of the foul assassin, Jackson, but by that of a thousand rebels. . . . Let the watchword be, 'Vengeance for the assassination of Colonel Ellsworth!'"[71] The Milwaukee *Morning Sentinel* noted that James Jackson's act in killing Ellsworth "was in strict harmony with all the conduct and policy of the rebels . . . and for it there will undoubtedly be a

fearful retribution"; the paper continued a few days later that "The Fire Zouaves will have a wilder and more lasting revenge for the death of their gifted
and gallant young colonel."[72] The motivating effect was strongest among soldiers, claimed the paper: "His death will animate every soldier throughout
all the loyal States with a keener hatred of the cowardly traitors."[73]

Ellsworth's death was explicitly used by war boosters as a way to unite public opinion behind the Union Cause: one man in Ellsworth's hometown who
dared to express "sentiments favorable to the South" during the public mourning was run out of town, accompanied by a band playing "The Rogue's
March."[74] The *New York Evangelist* newspaper published a letter to the editor
from a Chicago writer who claimed that "Providence" had permitted Ellsworth's death in order to rouse volunteers for the Union Cause: "What could
so consolidate, and arouse as one man, our already united people, as this
memorable assassination?"[75]

Some evidence exists that Ellsworth's "martyrdom" continued to inspire
other Union troops, although his own Eleventh New York Fire Zouaves performed poorly at Bull Run, failed to distinguish themselves in subsequent
battle, and were disbanded in 1862.[76] A newly organized regiment of Zouaves
(the Forty-Fourth) dubbed themselves the "Ellsworth Avengers." This regiment, in turn, inspired at least two versions of a popular Ellsworth revenge
song, which was reprinted as a leaflet and likely used in recruiting.[77] In reporting that the Ninth and Eleventh Pennsylvania Regiments received their
orders at West Chester on May 26, 1861, the *Philadelphia Inquirer* noted that
"over the camp ran a murmur of satisfaction that they would soon have an
opportunity to revenge the cowardly murder of Col. ELLSWORTH."[78] Lincoln
biographer Michael Burlingame claims that "indignation at Ellsworth's murder helped swell the enlistment rolls. . . . Though Lincoln had called for only
42,000 volunteers, by July 1 over 200,000 had joined up."[79]

Soldiers were not alone, however, in their capacity to be inspired by Ellsworth's sacrifice. Civilian women also responded by assuming a role related
to mourning they would increasingly claim as the war proceeded—keeping
his memory alive. Women wrote songs and poetry to immortalize Ellsworth
as a public martyr.[80] One apocryphal newspaper anecdote claimed that Ellsworth's mother responded to his death by declaring, "I wish I was a man, I'd
go immediately and avenge his death."[81] A paper published near Ellsworth's
hometown claimed that "a South Carolina lady" who visited New York was
converted by the news of his death not only to be a Union supporter but also
to declare, "I want to fight too, and if I were one of the Zouaves, I do believe
I would revenge his death. . . . I am no Southern Rebel now."[82] The idea of
feminine revenge testified to the power of sympathy to motivate action and
included women in the public mourning that imagined a national commu-

nity that seemed even more inclusive and unanimous because of female participation.

Simultaneously, James Jackson, known in the North as Ellsworth's assassin, was held up as a similar kind of martyr as Ellsworth himself but to the Confederate "cause," and his death sparked Confederate nationalism and military commitment. Northern newspapers called Jackson "Ellsworth's Assassin," but Southern papers talked of "the Butchery of Jackson" and hailed his bravery in protecting the Confederate cause in his own home.[83]

James Jackson's Confederate memory was less visual and material than Ellsworth's, in part because Southern printers faced hardship as the war ramped up, and the mechanisms of popular print culture were disrupted. But some Confederates used Northern print culture to their own nationalist purpose. Many of the engravings meant to lionize Ellsworth might *also* be used by Southern consumers to celebrate Jackson. The very same scene could fire both sides to righteous indignation, depending on the meanings assigned by its viewers. The hotelkeeper's actions, after all, could be interpreted as a civilian defending his home against northern invaders who trampled on the Confederate national flag. The Augusta, Georgia, *Daily Constitutionalist* noted that Northern images of Jackson actually made him seem heroic to Confederates, noting that as portrayed, "Jackson's act was not the impulse of a man half awakened from sleep, but that of one resolved to defend his rights against all odds, and at every hazard."[84]

Jackson quickly became a Confederate hero with public mourning of his own. Michael E. Woods has argued that some secessionists had mourned the death of the union as the death of a loved one and had used related mourning rituals to convert Unionists to their cause in the previous months, and now these rituals were intensified with Jackson as their subject.[85] Newspapers all over the South appealed to the public for monetary contributions for Jackson's widow "for presentation by the Southern people" as a tribute of gratitude, and contributions came from citizens in Virginia, Georgia, South Carolina, Alabama, and Louisiana.[86]

The Southern press took part in making James Jackson into, as one Kentucky newspaper called him, an "immortal hero."[87] A Memphis newspaper story argued forcefully that Jackson's defense of the Confederate flag and attack on Ellsworth was "the first blow struck in defence of Virginia. It was an act of single daring and heroic self-sacrifice. . . . This was a deed of remarkable daring and heroic patriotism, which . . . sent a thrill of sympathetic patriotism through the Southern heart. It taught the sons of Virginia how to strike in her defence, and to die for her cause."[88] The Richmond *Daily Whig* called Jackson a "martyr and a hero."[89] Several papers quoted Jackson's oft-stated sentiment, which also graced his Marshall House business card: "Virginia is determined, and will conquer, under the command of JEFF DAVIS."[90] Just as the Northern press had done with Ellsworth, these words (inaccurate and hyperbolic as they were) tried to link Jackson's sacrifice to some larger cause for which all Confederates should be prepared to give their lives.

James Jackson inspired Confederate public grief. Edward H. House, a reporter for the *New York Tribune*, had accompanied Ellsworth's men on their sortie to Alexandria, and he reported on Mrs. Jackson's considerable sorrow. When she saw her husband dead in the stairwell of their home, she "cried aloud with an agony so heart-rending that no person could witness it without emotion." Her grief was deep and uncontrolled: "She flung her arms in the air, struck her brow madly, and seemed utterly abandoned to desolation and frenzy. . . . She offered no reproaches and yielded only to her own frantic despair."[91] Other newspapers reported that when Jackson's wife discovered his body after Cpl. Francis E. Brownell shot and stabbed him, she "uttered the most agonizing cries . . . she remained a long time in the wildest state of frenzy."[92] Jackson's wife and daughters wore the same clothes, bloodstained from clutching his body at the scene, for two days after his death until his burial near Fairfax Courthouse.[93]

Collective mourning was also supposed to raise Confederates to act. The Jackson family's defense of the flag and James Jackson's sacrifice for it were used as positive examples of Confederate patriotism. Several newspaper accounts linked Jackson's killing to Union disrespect for the Confederate flag. The *Macon Daily Telegraph* reported the day after the invasion of Alexandria that, after trying to protect the "secession flag . . . Jackson was cut to pieces by the bayonets of Ellsworth's Zouaves," increasing the identification between the martyr and the flag.[94] Jackson's display and defense of the Confederate flag made him an excellent symbol of developing Confederate nationalism, and his close association with the flag became an important part of his martyrdom. One Charleston, South Carolina, newspaper relayed a rumor that Mrs. Jackson and her sister tried to prevent the Union men from removing the flag, first by drawing revolvers and then by tearing "the flag into shreds, determined that it should not pass into the hands of Lincoln's ruffians."[95] Jackson's blood sacrifice for the Confederate flag was held up before mustering soldiers in Virginia, Georgia, and Texas as an ideal they might have to match as they joined the Confederate military with Confederate nationalism in mind.[96]

Mourning went to the heart of the imagined U.S. and Confederate identities—formed out of opposing national ideals that nonetheless resembled one another in form. Objects touched by Ellsworth's and Jackson's blood became sanctified and collected as relics in both regions, material reminders of opposing national identities.[97] For both Ellsworth and Jackson, the public ratified the idea that martyrs' blood could create strong interest in physical objects that had touched it. In the weeks following the Marshall House incident, curiosity seekers and relic hunters dismantled much of the building and carried off pieces of wood and fabric stained with Ellsworth's and Jackson's blood, taking their mania for souvenirs to "ridiculous excess," according to at least one observer.[98] Elijah S. Brown, a volunteer from Woodbury, Vermont, made a special visit to the Marshall House and sent home "a piece of the pole" that Ellsworth "took the flag from."[99] The *Hartford Daily Courant* reported that "almost every man that visits Alexandria brings away some momento [*sic*] of the place. . . . The oil cloth on the hall where Ellsworth fell has been cut up and divided. On some pieces the blood is as thick as a knife-blade. . . . Pieces of the stairs covered with his blood, are also cut off and brought away."[100] Another paper claimed that "a large crowd of curiosity seekers" had carried away the Marshall House sign and much of the "furniture in the rooms where Ellsworth and Jackson laid, and everything stained by their blood is treasured up." Even the carpets and the newel post were cut up and taken by souvenir hunters.[101] After the war, relic hunters continued to swamp the Marshall House, and some newspapers accused the innkeepers of selling false relics "smeared with beef blood" to eager collectors.[102] Jackson's Confederate flag, stained with Ellsworth's blood, was carried in Ellsworth's funeral processions as a relic, and several of Ellsworth's men cut off pieces to keep as souvenirs of their commander. Part of the flag was presented to the Lincoln family.[103]

The cultural clash between Elmer Ellsworth as martyr for the Union Cause and James Jackson as martyr to the Confederate cause was intensely political and highlighted specific aspects of the breakdown in national unity. Ellsworth clearly stood as a symbol of union, and fighting for his vengeance meant fighting for union. Just as observers of Ellsworth's mortal remains looked through the window of his casket to assure themselves that the martyr's body would not decompose, so, too, they sought reassurance that sacrifice would bring reunion. The prominent display at his funerals of the American flag along with Ellsworth's captured Confederate flag, consecrated with his blood, argued that blood could reunite the sections—the great goal of moderate Republicans. Jackson's body, the relics of his hair, and the shards of blood-soaked stairs carried off by souvenir hunters, alternately, argued that Union forces were "invading foes." Their reverence supported a form of Confederate nationalism that emphasized independence and resistance but was not the most fire-eating or aggressive Confederate ideal.

At the beginning of the Civil War, the clash between Ellsworth and Jackson demonstrated how Nina Silber's observation that "going into battle . . . played crucial roles in shaping male identities" took on a racial dimension.[104] The celebration of these two opposed martyrs rested political and military inspiration upon the maiming and death of strong, white men. The symbolic public images of both Ellsworth and Jackson, with the public focused on their strong, white bodies struck down in their prime, drew attention away from the fact that slavery was at the heart of the conflict. Ellsworth and Jackson diverted the public gaze from both the politics of slavery that caused the war and the individual experience of the institution. It was not the blood and sacrifice of Black bodies, well documented by decades of narratives published by enslaved people, that drove the conflict when Ellsworth and Jackson took the stage.[105] Their symbolic clash over what the nation should be was all about the sacrifice of white manhood. Even though, as one newspaper noticed, enslaved people were the only residents of Alexandria who seemed happy with the Union occupation, most news stories constructed the scene as entirely a test of white manhood.[106]

Ellsworth's and Jackson's twinned martyrdoms set the precedent for one of the strongest strains of Civil War memory during and after the war. As the *first* martyrs of the Civil War, Ellsworth and Jackson set precedents for many who would come after them: from battlefield deaths to Abraham Lincoln himself. David Blight has argued that a sentimental regard for the mutual sacrifice of white soldiers came to define much of Civil War memory, to the detriment of memories of emancipation and African American participation in the war. Blight claims that by the 1880s, white "soldiers' nostalgia for the war came increasingly to be wrapped in patriotic visions of what they had accomplished for the larger society," fueled by both Union and Confederate patriotism.[107] What the veneration of Ellsworth and Jackson shows is how that process had its seeds even in the first days of the war, as each side persuaded men to fight in the first place. Civil War memory and its relationship to the "imagined reconstitution of the nation" began to be determined, even as the war just began.

Public mourning split American national identity. Ellsworth's martyrdom, both in 1861 and as it would live in Union memory, condemned the Confederacy and helped to define the Union national cause. The notion that Ellsworth had died as a martyr to the sacred cause of the Civil War was bolstered by his last letter to his parents, widely reprinted in the press, in which he wrote: "Whatever may happen, cherish the consolation that I was engaged in the performance of a sacred duty."[108] The exact "cause" that constituted his sacred duty was left somewhat vague—although it very clearly included fighting secession. Whether Republicans and Northerners interpreted the ultimate "cause" as the preservation of the Union or as the abolition of slavery, both motivations served to give the war higher meaning and to turn the Confederates into enemies. As one New Jersey newspaper put it: "The news of the murder of Col. Elmer E. Ellsworth . . . reveals to us another phase of Southern treachery and fanaticism."[109]

Ellsworth's martyrdom seemed to indict the Confederacy and arouse a Union "spirit of revenge."[110] The *New York Times* noted that because Jackson was a conspiratorial assassin (in its opinion), he proved how the "career of secession" was "to be carried out in a spirit of bloodthirstiness and private revenge."[111] The Republican newspaper editors in Springfield, Massachusetts, used Ellsworth's death to argue that secessionists had done everything in the war thus far "so meanly and so unfairly, that the feelings of all decent men have been outraged," and that the thirst for revenge among Ellsworth's men "must necessarily be shared by the whole army."[112]

The irony was, however, that James Jackson, Ellsworth's so-called assassin, was held up as the same kind of martyr to the *Confederate* cause, and his death sparked Confederate patriotism and military commitment that were explicitly opposed to the Union. The *Richmond Daily Whig*, a virulent pro-secessionist newspaper, wrote that "the heroic citizen of Alexandria who shot down the brigand Ellsworth, and was afterwards butchered by his bravos, merits the boundless and everlasting thanks of every Virginian." The paper's high esteem for Jackson was more than matched by the contempt expressed for Ellsworth: "He met, in the first hour of his ruthless invasion, the fate he deserved—a dog's death!"[113]

The theme of martyrdom for the cause of Confederate defense was echoed in the *Richmond Examiner*, which praised Jackson for standing "by his flag" and defending his home from "the horde of thieves, robbers and assassins in the pay of Abraham Lincoln."[114] The *Examiner* continued that Jackson "neither fled nor submitted" even as Ellsworth shot him and as the Yankee soldiers supposedly "surrounded him, and hacked him to pieces with swords and bayonets on the spot, in his own violated home."[115] Just as the Northern press had done with Ellsworth, these words tried to link Jackson's sacrifice to some larger cause for which all Confederates should be prepared to give their lives. The theme of home defense was not just specific to the Marshall House—it could easily be turned into a metaphor for the entire Confederacy.

Defense of home was quickly becoming, overall, one of the bedrocks of Confederate nationalism, and Jackson's story fit neatly as an inspiration for men to join the fight against the invading "hordes" from the North. In reporting on the incident at Alexandria, the *Richmond Enquirer* used a home metaphor to demand an armed response from other Confederate men: "Virginians, arise in your strength, and welcome the invader with 'bloody hands to hospitable graves'. . . . Meet the invader at the threshold. Welcome him with bayonet and bullet. Swear eternal hatred of a treacherous foe."[116] The coroner's jury report on Jackson's death made a point of noting that he was killed by "troops of the United States" as he defended "his private property, in his own house."[117]

Secessionists emphasized that the scene of Jackson's murder while protecting the Confederate flag and his family should warn all Southerners that "the bloody standard of tyranny is erected upon your soil." The *Richmond Daily Whig* amplified the message about Yankee intentions when reporting about the Marshall House scene: "They come to butcher and enslave—they come to desolate your homes, to slaughter your children—to pollute your wives and daughters. . . . To arms! Let their accursed blood quench the thirst of your fields!"[118]

Neither proponents of the Union nor the Confederate cause were completely blind to the irony of creating martyrs who opposed one another directly and turning the incident into a symbol of how each side should oppose the other. Some commentators noted the contradiction in the situation, while still refusing to give up any of their own politics or the heroism of Ellsworth or Jackson. In 1862, Jackson's biographer wrote:

> The name of James William Jackson is, perhaps, at this time, as widely celebrated throughout the Confederate and the United States, as that of any man, either living or dead. In the one country he is anathematized, vilified and detested as the assassin of a gallant soldier: in the other he is lauded as a hero, loved for his devotion to the flag of his country, and the terrible determination with which he defended it, and glorified as the first martyr in the cause to which the blood of all her true sons is pledged. . . . [He is] cursed in Boston, Philadelphia and New York . . . bewept in Charleston, Montgomery, and New Orleans.[119]

It was possible for some Confederate and Union partisans to see how Ellsworth and Jackson needed one another to create two opposing causes worth fighting for, even though they might never have agreed on the legitimacy of the other side.

John Hay's *Atlantic Monthly* magazine article, written just two months after the incident, said that Ellsworth and Jackson would stand as national symbols, ever opposed to one another. Hay claimed that Ellsworth

> tore down the first rebel flag. . . . He added to the glories of that morning the seal of his blood. . . . The poor wretch [Jackson] who stumbled upon an immortality of infamy by murdering him died at the same instant. . . . The two stand in the light of that event—clearly revealed—types of the two systems in conflict to-day: the one, brave, refined, courtly, generous, tender, and true; the other, not lacking in brute courage, reckless, besotted, ignorant, and cruel. . . . Let the two systems, Freedom and Slavery, stand thus typified forever, in the red light of that dawn, as on a Mount of Transfiguration.[120]

Hay did not shy away from racial issues as he juxtaposed Ellsworth and Jackson as great symbols of slavery and freedom. But he was the only major commentator who explicitly infused racial issues into the clash over Ellsworth's and Jackson's sacrifices. Although a few abolitionists praised Ellsworth in the press, they preferred to rely on John Brown and his rebels as symbols of martyrdom to the cause of liberty, and they looked forward to Black men being allowed to lay their lives on the line in the national cause of warfare.[121]

"Blubbering at His Post": Tears and Manhood

The spectacle of public grief for Elmer Ellsworth, and for his twin martyr James W. Jackson, harnessed aspects of the nineteenth-century culture of sentimentality by converting sorrow into manly action. But public mourning posed a conundrum: there was a fine line between useful, manly sorrow and "womanish," unacceptable grief. Like reading a sentimental novel did for women, participating in rituals of mourning for Civil War martyrs produced a bodily reaction from men, but instead of feminine emotion, this reaction was meant to take the form of martial behavior.[122]

When Lincoln cried over Ellsworth's death, the president's tears could become the emotional gateway to military resolve. Still, the *Herald* correspondent worried that writing about Lincoln's crying outburst in the newspaper might be "regarded as a breach of strict propriety" by many. But he felt it was important for him to describe the president's emotion because "our brave soldiers will appreciate the fact, that in all the length and breadth of the land there is not one who follows their marches with keener interest, who rejoices more heartily in their triumphs, or who mourns more sincerely over their losses" than the president.[123] The *Herald* correspondent called Lincoln's tears an "unusual spectacle" and wondered at the propriety of reporting them, concerned that the very emotion that was to spur men to action might also threaten to "unman" them at the very moment manly action was necessary. Lincoln had called his own tears a sign of "weakness" because they threatened to obscure action with emotion that might sap rather than strengthen his manly resolve. Thus, performance of public sorrow by political and military men both created and threatened military masculinity.[124]

Masculine sorrow was particularly powerful, and conflicted, in the case of public grief for the death of Elmer Ellsworth. Even beyond the incident of the president weeping in the White House recounted by the *Herald* correspondent, newspapers took special notice of President Lincoln's emotion at Ellsworth's death. Lincoln, known to be quite melancholy in general, mourned Ellsworth "like a son," as John Hay put it.[125] Several writers took special notice of Lincoln's crying from the first news until Ellsworth's D.C. funeral. The

Independent noted to its readers that "the President was affected to tears when informed of the death of Col. Ellsworth."[126] The *New York Illustrated News* reported that at the news of Ellsworth's death "the President himself wept, and was deeply affected."[127]

Lincoln was not alone in his tears. The press recounted several incidents of "brave" men crying upon hearing the news of Ellsworth's death—prefiguring in many ways the collective reaction to Lincoln's own death by assassination that would mark the end of the war four years later.[128] Several newspapers around the country reprinted the story that Col. Ellsworth's father first received the news of his son's death by visiting the telegraph office in Mechanicville and noticing the telegraph "operator weeping" over his dispatches.[129] A capital city correspondent wrote to Philadelphians as Ellsworth's body was being held at the Navy Yard on the afternoon of his death, "Our city is in a state of intense feeling, and brave soldiers are melted to tears at the sudden and melancholy death of one in whom all felt an especial interest, and respected and loved as an ornament to his profession, and noble pattern of loyalty and heroism."[130] The image of soldiers being "melted to tears" just when their active resolve might be needed in the field was sad, but also possibly threatening to the Union war cause.

Even after the initial shock of the news, some men reported being spontaneously moved to tears when they thought about Ellsworth's demise. Lincoln's confidant and private secretary, John G. Nicolay, had come to know Ellsworth well in the months leading up to the war.[131] Nicolay wrote to his future wife, Therena, after being a pallbearer at Ellsworth's Washington, D.C., funeral that he was overwhelmed by sadness at Ellsworth's loss. Somehow, Ellsworth's heroic death seemed to pierce Nicolay's carefully constructed, cool resolve in the face of war: "I had thought myself to have grown quite indifferent and callous and hard-hearted, until I heard of the sad fate of Colonel Ellsworth. . . . But since that time I have been quite unable to keep the tears out of my eyes whenever I have thought or heard or read about it, until I have almost concluded that I am quite a weak and womanish sort of creature."[132]

Ellsworth's death inspired action, but public mourning also carried danger if it went so far as to question manliness itself. Megan Kate Nelson and other scholars have shown how the war—the experience of battle, wounds, and death—constituted a long-lasting challenge to the strong image of American masculinity.[133] James W. Jackson's biographer scoffed at President Lincoln's tears for Ellsworth, calling the image of the weeping president "a mournful farce," and praised, instead, proper female grief, the sincere "tears and lamentations" of Jackson's female relatives.[134] Reactions to the death of Elmer Ellsworth indicate that the threat that Civil War grief and pain posed to masculinity was present from the very beginning of the war. As the conflict grew worse, the scale of emotion obviously would accelerate as scores were wounded and killed, and grief over Ellsworth prefigured the emotion and gender turmoil to come.

Some tried to control the damage. Even when the open display of tears threatened to impugn the masculinity of politicians and military men, press accounts took great pains to emphasize that, even if the tears seemed to exceed the bounds of acceptable manly sentimentality, they were actually a gateway to militant rage and vengeance that Ellsworth's memory would conjure. Instead of being "womanish," crying men might actually be moved to fight harder.

Lincoln's secretary, William O. Stoddard, reported on the scene in Washington after Ellsworth's death in the *New York Examiner* in one of the many anonymous dispatches he published under the pseudonym "Illinois." Stoddard reported that the news of Ellsworth's "assassination . . . threw the whole city into an indescribable excitement and agitation," and he noted widespread fears that "it will do much to inflame the passions of our soldiers." Stoddard linked the open grief of Ellsworth's Zouaves to their manly resolve for revenge and conjured up a scene in which emotion that might be interpreted as feminine sentimentality was instead mobilized to fire masculine military rage.

Stoddard wrote: "The Zouaves in particular swear (literally) eternal vengeance for their leader, to whom, rough as they unquestionably are, they were becoming much attached." He painted an ironic, almost comical scene, in particular, of one rough fireman who grieved for Ellsworth: "One great, Herculean fireman was found blubbering at his post this morning, vowing that he and his comrades 'would have a life for every hair on the head of the dear little Colonel.'"[135]

Calling the fireman soldier "Herculean" reminded readers how the volunteers seemed to match classical heroes in their physical prowess; Walt Whitman referred to New York firemen as "Roman gladiators."[136] The image of the tough, swearing, enormous fireman "blubbering" in memory of Ellsworth could not overshadow the purpose of the manly tears—to impel both Ellsworth's men and Stoddard's readers into military action and make them ready for more killing. One report told the public that, tears aside, "100 of the Zouaves have made a solemn vow that the blood of Gen. Lee shall atone for that of Ellsworth."[137] Ellsworth himself had claimed that he chose to recruit his regiment from New York City firemen because they were tough, as the biography appended to his drill manual claimed in 1861: "He thought that men accustomed to a rough life and exposed to hardships were best calculated for hard fighting, and all those privations which are inseparable from an active soldier's life."[138]

Indeed, some observers noted how Ellsworth himself was a great example of the possibility of unity between manly sentimentality and military resolve. The press gave many examples of Ellsworth's vigorous manliness, combined with his self-control. As portrayed in the press, Ellsworth was a sensitive man who refrained from alcohol and swearing and took pleasure in physical pursuits such as chopping wood and gymnastic exercise.[139] One of Ellsworth's friends, just four days after his death, praised the fact that his sacrifice had "already stirred the hearts of the North for vengeance." But the same friend noted that Ellsworth's "heart which poured out its blood on the altar of heroism—was ever fresh with the purest sympathy, love, and affection, that human desires could yearn for."[140] Ellsworth's touching and emotional last letter to his parents was reprinted in countless news articles and even appeared on a commemorative envelope for sale as a commercial reminder of sentimental manliness. Many newspapers noted how Ellsworth's personal moderation tamed the rough-and-tumble New York firemen-turned-soldiers under his command, referred to as his "pet lambs."[141] John Hay called the Fire Zouaves "the gallant Colonel's Bloodtubs," a theatrical phrase and the name of a violent 1850s Baltimore political gang that mixed admiration for Ellsworth's refined manly bearing with a hint of fear for the potentially sensational violence of his New York City toughs.[142]

Confederates, however, exploited the emotional tension at the heart of Northern masculinity by criticizing Ellsworth, and even more his "pet lambs," a term used with bitter disdain by Confederates who denounced the rowdy New Yorkers for their dangerous and uncontrolled masculine impulses.[143] For many Southerners, New York City firemen represented the worst excesses of Northern urban life and possessed a form of untamed masculinity that was beneath contempt. The *Richmond Daily Whig* assured its readers that Ellsworth had explicitly recruited New York City toughs because they would constitute a "company of ruffians" to assault refined Southern honor.[144] *DeBow's Review*, a prominent Southern agricultural magazine, called the Fire Zouaves "rogues, paupers and murderers whom Col. Ellsworth has brought to Washington to cleanse New York of its criminals and to pillage the South . . . men who live on excitement whether of liquor or of battle . . . human blood hounds, whose supreme happiness consists in shedding human blood without cause or provocation."[145] Several Northern papers were defensive about such comments and tried to reassure their readers about the Fire Zouaves that "they are a pretty rough set, but not nearly so bad as they are made out to be," while others emphasized that their tough qualities were worth the risk, for example, citing their positive action to save the Willard Hotel in Washington, D.C., from burning down just days before the invasion of Alexandria.[146]

Confederates glossed over the contradiction of their argument when they portrayed Ellsworth's men simultaneously as weepy in a feminine sense and as dangerously rough. One Georgia newspaper noted that when Corporal Brownell delivered Ellsworth's body to the Navy Yard just after his death, he

Matthew Brady cartes de visite photograph, "[Lieutenant Francis Brownell of Co. A, 11th New York Infantry Regiment]," 1861. Library of Congress, Prints and Photographs Division, LC-DIG-ppmsca-35582.

"fairly bit his lip through to keep from crying audibly."[147] Despite this overly emotional image of James Jackson's killer, his biographer singled out Brownell as an example of the ugly toughness personified by the firemen, calling him "the true type of a New York *sub*-fire-boy. . . . He wore then, over his uniform jacket, a rough, black over-coat, and his pants turned up, and a white felt hat cocked on one side of his head. . . . He talked in a sing-song way, had a down-cast look, and when he opened his mouth to roll over the stump of the cigar he held in it, you could perceive that several of his front teeth were gone."[148]

This description of Brownell employed every negative stereotype of a New York City Bowery tough: he was threatening, dandyish, and uncouth. John Kasson noted in his seminal study of nineteenth-century manners that a Bowery tough "drew attention to himself by 'swagger[ing] along the street, shouting and laughing with his companions, his hat on one side, a cigar between his fingers,'" while urban dandies "affected a slouching posture," and poor, impolite men "shuffled with downcast eyes."[149]

Even though the Bowery Boy was sometimes a figure of cultural fascination in the antebellum period, Southern print culture made Brownell seem like the worst stereotype of New York street tough come to Virginia. Even Northerners saw that potential in Ellsworth's men; when John Hay called them "Bloodtubs" he evoked the sensational violence of a theatrical stage. Confederates painted Brownell, and all of Ellsworth's Fire Zouaves, as foppishly concerned about fashion and urban fads, while simultaneously being threatening and violent. Except now, instead of performing their dangerous masculinity on the Bowery stage or in the streets of New York City, the boys were invading Southern territory. True Southern men would have to fight back, and that is exactly what they would do as the war intensified over the next few years.

"All the Honor Practicable":
Public Mourning for Stonewall Jackson

Thomas J. "Stonewall" Jackson exemplified just the sort of resolved, tough Confederate masculinity that seemed to answer the Union threat, and his own death in 1863 would become a high-water mark for Confederate mourning. Public grief for Stonewall Jackson intertwined with expressions of support for the Confederacy itself, seemingly indivisible from the martial cause. Jackson died on May 10, 1863, after being accidentally shot by his own men in the confusion during the battle at Chancellorsville. His arm was amputated, and he developed complications (pneumonia and likely a septic infection). Jackson's death was followed by the largest funeral ceremonies and outpouring of public mourning that Confederates could muster in the middle of armed conflict, and it had huge military, cultural, and political consequences. This death was a personal blow to Robert E. Lee, but it also held potential to be, as President Jefferson Davis called it in a telegram to him, "a national calamity" for the Confederacy.[150]

Lee grasped, at once, that mourning Jackson was a matter of military importance. On May 11, 1863, he announced Jackson's death to the entire army in General Order No. 61:

> With deep grief, the commanding general announces to the army the death of Lieut. Gen. T. J. Jackson, who expired on the 10th instant, at 3:15 p.m. The daring, skill, and energy of this great and good soldier, by the decree of an all-wise Providence, are now lost to us. But while we mourn his death, we feel that his spirit still lives, and will inspire the whole army with his indomitable courage and unshaken confidence in God as our hope and strength. Let his name be a watchword to his corps, who have followed him to victory on so many fields. Let officers and soldiers emulate his invincible determination to do everything in the defense of our beloved country.[151]

Lee's order expressed his personal "deep grief" at losing the man he called his "right arm," which obviously still afflicted him weeks later when he wept with General Pendleton. But the order also modeled for Lee's soldiers, and for the larger Confederate population, that although they would be frightened by the loss of Jackson's military talents, they must use his death as an inspiration: soldiers must use grief for Stonewall Jackson to impel them back into the fight. It was fine to cry, but tears must not divert any of the "invincible determination" it would take to continue the fight. Lee assured Jackson's men that their commander would receive "all the honor practicable" from the Confederate public, but that fighting men could not afford a long pause for grief; they must get right back in the fight.[152]

In some surprising ways, public grief for Stonewall Jackson echoed themes in the mourning for Elmer Ellsworth in the North at the beginning of the war. Just as tears for Ellsworth helped to define a militaristic national identity at the war's outset, the tears and public mourning for Stonewall Jackson became important factors in the continuance of Confederate nationalism during a treacherous time in the war. Hundreds of thousands of lives had been lost between May 1861 and 1863, and the nature of the war as a protracted struggle had become all too clear.

Jackson's funeral concentrated Confederate sorrow for personal losses, demonstrated both fear and resolve for the future of the war, and inaugurated the links between Confederate nationalism and the nascent Lost Cause ideology that would become a potent force after the war was over. Alan T. Nolan has identified Jackson's "sainthood" as one of the bedrocks of the later mythology of the Lost Cause, but the consecration happened immediately after Jackson's death, during the war. Stonewall Jackson's funeral defined the Confederacy, but in a way that fit with American traditions of public mourning—therefore paving the way for aspects of the Lost Cause and its reverence for a doomed, mythic Confederate nation to become part of American national identity and Civil War memory.[153]

Although historians have paid attention to Stonewall Jackson's funeral rituals and their importance to Confederate ideology, no one has explained how mourning for him fit into the tradition of public funerals that defined American national identity. Jackson's funeral was not entirely exceptional, but it was, indeed, significant.

Stonewall Jackson's most recent biographer, S. C. Gwynne, compares the general's funerals favorably to those held for Zachary Taylor and John Quincy Adams and argues that "Jackson triggered the first great national outpouring of grief for a fallen leader in the country's history." Even granting that Gwynne may be referring to the Confederacy when he speaks of the "country's history" in that phrase, he is wrong. Gwynne took Rev. Robert Lewis Dabney's 1865 pronouncement about Stonewall Jackson's funeral that "no such homage was ever paid to an American" too much at face value. Dabney was trying to contribute to Confederate veneration and mythology by emphasizing the exceptionalism of Jackson's mourning—his was not any kind of objective historical assessment, but rather an extension of the mythic mourning rituals themselves.[154]

Jackson's funeral was of great national importance—both to the Confederacy and to the United States—but in form and substance it built upon a funerary tradition established before the war by mourning for national heroes like Henry Clay and at the beginning of the war by mourning for Elmer Ellsworth. Mourning for Jackson also built upon two years' worth of public and private grief for dead Confederates, like James W. Jackson or cavalry commander Turner Ashby, who had been buried with significant public ceremony in Charlottesville just the year before.[155] Stonewall Jackson's remains also became the focus of public fascination in a familiar manner as they traveled, and press accounts and obituaries magnified their importance. In truth, Stonewall Jackson's funeral is a significant entry in a tradition of American public mourning. That it has been viewed as special is more a testimony to its long-term role in creating Confederate ideology and Civil War memory than an accurate assessment of its scale and meaning in 1863.

Gwynne may be more correct when he compares Confederate mourning for Stonewall Jackson to national mourning for Abraham Lincoln in 1865.[156] But Stonewall Jackson's funeral can be called as much a sequel to Elmer Ellsworth's funeral as a precursor to Lincoln's. Public tears for all three men defined themes of national identity in times of military anxiety. Public mourning took on some similar public forms: the traveling corpse providing the focus of national attention in person and in print culture. But Jackson's funerals, while certainly deeply meaningful for Confederate nationalism, were actually much smaller in scale than either Ellsworth's or Lincoln's. Robert E. Lee's tears for the dead Jackson indeed echoed Lincoln's own tears for Ellsworth, but even though both men cried for the loss of a beloved commander, Ellsworth's death held far fewer important military consequences than did Jackson's.

The Death of Stonewall Jackson

Stonewall Jackson was an archetype of a Southern Christian soldier, and he offered a counterpoint to Elmer Ellsworth. He was the Confederate answer to the threatening masculinity of Ellsworth and his Union Fire Zouaves.[157] Jackson graduated from West Point in 1846, commanded artillery in the Mexican War, and accepted a professorship at the Virginia Military Institute in Lexington in 1851. There, he converted to Presbyterianism and married Eleanor Junkin, the daughter of the Washington College president. After Eleanor died in childbirth, Jackson married Mary Anna Morrison who encouraged his Presbyterian devotion—to the point that some considered him a religious "fanatic." Jackson's religion mixed with his view of politics when he threw in with the Confederate military in April 1861, and it would also influence his ruthless approach to warfare as the war and his own military responsibility accelerated and he proved himself adept at pursuing attacks against forces that often outnumbered him.[158] Jackson earned the nickname "Stonewall" by routing Union forces at the First Battle of Bull Run, and he quickly ascended through the ranks of Confederate command. His 1862 Valley campaign against vastly superior numbers temporarily destroyed U.S. hopes of capturing the Confederate capital at Richmond and cemented his own heroic reputation.

Soon after, Gen. Robert E. Lee came to rely on Jackson to help pursue Confederate strategy in late 1862. Jackson recovered from losses in the Seven Days' Campaign to defeat Union Gen. John Pope at the Second Battle of Bull Run before helping to lead Lee's invasion of Maryland that fall. After providing key reinforcement to Lee at Antietam, Jackson was promoted to lieutenant general and proved his worth by defeating Maj. Gen. Ambrose Burnside at Fredericksburg in December.

By the beginning of 1863, Jackson was hailed as a military genius and publicly lauded for his ability to carry out Lee's aggressive strategies toward often superior numbers of Union forces. The greatest evidence of Jackson's talents in this regard came in the same battle that killed him at Chancellorsville that spring. On May 2, he executed a brilliant flanking maneuver around the force of federal Maj. Gen. Joseph Hooker and conducted a withering attack on Hooker's right flank through a wooded area known as the Wilderness. As Hooker's force was routed, Jackson continued to press the attack even after dark, and as he rode back toward Confederate forces to encourage the advance, his party was mistaken for a Union advance, and Jackson was shot by men in the North Carolina Eighteenth, receiving one wound in the right hand, two in the left arm, and a severe blow to the head from a tree branch.[159]

Jackson was clumsily evacuated to the military hospital at the rear of the action in Wilderness Old Tavern, where his left arm was amputated. The next day, perhaps realizing that whether his commander lived or died, Jackson's arm would become a relic, chaplain Beverly Tucker Lacy took the limb to his brother's nearby property at Ellwood Manor and buried it.[160] Jackson stayed at the hospital, complaining of pain in his side, for two days until he was moved in a covered ambulance carriage twenty-five miles to the home of Thomas Coleman Chandler near Guiney's Station. Jackson seemed to improve for several days until he took a turn for the worse and began to cough just before his wife, Anna, arrived on May 7. He developed a fever and declined over the next three days, as pneumonia or another lung affliction set in.[161] He discussed God frequently and expressed to Anna his wish to be buried in Lexington. All during Jackson's convalescence, Southern newspapers paid great attention to him, and soldiers and civilians expressed prayers for his recovery, and when he died on May 10, news flashed across the North and South.[162] As he expired, Jackson still seemed engaged in military command, issuing orders to A. P. Hill's corps and urging with his dying breath, "Let us cross over the river, and rest under the shade of the trees."[163]

Jackson, whose funeral cloaked him in the Confederate flag and in heroic glory, was instantly hailed as a Confederate martyr. Jackson's religious devotion, his record for military heroism and success, and his enigmatic personality all contributed to the perception that he died a martyr, although he did not literally die for a cause, but rather in a hail of friendly fire. The rituals of mourning elevated Jackson as the embodiment of a Confederate cause for which so many others were also being sacrificed. His public funerals in 1863 focused Confederate attention on the national implications of personal sacrifice.

Jackson's death almost had to be fit into a pattern of martyrdom, since to acknowledge the pure mistake in his death would risk questioning the sense of the sacrifice—not just his but that of so many Confederate men. The *Richmond Enquirer* took an almost perverse pride in the fact that Jackson had been shot by his own men by mistake, claiming that it proved Northerners could not stop him: "Our base foe will exult in the disaster to Jackson; yet the accursed bullet that brought him down was never moulded by a Yankee."[164] Removing Jackson from the field might have profound military consequences, but it would also remove him from the possibility of being conquered by any Union foe. This theme would underlie many of his funeral commemorations and plant seeds of future Lost Cause ideas about what Alan T. Nolan calls the "tragic and self-destructive" heroism of the Confederacy.[165] Jackson was painted as a tragic hero in his 1863 funerals.

"Poor Honors" for a Great Hero

In the immediate aftermath of Stonewall Jackson's death on May 10, his funeral presented some logistical challenges that had not faced American mourners for Elmer Ellsworth in 1861. How could a proper public funeral be conducted in a war zone? As Robert E. Lee's Order No. 61 announcing Jackson's death to the Confederate armies had demonstrated, it was taken for granted that there would be widespread and spontaneous mourning. Both soldiers and civilians showed signs of personal and public grief upon receiving the news of Jackson's demise. The *New York Times* told readers that the military bands in Fredericksburg were "performing dirges a greater portion of the afternoon" when the news of Jackson's death circulated within the city.[166] General Raleigh Colston wrote that his men's "bronzed cheeks were now wet with burning tears" and their "dauntless breasts were heaving with uncontrollable sobs" when they got the news.[167]

Immediately after death, Jackson was laid out in the parlor of the Chandler house, in a plain wooden coffin adorned with flowers. But his body would have to be moved 200 miles before it could be buried in Lexington, and certainly the Confederate capital of Richmond, which had been the site of other Confederate public funerals of note, would also expect to be included in the rituals of mourning.[168] The immediate threat of battle meant that Jackson's remains could not be moved as far as Ellsworth's had in 1861, nor was there the wartime capacity for Confederates to produce the amount of visual and material culture that had accompanied Ellsworth's martyrdom early in the war. But Confederates mustered all the ceremony they could. Stonewall Jackson would have to be enshrined as a Confederate hero while his mourners were under direct threat of both renewed battle and severe privation.

The ceremonial movement of Jackson's remains took place in the context of battle, troop movements, and population displacement in 1863. More than 200,000 Virginians, more than in any other Confederate state, fled their homes over the war's course. Even granting that a significant portion of that number were enslaved people seeking freedom, many of whom readily accepted the hardship of dislocation as an alternative to enslavement—this

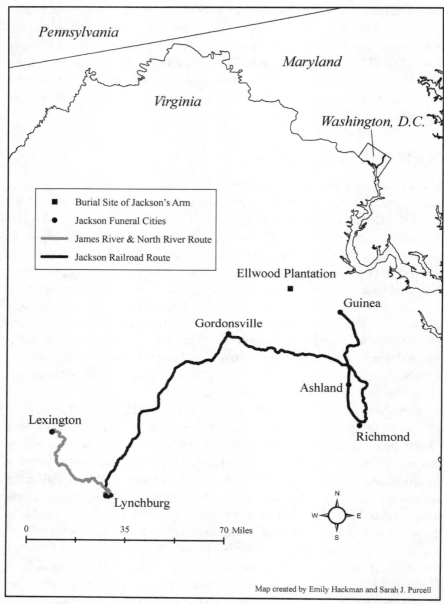

Thomas J. "Stonewall" Jackson funeral route, 1863. Data from IPUMS,
National Historical Geographic Information System. Map by Sarah J. Purcell
and Emily Hackman.

constituted a severe disruption in the population of the state. The city of Richmond had doubled its population since 1861, and both crowding and continued military threat meant that mourning rituals would be harder to pull off.[169] There seemed to be no question that Stonewall Jackson would be mourned publicly with as much pomp as possible, but the funeral commemorations were more contained than they would have been in other circumstances.

Officials also had to be cautious about public gatherings and ceremony in Richmond, given that just over a month earlier, on April 2, hundreds of people, mainly women, had broken into stores to appropriate food and clothing before marching on government buildings. Poor women in Richmond, many of them married to soldiers, were armed and well organized in their collective action. The Richmond bread riot concerned President Davis, Virginia governor John Letcher, and Richmond mayor Joseph Mayo, all of whom confronted the women but were unable to convince them to stop. Ultimately, soldiers with fixed bayonets ended the tumult, and sixty-eight women were arrested. Confederate officials kept the unrest out of the newspapers for the most part, but it might have seemed risky to spend public resources on ceremony and to encourage congregation in the streets for Jackson's public funeral, as officials were still struggling to prevent further unrest by granting food assistance to the poor.[170] Even if mourning Jackson offered the opportunity to boost Confederate fellow feeling and morale, calling masses of people together in the streets of Richmond might be risky.

Mourning had to proceed carefully, and Lee circumscribed Jackson's funerary send-off. In the aftermath of the Chancellorsville battle, Lee decided that the threat of renewed Union attacks meant that he could "not leave my Headquarters long enough to ride to the depot and pay my dear friend the poor tribute of seeing his body placed upon the cars," and he denied the request of officers of the Stonewall Brigade to have their men accompany the body on its way to interment.[171] Jackson's remains were entrusted to his adjutant general, Sandie Pendleton, and his aide-de-camp, Lieutenant James Power Smith, to move to Richmond, then Lynchburg and Lexington.[172]

Although truncated, the recognizable form of public mourning—a sort of superextended funeral procession—was visible in the movement of Stonewall Jackson's remains. A special train with just one car and a locomotive accepted the remains at Guiney's Station and headed for Richmond. As the train bearing Jackson's body moved through the countryside, residents followed its progress and, where possible, turned out to pay tribute to the dead general. Henry Kyd Douglas reported in his memoir that "crowds of people were at all the stations as the special train passed."[173] Confederate diarist Judith McGuire, herself displaced from her Alexandria home by the war, noted "almost every lady in Ashland visited the car, with a wreath or a cross of the most beautiful flowers, as a tribute to the illustrious dead."[174]

Even as immediate preparations commenced, the *Richmond Examiner* confronted the possibility that the war-stressed Confederate capital would not be able to summon enough resources to offer proper tribute to Jackson. But it was important to offer as much public mourning as possible, given the trying times. The *New York Times* commented that people offered "all the poor honors that Virginia, sorely troubled and pressed hard, could afford her most glorious and beloved son."[175]

Mourning Jackson: Before the Cause Was Lost

The loss of Stonewall Jackson produced a crack in Confederate public confidence: If he was not invincible, did that mean the Confederacy itself also might not be invincible? Although the Confederate "cause" itself was not yet lost, not by a long shot, the public mourning for Jackson celebrated the general in a way that presaged many of the themes in postwar Lost Cause culture, chief among them a gloriously doomed heroism. Drew Gilpin Faust has argued that the best way to study Confederate nationalism is to study the "revealing record of southerners struggling to explain themselves to themselves," and public mourning for Stonewall Jackson provides the perfect chance to see that process in action.[176] Confederates celebrated the man who seemed to stand for bravery, Christian faith, belligerence, and capability, things they wished for the Confederacy and for themselves. In the process, they also celebrated white sacrifice in the war and thereby continued to intertwine Confederate identity and white supremacy. Jackson's death also mixed a foreshadowing of doom that mixed with Confederate defiance.

Inhabitants of the Confederate capital, Richmond, would stand in for the Confederate nation itself in welcoming Jackson's remains into their city, and Southern newspapers did their best to multiply the effect. A huge crowd had gathered at the Richmond train depot by noon on May 11 but had to be dispersed when officials announced the body would not arrive until late afternoon.[177] Only a month after the bread riot, uncontrolled crowds could not be tolerated for long, even when they seemed mournful and respectful. The funeral train stopped outside the city to let Anna Jackson disembark and enter the town unobtrusively in a carriage with Governor Letcher's wife. Around the capitol building, flags were flying at half-mast, and the Richmond city council resolved that all business in the city would be suspended to pay respects to Stonewall Jackson, and so the city could assist with his public funeral. Novelist John Beauchamp Jones, who was serving as a clerk in the Confederate War Department, noted that by three o'clock government and business offices were closed and "a multitude of people, mostly women and children, are standing silently in the streets, awaiting the arrival of the hero, destined never again to defend their homes and honor."[178] Whether the causes of "home" and "honor" would be more vulnerable without Jackson to defend them remained to be seen.

Public mourning explicitly tied Jackson to Confederate nationalist symbols, especially the Confederate flag. The train was stopped at the corner of Fourth and Broad Streets, and Jackson's coffin was removed to a hearse "surmounted by raven plumes, and drawn by two white horses."[179] As it was placed in the hearse, the coffin was wrapped in the newly adopted national flag of the Confederacy, dubbed the "Stainless Banner" because it featured a red Southern Cross on a large field of white, a tribute to the supposed purity of the Confederate military cause, with a nod to white supremacy. The flag, which incorporated the Southern Cross that had been used as a fighting emblem by Lee's Army of Northern Virginia, had been adopted as the second national flag of the Confederacy on May 1, just ten days earlier. President Jefferson Davis presented the first "Stainless Banner" ever manufactured to Jackson's family to shroud his coffin—a fact that drew great notice in newspapers and from funeral participants.[180]

Jackson's corpse and the flag glorified one another. Robert E. Bonner has argued that Confederates' use of the "Stainless Banner" in Jackson's funeral "helped fix the reputation of the new national flag as a symbol of the warlike religiosity that Stonewall epitomized" and said "something important about the centrality of blood sacrifice to their collective sense of identity."[181] Jackson's mourning rituals helped shape the meaning of a national flag, as had rituals for James W. Jackson and Elmer Ellsworth before him. The Confederate national flag draped Stonewall Jackson's body as a form of Confederate nationalist symbolic investment in his perceived heroic martyrdom.

After the flag presentation, Jackson's hearse, preceded by military and government escorts, moved to Capitol Square, past the Virginia monument to George Washington and to the Governor's Mansion. Jackson's hearse was followed by his riderless horse, led by Jim Lewis, an enslaved man who Jackson rented and who was portrayed in the press as devoted and subservient to reinforce white supremacy by reminding the public of the "proper" position of Black people in relation to white heroism.[182] The *Richmond Examiner* reported that so many thousands of people followed the cortege to Capitol Square that "it was with difficulty that the guard at the gate kept back the crowd there."[183] Jackson's body was laid in the governor's reception room. Late into the night, Jackson's widow received friends and dignitaries, as hundreds of people remained in the square with bells tolling. Jefferson Davis stood by the body for some time before "leaving the house in silence."[184] Overnight, Frederick Volck made a death mask of Jackson before his remains were placed in what Henry Kyd Douglas called "a neat metallic coffin."[185]

The next morning at eleven, Jackson's body was again processed through the streets with ceremonial escorts from the Governor's Mansion to the capitol (previously the Virginia statehouse), where he would lie in state. His family and close friends were given some time with the remains before the doors were opened to tens of thousands of people who passed to pay their respects and to view Jackson's face through the glass window in his coffin. The crowd was very large, perhaps the biggest turnout ever in Capitol Square, and the *Richmond Enquirer* called the scene a "tumultuous outburst of mourning." But the *Richmond Daily Dispatch* took pains to note that "good order was observed, and the dense crowd slowly made its way through the rotunda into the large hall where the coffin lay."[186] Many observers noted the large quantity of flowers left in tribute: as visible evidence of collective grief, the coffin was "literally covered with lilies of the valley and other beautiful Spring flowers."[187] John Beauchamp Jones described the scene: "The funeral was very solemn and imposing, because the mourning was sincere and heartfelt. There was no vain ostentation. The pall bearers were generals. The President followed near the hearse in a carriage, looking thin and frail in health. The heads of departments, two and two, followed on foot—Benjamin and Seddon first—at the head of the column of young clerks (who ought to be in the field), the State authorities, municipal authorities, and thousands of soldiers and citizens. . . . flags and black feathers abounded."[188] Jefferson Davis, who carried Anna Jackson and her baby daughter in his carriage, noted how "sincere" the mourning in Richmond was since Jackson's death had been announced, and he believed that the same fervent grief would "extend throughout the whole land" as news spread.[189]

Jackson's funeral blocked out other public activity in the Confederate capital. Just before the funeral procession, a group of thousands of Union prisoners of war arrived in Richmond and were marched through the streets, but Jones reported that "these attracted slight attention—Jackson, the great hero, was the absorbing thought."[190] More than 20,000 residents of the city filed past Jackson's coffin as it lay in the chamber of the Confederate House of Representatives, and even when the doors were closed, "the multitude was still streaming in." One veteran, who arrived late and just missed the opportunity to view Jackson's remains, pointed to his own amputated arm "which I lost for my Country" and demanded "the privilege of seeing my General once more!" Governor Letcher allowed him into the chamber.[191] Anna Jackson sought quiet consolation that evening, but the crowds gathered outside granted her little peace.[192]

The next day, Wednesday, May 13, Jackson's remains were conveyed to the Richmond train station and sent on to Lynchburg, via Gordonsville, stopping at several small towns along the way. Anna Jackson wrote in her postwar memoir that crowds assembled along the tracks to present "floral offerings" for Stonewall's bier and to ask to kiss her daughter. A "vast throng" met the train at Lynchburg, where the remains and accompanying party were transferred to the packet boat *Marshall* to continue overnight along the Kanawha Canal to Lexington.[193]

The boat bearing Jackson's body arrived in Lexington on the morning of Thursday, May 14, accompanied by his wife and daughter, his personal staff, Governor Letcher, and a delegation of citizens from Lynchburg. Jackson's remains were received by the whole body of Virginia Military Institute (VMI) cadets, who solemnly marched to their campus and placed the general to rest overnight in his former lecture hall, which had been heavily decorated in mourning for the occasion.[194] VMI cadet Samuel Baldwin Hannah, who was serving as officer of the day when Jackson's body arrived on campus, wrote to his mother that he was disappointed Jackson's face could not be uncovered for viewing (despite being uncovered the day before in Richmond) because, despite the embalming, "decomposition had already taken place. . . . the features were said not to be natural." Hannah noted that "the coffin was a perfect flower bed" and that even though the Confederate flag underneath could barely be seen, none of the flowers were touched, even though cadets were mightily tempted to remove some as souvenirs.[195]

On the morning of Friday, May 15, Maj. Scott Ship, who had been Jackson's student, served under him in the Valley campaign, and succeeded him as commandant of VMI cadets, led the funeral procession to Jackson's Presbyterian church for the funeral service, and then to the cemetery for burial. The *Lexington Gazette* reported that "the Body enveloped in the Confederate Flag and covered with flowers, was borne on a caisson of the Cadet Battery, draped in mourning" and was preceded by military men, VMI cadets, and citizens of Lexington and the surrounding counties.[196] As many as 4,000 people crowded around the exterior of the church. Participants recorded that the two-hour service, conducted by Jackson's pastor William S. White, was exceptionally somber, as the congregation joined in "subdued, sobbing voices."[197] White preached upon First Corinthians and expressed deep grief for Jackson by linking his death to many other families' losses, including the death of his own son, Capt. Hugh White, who had been killed at Second Manassas.[198] When approaching the coffin, the people of Lexington added their floral offerings "to the multitudes of wreaths and flowers which had been piled upon it all along the sad journey to Richmond and thence to Lexington."[199]

After the service, Jackson's remains were processed to the Presbyterian cemetery in Lexington, where they were given a simple burial. The coffin was buried, still wrapped in the Confederate national flag, next to the grave of his first wife, Eleanor. Funeral flowers were heaped over his grave, and Margaret Junkin Preston, Eleanor's sister and the "poet laureate of the Confederacy," recorded that "sincerer mourning was never manifested for any one."[200]

"The Country Weeps":
Tears and the Future of the Confederacy

That demonstration of "sincere" mourning from the battlefield at Chancellorsville to the streets of Richmond to the graveyard in Lexington put Stonewall Jackson right at the heart of Confederate nationalism in 1863. Ian Binnington has argued that "the dead Jackson instilled ideas of a mythic present in the minds of white Confederates during the war years."[201] Public mourning for Jackson made it clear that the present, for many of these Confederates, would always be defined by grief. The past was filled with sacrifice of life, and Jackson's heroic mourning concentrated the grief of many Confederates onto their hopes for the Confederate nation itself. The question remained, however, whether the Confederate present, sanctified by past sacrifice, would provide a stable basis for a Confederate future. Could the Confederacy continue with only grief and the memory of Stonewall Jackson, not the man himself, to animate it?

Some mourners openly wondered if they could continue without Jackson. Judith W. McGuire wrote in her diary: "How can I record the sorrow which has befallen our country! General T. J. Jackson is no more. . . . Humanly speaking, we cannot do without him."[202] John Beauchamp Jones wrote in his diary that as Jackson's body passed through Richmond, "the grief is universal, and the victory involving such a loss is regarded as a calamity."[203]

Preachers argued that the answer to the survival and continued greatness of the Confederacy lay in Jackson's own piety and religious inspiration—the potential basis for a civil-religious devotion to the Confederate cause itself. Daniel Stowell has argued that James B. Ramsey and Robert Lewis Dabney (both Presbyterians who would later preach the Lost Cause) argued to the Confederate public that Jackson's death should animate them to "trust in no man, but in God alone" to carry forth the fight.[204] Dabney noted in his 1866 biography of Stonewall Jackson that right after Jackson expired, "men were everywhere speculating with solemn anxiety upon the meaning of his death."[205] With grief came anxiety.

Anxiety was not only focused on religious salvation but also encompassed concern for the Confederate nation itself. Mourning for Jackson took on a collective aspect that allowed renewed imaginative devotion to the fight. In gathering to mourn Jackson, loyal Confederates processed personal and collective losses, but they also tried to imagine how they could move forward.

Robert E. Lee had recognized that the fight had to press on or real calamity would come next, and he took little time to publicly grieve. But the Confederate public mustered as much mourning as it could before plunging back into the fray. The political aspect of mourning might provide inspiration for martial resilience. The collectivity of the grief for Jackson mattered immensely, as the Confederate community reinforced itself by shedding tears for the dead hero. Margaret Junkin Preston wrote in her diary that upon hearing the news of Jackson's death in Lexington "the grief in this community is intense; everybody is in tears."[206]

Crying over Jackson allowed grief for the past to mix with anxiety for the future, while still reinforcing an emotional sense of resolve. When Jackson lay in state in Richmond, the *Richmond Daily Dispatch* gave special coverage to the shedding of tears: "Many of the ladies, as they passed, shed tears over the remains, and, in token of their deep regard for the memory of the noble chieftain, pressed their lips upon the lid of his coffin." The paper noted a public consolation for the weeping "fair daughters of Virginia" when "an elderly and respectable-looking gentleman addressed them in tones of condolence, as follows: 'Weep not; all is for the best. . . . Though Jackson has been taken from the head of his corps, his spirit is now pleading our cause at the bar of God.'"[207] Anna Jackson noted of the mourners who passed her husband's coffin in Richmond: "The tears which were dropped over his bier by strong men and gentle women were the most true and honorable tributes that could have been paid him."[208] Tears expressed not a sense of crazed emotion and fear, but rather respect, honor, and resolve.

There was plenty of personal sacrifice to cry about. In 1863, the majority of Confederate soldiers (and Union soldiers for that matter) were sick and miserable most of the time. Even if they were not wounded or dying from battle, just existing in the conflict created profound mental and physical challenges well documented by Kathryn Shively Meier and other historians.[209] Battle casualties were accelerating in 1863, and as much as 22 percent of the Confederate male population aged twenty to twenty-four would be dead before the war ended almost two years later.[210]

Collective grief for Stonewall Jackson mingled with personal and familial grief in the midst of war and helped to turn loss into motivation, but in a slightly different way than mourning for Elmer Ellsworth had motivated vengeance in 1861. Stonewall Jackson's death called not just for vengeance for his own sacrifice but also for continued Confederate resolve in the face of the deaths of tremendous numbers of other men. He both focused their grief for their family members and provided an opportunity to hope for the future.

If the Confederacy itself was lost because Stonewall Jackson was dead, then all the personal grief and sacrifice would be for naught. The *Knoxville Register* praised him as an "incomparable" form of Christian soldier and asked, "What sacrifices shall we yet be called upon to make on the altar of independence?"[211] Judges in Richmond proclaimed a similar message, that Jackson's sacrifice amplified and stood in for all the other personal and family sacrifices of the war: "Again and again in this unholy war has Virginia been called to weep for some noble son sacrificed to liberty. . . . Now she mourns 'the noblest Roman of them all.'"[212] Confederates had no choice but to bear the losses if they wanted to continue building a nation.

National grief for Jackson also went beyond the personal, as one Richmond paper claimed that "eyes unused to weep were suffused with tears, and the great popular heart pulsated with emotions of grief too deep for utterance" upon contemplation of Jackson's remains.[213] As the *Charleston Courier* put it, "No tidings of a personal loss that could reach our readers would bring deeper and more general and sincere sorrow than will be felt on learning of the death of General Thomas J. Jackson."[214] The *Richmond Examiner* described the mourning scene in the capital by noting, "It was as though death had come home to every household, and snatched the one dearest away."[215] Jackson's death seemed to affect loyal Confederates with a sense of loss and dread.

Collective grief translated into a call for collective action, across state lines. The *Richmond Daily Dispatch* took great pains to cover the tears shed for Stonewall Jackson by Confederates far and wide, noting that "we have never before seen such an exhibition of heartfelt and general sorrow in reference to any other event."[216] In the May 15 issue, published just two days after Jackson's funeral in Richmond, the paper reprinted remarkably similar articles from other metropolitan areas, testifying to the "tears" of fellow Confederates. The *Charleston Courier* reported that "the country weeps . . . everyone feels as though he had sustained a personal bereavement," and the *Knoxville Register* agreed that "for the first time since the war began this whole nation weeps as one man. . . . a nation has appropriated him."[217] Another South Carolina paper noted that the news of Jackson's death "fell like a thunderbolt upon the hearts of the people of the Confederacy."[218] The *Savannah Republican* used Jackson's death to urge readers to continue their own sacrifices for Confederate independence.[219]

Much as the grief for Elmer Ellsworth and James Jackson had motivated fighting in the first months of the war, grief for Stonewall Jackson was publicized as a spur to action—albeit with seemingly higher stakes for a midwar Confederacy. A widely reprinted Richmond *Whig* obituary claimed that "since the death of WASHINGTON no similar event has so profoundly and sorrowfully impressed the people of Virginia as the death of Jackson. . . . Jackson, though dead, will still fight in the men whom he so often led to victory."[220]

The *Macon Telegraph* argued something similar, urging readers to consider how "a dead Jackson shall win the field."[221] John Beauchamp Jones tried to reassure himself in his diary that "there are other Jacksons in the army, who will win victories,—no one doubts it."[222] One private from Louisiana wrote to a friend, "The Enemy May think that Now Gen Jackson is Dead that they Can whip us but whenever they attempt it they will find that Though Jackson is Dead his Spirit is with his Men and whenever they go into Battle they will feel that the spirit of the Departed Hero is hovering over them."[223] Popular Confederate clergyman and writer James Dabney McCabe wrote in a biography of Jackson published just after his death, "He has gone, but his spirit is still with his countrymen. . . . Oh! May it animate each heart and nerve each arm to strike, as he struck, for the freedom of the land."[224] Defiance, a theme of Confederate nationalism, was thereby linked to loss, paving the way for another theme of the nascent Lost Cause.

Henry Kyd Douglas, a member of the Stonewall Brigade, penned a fable of how Jackson's death could serve a higher purpose. He told an apocryphal fable in his memoir when reflecting on how the death of Jackson affected Confederates, who knew "that it was the first mortal wound the Southern Confederacy had received." Douglas recounted the following:

> It is said that a semi-lunatic was walking on the lawn of an asylum near Baltimore when someone announced to him the death of Stonewall Jackson. At the news he was dazed, disturbed, and his feeble mind seemed to be groping in the dark for some explanation for such a calamity. . . . Deep sadness settled upon his face. Then suddenly a light broke over [his face] and lifting his head and looking up into the sky he exclaimed, 'Oh, what a battle must have been raging in Heaven, when the Archangel of the Lord needed the services of Stonewall Jackson!'[225]

Even in some Confederate areas under Union occupation, discussions of grief for Stonewall Jackson could be used as coded language for Confederate resolve. In New Orleans, occupied by U.S. troops for over a year already, the *Times Picayune* praised Jackson's military and personal virtues but exercised caution in declaring what his death meant for the Confederate nation. The editors ended his obituary with the statement that "those who really respect and revere his memory can safely leave to the future and to less troubled days the duty of writing his epitaph and pronouncing his eulogy," testifying in their reluctance the very bond between Jackson's memory and the Confederate national cause.[226] In occupied New Orleans, collective grief over Jackson indicated not only sadness but also hope for the "less troubled days" in the future Confederacy.

Union Response

Many Northerners, upon Jackson's death, also conflated him with the Confederacy and looked for signs of its future in his demise—which only further associated Jackson's public mourning with Confederate identity. Northern newspapers took wide notice of Jackson's passing and commented extensively on Confederate mourning, measuring Confederate public opinion and resolve in the observation of funeral sorrow. With Union casualties mounting and prospects for winning the war yet a dim future possibility, many Northerners seemed to grasp Jackson's death as a possible spur toward hoped-for victory. Jackson merited American national eulogy, both respectful and critical, because Union supporters hoped his death would help hasten the failure of the Confederacy and the reunification of the country. Many Northern eulogists noted Jackson's heroism, paying supposedly "due respect" to a Confederate greatness they perceived as doomed to defeat. When New York lieutenant John T. Norton in a letter to his father called Jackson "the bravest of the brave" upon his death, it was both a compliment and a sigh of relief that he was gone.[227] Triumphing over brave Confederates helped boost the righteousness of the Union Cause.

The Northern press paid Jackson respect and noted his death as one of great consequence to the South. Some reprinted Lee's announcement of Jackson's death, or reproduced simple reports of his passing.[228] *Harper's Weekly* published a largely respectful illustrated biography of Jackson on May 30, and the New York journal *Knickerbocker Monthly* wrote that "Northern and Union though we are, we cannot but respect the memory of one so brave and skillful . . . for admiration for the individual is entirely distinct from that for the cause."[229] The *Nassau Literary Magazine* struck a similar note, hoping that "it is permitted us, like Brutus, to have tears for the man, and daggers for his cause."[230] The *Providence Daily Journal* denied that Jackson was "strategic genius" but told Rhode Islanders that he was "worth an army to his cause."[231] Many Northerners praised Jackson's military talent but paused to note his "fanaticism" for religion and for the wrongheaded Confederacy.[232] Others, including Washington editor John W. Forney, whose eulogy for Jackson was praised by President Lincoln, styled Jackson's religiosity and bravery as good qualities.[233]

Eulogizing Jackson's great talents in the North might be possible, even necessary, but Jackson eulogies also provided an opportunity for many Northern papers (especially Republican ones) to denounce the cause Jackson fought for and to point out that he was a traitor. To them, Jackson may have had admirable qualities, but he used them for an ill purpose. The *Chicago Tribune*, for instance, noted that Jackson's loss was one "the rebels may well mourn, for he was not a man easily to be replaced. . . . History, when she records her final verdict against the infamous rebellion, will rank him among the most active and determined of its misguided agents."[234] When the paper received a critical letter from "some resident rebel" denouncing the critique of Jackson, the editors re-upped a few days later and tied Jackson directly to the perpetuation of slavery. The *Tribune* raged about Jackson "that he prostituted his talents . . . in the behest of the most infamous and atrocious of all systems that ever blackened the page of civilization," claiming that "the great shade of Washington will own no kinship with modern Virginians," even in their grief.[235]

To some Northern papers, Jackson stood in for all Confederates, perhaps not surprising since the outpouring of grief emphasized collective Confederate resolve. The *New York Times* printed a lengthy obituary of Jackson on May 14, praising his military talents and Christian devotion, but pronounced, "He will figure in history as one of the ablest of modern military leaders; and it will only be the brand of *traitor* on his brow that will consign him to infamy, as it has brought him to an untimely grave."[236] The *Detroit Free Press* called Jackson a "dangerous foeman" but lamented "his prostitution against his country of the talents and skill she had educated and trained."[237] The humor magazine *Vanity Fair* joked about Jackson that "considering that he is dead, he is not so bad as the live Rebels. . . . Stonewall Jackson had every reason for being a Union man, save that he was a Rebel."[238] The *Sacramento Daily Union* proclaimed in Jackson's eulogy that he had never really lived up to his own promise as a military commander but that he retained "the confidence of his men" and "continued to be the pet of the rebel masses and the hero of the rebellion in foreign estimation."[239]

Some Democratic papers foreshadowed postwar sectional reconciliation that was based on mutual respect for all soldiers' sacrifices and emphasized the positive, as in the *New York World*'s claim that "the Northern people honored in Jackson qualities which the worst cause cannot obscure."[240] Some of the most admiring of the Northern papers took pains to explain how greatly the loss of Jackson would impede the Confederate military cause and to beg: "Would to God that the eyes of the *good* men in the South might be opened to the sin and folly of secession and rebellion."[241] The *New York World* reported that General McClellan proclaimed upon hearing the news of Jackson's death, "No one can help admiring a man like Jackson . . . yet no one has disappointed me more than he has."[242]

Southern papers, in turn, reprinted Northern eulogies to argue how Northerners were afraid of Confederate military prowess, and they sometimes left in the accusations of treason to egg on Confederate vengeance.[243] Confederates worried about who would replace Jackson, even while praising the power of his loss to motivate the fight. Gen. William Nelson Pendleton wrote a mournful letter to his wife about Jackson's death and mused: "Who will fill his place we do not yet know. . . . At any rate, Jackson's example will be mighty in animating alike commanders and men."[244] Confederates faced almost two more years of war without Jackson. The absence of Stonewall Jackson, especially two months later at Gettysburg, became a cornerstone of Lost Cause ideology as people asked what would have happened differently if he had been there.[245]

Jackson's Grave: Confederate Memorial

After Jackson's burial in May 1863, public mourning for him continued to play a role in Confederate nationalism during the war's final two years and after. Reverence for the dead Jackson could turn easily into a form of reverence for the passing, or dead, Confederacy itself. Dying froze Jackson's heroic image in time, which became useful as the Confederacy faltered and fell, only to be revived in memory and imagination. Lt. Gen. Richard Taylor wrote in the *North American Review* in 1878 that Jackson was "fortunate in his death, he fell at the summit of glory, before the sun of the Confederacy had set; ere defeat, and suffering, and selfishness, could turn their fangs upon him. . . . As one man, the South wept for him . . . even Federals praised him."[246] To many Confederate nationalists Jackson's death, and the victory at Chancellorsville, became the apex of Confederate achievement—with calamitous national loss to come thereafter. The calamity became part of the romanticized myth of doomed Confederate glory, with Jackson as one of its patron saints.

As such, Jackson's grave site in Lexington began immediately to attract attention as a site of Confederate devotion. The *Richmond Examiner* wrote on the day of Jackson's funeral that his grave would be "consecrated a Mecca and a shrine" by future generations.[247] Robert Lewis Dabney (Jackson's chief of staff, Presbyterian theologian, and apostle of the Lost Cause) praised the simplicity of Jackson's grave in Lexington in the biography of the general he published in 1864, noting that the grave needed no marker but the "path" created by visitors, for "no Confederate ever passes the spot without turning aside to seek a new lesson of patriotism and fortitude from the suggestions of the scene."[248] Wallace Hettle has documented how Dabney used Jackson's "martyrdom to reframe the idea of courage" as one of the cornerstones of Lost Cause ideology from 1863 until Dabney's death in 1898.[249] It is notable that Jackson's grave site became a site of Confederate veneration in the first year after his death, before the war was even over.

Jackson's grave provided a marker for Confederate identity. As such, some Confederate nationalists in 1863 lamented that Jackson was not buried in Rich-

"The Grave of Stonewall Jackson: Lexington, Virginia" engraving by Currier and Ives, c. 1870. Library of Congress, Prints and Photographs Division, LC-DIG-pga-09016.

mond in the gorgeous, parklike Hollywood cemetery, worrying that Lexington was too far away from the heart of the Confederacy to afford proper hero worship.[250] The *Richmond Enquirer* lamented that Jackson would not be interred in Hollywood, where he could join U.S. presidents already, for "there sleep Monroe and Tyler. . . . We have neither a Westminster nor a Pantheon, but all would wish to see the best that we could give conferred on Jackson."[251] The Hollywood Cemetery, founded in the late 1840s, became the focus of many Confederate memorial activities in Richmond immediately after the war, especially those sponsored by the Hollywood Memorial Association, one of the many Ladies' Memorial Associations founded to carry on the work of Confederate memory and veneration of the dead after 1865.[252] Even as the war was ending, embryonic plans to make Hollywood Cemetery the heart of mourning for the Confederate dead were shaping up, but without a link to Stonewall Jackson, some feared the plans would not be as effective. Jackson's burial ignited a tension between Lexington and Richmond—as each city claimed to be the sentimental heart of the Confederacy.

Stonewall Jackson's grave and the memory of his death played a signal role immediately after the war in the establishment of Confederate memorial practices that would help turn Confederate nationalism into the long-lasting Confederate memory that fed the Lost Cause. In the year after the war, as Caroline Janney has demonstrated, Ladies' Memorial Associations and other organizations directly linked the sanctification of graves and the reburial of the Confederate dead to politicized memorials throughout Virginia.[253] By 1866, the Ladies' Memorial Associations were already beginning what would become "their most visible and popular activity," the observance of Memorial Day, a day to decorate Confederate graves and pay honor to the dead.[254]

Stonewall Jackson's grave and the anniversary of his death proved central to Confederate memory and identity by providing a rallying point for Confederate Memorial Day observances. One of the very first observances of a Confederate Memorial Day was held on May 10, 1866, the third anniversary of Jackson's death. That day, the men and women of Lexington, Virginia, along with VMI cadets, Washington College students, and honored guests, paid homage to Jackson in a ceremony that resembled a replay of Jackson's funeral. In other locations, Jackson's commemoration was also "set apart as a suitable occasion for showing respect and honor" to all the Confederate dead, an important association that would intensify in years to come.[255] In Lexington, after a Presbyterian service featuring remarks by the Reverends Pemberton and White, who had both preached at Jackson's funeral, the crowd processed to the cemetery and paid respects at Jackson's grave site, which had "recently been enclosed by a neat and simple iron railing, with plain marble slabs placed at the head and feet to mark the spot." The headstone had the simple inscription "Lieutenant-General Jackson," and the Lexington Gazette noted: "It has no epitaph, and needs none. Angel hands have recorded it in Heaven."[256] Jackson's grave was sanctified space of Confederate memory.

Although connected to a real wave of activism to reinter Confederate soldiers who had been quickly buried during the war, this memorial observance and the way it was tied to Jackson's memory far exceeded simple respect for the dead. Tying reverence for the Confederate dead to Jackson's memory in such a material way elevated the occasion into a celebration of the Confederacy itself. According to the newspapers that called him "the great leader of the Southern armies," Robert E. Lee, who had recently become president of Washington College in Lexington, "stood with uncovered head, as he tendered silent homage to the heroick sleeper" at Jackson's grave. As VMI cadets and veterans of the Stonewall Brigade laid flowers and wreaths prepared by the women of Lexington for the occasion on Confederate graves, they "honored themselves" by preserving the memory of political sacrifice and carrying it into the future.[257]

Repeating similar mourning rituals became a defiant aspect of Confederate memory. Using the anniversary of Jackson's death as the date to mark Memorial Day was a way to tie the decoration of graves to Jackson's heroic image and a way to continue Confederate nationalism in a postwar context. David Blight has reminded us that "a unique version of the war's meaning, rooted in resistance to Reconstruction, coalesced around Memorial Day practice," and marking the day on Jackson's death date of May 10 was part of that process.[258] Beyond Lexington, on May 10, 1866, Ladies' Memorial Associations in Fredericksburg, Lynchburg, Charlottesville, and Richmond all adopted the date as the occasion to revere local Confederate graves, and a memorial association was established in Gordonsville on that date, as well.[259] The Richmond *Times* and other Southern papers campaigned to make May 10 a public holiday, "an anniversary always to be remembered."[260] On May 10, 1866, former Confederates also decorated family graves of President Andrew Johnson to show "their gratitude for his magnanimous Southern policy."[261] As the observance of Confederate Memorial Day spread across the South in subsequent years, the date varied, but many Virginia towns and the state of North Carolina adopted May 10 as the date of the holiday to honor the Confederate dead.[262] As the former states of the Confederacy were reincorporated into the United States, Jackson's grave and the anniversary of his death would mark how Confederate memory and the Lost Cause would also begin to play roles in versions of American national identity. With Confederate states back in the union, defiant rituals like Confederate Memorial Day became part of the American holiday calendar. Confederates rejoined the American nation, and their military mourning rejoined the fight for the "imaginative reconstitution of the nation."

————

Public mourning for Elmer Ellsworth and for Stonewall Jackson show clearly how rituals of unity around dead, heroic military men contributed to polarization and opposed versions of American and Confederate national identity during the Civil War. The war itself tore the Union and the Confederacy apart, and mourning helped assign meanings to the rift. Funeral rituals, print culture, grave sites, and veneration of remains all helped stoke patriotism and anger at the opposing side—helping to define what the war was about. Mourning rituals that had begun in the Revolutionary War as unifying elements in American national identity worked to solidify the fissures between Americans during the time of Civil War. Ellsworth and Jackson, and the culture of mourning and revenge that rose up around them, helped to impel countless others into the fray.

These wartime funeral rituals also show how public mourning for great Union and Confederate figures helped to mutually constitute identities for each side. The Union Cause and the Lost Cause might be opposed, but the fact that they mirrored one another mattered immensely. People in the United States and the Confederate States of America all shed public tears for dead heroes, even if the values they supposedly embodied were polar opposites. The form of the public funeral proved immensely powerful.

The process of mourning and the value of sacrifice were held in common. Citizens of the Union and the Confederacy were certainly opposed, but they shared the experience of defining themselves by publicly mourning white, manly heroes. The theme of common sacrifice of white soldiers during the Civil War that would become—as David Blight has argued—such a potent force in reconciliation of the nation thirty years later had its roots in wartime funerals for Ellsworth and Jackson.[263] Public funeral rituals helped to tear people apart, and they also gave them lessons in how to imagine coming together.

Chapter 3

George Peabody, Robert E. Lee, and
the Boundaries of Reconciliation

Hundreds of trustees, teachers, musicians, students, and members of the public filled the Peabody Institute Hall in Baltimore, Maryland, on February 18, 1870, to commemorate the man whose financial donation had established the institute just eight years earlier. George Peabody, a New Englander who had spent almost half his life in London as he built huge merchant and financial businesses, had died in England four months before. Americans had spent months riveted by press coverage of Peabody's elaborate London funeral and temporary interment in Westminster Abbey. The press reported every step as Queen Victoria ordered Peabody's remains to be returned to New England aboard the warship *Monarch*, which crossed the Atlantic with a U.S. naval escort. When Peabody's remains arrived in New England, a delegation of the Baltimore Institute trustees attended his funeral and burial in Harmony Grove cemetery in Peabody, Massachusetts. Ten days after Peabody's burial, the city of Baltimore officially declared a day of mourning, and efforts were underway to erect a statue of Peabody near the city's monument to George Washington. Baltimore, the Southern city that had launched Peabody's career as a transatlantic merchant, associated the famous New Englander with its own post–Civil War Southern identity.[1]

Peabody is largely forgotten today, but he was tremendously important in the nineteenth century, and his funeral commemorations were important rituals of post–Civil War reunion. Commemorating George Peabody highlighted contradictions even as the ritual was very tied up with Civil War memory: he was a famous Northerner who lived in Great Britain and who supported the South. Peabody was a son of New England whose statue stood in London and whose portrait graced Robert E. Lee's office wall. Severn Teackle Wallis, chosen by his fellow Peabody Institute trustees to deliver the eulogy for Peabody in Baltimore, used the speech to emphasize reconciliation between Britain and the United States and between the American North and South. Wallis argued that the transatlantic public mourning for Peabody contained enormous cultural significance and the power to reunite political opponents. Wallis noted that the "cavils of diplomacy and the mutterings of discord" between Britain and the United States were "hushed" by sincere mourning rituals for George Peabody, "whose death touched the hearts of two great nations, that either could call unto the other to join hands with it across his grave."[2] In words that echoed Horace Greeley's sentiment, first expressed in 1865, that the North and South could reunite to "clasp hands" over the grave of slavery, Wallis maintained that public mourning must have a calming effect on post–Civil War relations between the United States and Britain, which were embroiled in a diplomatic dispute over the *Alabama* claims and other U.S. demands for reparations for the damage done by British raiders that had aided the Confederacy.[3]

Wallis also argued that Peabody's memory could reunite Northerners and Southerners divided by bitter memories of the Civil War. He noted that in the 1820s, Peabody had lived in Baltimore "a Northern man among a Southern people," and when he returned to the city only a few months before his death, "He returned to find us sullen and divided. The wounds of our then recent civil strife were yet unhealed. Political antagonisms, social resentments—personal and even domestic animosities—were still rankling, and it was next to impossible for any man to speak, without offence to some one whom he cared for." Peabody donated huge sums of money to Southern postwar recovery, especially educational efforts, and Wallis wanted other Northerners to absorb his spirit of generosity toward the South.

According to Wallis, the remarkable burial commemorations for Peabody should inspire Americans to a spirit of reunification and a willingness to preserve Southern respect: "While he proclaimed that his sympathies had been always with the Union and his hopes with the success of its armies, he dared to proclaim, at the same time, his respect for the integrity and manhood of the vanquished." Wallis claimed that Peabody's own efforts to "dry the waters of bitterness" between North and South "reconciled" many people who were estranged on account of the Civil War.[4]

Of course, Wallis was no neutral observer of post–Civil War sectional strife. The Baltimore lawyer had been, as Michael D. Robinson calls him, "one of the Border South's most outspoken proponents of secession," who was imprisoned by Union forces as disloyal during the war.[5] After the war, in 1867, Wallis helped the Democratic Party quickly regain control of Maryland politics from Maryland Republicans who had, indeed, bitterly expelled former Confederates from politics in 1865.[6] Neither party in Maryland advanced African American rights—Black suffrage was not extended after the war, and both public education and the private education funded by Peabody in the state were segregated and vastly unequal.

Wallis framed mourning for George Peabody as a ritual of reunification between North and South and the United States and Great Britain—and it surely was—but only for some. Reunion meant different things to different people. Not everyone was sure that British-American relations, so hurt by British support for the Confederacy, could be repaired by "joining hands" across Peabody's grave. Some Radical Republicans and former abolitionists denounced the national mourning for Peabody precisely because it dramatized North-South reunion—but on terms too friendly to former Confederates whom they suspected of possessing Peabody's true sympathies. Dissenters, who also pointed out how strongly associated Peabody was with former Confederate general Robert E. Lee, worried that the public funeral provided Southern men like Severn Teackle Wallis a way to dramatize their fantasy of national reunion with former Confederates returned to national power. When Lee died just months after Peabody, his own public funerals prompted some similar conflicts.

In the years following the Civil War, at a time when the nation was attempting Reconstruction with considerable pain, politicized public funeral rituals continued to offer a platform on which different forms of national identity could be rebuilt. The reunification process was made much more difficult by the deep divisions sown by the war. National identities formed before the war mixed with Civil War memory to reconfigure what it meant to be American. Strong Southern pride that would feed the Lost Cause for many decades to come survived the Confederacy itself and worked its way into the larger stream of American national identity. The conflicting strains of regionalism, identity, reunion, and the beginnings of reconciliation are all vitally evident in the 1869–70 funerals and public mourning dedicated to George Peabody and Robert E. Lee. Mourning culture and public funerals created rituals that became the terrain of contest over the meaning of the war and its end. Public funerals for George Peabody and for Robert E. Lee allowed Americans to express identities that all related to the nation in various (even some conflicting) ways. Animosities forged during the war—North versus South and American versus British—shaped public mourning as the nation was reconstituted after wartime frictions. Tensions between themes of reunion and reconciliation, often expressed in the same funeral rites, reflected divided feelings about the American nation itself.

As Americans worked to reunite the nation, even during the height of Republican control of Reconstruction in 1869–70, they also started to open the door to sectional reconciliation and forgiveness in some surprising ways. The tensions between sectional reunion and sectional resentment have formed the basis for one of the most important historiographical debates over the meaning of Civil War memory in recent years. Some scholars have argued, following David Blight, that the theme of reconciliation privileged white Southern memory and dominated emancipationist culture, while others, following Barbara Gannon and Caroline Janney, have emphasized a more limited strain of reunion, arguing that both Northerners and Southerners held on to their sectional causes and resentments.[7] Recently, Nina Silber has argued that reconciliation and reunion were, perhaps, not as opposed as the debate has sometimes made them seem, and she has refocused our attention on "the imaginative reconstitution of the nation" as new American national identities were created out of many strands of Civil War memory, sectional and nationalist alike.[8] Examining the funerals and public mourning rites for George Peabody and Robert E. Lee in 1870 shows that, indeed, Silber's call to refocus on national identity as a product of Civil War memory is helpful.

Public funerals in 1869 and 1870 provided powerful occasions for rival versions of "the imagined reconstitution of the nation." Even in the first years after the war, before rituals of memory had had time to fully develop, seemingly mutually exclusive visions of American unity and sectional resentment both circulated as themes in the rituals of mourning that helped to re-create American national identity. Funeral rituals for George Peabody and for Robert E. Lee specifically show how national identity could take shape against a backdrop of difficult international, sectional, and racial relations. Peabody was a Northerner who loved England and became a fixture there, and his funeral was a pageant of reconciliation with England that allowed Americans to fantasize about finding a new place in the world. But his commemoration also occasioned public controversy over British naval power and over Peabody's supposed Southern sympathies. Perhaps even more remarkably, Robert E. Lee's 1870 funeral also showed reconciliationist signs—while simultaneously fueling the Lost Cause mythology that would feed Southern sectionalism and a post-Confederate civic identity in Virginia. Even while under control of Republican Reconstruction policies, former Confederates used mourning for Lee as a way to make their Lost Cause post-Confederate sentiments heard— and a surprising number of Northerners were willing to listen to, and even spread, their pro-Confederate messages.

The funerals for Peabody and Lee demonstrate how both reunion and reconciliation were already at play in 1870, just five years after the war. Many historians have noted how Lee became an important secular saint of the Lost Cause with cross-sectional appeal by the turn of the twentieth century. But the mix of reunion and reconciliation, sectionalism and nationalism, had already started in 1870. The funerals of Peabody and Lee demonstrate why it is a mistake to exclusively emphasize either reunion or reconciliation as a theme in Civil War memory, even in its early years, because the two could combine in complex ways as the American nation remade itself in the minds and ritual practices of its citizens.

George Peabody and Reconciliation

Examining public funerals as expressions of Civil War memory allows us to see how cultural contests over war memory sometimes took place in unexpected places. In the twenty-first century we might not see why George Peabody's funeral was so important, but no one in the nineteenth century would have denied it. Peabody, a wealthy financier who lived for more than thirty years in London and who never served in the military or in any government position, might seem to be a surprising figure to receive a large-scale funeral that helped to configure Civil War memory and national identity during Reconstruction. But he was a key figure in the links between the United States and Great Britain and helped to configure some key aspects of the reunification of North and South.

Peabody's funerals created one of the largest transatlantic spectacles of the nineteenth century. Anglo-American reunification and Union-Confederate reunification were tied up together in 1869–70, as the United States pursued international legal claims against the British for helping the Confederate navy. The ability of a reunited United States to stand up to Britain was a test of power, even as some former Confederates still took pleasure in seeing the United States humbled internationally. Many Americans debated the terms of Civil War memory and reunification by mourning for George Peabody, and even though he is not well remembered today, to miss out on his importance in 1869-70 would be a mistake. Peabody's funeral simultaneously dramatized sectional and transatlantic reunification and contributed to contested versions of American national identity.

George Peabody was born in 1795 in Danvers (now Peabody), Massachusetts, to a very poor family, but he worked his way from being a grocery and dry goods apprentice to the principal in a wholesaling and import business in Baltimore by 1829. Peabody soon began to deal in finance, negotiating an $8 million loan for the state of Maryland from London banks in 1835. He moved to London, more or less permanently, in 1837 and deepened his financial business selling bonds and American securities (including speculative railroad coupons) and exporting British steel. In 1854, Peabody partnered as a merchant banker with J. S. Morgan, and when Peabody retired in 1864, Morgan continued the business on his own. Peabody's net worth upon his death in 1869 was $16 million (the equivalent of almost $6.5 billion in 2015 dollars).[9]

Peabody was extremely famous because he used his exceptional wealth in a relatively novel way: he dispersed lavish philanthropic gifts on both sides of the Atlantic. Predating generous men of capital like Andrew Carnegie and John D. Rockefeller by at least forty years, Peabody began to give away his fortune in the 1850s, even as he was still accumulating great wealth. In that decade, he gave $250,000 to establish the Peabody Institute, an educational and civic center, in his Massachusetts hometown and endowed another Peabody Institute in Baltimore for $1.5 million. In 1862, Peabody established a $2.5 million Peabody Trust that was earmarked to provide well-appointed low-cost housing for poor workers in London, a gift that won him plaudits: the Freedom of the City of London, a statue of him erected in London, and accolades from Queen Victoria (he declined a baronetcy). The U.S. Congress voted thanks to Peabody for his exceptional American philanthropy and presented him with a gold medal in 1867.[10]

Politically, George Peabody was a trimmer, who tended to favor stability in support of international business interests over ideological commitment, even during the Civil War. He opposed secessionism but disliked abolitionism. Despite wishing that the Civil War could have been avoided, Peabody told many that he supported the Union Cause. Throughout the war, he maintained strong friendships with wealthy Confederates, and he was accused by no less than Secretary of State William Henry Seward of being a war profiteer. Despite being seen as wanting to play both sides during the Civil War, Peabody refused to negotiate loans for the Confederacy in London, and he maintained close ties with U.S. diplomats in the British capital. Peabody supported the Union Cause, but he did so without enthusiasm and seemingly without much awareness that his actions were sometimes perceived as very pro-Confederate.[11]

Peabody intensified his philanthropy after the Civil War, as he focused on U.S. education—especially in the South. In consultation with his scientist nephew, O. C. Marsh, Peabody donated $150,000 each to Harvard and Yale to found scientific museums, and he donated almost as much to start the Peabody Academy of Science in Salem, Massachusetts. In 1867, Peabody expressed his hopes that the reconstructed South would soon rejoin the North on equal terms by donating $2.1 million to establish the Peabody Education Fund for public schools and teachers' colleges, including George Peabody College for Teachers (now merged with Vanderbilt University). Although the fund itself did not exclude African Americans from receiving aid, it did acquiesce to state segregation, and it funded Black schools at least one-third less than it funded equivalent white schools.

Within the few years before his death, Peabody would raise the Southern education endowment to $3.5 million, equal to more than one-tenth of the entire federal budget in the year he died. His $60,000 gift to Washington College (where Robert E. Lee was president) a few months before his death at a time when the college was in precarious financial straits marked it as a particular favorite, but it was only one of the Southern institutions Peabody readily funded. His friend Robert C. Winthrop, who became lead trustee of the Peabody Education Fund, noted that Peabody's educational philanthropy had "neither precedent nor parallel."[12] Peabody's philanthropy intervened in Reconstruction, and by funding education he promoted a vision of a restored South, ruled by "the best men"—whites who would restore social order and reunite with the North on equal terms—a vision that foreshadowed a national mood of Northern and Southern veterans' reunion that would gain wider traction by the turn of the twentieth century.[13]

Although Great Britain never formally recognized the Confederacy, British financial and other support for the Confederacy caused a deep fracture in U.S.-British relations that was painful to George Peabody. Peabody was beloved in England and in America for his philanthropy, and he had become since the late 1830s both a symbol and a promoter of British-American relations. He championed U.S. and state finances to London banks during perilous economic times in the 1840s, he personally funded the American exhibit at the Crystal Palace Exhibition in 1851, and his annual London dinners in honor of the Fourth of July brought together the transatlantic upper crust.[14] Peabody himself declared (in openly racialized terms) that he hoped his donations to British charities would "soften asperities of feeling which had unhappily arisen between the two great nations of the Anglo-Saxon family."[15] He wished to bring England and the United States closer before and after the Civil War.

George Peabody viewed repairing the rifts between Britain and the United States and between North and South as part of the same healing project. He told President Andrew Johnson at a private meeting in 1867 that he appreciated Johnson's efforts to restore the Southern states to "full relations" with the federal government, since that restoration also helped British-U.S. relations.[16] Peabody's vision of Southern forgiveness matched Johnson's, and he intertwined international recovery with sectional forgiveness.

When George M. Brown, president of the Eastern Railroad Company, commented about the arrangements for George Peabody's funeral, he noted, "Nations contend to do honor to the memory of the great philanthropist in transporting his remains across the ocean." Brown's language was revelatory. Although Peabody wanted to reunite the two nations, he also inspired a contest. The transatlantic funerals for George Peabody allowed the United States and Britain to express the pageantry of reconciliation. But at the same time, parts of that pageant were highly contested—and there was an unveiled note of naval competition in the convoy that conveyed Peabody across the Atlantic. Peabody's funeral also introduced a similar note of reconciliation alongside contest between the Confederate "nation" and the United States. Indeed, nations contended to do him honor.[17]

The international grief for George Peabody created a very particular vision of Civil War memory: one that emphasized U.S. forgiveness of both Britain and the Confederacy, while still containing a thinly veiled theme of international and sectional competition below the surface. Contests over how Peabody ought to be mourned became good venues for arguing about the terms of national forgiveness that would be so important to the postwar United States.

Transatlantic Mourning

When George Peabody died on November 4, 1869, his demise made huge news in London and quickly spread by telegraph across the Atlantic, appearing prominently in the pages of American newspapers by the next day.[18] Around London, flags flew at half-staff in his honor, and prominent buildings were draped in mourning as the news spread.[19] Obituaries praised him as a philanthropist and unifier, and papers on both sides of the Atlantic immediately began to report on funeral arrangements, noting that the details of Peabody's mourning would matter "wherever integrity and benevolence are appreciated."[20]

Peabody received a public London funeral that was exceptional for an American and a commoner. Six days after his death, his remains were taken from Sir Curtis Lampson's home in Eaton Square to Westminster Abbey, where they were, at Queen Victoria's request, temporarily interred after an elaborate funeral ceremony.[21] Peabody's funeral cortege of a coach and five mourning carriages, accompanied by the coaches of many London dignitaries, traveled through London streets "lined with silent crowds of spectators" to reach Westminster Abbey, burial site of kings and since the 1260s the most sanctified space of English national mourning.[22]

The abbey was draped in mourning and so crowded that tickets had to be issued for Peabody's burial service. Prime Minister Gladstone, British foreign secretary Lord Clarendon, U.S. minister to Britain John Lothrop Motley, Queen Victoria's private secretary, the lord mayor and aldermen of London, and many businessmen and aristocrats attended the ceremonies, performed by the cathedral canon and subdean, Lord John Thynne. Both British and American papers stressed that tears were shed as "the solemnity of the occasion was profoundly felt by the vast assembly."[23]

The bishop of London preached a funeral sermon for Peabody on the following Sunday and noted that "no untitled commoner drew around his grave as large a concourse of sincere mourners as George Peabody."[24] Some American editors seized on the bishop's claim and enhanced it, maintaining that "no private citizen of either country has ever before received such distinction."[25] On the same Sunday, the famous dissenting minister Newman Hall, who had been a staunch supporter of the Union Cause in the Civil War, preached on Peabody to a packed house at St. James' Hall, emphasizing that Peabody's funeral mourning would unite the two countries in peace.[26]

These rituals seemed to provide the opportunity for a show of international unity, even as the United States and Britain continued to be locked in conflict over war reparations, especially for the support Britain had offered to Confederate naval operations. Americans took note of the British pomp and respect for Peabody, and many claimed that it deserved to be repaid by a move

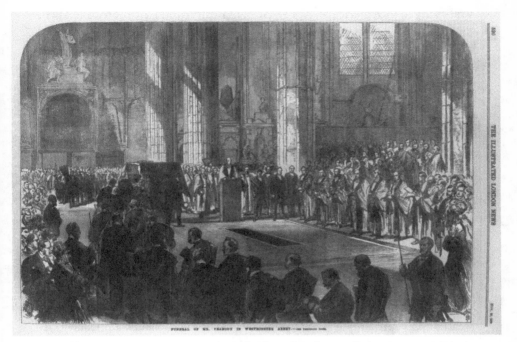

"Funeral of Mr. Peabody in Westminster Abbey," *London Illustrated News*, 1869.
Library of Congress, Prints and Photographs Division, LC-USZ62-62245.

to repair U.S.-British relations. Several American, and even some British, newspapers noted that Queen Victoria showed her "kindhearted" nature as the "crown of womanhood" by paying tribute to Peabody and argued that she (and the British nation with her) earned American respect by their regard for Peabody.[27] The *New York Herald*, particularly, offered praise for Queen Victoria and noted that the Westminster funeral would have been "a mockery" had "her affection for his character" not been so great.[28]

Prime Minister Gladstone lamented in a speech several days after Peabody's death that diplomacy had often failed to maintain close relations between Britain and the United States, but he hoped that Peabody's death would have a calming effect, and "with Mr. Peabody's country we are not likely to quarrel."[29] The *New York Times* editorialized that "Mr. Gladstone is quite right in saying" that Peabody's philanthropy and mourning for his death "do more than all the oumbrous efforts of diplomatists to promote a right understanding between nations."[30]

Many Americans reacted to the call for unity. Charles Pettit MacIlvaine, the Episcopal bishop and Anglophile, who also served on the board of the Peabody trust, wrote that Peabody's funeral at Westminster Abbey was "very gratifying to us Americans."[31] The cities of Boston and Baltimore tolled bells and flew public flags at half-staff in Peabody's honor on the day of his London funeral.[32] Dozens of American newspapers reprinted sympathetic coverage of the London funeral, and *Harper's Weekly* published a multipage pictorial of Peabody's burial in Westminster Abbey.[33] The American press argued that the "international mourning" for Peabody reflected equal glory upon Britain and the United States.[34]

Westminster Abbey was not slated to be Peabody's final resting place; he wanted to be buried in Massachusetts. The transportation of Peabody's remains, however, tested whether Britain and the U.S. could set aside tension to peacefully mourn him. Within days of Peabody's death, reports swirled that Queen Victoria would order a man-of-war, perhaps the *Inconstant*, to transport Peabody's remains for final burial in Massachusetts.[35] The Grant administration dispatched an American warship to London—preferring not to cede the transport to a British ship of the line.[36] The day after Peabody's Westminster funeral, Secretary of the Navy George Maxwell Robeson cabled Admiral William Radford, commander of the U.S. fleet in Europe, to send a U.S. warship from France to England to pick up Peabody's body. But stormy weather prevented any American ship from arriving in Britain until early December, by which time the British ship *Monarch* was already specially outfitted to carry Peabody's remains.[37]

It became clear that the British warship *Monarch* would transport Peabody's remains, and the American ship *Plymouth* would merely act as a naval escort—a fact that became ripe with symbolism and made the transportation of Peabody's body the subject of a kind of peaceful naval competition. On December 11, the *Monarch* received Peabody's remains at Portsmouth, England, accompanied by another set of funeral events there.[38] The ship, which held Peabody's casket in a special funeral chapel constructed on its main deck, waited for the *Plymouth* to arrive before departing for America. The *Plymouth* joined the *Monarch* at Spithead on December 16. Again, U.S. newspapers followed every step of the naval rendezvous and printed them as part of the massive coverage of the journey to repatriate Peabody's remains.[39]

The international squadron conveying Peabody's remains across the Atlantic simultaneously showed the ability of the nations to work together and allowed them an opportunity to showcase and compare their navies. British and American newspapers vied in their descriptions of the ships along the Peabody funeral journey. American newspapers covered the ships in ways that emphasized the relative power of the "steel frigate" *Monarch* as compared with "American vessels from the Mediterranean Squadron," and made special note of the *Monarch*'s impressive steam power and "very heavy armament."[40] The

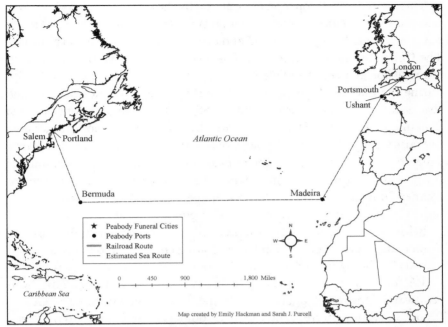

Transatlantic journey of George Peabody's remains, 1869–70. Data from IPUMS, National Historical Geographic Information System; Jeremy Atack, "Historical Geographic Information Systems (GIS) database of U.S. Railroads for 1873 (May 2016); University of Nebraska, Railroads and the Making of Modern America," http://railroads.unl.edu /resources/; OpenStreetMap, www.openstreetmap.org; National Geospatial-Intelligence Agency, World Port Index. Map by Sarah J. Purcell and Emily Hackman.

New York Times reported that "in naval circles considerable interest" was aroused by the idea of an American ship acting as "consort" to a British man-of-war.[41] As the *Monarch* prepared to sail with her American escort, the *New York Times* reminded its readers of the British claim that the *Monarch* was the nation's "finest turreted ship," but the *Chicago Tribune* also noted that the *Plymouth* was "perfectly able" to keep up with her.[42] British naval officials took some pride in an American naval report on the Peabody expedition that dubbed the "*Monarch* the most formidable and effective iron-clad vessel-of-war for ocean service in the world."[43]

The U.S. Congress offered a joint resolution on December 23, paying tribute to Peabody and directing the president to pay for the reception of the remains in the United States, since "the Queen of Great Britain, the authorities of London, and the Emperor of France have made extraordinary provision for the transfer of his remains to his native land."[44] Even in tribute, the spirit of naval competition was not lost.

This naval competition took place at exactly the time when post–Civil War tensions in the Anglo-American relationship, especially as they related to the naval war, were being confronted and brought to international arbitration. The United States sought, in 1869, financial claims against the British government for allowing Confederate raiders to capture U.S. merchant ships during the war. The legal claims took on the name of the most famous and successful raider, the Liverpool-made CSS *Alabama*, and tensions between Britain and the United States were generally high just as diplomats gathered to praise George Peabody.[45] Adrian Cook, a historian of the *Alabama* claims, called the winter of 1869–70 "the critical year" in *Alabama* negotiations, as the new Grant administration sought to balance fiery outrage from Senator Charles Sumner and other radicals at home (many of whom wanted to acquire Canada) and relatively ineffectual English diplomats abroad.[46]

British and Americans, Northerners and Southerners, Republicans and Democrats all perceived that jointly celebrating George Peabody's death could provide a calming influence on the situation, even as all sides also used Peabody's funerals as an opportunity to jockey for position. The *Pall Mall Gazette* warned the British public not to let the "hokum" of mourning for George Peabody divert them from the very real conflicts between the two nations.[47] The same paper remarked, however, in December when President Grant sought in a public message to calm the tensions over the *Alabama* claims, that "demonstrations in honor of George Peabody will tend to mitigate the irritation" that existed between the nations.[48]

The chance for the U.S. government to signal its reconciliation with Britain through participation in Peabody's mourning, however, almost foundered because of congressional disagreement over the strength of Peabody's Union sympathies. Just days after Grant's somewhat conciliatory public message about transatlantic mourning for Peabody, Thomas L. Jones, a Democratic congressman from Kentucky, introduced a joint resolution in the U.S. House of Representatives directing the president to send "a fleet of war vessels" to escort the *Monarch* when it reached American waters.[49] Although the House offered unanimous consent, Jones's proposal faced stiff opposition from two former Union generals now serving as Republican representatives, General Benjamin Butler (Massachusetts) and Robert C. Schenck (Ohio), who argued that sending war ships would cost too much and that Peabody had not sufficiently supported the Union in the Civil War. Schenck was well versed in sectional strife and funeral politics, having been embroiled in controversy for refusing to vote to adjourn the House of Representatives for the death of President Zachary Taylor in 1850.[50] For fear of causing international embarrassment, the House referred the matter to President Grant, who without much enthusiasm instructed the navy to send vessels to rendezvous with the *Monarch*.[51]

The contest between the nations to deploy ships to carry Peabody's remains struck a note of military contest that resonated in the transatlantic relationship in the particular context of the rift over the *Alabama* claims in 1869–70.[52] Even some of the same newspapers that lavished praise upon the British for their extensive mourning of Peabody kept to their Republican principles by being skeptical of British naval goodwill. One commentator in the *Chicago Tribune* claimed, "It is nonsense for Mr. Gladstone to say that Great Britain can never quarrel with 'the country of George Peabody' . . . What in the world has Mr. Peabody, alive or dead, to do with the question of peace or war between England and the United States?"[53] In reality, he did have something to do with the question; Peabody had sought to strengthen U.S.-British relations for decades. Transatlantic bankers who had worked with George Peabody pressed for a resolution to the *Alabama* claims and helped push the matter into international arbitration, arguing that Britain and the United States needed one another both diplomatically and financially.[54]

The interaction between Peabody's funerals and British-American tensions also played into North-South tensions in the aftermath of the Civil War. Some former Confederates were still hoping, as they had during the war, that Britain might teach the American government a lesson. One South Carolina newspaper noted that the British had sent "a powerful hint" by sending the impressive ironclad *Monarch* to convey George Peabody to American shores: "She has startled the Yankees with her superior capacities for sailing and fighting. As there are plenty more like her in Old England, we shall hear no more of a war with John Bull."[55] The "powerful hint" was not lost on the Northern press, but Northern editors tried to put a more positive gloss on the Anglo-American warship encounter by emphasizing, for example, how the *Monarch*'s captain declared the American ironclad *Terror* was "a 'match' for the most powerful iron-clad in the royal navy."[56]

Far more commentators (in both countries) emphasized the cooperation necessary to use such naval power to convey Peabody's remains to the United States, turning the funeral convoy into a symbol of war machines used for purposes of peaceful transatlantic reconciliation. Many followed the lead of Newman Hall, who had preached that "George Peabody is a link of peace and love between the two nations that must never be broken."[57] *Punch* magazine emphasized the amazing power of the "Old World's warship" transporting Peabody's remains but also hoped that the journey would "turn each foe to friend."[58]

The Reverend Henry Foote, head minister of King's Chapel in Boston, preached a funeral sermon for Peabody maintaining that the fact that Britain chose "to send home his mortal remains in a vessel of war" was actually a "happy omen of the gracious friendliness which hereafter shall take the place of past discords and quarrels!"[59] One Massachusetts paper wrote that by joining British and American vessels together, "these nations thus unite in honoring the memory of the merchant and philanthropist. The fact is a memorable one."[60] As Captain John Edmund Commerell received Peabody's remains onto the *Monarch* for the funeral journey, he assured the U.S. minister to Britain that Peabody's "memory would ever be held dear by the people of my country."[61] Even with some hints of dissent, there was a clear transatlantic hope that the mourning pageantry for Peabody might strike a new note of Anglo-American unity.

Transatlantic Remains and Civil War Memory

The transoceanic funeral transport and its Anglo-American importance magnified the scale of public mourning being prepared in the United States. As the *Monarch* and the *Plymouth* made their journey across the Atlantic, Americans prepared for the arrival of Peabody's remains as American newspapers both speculated on the progress at sea and reported on the funeral preparations "intended to eclipse anything of the kind heretofore known."[62] Boston had hoped to host Peabody's funeral squadron, but its port was not deep enough for the massive *Monarch*, and among New England ports only Portland, Maine, could dock the heavy warships.[63] By mid-December, officials in Portland watched the telegraph for the fleet's progress and put considerable effort into civic preparations for the arrival of Peabody's remains.[64]

The U.S. Navy prepared to send several ironclad steamers to Portland to receive the remains from the British, hoping to match the grandeur of the *Monarch*. President Grant placed Admiral David Farragut, the Civil War hero who had served in the navy since 1812, in charge of the naval operations to receive Peabody's remains.[65] Farragut, who also served as one of the trustees of the Peabody Educational Trust, was elderly and very ill, but he accepted the command of the American naval delegation for Peabody as his last assignment.[66]

In early January, news came from the Navy Department that the "Anglo American funeral convoy" bearing Peabody's remains had taken a southern route, stopping at Madeira and Bermuda for refueling, and would not arrive in Maine for several more weeks.[67] Meanwhile, the institute trustees and Peabody's nephew George Peabody Russell were also preparing in earnest for large funeral and civic ceremonies in Peabody, Massachusetts, where the remains would travel by special train from Portland.[68] The American press passed the time by reporting on the preparations in Maine and Massachusetts and by speculating on the progress of the ships.[69] The January 15 issues of both *Harper's Weekly* and *Frank Leslie's Illustrated Newspaper* detailed the decor and mourning rituals on board the *Monarch* accompanied by illustrations of the ship and its special mortuary chapel that housed Peabody's remains in a sealed metal casket during the voyage.[70]

Having Peabody's funeral convoy arrive in Maine connected the arrival to Civil War memory in a very specific context that heightened some of the tensions present in Peabody's own legacy and in the contested narratives of Anglo-American and sectional cooperation created by the naval journey. Portland harbor saw several naval clashes during the Civil War. In 1863, a Confederate raider exploded the federal revenue cutter *Caleb Cushing* in the harbor, and Portland merchant ships were under constant threat during the war. Eleven of the fifty-two merchant ships sunk by the Confederate raider *Alabama* were from Maine, which put a spin on the show of British naval strength in transporting Peabody's remains as the *Alabama* claims simmered.[71]

While officials in Maine sought to make the most of their opportunity in the national spotlight and hoped that their ceremonial reception of Peabody's remains would "reflect the greatest credit upon the city and State," political divisions in the state between Radical Republicans, more conservative Republicans, and minority Democrats also prevented a unified show of mourning.[72] Joshua Chamberlain, the heroic commander of Maine troops at the Battle of Gettysburg, was serving his fourth term as Maine's Republican governor as Peabody's remains approached Portland, but even he could not easily unify the Maine legislature around Peabody's memory. Despite his Republican loyalty and his support of the Fourteenth Amendment, Chamberlain was no proponent of Black voting rights, and by early 1870 he held views, similar to Peabody's, that talented men in the North and South should "restore fraternal confidence and enterprise . . . for the better bond of union and the future prestige of the Nation" without regard for the rights of African Americans.[73] Both Peabody and Chamberlain opposed radical Reconstruction and favored placing confidence in white Southerners in 1869, well before the end of Reconstruction and well before the time when many historians have identified a more widespread embrace by Northerners of white supremacist reconciliation.[74]

Chamberlain ordered state officials to cooperate with the committee planning Peabody's arrival in Portland, but he faced some opposition in the state legislature.[75] Even as the Massachusetts Common Council, the Maryland General Assembly, and the New York legislature all easily approved committees to represent them at the funeral observances, the Maine legislature dithered.[76] In the first week of January, a resolution to have members of both houses of the Maine legislature attend the Portland funeral along with Chamberlain and state judges was laid on the table, and a compromise committee recommended against legislative representation at the funeral in light of

Governor Chamberlain's attendance, a fact that outraged some Democrats enough to protest in the state's newspapers.[77] One Maine legislator sought to resolve the impasse by moving to adjourn the legislature so that members might attend the Peabody funeral as private citizens.[78] Finally, on January 22, the Maine legislature did vote to attend the Peabody ceremonies en masse.[79] Some of the fuss was doubtless due to political infighting, but politicians may have also been reluctant to receive a British warship in the port where Confederates (helped by the British) had plagued their state.

The symbolic stakes were high as the funeral fleet arrived in Portland on January 25, 1870, continuing the spirit of transatlantic naval competition contained within a show of Anglo-American togetherness. As it entered Portland's harbor, the *Monarch* exchanged ceremonial salutes with the American warships *Miantonomoh* and *Terror* and with Fort Preble, all three symbols of American naval might. The *Miantonomoh*, one of the most impressive iron-clad monitor ships in the American navy, had visited British ports in 1866 and had helped to inspire the construction of the even more heavily armored, turreted *Monarch* itself. As the imposing American and British ships saluted one another, a huge crowd gathered along the shore to observe the striking "spectacle."[80] The following day Admiral Farragut boarded the *Monarch*, after it anchored by Fort Gorges, to discuss the funeral arrangements and to dine with the *Monarch*'s Captain Commerell.[81]

As the *Monarch* opened its decks for citizens to come on board and view Peabody's embalmed body in the special pavilion on deck, the newspapers continued to describe in loving detail the impressive nature of the British ship, noting that Captain William Macomb of the *Plymouth* was "surprised at the admirable qualities which she exhibited."[82] One newspaper noted that "the excellent opportunity to visit one of the finest vessels in the world" doubtlessly increased public attention to Peabody's remains, and another noted that "steamers, tugs and sailing craft of every description, crowded with visitors, were plying all day between the war ships and the city."[83] Both *Harper's Weekly* and *Frank Leslie's* published engravings of the ships in harbor at Portland, as they had of the Westminster Abbey funeral, seeking to satisfy the wide curiosity of readers who wanted to view the *Monarch* and its American escorts.[84]

The spirit of competition continued in the funeral exercises, as Americans vied to meet the standard of British ceremonial grief and as Northerners and Southerners flocked to praise Peabody. The *New York Herald* stressed the national importance of meeting the British level of praise for Peabody when announcing that "it remains for his own native country to complete his obsequies and to pay him as much honor and show his memory as much affection."[85] Robert C. Winthrop, along with several of his fellow trustees of the Peabody Trust, and officers of the Peabody Institute attended the body on

THE ILLUSTRATED LONDON NEWS.

No. 1573.—VOL. LV. SATURDAY, DECEMBER 25, 1869.

"Reception of Mr. George Peabody's Remains," *London Illustrated News*, 1869. Library of Congress, Prints and Photographs Division, LC-USZ62-62244.

board the *Monarch*, after arriving in Portland on the special train that would conduct the remains back to Massachusetts.[86] The mayor of Baltimore; prominent men from many states; and the British, French, and Spanish consuls to the United States also attended Peabody's remains in Portland.[87]

The public mourning expanded on January 29 as the body was delivered to American custody, with Fort Preble and scores of ships firing in salute. Farragut, the Union naval hero, accompanied the British warship captain to deliver Peabody's remains to the hero of Gettysburg, Governor Chamberlain, who delivered a message of international peace and gratitude to the British.

Chamberlain received the remains with these words: "I thank you, captain, for your generous courtesy in allowing our people to see the almost royal state in which you have borne hither the remains of this good man. . . . You will return from a mightier victory than your guns shall ever win. You will bear a nation's gratitude, reverence and love."[88] The official transfer of Peabody's remains emphasized the narrative of national gratitude and emphasized that a special love existed between the United States and Britain, a narrative that sought to smooth over very real financial and naval conflicts as a legacy of the Civil War.

After the formal reception, Peabody's coffin traveled on a funeral car through the streets of town in a procession to Portland City Hall, where it again lay in honor open to an "unceasing stream" of visitors for a day until the formal ceremonies there.[89] Crowds were so large that pickpockets had a heyday, but generally onlookers commented that the ceremonies featuring British marines, high governmental officials, naval officers, and military and town bands were "quite imposing."[90] Governor Chamberlain entertained Farragut and the other American and British naval officers at a dinner.[91] The *New York Herald*, which had followed the progress of Peabody's remains with particularly close attention, commented that in Portland "everywhere there were evidences of sorrow, scarcely less conspicuous than those which were displayed upon the occasion of the death of President Lincoln."[92]

Although the funeral ceremonies were full of grandeur, commentators also sought to positively contrast the simplicity of the American honors for Peabody to the British pomp. He might be taken to his "little village" in Massachusetts in a special Eastern Railroad car decorated with black velvet, silver fringe, and British and American flags peeking through black crepe, but he would ultimately be buried in an "unpretentious monument" at his family cemetery.[93] Newspapers reported on every detail of the railcar decorated in "somber richness," and the plans for all railroad employees to dress in full mourning.[94] The train with Peabody's remains and several cars full of mourners left Portland in a raging snowstorm and arrived in Salem, Massachusetts, on the afternoon of February 1. The body was removed in a mile-long procession to the Peabody Institute Library (in the neighboring town that bore Peabody's name), where it again lay in repose for a full week, until his final funeral ceremony on February 8.[95]

Thousands of people viewed Peabody's remains at the institute, which was decorated inside and out and filled with incense.[96] The library building of the Peabody Institute was heavily draped with black fabric, and a ten-foot-high catafalque to hold the coffin was erected in front of the display case holding the gold medal presented to Peabody by Queen Victoria and the portrait of her that was a personal gift to him.[97] On February 9, Peabody received his final funeral service at the South Congregational Church, attended by Queen Victoria's son Prince Arthur, several state governors, British and American naval officers, and many other dignitaries.[98] Robert C. Winthrop delivered a forty-five-minute eulogy praising Peabody's philanthropy and his ability to unite Britain and America, North and South.[99] The body was then processed through the streets of Peabody in the snow (followed by 125 carriages), up the hill to Harmony Grove Cemetery, where it was placed in a family vault. The ceremonies concluded with an elaborate dinner for Prince Arthur that evening.[100]

British officers and officials who had accompanied Peabody's remains aboard the *Monarch* reported to Parliament and British naval authorities that they had been treated extremely well by the Americans who mourned Peabody. The *Monarch* even continued on to be shown off at Annapolis, Maryland, after its funeral duties had concluded, and naval pageantry had seemed to restore at least some measure of good feeling between Britain and the United States.[101]

Sectional Healing or Sectional Conflict?

Although the press and the public had certainly been swept up in the messages of Anglo-American healing and unity as part of the Peabody funeral rituals, not everyone—like Benjamin Butler and Robert Schenck—was convinced. Some critics felt that the excessive celebrations were undignified, while others went so far as to question whether Peabody merited the pageantry. Did this private citizen, however wealthy and philanthropic, really merit mourning on a par with President Lincoln's, or was the funeral more of a purely entertaining spectacle? One editor opined: "Into the burial service of an English American is mixed a conglomeration of engineering, dancing, drinking, and general carnival, until to the looker on it has more the appearance of an effort to resurrect him, than to entomb his remains. It is a grand *gala-fandango* in which a portion of the people have become excited, and are reaching far beyond the necessity of the case."[102] At least some participants seemed to be taking Peabody's funeral more as an entertainment than a serious ritual of international cooperation and mourning. Questions emerged: Was Peabody's mourning full of empty pomp, or could it also contain the power to promote sectional peace within the United States?

Even mourning itself seemed at issue, as some participants argued over possible excess. One Cleveland newspaper correspondent had his "moral consciousness" shocked by the drinking and carousing of those staying in Portland, Maine, for the Peabody funeral, and he felt that "the memory of the dead philanthropist was forgotten in the self-praise of a Mutual Admiration

Society."[103] Other critics argued that governmental officials were merely looking to aggrandize themselves in all the fuss. Still others questioned the lionization of wealth and the cost of Peabody's funerals. One newspaper calculated wryly that the funeral celebrations in Maine and Massachusetts alone must have cost at least $6,200, while another noted that surely citizens would have objected if they had been asked whether or not to use tax money to laud Peabody: "A *dead rich man* must have magnificent funeral service, while the *living poor man* must be taxed to pay the bill."[104] Peabody's philanthropy did not erase all public critique of the misuse of his wealth.

The loudest critics of the Peabody mourning rituals, however, were Northerners with Radical Republican sympathies who painted Peabody as a Confederate sympathizer in the Civil War. Peabody's own vision of quickly restoring the "best men" of the South to power and his disregard for radical Reconstruction opened him to the critique and questioned, for some, his memory-worthiness. When Robert C. Winthrop claimed that Peabody's "friends at the South" would miss him greatly, critics who were at odds with Winthrop's own brand of political conservativism claimed that was exactly the problem. Peabody's Southern ties exemplified the exact wrong kind of reunion: one that conceded too much to former Confederates.[105]

Prominent critics of Peabody used the occasion of his funeral to argue that he had advanced the interests of the Confederacy during the war and that his donations to Southern education and other Southern causes after the war were suspect. George Francis Train, an eccentric entrepreneur and politician, called "the fact of George Peabody's remains being brought over on a British ship of war the greatest insult ever offered to America" because "George Peabody was a secessionist."[106] Peabody had not supported secession, but Train's questioning of his loyalty was a way to air grievances against Northerners who found common cause with the South.

William Lloyd Garrison, the abolitionist leader and *Liberator* publisher, was the most prominent of Peabody's critics, and he directly linked his critique of the philanthropist's pro-Confederate attitudes to the unnecessary excess of Peabody's funerals. Just prior to Peabody's final illness, in August 1869, Peabody had visited White Sulphur Springs, Virginia, where he met with Robert E. Lee and other former Confederate leaders who supported his Southern philanthropy. Prominent Southerners held a ball there in his honor. During Peabody's visit, Garrison published an essay titled "Mr. Peabody and the South" in the radical New York *Independent* claiming that both during and after the war "Peabody was with the South in feeling and sentiment" and accusing him of withholding financial, political, and moral support from the Union Cause. Garrison denounced Peabody for, among many other things, withholding any expression of sorrow during the public mourning for Abraham Lincoln.[107] In the final months before Peabody's death, Garrison was already on record questioning Peabody's loyalty.

Garrison amplified his criticism when he saw the public so taken with mourning for Peabody. On February 10, 1870, just after Peabody was buried in Massachusetts, Garrison again took to the pages of the *Independent* to denounce both Peabody and the funeral fuss, which Garrison deemed completely over the top when "no such honors have ever before been paid to any private individual, scarcely to the most renowned of any nation or age."[108] Garrison argued that there was nothing in Peabody's "life or character" to justify such "unprecedented respect and honor . . . on both sides of the Atlantic."[109] As evidence that the pomp outpaced the man, Garrison contended that Peabody's "sympathies in his own country were much more strongly with a pro-slavery South than with an Anti-slavery North," that he had defended the Fugitive Slave Act, that he had refused to fund American war needs, and that even his philanthropy could not erase the stain of this memory.[110] Garrison was outraged that so much public mourning and admiration was expended upon a New Englander whom he considered to be too conservative and too friendly to slaveholding interests both before and after the war.

Garrison's accusations probably overstated the degree of Peabody's Southern sympathies during the Civil War—he did help to arrange war loans for the United States and he offered quiet support to the Northern cause—but Garrison also tapped a nerve. He and other critics such as Schenck and Butler, who had opposed federal aid to the funeral fleet, read Peabody's pro-Southern behavior *after* the war back into the war years. Robert Schenck had, as commander of the Middle Department in Maryland, taken a hand in suppressing pro-Confederate behavior by men like Severn Teackle Wallis: exactly the kind of Southerner who now wanted to use Peabody's reputation to help raise up former Confederates.[111] Schenck was among the group of Northern veterans whom scholars have identified as unwilling to compromise the Union Cause for public memory that they considered too pro-Confederate.[112]

The contest over the memory of Peabody's wartime sympathies seemed to have national political consequences. Conservative New York Republican party boss and journalist Thurlow Weed, who had spent much of the war in Britain and France and was now retired to Albany, defended Peabody's reputation when Schenck opposed the funeral ships. Weed, certainly no friend of secession, claimed in a letter to the *Commercial Advertiser* that was widely reprinted that "Mr. Peabody's accusers discern . . . evidence of rebel sympathies in his great educational gift for the poor of the formerly slave states," but that he had seen Peabody consistently support the Union Cause politically and monetarily in London during the war.[113] Other Peabody critics sought to refute Weed's defense; one London newspaper correspondent claimed that all loyal Americans in Britain felt "grieved and insulted by the national honors" being paid to Peabody because he was widely believed to have supported the Confederacy, and another refuted Weed's testimony about Peabody's loyalty.[114] Arguing about Peabody's loyalty in the context of public mourning allowed debate about the terms of sectional reunification.

Peabody's funerals allowed sectional debate about the terms of national reunion. The very thing that William Lloyd Garrison, Robert Schenck, and other radical Republican critics of Peabody and his funeral feared—Peabody's Southern sympathies—actually shored up support among some for Peabody's mourning as a symbol of national reunion. At least some Northerners and Southerners saw Peabody's pro-Southern stance as a positive, and his funerals offered a chance to praise a vision of reunion and forgiveness on terms favorable to the "best" former Confederates. Praise for Peabody's postwar Southern philanthropy afforded an opportunity to praise an alternative to federal Reconstruction measures that were greatly disliked by former Confederates who wanted to get back into power. Upon Peabody's death, Robert E. Lee wrote to George Peabody Russell about his uncle that "nowhere have his generous deeds . . . elicited more heartfelt admiration than at the South."[115]

Sidestepping the debate over Peabody's sympathies *during* the war, many prominent white Southerners especially praised his postwar Southern donations as proof that prominent Northerners could support their goals. Former Confederates, who were fighting for President Grant's proposal of general amnesty that was dropped just a month after Peabody's funeral, might take some heart from the spectacle of thousands of people on both sides of the Atlantic publicly praising the man who supported their postwar ambitions.[116] As Severn Teackle Wallis argued in his Baltimore eulogy, Peabody's funeral offered a chance to show how prominent Northerners could reunite, reconcile themselves to former Confederates, and just move on (which is exactly what William Lloyd Garrison feared).

Federal judge and former congressman William Branch Giles eulogized Peabody at a memorial celebration held by the Maryland Historical Society while Peabody's remains were still at sea and noted that Peabody was a particularly apt symbol of reunification because he had avoided the war by remaining in Europe: "But when our civil strife closed, and he found it left our Southern country without the means of educating its children, the depths of his noble nature were moved at the sad spectacle, and he made his magnificent donation to meet this great want . . . he knew no North, no South, no East, no West . . . all were his countrymen and entitled to share in the bounty that was blessing the world."[117] Augustus W. Bradford, the Civil War governor of Maryland, said at the same event that Peabody was "a Northern man" who supported the United States as long as armed conflict endured, but who, after the war, realized that he had to help the South in a time of "destitution, despondency, humiliation, and in some places proximate famine; when its adult population was decimated, and its children adrift upon the Dead Sea of ignorance and vice."[118] Peabody's mourning provided a chance for direct critique of the supposed "humiliation" of the white South both during the war and during Reconstruction.

Praising Peabody, for some, became a way to praise Confederate forgiveness, and even to praise the South itself. Southern states that benefited from Peabody's monetary gifts rushed to participate in the funeral honors for him. The Tennessee legislature adopted resolutions to honor Peabody during his public festival of mourning, and some Southern school districts declared a school holiday in Peabody's memory.[119] The *Southern Review* magazine declared the Southern standard of mourning for Peabody to be far superior to the lesser Northern eulogies that paid him tribute.[120]

Even some Northerners and Republicans, who otherwise might have critiqued Peabody for his pro-Southern opinion, painted him as an example of enlightened magnanimity—a magnanimity that encouraged postwar unity with the South. Might he provide a model for forgiveness? The *Philadelphia Inquirer*, for example, maintained that the claim Peabody was "yet a sympathizer with the South . . . is undoubtedly true." But even though he supported the Confederacy, his charity was so generous that it was more important as an example to reunite the sections.[121] The *London Times* opined right after his death that Peabody was "a New Englander who, when the south was bowed down to the dust, stepped forward and claimed the right to succor it."[122] Other defenders were quick to note that his philanthropic gifts made "no distinction of class, of creed, of clime, of section, of race or *nationality*."[123] *Frank Leslie's Illustrated* reminded its readers of Peabody's Southern affinity by publishing a spread on his November 1869 visit to White Sulphur Springs that associated him with Robert E. Lee amid all the news of his London funeral.[124]

In fact, the question of whether Robert E. Lee would attend Peabody's funeral—an issue hotly debated in the press coverage of the mourning preparations—became a test of the ability of Peabody's obsequies to act as a symbol of sectional reunification. The trustees of the Peabody Institute in Massachusetts sent a letter of invitation to Peabody's funeral to General Lee and the trustees of Washington College, to acknowledge Peabody's philanthropic connection to them. Lee, who was himself ill by that time, sent his regrets to the committee, but the Washington College trustees did send a delegation to the New England funeral commemorations.[125] Lee highly regarded Peabody and kept Peabody's portrait as one of the only pieces of art on the wall of his office at Washington College.[126]

The public was fascinated by the link between Lee and Peabody. As Peabody's remains were still at sea, the *Peabody Press* republished stories from Staunton, Virginia, and Boston newspapers speculating about whether Lee had in fact been invited to the Massachusetts funeral and whether he would attend, and other papers fueled the rumors. The *Boston Traveller* claimed that "he has as good a right to come as any other person, although we are *quite* sure he won't be here."[127] The *New York Times* reprinted Lee's letter of condolence to Peabody's nephew, saying that Peabody himself would have prized Lee's praise more highly than any other.[128] Just a few days before Peabody's remains landed at Portland, at least one newspaper was still claiming that Lee would attend the funeral.[129] Lee himself wrote to the Peabody Institute trustees that Peabody's "memory" would "live in the hearts of the Southern people and his virtues . . . revered by unborn generations."[130] Robert C. Winthrop was outright afraid that Lee would attend the funeral because if the former Confederate commander appeared in Massachusetts, "something unpleasant might occur."[131] Uniting the "best men" from the North and South was one thing, but perhaps hosting Robert E. Lee at a Massachusetts funeral was another. Winthrop was doubtless relieved when Lee did not attend: without a direct confrontation with the ex-Confederate leader, Peabody's funeral could encourage a general air of sectional forgiveness without any direct postwar "unpleasantness" to disrupt the feeling of amity between Northern and Southern elites.

Robert E. Lee and Civil War Mourning

Within nine months of George Peabody's public funeral celebrations, Robert E. Lee was dead, and Lee's funeral took on national importance. Lee's actual burial service was quite small, much more subdued than Peabody's had been, but the print and public culture surrounding his funeral was nationalized all the same. Mourning for Robert E. Lee provided a major platform for the Lost Cause mythology that would dominate Southern culture for many decades to come, but it also showed how Southern Lost Cause memory sometimes intertwined with U.S. national identity in unexpected ways.

Public mourning for Robert E. Lee allowed former Confederates—and even some Northerners—to fuse several strands of Civil War memory that glorified the so-called doomed Confederacy. Brian Craig Miller notes that "in the wake of Lee's death, a new battlefield for memory construction emerged," and it is notable that the battlefield was immediately occupied during Lee's funeral commemorations.[132] By 1870, the Lost Cause as a literary and cultural movement was only getting started, but its emphasis on the nobility of Confederate military sacrifice played right into a rising tide of reunification and the beginnings of reconciliationist Civil War memory.[133]

Public mourning for Lee gave many former Confederates a platform, just as many of them also opposed Reconstruction. Visions of reconciliation on pro-Confederate terms and the beginnings of the Lost Cause coalesced in Lee's funeral commemorations. Edward Ayers has written that Lee saw Reconstruction as "a bargain that would have restored things as close to the way they had been in 1861 as possible," and after the war he engaged in nostalgia for the antebellum social and political order as he chafed against Reconstruction policies.[134] The festival of mourning for Lee allowed former Confederates ceremonial space to stage a public comeback. Most former Confederates came to see Lee as the consummate military hero, who proved his status as a Christian gentleman by retiring to the presidency of Washington College and graciously accepting defeat.

Public mourning for Lee immediately after his death in October 1870 showed how quickly defeat, nostalgia, and resentment could recombine into a potent cultural force in the Lost Cause. For white Southerners, and even for many Northerners, Lee's death and burial occasioned expressions of Southern identity that foreshadowed how national reconciliation would largely take place on terms agreeable to the South. Many of the themes begun in mourning for Stonewall Jackson in 1863—the vision of the Confederacy as heroic but doomed, nostalgia for slavery and antebellum social order, the vision of Confederate officers as tragic heroes—took on new force now that they could be associated with Robert E. Lee. In Lee's case, however, the Lost Cause also proved to have national appeal, as its proponents took part in the postwar rebuilding of U.S. national identity itself. We can see in the early mourning for Lee some of the truth in historian William R. Black's statement that "the Lost Cause itself was a project of American nationalism."[135]

By the turn of the twentieth century, when most white Northerners had turned away from Reconstruction and had embraced a reconciliatory memory of the war that emphasized the sacrifice of common white soldiers, Lee became a figure of wide admiration in the North.[136] But that process started in 1870 with Lee's death. In 1870, mourning for Robert E. Lee in the North and South showed that both the idea of reuniting the nation around the sorrowful memory of the dead Confederate hero and, even, the larger cult of Southern honor-in-loss made up part of the national fabric.[137] Lee's public funerals, by coaxing positive expressions of grief for the Confederate hero, put Lost Cause ideas at the heart of an important ritual of U.S. national identity.

Robert Edward Lee was, of course, the most important Virginian and Confederate general during the Civil War, commander of the Army of Northern Virginia from June 1862 until his surrender in April 1865, and the closest military adviser to Confederate president Jefferson Davis. Lee was born on the Stratford Hall estate in 1807 (twelve years after George Peabody) to Revolutionary general Henry "Light Horse Harry" Lee and Ann Hill Carter Lee. He distinguished himself as a West Point cadet and graduated second in his class in 1829, accepting a commission as second lieutenant in the U.S. Army Corps of Engineers in July of that year. Three years later, he married Mary Anne Randolph Custis, daughter of George Washington Parke Custis, the orphaned grandson of Martha Washington who had been raised as a son by her and George Washington. The Lees' 1831 marriage united two extraordinarily distinguished Revolutionary Virginia families. Mary Randolph Custis Lee and several of her seven children would play an important role in her husband's mourning and commemoration after his death.

Unlike George Peabody's, Lee's biography and Civil War exploits are well known, but they still bear a brief repeating. After a successful career as an army engineer, rising to the rank of brevet colonel in the Mexican-American War, Lee served as superintendent of West Point from 1852 to 1855 before becoming an officer of the Second U.S. Cavalry in Texas. Lee commanded the cavalry units that captured John Brown at Harpers Ferry, Virginia, in 1859. By March 1861, with secession looming, Lee was commissioned colonel in the U.S. Army and commander of the First Cavalry. He resigned his commission on April 20, 1861, and took command of Virginia's state forces the next day. Within a month he was commissioned brigadier general in the Confederate army and given command of Confederate forces in Virginia, and by 1862 he commanded the Army of Northern Virginia.

In 1862, Lee expertly defended Richmond and proved his strategic prowess in the Seven Days Battles. Then Lee gained public acclaim from a string of strong performances if not outright victories, despite being at a disadvantage in numbers and supply: first defending northern Virginia from John Pope, then invading Maryland and fighting McClellan to a bloody draw at Antietam, and winning decisively at Chancellorsville and Fredericksburg. By mid-1863, Lee had convinced Davis that the best hope for Southern victory came in offensive strategy, and he again invaded Northern territory, only to suffer his greatest loss to date at the July Battle of Gettysburg.[138]

In the spring of 1864, Lee faced even fiercer opposition in the newly appointed Union general-in-chief Ulysses S. Grant, but Lee's tenacity and tactics slowed Grant's movements and enforced great casualties on Northern forces from the battles of the Wilderness in May through Cold Harbor in early June. By mid-June, Lee's forces were beginning to wear heavily, although he again triumphed at Petersburg. Lee entrenched to protect Petersburg and the Confederate capitol at Richmond for a further ten months, while Grant sent Sherman through the Carolinas and Georgia. In February 1865, President Davis named Lee as commander in chief of the Confederate armies, but by then Grant's forces had been reinforced to more than two and half times the size of Lee's army. U.S. forces captured Richmond, and Lee tried to retreat southwest to join Joseph Johnston's forces in the Carolinas, but he was virtually surrounded at Appomattox Courthouse in April. Lee surrendered his army to Grant on April 9, 1865.

Immediately after the war, Lee was paroled as a prisoner of war, and although he was excluded from amnesty by President Andrew Johnston and indicted for treason by a U.S. district court in June, the indictment was never pursued. By October 1865, he had taken up the presidency of Washington College in Lexington, Virginia.[139]

This rehearsal of Lee's biography barely captures his status as the most lionized hero of the Confederacy. Many scholars have parsed Lee's reputation and his links to the creation of the Lost Cause, and some of the scholarship on Lee re-creates the veneration of its subject. As Lee biographer Emory Thomas comments, "Lee has been several sorts of American hero, and within the American South he has attained the status of demigod. Over time Lee has been a Christ figure, a symbol of national reconciliation, an exalted expression of bourgeois values, and much, much more."[140]

Fewer scholars have noticed that, immediately upon Lee's death, some Northerners were surprisingly willing to praise him as a Christian gentleman, a stoic defeated hero, and even a military leader.[141] It is important to notice that many Northerners praised Lee as soon as he died. Even though some praise was couched in triumphal terms that glorified the North for beating Lee, he was still praised, as the *New York Herald* put it: "As a brave enemy . . . deserving of a tribute."[142] Obituaries for Lee were ubiquitous and positive enough in the North in the months after his death that Frederick Douglass raged: "We can scarcely take up a newspaper . . . that is not filled with *nauseating* flatteries of the late Robert E. Lee."[143] Douglass asked, "Is it not about time that this bombastic laudation of the rebel chief should now cease?"[144]

It did not cease, and mourning for Lee became a battleground over Southern civic identity, the cultural power of the Lost Cause, and the place of Confederate memory in the American nation itself. The stakes were high in mourning Robert E. Lee.

The Death of General Lee

Lee died not in the midst of war but in its aftermath, when the legacy of the war was up for grabs. Lee's relative retreat from national attention and lack of loud critique of Reconstruction helped set him up to be a usable symbol of reunification and possible reconciliation by the time of his death, although it is an exaggeration to say, as one chronicler of Lee's last years does, that "the decisions he made from the Appomattox surrender until his death in

October 1870 place Robert E. Lee as the leading 'nation-healer' of his time."[145] Lee worked wonders for Washington College during the five years of his presidency, allowing faculty to modernize the curriculum, growing the student body fourfold, and improving the still-shaky finances, not the least through donations from George Peabody. Lee wrote and posed for portraits, remaining a public figure, but not doing much to stoke his own notoriety until he made a swing around the South with his daughter, Agnes, in the spring of 1870—seeking a health retreat but also finding great public acclaim everywhere he went from Virginia to Georgia to Florida to North Carolina to Maryland.[146] Back in Lexington, his illness, likely a combination of heart and circulation issues, worsened at the end of September. He suffered a stroke or thrombosis in his last days.[147]

Lee died quietly at home in Lexington on October 12, 1870. A grief-stricken Mary Randolph Custis Lee desired to keep the funeral commemoration relatively simple, with no elaborate funeral oration, in deference to Robert's wishes and in keeping with his devout Episcopal faith. Mary Custis Lee would learn the lesson that both first ladies Martha Washington and Mary Lincoln had learned that even if she could control the location of her husband's burial, she could not control the wider public reaction. General Lee had expressed wishes to contain public mourning on his behalf to a simple funeral on the college campus in Lexington, but he also had no such power from beyond the grave.

Despite heavy rain and severe flooding that slowed communications, word spread quickly of Lee's demise, and public fascination grew as the solemn funeral arrangements in Lexington proceeded. The chapel at Washington College, site of Lee's funeral and burial, soon began to attract attention as the focus of a cult of veneration.[148] The day after Lee's death, a monument association in his honor had formed in Lexington, and within a year Mary Randolph Custis Lee agreed to have the association commission a reclining marble funerary monument by Richmond sculptor Edward Valentine. The statue was completed in 1875 and installed in a chapel mausoleum in 1883 that would serve—to this day—as a draw for pilgrims of the Lost Cause.[149]

Much of the public funeral mourning for Lee in 1870 took place far from his grave. In drastic contrast to the postmortem journey of George Peabody (or Henry Clay or Abraham Lincoln), Robert E. Lee's remains traveled nowhere, not moving more than a few streets over from his cottage to the college chapel. But his reputation, the press coverage, and public commemorations in his honor spread just as far as Peabody's. All over the country, newspapers ran multiple stories that reported on Lee's death and burial, and the celebrations in his honor, in urgent, breathless tones. Lee's memory and rituals of mourning traveled much farther than his remains. The localized funeral in Lexington became the focus of intense national (and even international)

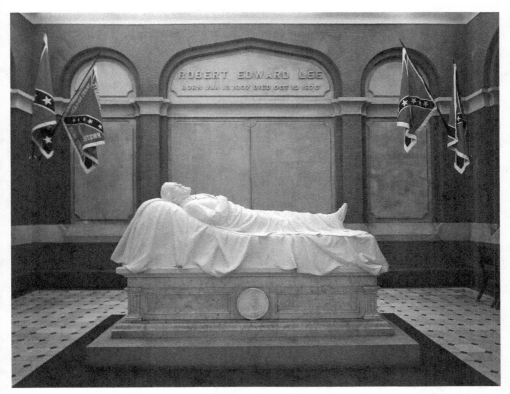

Edward Valentine's statue "Recumbent Lee," Carol M. Highsmith, "Recumbent Robert E. Lee, Washington & Lee University, Lexington, Virginia," photograph, 1980–2006. Library of Congress, Prints and Photographs Division, photograph by Carol M. Highsmith, LC-DIG-highsm-11812.

curiosity and discussion, each detail unpacked in the press, even as his remains were stationary and the actual funeral rites were relatively simple.[150]

Lexington had already drawn considerable attention as the burial site of Stonewall Jackson, and now Lee's burial amplified the town as a Confederate sacred space. On the morning after Lee died, October 13, his remains were escorted by cadets from the neighboring Virginia Military Institute from his home to the chapel at Washington College, where he lay in repose as student mourners braved the driving rain to look upon his face. Classes and public exercises on both campuses were suspended. The chapel service featured eulogies from Lee's beloved artillery chief Brig. Gen. William Nelson Pendleton (now returned to his duties as rector of the Episcopal church in Lexington) and Episcopal cleric W. S. White, along with Baptist VMI chaplain and former Confederate J. William Jones. Cadets were assigned to guard the body through the night and all the next day. The chapel, the campus, and indeed the entire town of Lexington, were draped in black fabric, so much that students were afraid they would run out of cloth.[151] Both the citizens of Lexington and the town's Confederate veterans held memorial meetings in town.[152]

At ten o'clock on October 15, Lee's long funeral procession marched from his home to the campus of Washington College, filled with dignitaries and Confederate veterans, trustees, faculty, and students from VMI and Washington College, who all marched past the remains before forming a gauntlet at the chapel entrance for the ministers and dignitaries.[153] The Confederate veterans in the procession did not march in uniform, and Lee himself was laid out in a simple dark suit. The procession was led by an empty hearse, Lee's remains already having been on display in the chapel for the previous two days.[154] The service itself was relatively short: Pendleton read the Episcopal burial rite, and the remains were placed in a crypt in the college library, beneath the chapel.[155]

"Every Section of the Country": National and Sectional Mourning

Lee's death and burial garnered huge press coverage and attention across the entire country, even though Northern newspapers debated how much positive ink should be spilled over the former Confederate enemy. Some eulogies were measured, but nearly *all* newspapers took note. Despite the wishes of the *Santa Fe Post* that "nothing can be said in his honor;—let silence be preserved over his grave," plenty was said in all regions of the country.[156] The burgeoning Lost Cause vision of Southern victimhood surfaced in stories that both lamented Lee's passing and emphasized how much more praise he actually deserved on the national stage. One Petersburg, Virginia, newspaper imagined the alternative state funeral that might have been: "Had not cruel odds torn Victory from those tattered battle-flags . . . there would be to-day drooping flags, the stately pageant of public mourning, the slow booming of funeral guns" throughout the country.[157]

A great number of Northern papers were filled with positive assessments of Lee. One Arizona newspaper noted that his death "was mourned by men of all parties, in every section of the country."[158] Lee was respected in the North for his personal qualities, his military genius, and his leadership of Washington College. Some writers emphasized that Northerners were so great and victorious that they could afford to praise Lee, and the fact that Northerners did not hate their enemies only made them greater. The New York *Sun* noted that although Lee took the college presidency just for money, he was a faithful warden of the Episcopal Church in Lexington and noted that "very many people in the North will forget political differences beside the open grave of the dead chieftain, and drop a tear of sorrow on his bier."[159] The rival *New York Herald* said Lee "came nearer the ideal of the soldier and Christian general than any man we can think of" and eulogized him, noting, "As a brave enemy he is deserving of a tribute, and for his course since he surrendered his sword at Appomattox he deserves high honor."[160] In a eulogy that accompanied coverage of the funeral, *Frank Leslie's Illustrated Newspaper* praised Lee's nobility in the war, his peaceful retirement to Washington College, and his courteous manners and social life.[161]

Respecting Lee in this way was meant to provide evidence that reunion was working, as Northerners and Southerners sought to get over the war. Even as Southerners wrapped themselves in the Lost Cause during Lee's commemorations, they also sought to connect their Southern nationalism to a greater American national identity that they hoped to refashion in their own image. And, Northerners who struggled to decide whether or not it was proper to commemorate Lee often noted how important the question was for the project of national reunification. In these sectional commemorations of Lee, we can see participants imagining how his loss related to their own definitions of the United States.

For example, at a memorial service headed by Union general John T. Ward at New York's Cooper Union, "speeches were made by several persons, the gist of which was, that the death of Robert E. Lee furnished a fitting occasion for the reconciliation of all sections of the country and the burial of sectional animosities." Confederate general John D. Imboden also spoke at the Cooper Union memorial and presented the memorial resolutions drafted by the Lee memorial committee in New York City. Public memorial speeches for Lee on the same stage from which Abraham Lincoln had rallied the Republican Party in 1860 and stated his opposition to slavery expansion might indeed indicate a remarkable degree of reconciliation, but there was also backlash. One Maine newspaper raged about the Cooper Union service: "We can imagine no surer method of keeping alive the bitter memories of the war than the affront thus given to public opinion by such a demonstration in the principal city of the nation, over the death of one of the most active and prominent leaders of the rebellion."[162]

One of the ways Northerners who paid tribute to Lee sought to negotiate this tension was by stressing the magnanimity it took for the United States to praise Robert E. Lee. Mourning Lee showed forgiveness and provided the opportunity to, somewhat paradoxically, reflect glory on the American nation. Many Northern obituaries strained for a tone of self-congratulation for allowing the South to express its grief. Republican editors William Burnet and Thomas T. Kinney led their coverage of Lee's death in the *Newark Daily Advertiser* by praising the United States for holding no "malice" against Lee and allowing Southerners to grieve: "Rarely has any country exhibited such entire magnanimity . . . the most solemn observances of funeral rites will be permitted to his late adherents without interference or opposition from the Government."[163] The victors could afford to be magnanimous. Kentucky Democratic congressman Thomas Jones, the same man who had proposed federal support for George Peabody's funeral, favored paying tribute to Robert E. Lee. He supported returning captured "relics" of the Washington family from the Arlington estate to Mary Lee and wanted Americans to forget the "blood and tears and death" of the war so they could be united once more. On the floor of the House of Representatives, Jones called Robert E. Lee "the great captain of the rebellion" and asked: "Can we not afford to be as magnanimous as we have been victorious?"[164]

Some former Confederates seized upon this theme of magnanimity and tried to encourage mourning for Lee as a way to seek reunification and reintegration into national life—in a way that openly challenged Reconstruction. Public mourning for Lee in Louisville, Kentucky, provides a prominent example. Louisville was heavily draped in mourning when news of Lee's death reached the city on October 13, and Democratic mayor John Baxter presided over a city meeting in Lee's honor that featured speeches by University of Louisville president Isaac Caldwell (who argued against federal Reconstruction law in court two years later), John C. Breckinridge (who had resigned as U.S. vice president to renounce the Union and become a Confederate general), and several other former Confederate military leaders. The members of the memorial gathering resolved, "We people of Louisville occupy a middle geographic space and a middle opinion between two extremes . . . in the death of Robert E. Lee the American people, without regard to states or sections or antecedents or opinions, lose a great and good man, a distinguished and useful citizen, renowned not less in arms than in the arts of peace."[165] Louisville's former Confederates used Lee to make their claim on American national identity, framing an image of his venerated remains as "not merely those of a matchless soldier, but also of a great and good American."[166] The huge evening gathering in St. Paul's Episcopal Church, called by the former Confederate soldiers in the city, emphasized Lee's sacrifice, and the funeral sermon by rector H. W. Platt highlighted the Northern press's plaudits for Lee as it dwelled on the "glorified" nature of the Southern cause associated with him.[167] The Lee celebration in Louisville, far from being a neutral expression of Southern integration into the nation, took place in a hugely divided city—where former Confederates fought for dominance just as the Black population of the city had increased 120 percent in the previous ten years.[168] Despite insistence on Louisville's "middle" status between the Union and the Confederacy, the public commemoration of Lee's death emphasized the city's Southern identity and Democratic control, an increasingly potent factor in Kentucky as a whole.

Cities all over the South repeated this mourning process—as news spread of Lee's demise, women filled the streets with black crepe, and prominent former Confederate men spoke to huge gatherings containing both former allies and enemies to sing Lee's praises. Mourning for Lee in many cities was a symbol of reunification that also contained a clear challenge to Reconstruction policies and Republican control. Caroline Janney has written that with federal control loosening in many Southern cities, Confederate veterans "saw Lee's death as the first real opportunity to glorify their war effort and honor their own martial spirit—to breathe new life into the Lost Cause."[169] Michael Ross has shown how public mourning for Lee in New Orleans provided the opportunity for conservative ex-Confederates to openly contest the biracial Reconstruction government in that city and "to lure moderate whites" to the Democratic Party, as some African Americans and Republicans participated in public mourning rituals for Lee.[170] Indeed, the spontaneous mourning in cities around the South (and even some in the North) fueled the Lost Cause and specific Democratic campaigns for control in specific cities.

Former Confederates claimed attention at public funeral commemorations held in the days after Lee's death in cities from Lynchburg, Virginia, to Los Angeles, California.[171] In city after city, former Confederate military men emerged to deliver public eulogies to Lee to religious, civic, and government gatherings, praising the Lost Cause and enhancing their own political reputations, just in the process of being rehabilitated. Many of these funeral orators soon became congressmen, governors, or mayors as Democratic control returned to the South. They took to stages in the Deep South, in border states, and even in some Northern cities to declare Lee's greatness and to associate his memory with the glorious South.

The fusion of Lee's memory with the Lost Cause reached across many states. At a public memorial meeting packed with former Confederates in St. Louis, Trusten Polk, who had been expelled from the U.S. Senate in 1862 before taking up arms for the Confederacy, argued that "there is not a man in the country that does not in his heart honor and revere the name of Gen. Lee."[172] Both houses of the Georgia legislature adjourned to attend a Lee memorial gathering with more than 10,000 people in Atlanta on October 13, featuring a fiery eulogy by former general John B. Gordon. Another former Confederate general, A. R. Wright, addressed a civic meeting in Lee's honor in Augusta on October 18.[173] The bitter former Confederate general John T. Morgan, who would soon lead the charge to expunge Republicans from power in Alabama, gave the eulogy for Lee to a large crowd in the Selma Opera House.[174] Former cavalry general Wade Hampton, who would become the post-Reconstruction governor of South Carolina, likened Lee to George Washington in a eulogy in Columbia, South Carolina, and H. D. Lesesne called Lee the "patriarchal head" of the "large family" of the South in a mass meeting in Charleston.[175] In Chattanooga, former Confederate general John C. Brown, who was likely a leader of the Tennessee Ku Klux Klan, a Democratic candidate for governor, and a strong opponent of Reconstruction in the state's 1870 constitutional convention, publicly eulogized Lee at a "large demonstration of sorrow" on October 14.[176] Lee's army chief of staff, Col. Charles Marshall, spoke at a public gathering of Confederate veterans in Lee's honor in Baltimore on October 15.[177] Confederate general William Preston called Lee "a man perfect in Christian principles" at a civic memorial to the dead commander in Lexington, Kentucky.[178] In Charlestown, West Virginia, former Confederate major Wells Hawks, a great admirer of Lee's, led a public memorial in honor of his "irreparable loss," where several other former Confederates also gave speeches.[179] At the Kansas City meeting in Lee's honor in November, former Confederate cavalry commander Capt. George Baylor assured the gathered mourners that Lee would never die as long as Confederate Memorial Day lived on and "the sons and daughters of the South will delight to gather around Lee's grave."[180]

Several major cities also included eulogies and public speeches in Lee's honor given by Southerners who had disagreed with Lee during the war but were now willing to praise him. Former U.S. attorney general and recently returned U.S. minister to Great Britain Reverdy Johnson told a gathering of gentlemen appointing Maryland state delegates to Lee's memorial convention in Virginia that although they "might be surprised" that he was willing to eulogize the general with whom he "did not agree . . . in political views," he would gladly take the opportunity to emphasize reunion. Johnson's eulogy for Lee expressed rhetoric that would characterize the reconciliationist memory that David Blight has identified as emerging decades later.[181] Johnson proclaimed that honoring Lee was right for all loyal Americans because "it is the duty of every citizen of this land to seek to heal the wounds of the war, to forget past differences, and to forgive, as far as possible, the faults to which the War gave rise. In no other way can the Union be truly and permanently restored."[182] Even more clearly than had the public funeral celebrations for George Peabody, mourning for Lee provided an occasion for expressing healing sectional reunion on terms friendly to the South.

Many Southern mourners expressed defiantly pro-Confederate or sectionalist sentiments in public. Southern pride shared the stage with national (even international) feeling when the *Atlanta Constitution* wrote, "Lee was ours. This pride can never be torn from us," but that "the civilized world will still claim a share in him by right of an example so adorning to humanity."[183]

When Jefferson Davis, less than two years out of jail on charges of treason, addressed the civic memorial gathering for Lee in Richmond on November 3, the links to Confederate defiance of Reconstruction were clear. The *Richmond Dispatch* reported that "as Mr. Davis arose to walk to the stand, every person in the house stood, and there followed such a storm of applause as seemed to shake the very foundations of the building, while cheer upon cheer was echoed from the throats of veterans saluting one whom they delighted to honor." Davis addressed his audience as "soldiers and sailors of the Confederacy, comrades and friends" and emphasized that the incredible public mourning for Lee showed the crowd's ability "to discriminate between him who enjoys and him who deserves success," a clear reference to the superior merit of the Lost Cause over the more successful Union Cause.[184]

This open defiance tested the magnanimity of some Republicans and of Reconstruction authorities, who were wary of allowing public mourning for Lee to challenge their authority in areas still under military control. Magnanimity had its limits. One Republican paper in Galveston, Texas, noted that "while we in common with thousands in the land give him credit for his private virtues as a man, and his great ability as a soldier, we never did, and never can commend his course during the late rebellion."[185] In Savannah, Georgia, still under control of federal troops, workers at the customs house tried to lower the U.S. flag to half-staff in honor of Lee's death, but the federal customs collector, Col. T. P. Robb, ordered the flags restored to full position. Southern newspapers expressed outrage at the act and at the support Treasury secretary George Boutwell showed for the collector's decision not to lower the flag. But others recognized that "the revenue flag is the property of the U.S. government" and should not be used for mourning a former enemy of the United States, and one Texas Republican news editor opined that "we accord to individuals the right today, to honor the dead hero, as they see proper, but we hardly expect them to ask that the National flag . . . shall be at half-mast, in honor of him who was foremost in a war for its destruction."[186] Horace Greeley, among others, supported Boutwell's move.[187]

As Frederick Douglass's testy comments about the "bombastic laudation" in Lee's newspaper obituaries showed, some Northerners and Republicans expressed limits to their tolerance for public mourning of Lee, no matter where it took place. Some expressed the willingness to tolerate private mourning but denied that public attention should be paid to Lee in the United States. One Texas Republican editor wrote of Lee's funeral celebrations: "Let individuals mourn who wish to do so. But let that nation, whose government he sought to destroy, keep ever unsullied her national glory and unity; through which she conquered the mighty chieftain for whose death she now is asked to mourn."[188] The *Boston Daily Advertiser* praised Lee's postwar behavior and "the purity of his private character" but noted, "Yet the nation does not mourn for him."[189] One Cleveland editor wrote that Lee's death would be "regretted by very many in the North," but that many who truly valued him wished he would have died "before his previous fair fame had been stained with rebellion."[190] Northern Republicans, especially, walked a fine line that acknowledged Lee's personal greatness but denied him a place in any national narrative of heroism.

On the other hand, Northern Democrats effusively praised Lee and claimed him as a national figure. The *Argus*, the Democratic paper in Portland, Maine, criticized Northerners who spoke ill of Lee upon his death and emphasized his military prowess: "The attacks of certain loyal scribblers upon the dead Gen. Lee are contemptible and disgusting. These jackals, we venture to say, never faced the lion while he lived."[191] Democrats draped some houses and businesses in Indianapolis in mourning upon the receipt of the news of Lee's death.[192] The partisan contest for public attention and power could be fought with black ink and black fabric.

Some reactions to Lee's death, however, defied partisan expectations. While plenty of Republican newspapers continued to criticize Lee and his Confederate followers upon his death, some eulogized him in glowing terms.[193] The *Chicago Republican* noted that "it has not been common, even by the strongest partisans . . . to question his motives, doubt the sincerity of his convictions, or impugn the purity of his character. No prominent man upon that side came through the war with less of obloquy, or retained in a higher degree the respect of those against whom he was enlisted," and its eulogy maintained that even though some would remember Lee's Confederate service as a crime, "his memory will be cherished for his magnanimity as a soldier, and his virtues as a man."[194] The *Raleigh Standard*, a paper controlled by staunchly Republican editors, noted that "the death of such a man is always a public calamity" and praised Lee for encouraging "peace and good will toward the whole country" since the war.[195] The Philadelphia *North American and United States Gazette* wrote that Lee's embrace of peace after the war had erased the "odium of treason, and placed it in an honorable niche."[196]

Some obituary writers took pains to note Lee's wrongdoing in betraying the United States, but showed him personal respect. The San Francisco *Daily Evening Bulletin* noted that although he was a very flawed military commander, "He was a chivalrous, kindly, humane man . . . probably one of the most conscientious and unselfish of the Southern leaders who were led by sectional feelings and mistaken ideas of State Sovereignty and not mere private ambition," and the editor stressed that "no other Confederate leader enjoyed so largely the respect of the Unionists, during and after the war."[197] Another San Francisco weekly noted: "History will accord to the deceased General a distinguished place among the great military men of the world. However bad and wrong the cause in which he engaged, there can be no question of his consummate ability as a military leader . . . his course ever since the collapse of the rebellion, has been quiet, calm, dignified and irreproachable."[198] The *Bangor Daily Whig and Courier* told its readers that Northerners would undoubtedly mourn Lee because "death casts a generous mantle of charity over the past," allowing them to "shed their tears over the new made grave of another son of the South."[199] The popular Washington correspondent and columnist George Alfred Townsend claimed in a column after Lee's death that "his talent outlasted the spirit of his forces and the resolution of his government," making Lee an exceptional Confederate whose personal merit outshone the cause for which he fought.[200]

That Townsend's statement on Lee's merits was also reprinted in a Raymond, Mississippi, Democratic newspaper testified to how badly some Southerners wanted to see the mourning for Lee as national grief. Former Confederates wanted to prove that mourning Lee was a national activity. Some claimed that the grief was universal, like the Lynchburg, Virginia, newspaper that insisted, "Even the enemies who fought him so long and so hard will join in the tribute of regret and honor which we lay on his grave."[201] John Esten Cooke published a biography of Lee just after his death that included a detailed account of his funeral; he wanted to impart to readers that "the people of the North, not less than the people of the South, feel that Lee was truly great."[202] A staunchly Democratic newspaper in West Virginia noted (hyperbolically) that "the world will unite, with singular unanimity, in the sentiment that there has fallen the Greatest American."[203] The *Charleston Courier* assured the people of South Carolina that Lee's death was "lamented in a *Nation's* grief!"[204] A conservative Democratic political convention in Lynchburg, Virginia, celebrated the fact that his death was mourned "as a State and national calamity."[205]

Southern editors expressed gratitude, even pride, at the positive tone in some Northern eulogies of Lee. The New York *World*, the *Tribune*, and the *Herald* all published eulogies for Lee that acknowledged some "sincere regret" would be felt in Northern as well as Southern hearts at the news of Lee's death, although their praise of him fell along a spectrum from grudging acceptance to sincere admiration.[206] The *New York Times* closed its eulogy for Lee by noting that since the war he had devoted himself purely to higher education, "keeping so far as possible aloof from public notice, and by his unobtrusive modesty and purity of life . . . won the respect even of those who most bitterly deplore and reprobate his course in the rebellion."[207] Many Southern papers quickly reprinted the New York eulogies to show evidence of Northern respect for their most beloved hero.[208] Other papers added reprints of Lee eulogies from Pennsylvania and Connecticut and from Southern Republican papers to the New York articles.[209] The *Richmond Daily Dispatch* published a lengthy account of the gathering in Lee's honor at Cooper Union in New York City.[210] One former Confederate chaplain noted in his eulogy of Lee that he had heard "a distinguished Northern clergyman, of extreme radical politics," proclaim Lee to be "the most polished courtly gentleman, and one of the most charitable, high-toned, Christian men I ever met."[211] Several letters of condolence to Mary Randolph Custis Lee reported to her the praise offered to the general in the Northern press.[212]

As a marker of supposed unanimity, both Northern and Southern papers emphasized the participation of African Americans in Lee's mourning rituals. The Associated Press reported from Lexington, "The colored people joined in these demonstrations of sorrow."[213] A correspondent reported from Lexington to the Wilmington, North Carolina, *Journal* that "as indicating the universal grief of this community, that the colored barber-shops and the colored churches were all draped in mourning, and that the bell of the colored Methodist Church was tolled in unison with those of the white churches."[214] A Georgia legislator noted in a letter to the *Atlanta Constitution* that when the state House of Representatives voted a resolution of mourning for Lee, "it was evident that the colored members shared in the deep and wide-spread gloom which the announcement of the sad occasion occasioned."[215] These papers used images of Black grief (however scattered)—related to the trope of the loyal slave—in the service of Lee's memory, to emphasize white supremacy and to denote the supposed unanimity of public mourning.[216] If Northern Republicans and even African Americans mourned Lee, he—and by association the South—must truly be great.

Private Consolation, Public Grief

Lee's family, especially his widow, also became symbols of sectional and national grief. Hundreds of private citizens and public groups offered condolences to the Lee family, taking great pains to assign national meaning to the general's death. Private consolation offered to the Lee family mirrored many of the themes in the press eulogies for Lee and continued testing the boundaries of reunion and reconciliation. Even private letters connected the family to the public process of national mourning. Mary Randolph Custis Lee referred to hers as "a common sorrow," and she knew that her grief also partly belonged to the post-Confederate Southern public.[217] Just as the boundaries between reunion and reconciliation blurred in the creation of the Lost Cause, so did the boundaries between public and private. Not surprisingly for an ideology built on the mythic protection of white Southern womanhood and the Confederate home, Mary Randolph Custis Lee as widow functioned as a touch point for the public who associated the Lees with the Lost Cause.[218]

Many upper-class white women assumed special responsibilities in the postwar years for perpetuating Confederate memory, and Mary Randolph Custis Lee played a leading role—even just by attracting public attention.[219] She embodied Confederate womanhood not by joining a Ladies' Memorial Association as so many others had done but by her lineage and connection to her noble dead husband. Even before Mary had much of a chance to publicly mourn Robert (or to publicly wear widow's weeds as Mary Anna Jackson had when her husband was killed), she was immediately recognized as the focus of public sorrow. She was a public symbol of post-Confederate grief.

Confederate values attached to Mary Custis Lee in part because she supported them. She had been more vocal against Reconstruction than Robert E. Lee had been.[220] She maintained her commitment to the values of the Old South, and she harbored ill will against the federal government for confiscating her family estate, Arlington House, whose return she continued to pursue even after Robert's death. The outpouring of sympathetic consolation that flowed toward Mary Randolph Custis Lee exemplified her superadded cultural power as a grieving widow—perhaps the ultimate Confederate grieving widow.[221] That grief also nurtured Southern grievance as part of the Lost Cause.

The consolation letters, messages, and memorial resolutions that flooded in to Mary Randolph Custis Lee and her oldest daughter, Mary Custis Lee, showed how many Southerners (and even some Northerners) prized their association with the family and wanted to mark the occasion of Robert's death. Groups from New York to Florida sent the Lee family urgent messages of grief. Many of the letters of consolation crossed the boundary between private and public mourning, and they show how acts of mourning for Robert E. Lee were tied not only to personal grief but also to civic and public identities that also related to the creation of the Lost Cause. Many of the messages of consolation emphasized that grief at Lee's death was not the family's alone, and they claimed a share of public grief by connecting themselves with his family. Grief for Robert E. Lee became a way to further the connection of civic groups and prominent individuals to the general's memory. Consolation and memory mixed to help define a new sense of Southern nationalism—rooted in the past, yet charting a path forward based on collective grief.

Public-private grief for Robert E. Lee united Southerners, and as they expressed it in resolutions and condolences sent to his family, it might also connect them to a larger national community, which also grieved for Lee. As the city court officers of Alexandria, Virginia, wrote, they wanted to express public grief and extend condolences to Mary Lee to "mingle their sorrows with the lamentations of a bereaved and smitten people and in sympathy with our fellow citizens of the South and just of all lands."[222] One group of North

Carolinians wrote that "in common with our countrymen we feel that we have been stricken in the death of your esteemed and honored husband," and St. Louisans wrote that "the entire nation, North and South, East and West" would view Lee's death as "a public calamity."[223] A letter from the University of Nashville predicted that "no sectional animosity" would dare to sully Lee's memory.[224] The city officers of Nashville, Tennessee, emphasized in their mourning and condolences to the Lee family that, like George Washington, Robert E. Lee would be mourned "in both sections of our Republic whose soldiers' hands were red with the others blood."[225] This language predated by ten to fifteen years the national trend noted by David Blight of emphasizing national unity by noting common military sacrifice, but it nevertheless served the same cultural project: re-creating national identity out of a military memory that simultaneously stressed unity and privileged Southerners.[226] Memorials to Lee, then, mixed public and private, North and South, past and present to create powerful ideas of family, civic, and national identities. The memorials imagined a community of mourners for Lee that linked memories of him and the Confederate past to a vision of future national greatness following in his footsteps.

Most of the civic and educational groups that sent letters noted that they had adopted resolutions at public meetings and told the Lee family that they would also be publicly disseminating their messages of consolation, mixing private condolences with public rituals of grief. Mary Randolph Custis Lee and Mary Custis Lee received letters of consolation from twelve colleges or learned societies, including Washington College, the Virginia Military Institute, Davidson College, and the University of Mississippi. Many stressed the importance of transmitting the lessons of "the Model Man of the Age" to youth, so they could carry forward Southern greatness.[227] Twenty-three municipalities passed resolutions in honor of Lee and sent copies to the family, along with their condolences. Townspeople stressed the spontaneity of their grief and told the general's family how proud they were to have a chance to "unite with our fellow-citizens, all through this Southern land," to pay him respect.[228] The citizens of Covington, Kentucky, for example, simultaneously praised Lee for being a paragon of the white race and called his death "a great loss, not only to the immediate section in which he lived, but to the nation at large."[229] Many Southerners used the opportunity of writing to Lee's family to imagine themselves united with Northerners in praise for the dead general—creating a sense of national unity on pro-Confederate terms.

The imagined community of grief reached a far distance. Consolation resolutions and letters issued forth from reform societies, veterans organizations, churches, business groups, debating societies, and at least one baseball club—all of which wanted to shape the meaning of Lee's death. Many groups stressed that Robert E. Lee had provided an example of bravery, thrift, and Christian living. The opportunity to express condolences to the family led many civic organizations also to publicize how they found him to be "the highest type of the American soldier and citizen."[230] Several groups explicitly claimed their mourning for Lee would contribute to reverence for the "Lost Cause," the phrase that encompassed so much tragic former Confederate pride and formed the basis for the path to a glorious future, especially if power could be recaptured from the integrated forces of Reconstruction.[231] Messages of grief also came from Southerners living in San Francisco, California; Poughkeepsie, New York; and an Episcopal church in Detroit, Michigan.

The widow and her daughter received a flood of private letters of condolence from friends and important personages, including many former military colleagues or their widows. Many private condolences also commented on the public mourning and continued the linked themes of Southern pride and national unity. Charles Wesley Adams noted to the widow that "eulogiums" to her husband were everywhere, and former Confederate general P. G. T. Beauregard wrote that General Lee's death was "casting a universal gloom" over all of New Orleans.[232] Other correspondents mixed their private condolences with reports of the public outpourings of grief in their communities, telling the widow about tolling bells, civic gatherings, and memorial decor. Letter writers from rural areas and from cities imagined themselves, in direct address to Mary Randolph Custis Lee, to be participating in mourning rituals that would unite "the *millions* who have sympathized with your grief."[233] Veteran Confederate officers, and at least one former Union officer, wrote to assure the family they would continue to uphold Lee's values in public.[234] Some correspondents even noted that they felt writing a letter of condolence itself was a way to participate in a rite that would represent the collective sorrow of the South.[235] One friend wrote to the widow that "never in my long life have I beheld such universal feeling."[236] Even private condolence became a way to connect to the "universal" public culture of Civil War memory as condolences for Lee took on a larger meaning.

Mourning Lee and Southern Civic Identity

Mary Custis Lee lived in Lexington, Virginia, and she supported her town's status as the protector of Confederate memory. The outpouring of public grief for Robert E. Lee intensified the competition that had begun during Stonewall Jackson's funerals in 1863 between Richmond and Lexington over which city would stand as the ultimate repository of the Lost Cause. Richmond saw itself as the location of "the holiest shrines of the Lost Cause," but the graves of Stonewall Jackson and Robert E. Lee also gave Lexington a strong claim.[237]

Southern civic identity was clearly tied up in Confederate memory, even before the largest wave of public monument building and before a post-Reconstruction redemption movement began in the later 1870s. In mourning Lee, Lexington and Richmond contended to be the ultimate site of Confederate memory and Lost Cause identity.

Upon receiving telegraphs announcing Lee's death on the evening of October 12, 1870, mourning fell especially hard upon Richmond. The civic identity of Richmond's white population, tightly wrapped up with its having been the capital of the Confederacy, was now tested by Reconstruction federal control, but Lee's death provided a link to the Confederate past. State and local Democrats were plotting their route back to power, and some Black Richmond residents had complained that "former rebels" had continued to control the city, even as the African American population had almost doubled since 1865.[238] Public mourning and pleas to the Lee family for the general to be buried in Richmond were ways to link the community firmly to its Confederate past.

The *New York Times* correspondent reported that Richmond achieved a level of public mourning "hardly witnessed in this generation," a strong statement just five years after the huge funeral honors paid to Abraham Lincoln across the North and only months since the transatlantic pageant for George Peabody.[239] In the text of his city guidebook, Carlton McCarthy, veteran of the Army of Northern Virginia and future Richmond mayor, captured the scene in Richmond as the city was decorated in Lee's honor:

> The busiest streets were almost deserted . . . nearly all the stores on Main, Broad, and Cary Streets were closed, and upon the doors appeared badges of mourning . . . in many windows were to be seen faithful portraits handsomely framed and hung with black. Many private residences also were draped with mourning emblems, intertwined with wreaths of laurel and cypress. The public offices of the State Government were closed all day, and the bells at the Capitol Square bell house, and the police stations, were tolled from sunrise until sunset. The United States and Virginia flags on the Capitol were displayed at half-mast. . . . The whole community was prostrate beneath the dispensation of Providence.[240]

McCarthy praised the people of Richmond for properly mourning Lee and turned funeral observances into a direct form of community boosterism.

Newspapers amplified the idea that mourning Lee created local community. The *Richmond Daily Whig* emphasized the unanimity of the mourning by noting that the Black-owned Union Hotel, which catered to Black customers, flew its flag at half-mast, ignoring the fact that Black participation in Lee's mourning was vastly smaller than in the annual celebration of the end of slavery in Richmond. The paper further stressed civic unity the following day by commenting that "woman's taste and woman's skill was discernable" in the beautiful funeral decor in the city; the editor also noted that "the most conspicuously draped house in the city . . . is the dry goods establishment of the Levy Brothers," a Jewish merchant family whose three brothers served in the Confederate military.[241] The paper observed that even "Northern-born citizens" of the city draped their houses.[242]

When Virginia governor Gilbert Walker, himself a Northerner until 1865, communicated the news of Lee's death to the Virginia legislature, it immediately set to work on a plan to have Lee buried in Richmond in Hollywood Cemetery, which was in the process of becoming something of a "national" cemetery for the former Confederacy, the resting place of "so many of her heroic dead."[243] The legislature felt that Lee's tomb not only would honor the city of Richmond but that it could become the easily accessible site of pilgrimage inside Hollywood Cemetery. The desire of the state government to have Lee's remains in Richmond, Virginia, was reported on all over the country.[244]

The Hollywood Memorial Association was one of the most powerful of the influential Ladies' Memorial Associations that had aggressively pursued laudatory Confederate commemorations since the end of the war, and the Hollywood Memorial Association had succeeded in winning over the Virginia legislature to its agenda. Just the previous year, the association had installed a massive granite pyramidal monument "to the Confederate dead" and had raised money for the project by selling engraved likenesses of Lee.[245] Governor Walker emphasized in a public message that the entire "bereaved state" would "bow with reverence and humility" before Lee's death, but the president of Richmond's city council made it clear that city officials would "ask that his remains be deposited in the soil of our beautiful Hollywood, at the capital of his dear old mother, Virginia."[246] The *Richmond Daily Whig* reported that "a hundred" citizens in Richmond could be heard "suggesting simultaneously and without conference that the old hero ought to be buried at Hollywood."[247] The male and female civic leaders of Richmond seemed instantly united in the desire to see Lee buried in Hollywood Cemetery.

Leaders in Richmond were worried, and rightly so, that Lee would be buried in Lexington before they could properly communicate their appeal for his remains to the grieving Mary Randolph Custis Lee, who was trapped in Lexington by the flooding rains. They sent telegrams and letters to Lexington appealing to the widow to delay burying Lee, and former Confederate cavalry general Williams Carter Wickham, now the vice president of the Chesapeake and Ohio Railroad company, offered a special car to remove Lee's remains from Lexington if she would agree to the plan.[248] Although some papers carried false reports that Mary Lee had agreed to a Hollywood burial, officials in Richmond were unable to convince her, and Robert E. Lee's funeral in Lexington took place the day after they appealed to her.[249] Later proponents of the Lost Cause would emphasize that the heavy rains and damaging floods "gave cogency" to Mrs. Lee's decision to locate the general's remains in Lexington, although there is no sign she ever intended them to move elsewhere.[250]

That did not mean that civic leaders in Richmond gave up the stake in Lee's memory, or that they gave up hope that he might even be reinterred someday in their city. The Hollywood Cemetery women put out a call the week after Lee's funeral for funds to erect a monument in his honor on their grounds, and they appealed to a wide range of Confederate veterans, including Jubal Early, to contribute to the cause.[251] The female leaders of the Hollywood Memorial Association saw the effort as an extension of their years of work to commemorate and reinter the Confederate dead. At a Richmond meeting of veterans of the Army of Northern Virginia one week later, the attendees invited "the cooperation of all Confederate soldiers in this and other states in an appeal to the family of General Lee that they will permit his sacred remains to repose in Hollywood Cemetery . . . amid the many thousand brave men who followed him so cheerfully," even though they acknowledged that Lee himself had requested a Lexington burial.[252] Arising from the meeting, Jubal Early led veterans in Richmond to form a Lee monument association that rivaled the association formed just after Lee's death in Lexington, and the two groups did not work together until more than a year later.[253] Early's work with veterans to commemorate Lee helped start him along the path to becoming one of the most important champions of the Lost Cause, and Caroline Janney has pointed out how he used the Richmond Lee Monument Association to contest the institutional, feminized authority of the women of the Hollywood Memorial Association.[254]

The move to reinter Lee in Richmond never gained much traction, although at least one Petersburg newspaper supported the idea of making Hollywood into "a Westminster Abbey for Virginia" to gather Confederate remains that were "scattered all over the Commonwealth," including Lee's.[255] Four months after Lee's death, Jubal Early reassured Mary Randolph Custis Lee that Richmond authorities would gain plenty from erecting a monument to Lee in Hollywood and leaving his remains in Lexington, but Early battled with the Hollywood Memorial Association women for more than a decade about control of the Richmond monument fundraising efforts.[256] Mary Lee did accept a burial plot for herself at Hollywood in 1872 after her son, Rooney, had purchased one, but neither them was buried in Hollywood, nor did they allow any serious conversation about reinterring Robert E. Lee in Richmond.[257]

The failure of Hollywood Cemetery to win the remains of Robert E. Lee denied it a chance to become the one, central funeral shrine of the Lost Cause.

Instead, the Edward Valentine statue of Lee installed atop his grave in the Washington College chapel would continue to draw Lost Cause attention in decades to come, even as Hollywood also gained in popularity as a site of Confederate memory. By the 1890s, when Richmond erected a huge equine statue of Lee as the centerpiece of its new Monument Avenue, both cities had a claim to be an important shrine to Lee's place in the Lost Cause, but neither was exclusive. For sure, no city could become the locus of the Lost Cause without demonstrating a Lee connection.

————

The public mourning events for George Peabody and Robert E. Lee in 1869 and 1870, when considered together, show how various forms of American national identity could take root in the tensions of sectional and transnational reunification, resting on the contested and uneasy memory of different kinds of heroes. In some ways, mourning for great men could work to reunite North and South, Britain and the United States, at least in ritualized form. But the rituals of unity never completely papered over regional difference or hard-won memories of the war. The Lost Cause and the Union Cause both formed a part of public discourse; in some ways they mutually constituted one another. Funerals for the great philanthropist and the general amply demonstrated that postwar public culture contained deep contradictions, even as it often imagined unity.

Chapter 4

Charles Sumner and Joseph E. Johnston
Mourning, Memory, and Forgetting

On December 2, 1872, the first day of the third session of the Forty-Second Congress, Massachusetts senator Charles Sumner introduced two bills on the floor of the U.S. Senate that were among his last. He expected the most important act he introduced that day to be the supplement to the Civil Rights Bill, which he had advocated since 1865. Although he expected little notice for the other bill he introduced that day, it caused a firestorm. Sumner sought to obliterate an aspect of the military memory of the U.S. Civil War.

Sumner's proposed legislation sought to influence the memory of the U.S. Civil War by regulating the Army Register, the official record of conflicts and casualties, and the regimental flags of the United States. The very brief bill read, in full: "Whereas the national unity and good will among fellow-citizens can be assured only through oblivion of past differences, and it is contrary to the usage of civilized nations to perpetuate the memory of civil war: Therefore *Be it enacted, &c.* That the names of battles with fellow-citizens shall not be continued in the Army Register or placed on the regimental colors of the United States."[1]

On its face, Sumner's bill seemed concerned with national unity and recognized that Civil War memory—or the suppression thereof—would play an important role in the future "civilization" of the United States alongside the politics of African American equality that his Civil Rights Bill would seek to ensure. Sumner's move against military memory, however, turned out to be one of the worst political blunders of his entire career, one that threatened his own legacy. He was censured by the Massachusetts legislature, while old friends and supporters turned on him.

The controversy over the politics of Civil War memory that Sumner's resolution unleashed affected how he would be remembered upon his death two years later in 1874. Perhaps because he had long put his faith in politics rather than armed force, he underestimated the importance and durability of military memory. Sumner was probably trying to set aside military memory to let the politics of Reconstruction take center stage, but he miscalculated how much agitation would be caused by urging people to forget the war. His bid to erase Civil War battles from the Army Register and from regimental flags, which veterans held as deeply meaningful symbols of their national service, flipped his own political reputation as a radical and a Republican on its head. Republicans censured him, and Democrats praised him for striking a note of reconciliation as a way to score political points against Sumner, their traditional enemy.

In the process, Sumner's own utility as a symbol of the fight against slavery was compromised, as commemorations of his death in 1874 showed. Eulogies and funeral rituals for Sumner in 1874 could not avoid the controversy that his calls for wiping away the memory of the Civil War had unleashed. Upon Sumner's death, the flag resolution controversy stole public attention that might have been lavished upon his long fight for Black rights. The process mirrored the struggle for emancipationist memory to fight the impulse by many in the United States to forgive and forget the sins of slavery.[2]

In the period between 1872 and 1891, as Reconstruction waned and a rebalancing of American politics took place, public funerals continued to play a key role as repositories of Civil War memory and as sites to create American national identity. But Civil War memory was unstable, and even the best efforts of prominent men to control public memory proved ineffective. The "imagined reconstitution of the nation" in public funeral rituals, as in Sumner's flag resolution, was connected to processes of both remembering and forgetting.[3] Memory and forgetting combined in sometimes unexpected and counterintuitive ways, which only emphasized that any path to one, single national identity was impossible in the United States—national identity was created in the contests. Union and Confederate memories—and forgetting—became parts of the national narrative of a reuniting nation.

Public mourning for both Charles Sumner and Joseph E. Johnston demonstrates that, despite their personal efforts to support particular versions of Civil War memory, their deaths changed them into symbols of memory that could be used by others in ways they might not have approved of or anticipated. National identity simultaneously reflected reconciliation and fierce sectionalism: military memory contained contradictions that *were* the essence of American national identity at the end of Reconstruction. The public funeral celebrations for Senator Charles Sumner and General Joseph E. Johnston demonstrate how memory and forgetting themselves were politicized in ways that affected the national imagination. Both Sumner and Johnston wanted to promote messages of reconciliation, which they thought required forgetting aspects of the Civil War, but their own funerals prove that a controlled amnesia was not possible, and grievances persisted.

Sumner and Johnston also each sought to promote particular versions of Civil War memory—and forgetting—that they hoped would influence how they themselves would be commemorated upon their own deaths. Each man served as a national symbol, but neither man could control how his reputation would function symbolically. Both Charles Sumner and Joseph E. Johnston promoted forgetting parts of the Civil War as a form of national reconciliation, but mourning for each man showed how imperfect that formula for reconciliation was. The funerals of Charles Sumner and Joseph E. Johnston show the complex relationship between Civil War memory, reconciliation, and forgetting. Both men died in Washington, D.C., and then were moved to their respective regions for interment. Sumner was buried in the heart of abolitionist Boston, and Johnston was buried in Baltimore and heavily mourned in Richmond, the heart of the Confederacy. But neither had a straightforward legacy: each man embodied reconciliation with a belligerent sectional twist.

Charles Sumner: Memory and Forgetting

Charles Sumner had a long career as an abolitionist and antislavery senator. Sumner was born in Boston in 1811, and following his graduation from Harvard in 1833, his devotion to humanitarian philosophy transformed into antislavery politics as he practiced law and traveled in Europe. He believed that law was the basis of social order, and unlike many Garrisonian abolitionists, he saw politics and law as the best ways to fight the evils of slavery.[4] Sumner broke with the Whigs in the 1840s and became one of the founders of the Free Soil Party, under whose banner he was first elected to the U.S. Senate in 1851. His strong antislavery politics and fiery oratory earned him hatred in the South, where he was considered "a rank abolitionist."[5] He decried the 1850 Fugitive Slave Act, and he embraced the Republican Party upon its founding in 1856, becoming one of its most outspoken antislavery members.

Sumner became a vivid martyr for antislavery when, later that year, Rep. Preston Brooks of South Carolina viciously beat him with a cane on the floor of the Senate for denouncing "The Crime Against Kansas."[6] Sumner denounced proslavery settlers streaming into Kansas using a rape metaphor, and Brooks's aggressive response offered just one measure of how dangerous proslavery forces considered Sumner's oratorical and legislative powers to be. Sumner, disabled for quite a time by the beating, was hailed by many Northerners for his bodily sacrifice on behalf of the antislavery cause. Sumner remained in the Senate, and he returned to political action during the war. His promotion of the Freedmen's Bureau during the Civil War, and afterward his opposition to Andrew Johnson and other forces of moderate Reconstruction, and his continual insistence upon Black rights, including the franchise, ensured that Democrats continued to view him as an enemy, while Radical Republicans hailed him as a champion of freedom.

Yet Sumner underestimated the importance of the military conflict itself as the center of Reconstruction-era memory, favoring a political rather than military vision of the nation that he did not view as at odds with retaining an emphasis on emancipation and Black freedom. Sumner underestimated the allure of Civil War memory. Even though during the war he had twice proposed similar restrictions on regimental flags, his 1872 bill was considered a disavowal of Union heroism.[7] A bitter enemy of President Ulysses S. Grant, Sumner had been effectively ejected from the Senate Republican caucus following his support of the Liberal Republican Horace Greeley in the 1872 presidential election just a month earlier. Sumner claimed that he had never abandoned the fight for African American freedom when he opposed Grant and supported the Liberal Republicans, but the Republican break and the Liberal Republican "new departure" further opened him to charges of disloyalty, especially when other Republicans might question his commitment to honor military accomplishments.[8]

For Sumner, Grant was always too associated with warfare and therefore prevented sectional healing. Sumner's biographer David Herbert Donald explains the flag bill as part of Sumner's anti-Grant maneuvering, pointing out that he had told a campaign-season crowd in Massachusetts that the president could never "promote true reconciliation" because Grant himself was "a regimental color with the forbidden inscription" that would "flaunt in the face of the vanquished" their defeat in the war.[9] Sumner's 1872 flag bill made little progress in Congress; it was defeated by a joint resolution introduced in the House, which argued that "the national unity cannot fail to be strengthened by the remembrance of the services of those who fought the battles of Union in the late war of the rebellion."[10]

Even before Sumner's bill died in Congress, however, he faced stiff opposition back in his native state because his resolution violated the politics of strong Union memory. Massachusetts chapters of the Grand Army of the Republic (GAR), many of which had strong Radical Republican commitments, had for years pursued political action based on the belief that "we cannot forget the past with its privations and sacrifices, nor forgive the treason which caused them."[11] The Massachusetts GAR was gaining strength after opposing the Liberal Republican ticket, and therefore breaking with the senator, in the 1872 election.[12]

In condemning the flag resolution, Sumner's Republican opponents in the Massachusetts House hoped to gain traction in the upcoming senatorial elections and felt that they could mobilize support from outraged veterans. On December 18, they introduced a resolution of censure against Sumner, calling his bill "an insult to the loyal soldier of the nation."[13] The GAR as an organization tended to hold on to both Civil War memory and the Union Cause. The Massachusetts legislature, which happened to be meeting in special session, passed the resolution quickly in one day after a series of parliamentary maneuvers gave Sumner's supporters little chance to object. It took a fourteen-month petition campaign, led in part by John Greenleaf Whittier, and a series of heated hearings to get Massachusetts legislators to rescind the act against Sumner in February 1874, just one month before the senator's death.[14]

Charles Sumner worried that the memory of Civil War battles would continue sectional division and overshadow the efforts to win African American rights, so he wanted to forget one and remember the other. He thought that to guarantee the passage of the Civil Rights Bill and finally protect Blacks would require sectional reconciliation that sidestepped the memory of Southern military defeat, which could stir up bitter hatred. Sumner fretted that military memory would eclipse emancipation and correctly anticipated what, in fact, would happen over the next several decades, as dominant strains of Civil War military memory both inspired continued Southern hatred of the North (enshrined in the Lost Cause) and created an image of sectional reconciliation based on the shared sacrifices of white Union and Confederate soldiers in battle that frequently drowned out Black contributions and emancipation struggles.[15] He argued for a different kind of sectional reconciliation, one that suppressed the war and was cemented by political power.

Sumner was wrong, however, to believe that legislation could suppress military memory, let alone to think that Congress would be willing to try. He was shocked at the public outcry against his bill and against him, writing to Willard P. Phillips, "I cannot comprehend this tempest."[16] The press excoriated him; one paper called his resolution "an insult to every soldier and patriot who fought to save this Government."[17] Thomas Nast caricatured Sumner in the December 28, 1872, issue of *Harper's Weekly* as haughtily ignoring an amputee veteran, a soldier's widow, and a war orphan who beg for congressional relief. The cartoon portrayed Sumner as manipulating Civil War memory: a paper in front of him read, "The only record of the rebellion shall be Charles Sumner and his speeches," even as plans for "monuments and burying grounds for Union dead" and "U.S. History" lie in the wastebasket at his feet.[18] Ironically, Sumner's own reputation was the main thing threatened by his move to forget the war.

Political will to enforce issues of African American rights and equality, the great causes of Sumner's political career, was already waning as Reconstruction showed signs of expiring in 1873 and 1874. In fact, many felt that Sumner's Civil Rights Bill, passed by the Senate less than a year after his death, passed mainly out of deference to the dead senator (still nationally respected by Republicans even as he caused some controversy). In the following years the House of Representatives gutted the legislation, which it had never fully supported, and the Supreme Court declared it unconstitutional in 1883.[19] Some

African American leaders worried that with Sumner's death their last strong legislative advocate had expired.

By taking on the politics of Civil War memory and trying to obliterate military accomplishments Charles Sumner threatened his own legacy and actually hurt his prospects of being useful as an object of public memory after his death. Sumner was well accustomed to being cast as a political symbol, having been considered a martyr to the cause of liberty ever since his 1856 caning. The caning had done much to tie Sumner symbolically to the cause of emancipation and African American equality, both of which he continued to pursue with an aggressive fervor that united him to African Americans and sometimes alienated other white politicians.[20] When he passed away in 1874, a great outpouring of public mourning issued forth—stretching from congressional obsequies in Washington, D.C., to his burial in Massachusetts. But the memorials for Sumner were imbued with some of the same controversy that the senator himself had sought to prevent, in particular concerning what Americans should remember about the great issues of the Civil War. On a national scale and in Massachusetts, mourning Sumner was an occasion to celebrate the success of the antislavery movement and Black freedom; however, the long shadow of the flag bill controversy also dramatized the ongoing conflict about the legacy of the Civil War and the life span of Reconstruction.

Sumner was certainly hailed as a national hero by many African Americans and a revered son of Massachusetts, but he was not a strong enough symbol to suppress political conflict over race and Civil War memory. As seen in his funeral commemorations, Sumner symbolized a nation trying to reconcile, while still struggling with, the legacy of slavery. The mourning for him showed just how hard it was to balance reconciliation and emancipation— even when memorializing someone who had been one of the loudest white champions of Black freedom.

Charles Sumner died early on the morning on March 11, 1874. He had endured poor health since his 1856 beating on the U.S. Senate floor, and his death was preceded by severe bouts of chest pain.[21] Congress, already preparing to adjourn because of the death a few days earlier of former president Millard Fillmore, took immediate notice of Sumner's passing. As national newspapers filled with notices of the senator's death, Congress planned a grand funeral in the nation's capital. On March 13, Sumner's remains were brought from his D.C. home to the U.S. Capitol in a procession led by prominent African American men, including Frederick Douglass and P. B. S. Pinchback, who had defended Sumner when other Republicans had excoriated him for opposing Grant in 1872.[22] Sumner's body lay in state in the Capitol rotunda, attended by thousands of mourners, and spectators packed the Senate chamber—draped in black crepe for the occasion—to witness his funeral there. Congressional representatives, the president and vice president, members of the diplomatic corps, and other government officials also attended the rites. After the ceremony, Congress adjourned; a Massachusetts committee accompanied Sumner's remains on a special train to New York and then on to Boston.[23]

In Boston, "universal sorrow" descended on the inhabitants, and many homes and store windows were decorated in Sumner's honor.[24] Both the state legislature and the city government adjourned to prepare for the senator's funeral and burial, and several newspapers mentioned that any lingering bad feelings for Sumner had been pushed aside as the Commonwealth prepared to bury one of her most illustrious statesmen.[25] One paper in the western part of the state wrote, "Charles Sumner was never so much to Massachusetts as on this day of his funeral. . . . For the moment, at least, his death has broadened and deepened his power over her people."[26] Before Sumner's remains had even arrived in Boston, a huge public meeting in his honor had convened at Faneuil Hall, where Mayor Samuel C. Cobb, legislator and author Richard Henry Dana, and other city luminaries eulogized him.[27] After the funeral train arrived on March 14, Sumner's remains lay in state in the Doric Hall of the Massachusetts State House, where tens of thousands of disorderly and sometimes rowdy men and women paid their last respects.[28]

Sumner's service and burial on Monday, March 16, became one of the largest civic funerals in Boston's history. His body was moved from the state capitol to King's Chapel in the afternoon, and Beacon Street was so packed with onlookers for the procession that "vigilant exertions of a large police force" were necessary to keep the funeral route open.[29] So many mourners wanted to enter King's Chapel that only those issued tickets by the General Court of Massachusetts were allowed inside, and one paper claimed that even part of the choir was barred from entering.[30] After Rev. Henry C. Foote conducted the funeral service, Sumner's procession continued from the chapel on to Cambridge, where his body was interred in Mount Auburn Cemetery, the picturesque resting place that Sumner himself had often used as a city retreat.[31] The graveside service was concluded with prayers and hymns sung by the men of the Apollo Club.[32] The Boston City Council organized an additional memorial service held at the Music Hall on April 29, where Missouri senator Carl Schurz, who brought oratorical star power and a reputation for political controversy, delivered a lengthy eulogy.[33] It became the best-known speech in honor of Sumner, among dozens delivered at churches, clubs, and memorial meetings and on the floor of Congress, where official tributes were presented on April 27.[34]

Even in the midst of all the public mourning that celebrated Sumner's long political career, the flag bill controversy and the Massachusetts censure occupied a prominent place in the public memory of the senator. The Democratic New York *World* cast a doubt on the sincerity of many of the accolades, noting that Sumner had died with a shattered reputation: "The generous American instinct which forgets all political differences on the brink of the grave, insures to Mr. SUMNER the usual pomp of eulogy, but the encomiums which will come from the lips rather than the heart, cannot disguise the fact that, like poor Mr. GREELEY, he died a broken-hearted man."[35] Sumner's battles on behalf of African American rights and his caning by Preston Brooks occupied important space in his obituaries, but his more recent break with the Republican Party and the controversy over war memory clouded an unalloyed heroic picture of him in both Republican and Democratic papers.[36] The *World* raged that public eulogies of Sumner were an "empty mockery" because he "was isolated and estranged from the party which owed him a great debt of gratitude."[37] The editors sought to use Sumner's partial disgrace to score points against the Republican Party, even though party leaders denounced him for the flag bill, on the basis that "a party which thus casts aside its honored leaders has outlived its original principles."[38] One of the traditional purposes of public mourning for political figures in the United States was to symbolically reinforce unity that could seem to bind up partisan or sectional differences, but the last chapter of Sumner's career did not allow him entirely to fill that purpose.[39] Even as senators honored his dying words—"You must take care of the civil rights bill . . . don't let it fail!"—Sumner himself seemed to symbolize something of the disarray and partisanship of Reconstruction.[40]

Sumner's supporters tried to downplay the effect of the controversy on his reputation. John Greenleaf Whittier, who believed that the General Court "never did anything more unjust, uncalled for, foolish and wicked than that resolution of censure of her great senator," hoped that rescinding it would allow Massachusetts to keep "the memory of his tireless devotion to duty, his courage . . . stainless honor and tender regard for the rights of all" rather than the "stigma of ingratitude" the censure implied.[41] Further, Whittier believed that "the folly of the Extra Session of 1872" would be superseded by the power of public mourning for Sumner, which would suppress "all enemities [*sic*], jealousies and party hatreds."[42]

The timing of the censure's removal gave Americans ample opportunity to be reminded of the flag resolution and to ponder and debate anew what Sumner's attitude toward the Civil War's legacy had really been. Newspaper reports of Sumner's death were not able to heap praise on him without also refreshing the public memory of his censure. The day before his death, while on the U.S. Senate floor, Sumner had received the news from Massachusetts that the censure had been lifted. The *Chicago Daily Tribune* reported, "It is a rather singular fact that, on this last day in the Senate, and the last day that he was alive on earth and in the discharge of his duties, the resolution expunging the censure voted by the Massachusetts Legislature on account of his battle-flag resolutions were presented by his colleague, Mr. Boutwell, and read in his presence."[43]

That day, Sumner told several associates that he had not been feeling well, but, as the *New York Times* reported, "after the presentation in the Senate of the resolutions of the Legislature of Massachusetts expunging from its records the resolutions of censure . . . the Senator was feeling much better."[44] The Chicago *Inter-Ocean* noted that the excitement of the day proved, perhaps, too much for Sumner, even though "it is regarded as a remarkable and fortunate coincidence that the resolution . . . should have been presented and read in the Senate before he left it on the last day of his presence in the chamber as a member of the body." After the announcement, he "was greatly affected by this event, and talked about it to his friends in quite a cheerful mood. . . . For some time before the session closed, however, the excitement seemed to have wearied and depressed him."[45] Several papers noted that Sumner left the Senate "in unusually cheerful spirits on account of the announcement of the passage of the rescinding resolutions by the Massachusetts legislature," after which he went home to dine with friends.[46] Sumner took ill after his dinner and never recovered.

In the days following his death, many of his supporters expressed thanks that the censure had been lifted while Sumner was still alive. When he heard that the senator had passed away, Kenneth Allen, a student from Worcester, Massachusetts, rehearsed Sumner's biography in his diary as he prepared to travel to Boston for the funeral exercises. Allen noted, "The unjust resolution of censure which was put on him a year and a half ago was repealed" just before he died.[47] Thomas Russell eulogized Sumner at the Commercial Club in Boston on March 21 and remarked that "those who voted for the censure join us in rejoicing that it was removed in time to cheer the last days of our great senator with the thought that his heart and the heart of Massachusetts beat in harmony."[48] Noted Boston preacher Caleb Bradlee praised Massachusetts legislators in a sermon for "wiping clean the former mistake" of censuring Sumner and thanked God that the senator had lived to hear the news.[49]

Some of Sumner's most important Massachusetts critics had, indeed, had a change of heart about him during his last months and in the period just following his death. The *New York Times* reported that when the state legislature met to arrange for Sumner's funeral solemnities, "the fact the resolutions rescinding the censure of the dead statesman had been so recently passed, was the subject of congratulation among the members."[50] The president of the Massachusetts Historical Society, Robert C. Winthrop, who had been a bitter enemy of Sumner's since the 1840s, had reconciled with the senator in the last months of his life and had finally supported his election as a member of the society in September 1873. Winthrop, the conservative political independent who also presided over the Peabody Educational Trust and had helped organize Peabody's American funeral, announced Sumner's death at a meeting of the Massachusetts Historical Society and acknowledged that few leaders were so much "on the lips of the people in all parts of the country,—sometimes for criticism and even censure," but that he ought to be remembered well now.[51] Prominent society members "all made complimentary remarks," and Winthrop served as a pallbearer at the senator's funeral.[52] Sumner's former critics, whether in the General Court or in the Massachusetts Historical Society, realized that continuing the enmity over Sumner's support of the Liberal Republicans or over his flag resolutions would work at cross-purposes with their desire to hold him up as a posthumous hero for any number of causes: Black rights, Republicanism, or the glory of the state of Massachusetts. Even if Sumner wanted to forget the war, he, himself, could not be forgotten.

Some Democrats and Southerners tried to use Sumner's death and the remnants of the flag bill controversy to push the idea that the Civil War must be put to rest in the interest of national reconciliation—on Southern terms. The simple sight of a Democratic newspaper supporting Sumner demonstrated forgetting the past, since Sumner had been a bitter Democratic enemy for more than twenty years. In 1851, one leading Boston Democratic paper had written, "For a Democrat to support Mr. Sumner is to place himself in direct hostility to the Democracy of the Land."[53] Now, the Democratic *Boston Statesman and Weekly Post* argued that Sumner had "closed his career with an effort to restore fraternity among the . . . sad memories of a destructive civil war" and called his efforts to wipe out battle commemoration "the noblest act in all his public career," one that would actually ensure his own long public memory.[54]

Sumner's political missteps in 1872 allowed him to be used as a symbol for a form of reconciliation that he did not actually support. Democrats and Southerners exaggerated Sumner's political transformation by the end of his life; he opposed Grant, but he was still a strong advocate of Black rights and wished to be affiliated with the Republican Party. But his flag resolution had created a rhetorical opening to paint him as an advocate of total Southern forgiveness: it was framed as similar to Horace Greeley's 1872 campaign plea that the North and South should "clasp hands across the bloody chasm"—an expression of unconditional absolution.[55] Sumner wanted to continue using state power to enforce racial equality and Reconstruction policies, but most other Liberal Republicans wanted to end Reconstruction and supported Greeley's notion that forgetting the war was the best path to reconciliation.[56] By supporting the Liberal Republicans in 1872 and then proposing the flag bill, Sumner endorsed a form of forgetting the past that could be used to argue for the end of Reconstruction—even though he himself never went that far.

Some newspapers used Sumner as a symbol of a remarkably new national reconciliation. One Connecticut obituary exaggerated Sumner's emphasis on Southern forgiveness, noting his achievements as a legislator and abolitionist and concluding, "Among his later efforts may be mentioned . . . his proposition to remove from public buildings the war flags captured from the confederate states during the rebellion."[57] The New Orleans *Picayune* pleaded, "Let the grave cover all that was inimical to Southern ideas and sentiments in the deceased senator, and let us only remember that he would have put away from the federal archives all show and sign of the triumph of countrymen over countrymen."[58] The Louisville *Courier Journal* editorialized, "Fifteen years ago the news that Charles Sumner was dead would have been received with something like rejoicing by the people of the South. . . . Today they will read it regretfully, and their comment will be: 'He was a great man. He was an honest man. As he has forgiven us, so have we long ago forgiven him.'"[59]

Even though some Democrats and former Confederates were willing to forgive Sumner, or at least to use his memory conveniently, others could not get over decades of viewing him as a nemesis. When Mississippian Lucius Q. C. Lamar, the first former Confederate to serve in the U.S. Senate, delivered a eulogy for Sumner on the floor during the official Senate day of mourning on April 27, he was attacked by fellow Southern Democrats for lauding their former bitter enemy. Lamar explained in a letter to Alabamian Clement Claiborne Clay that he had spoken up because he believed Sumner's political change of heart was real: "The most advanced & offensive assailant of our institutions . . . had become an advocate of amnesty & peace & fraternity with our people. His own legislature had censured him." Lamar felt that the occasion of Sumner's death would provide an excellent chance to explain the Southern point of view on Reconstruction to Northerners because "every word said about him [Sumner], on the occasion of his funeral, would be read all over the North."[60]

Lamar's eulogy used Sumner's death to make what newspapers called "an earnest appeal for the drawing together in brotherly love of the North and the South," something that would not have been possible without Sumner's own spin on Civil War memory.[61] Lamar praised Sumner's "spirit of magnanimity" toward the South, especially in the last two years of his life—a reference to Sumner's Liberal Republicanism and his flag resolution.[62] The flag resolution, and its place in the public mind around the time of Sumner's death, paved the way for former Confederates to make wider arguments that Americans should put the war behind them.

Republicans were not willing to let the memory of the flag resolution be used only to create a Southern version of reconciliationist memory. Some commentators fought back against the idea that Sumner wanted to forget the war, arguing that his flag resolutions were simply misunderstood. Sumner himself was mystified that the Massachusetts legislature had considered his resolutions to be antiveteran. He wrote to Willard P. Phillips just after the censure that he was "at a loss after all my work through the war" to explain how "any body can charge me with insulting the soldier."[63]

Sumner did not understand that it would be impossible to forget the war, or even to remove the names of battles from regimental flags, without many veterans taking that as a mark against their service. For veterans, flags "captured the main themes of love, courage, honor, and duty" that could not be separated from the memory of the war, and Northern veterans were among the most pro-Union citizens in their wartime recollections.[64] War memory overshadowed the political accomplishments of men such as Sumner, especially since his flirtation with the Liberal Republicans showed cracks in the political legacy of the war.

After his death, Republicans who wanted to use Sumner's memory to continue their political battles had to either apologize for his straying from the course or agree that his resolutions had been grossly misconstrued by the legislature and the public. In a widely reprinted Sumner eulogy, staunch Massachusetts Republican George William Curtis claimed, for example, that the state had "censured him for the resolutions which the people of the State did not understand, and which they believed, most unjustly to him, to be somehow a wrong to the precious dead."[65] It was not politically advantageous to leave the public thinking that Sumner had devalued military sacrifice—even though that was a hard presumption to overcome.

The *Chicago Tribune*, the city's main Republican newspaper, reexamined the flag resolution in a series of articles appearing just after Sumner's death and also argued that the public had severely misunderstood the senator's intent. At first, the *Tribune* editors argued that the "row" that erupted after the battle flag resolution had been proposed had really been unwarranted because his critics had blown Sumner's intentions all out of proportion. The paper's first editorial on the subject complained that "the average party organ informed its readers that the Senator was craftily plotting to destroy the flags of all the volunteer regiments of the country. . . . Their colors were to be torn down from public halls and State-Houses and defaced, lest the feelings of 'Rebels' should be hurt." The *Tribune* pointed out that simply removing the names of Civil War battles could hardly be an insult to "the loyal soldiery of the nation," since many volunteer regiments flew flags bearing the names of battles in which they had not even fought.[66]

The *Tribune* editors went even further in a second article, proposing that "the most fitting mark of respect to the great Senator would be the passage of his famous battle-flag resolution, word for word as it came from the brain which has now done with earthly thinking." Although the *Tribune* editors shared no political interest with men such as Lucius Q. Lamar, their rhetoric prefigured Lamar's congressional obituary of Sumner when they argued that after nine years "the one thing needful now is to heal the wounds made by the long struggle." They asked the public to "dispense" with "flaunting the memorials of fratricidal strife in the faces of our enemies and present friends."[67] Republicans who sympathized with Sumner's flag resolution showed signs of fatigue with Reconstruction. Ultimately, the Republicans who were most willing to promote Southern forgiveness were the ones who could most forthrightly deal with Sumner's flag resolution in the context of mourning his death.

It should not be surprising, then, that Carl Schurz agreed with the *Chicago Tribune* and that his eulogy of Sumner became the most widely disseminated prominent effort to rehabilitate the senator's posthumous reputation in regard to the flag resolution. Like Sumner, Schurz was a Republican operative who had lost faith in Grant by the time of the 1872 presidential election. He was an even stronger supporter of the Liberal Republican movement than Sumner had been, but, perhaps because he lived longer, he was able to integrate back into Republican power circles more successfully after the dissolution of the Liberal Republican movement and as Reconstruction came to an end. Boston city officials invited Schurz to deliver the main eulogy for Sumner at their celebration in his honor, which took place at the Music Hall on April 29, 1874, three weeks after the senator's death.

Of all the orators who eulogized Sumner in the months after his passing, Schurz, the former Union general and Missouri senator, took on Sumner's flag resolution and what it meant for Civil War memory in the most forthright terms. Schurz flat out refused the notion that the flag resolution had sullied Civil War memory, and therefore Charles Sumner. He left no doubt in his speech but that Sumner's memory left "a legacy to the American people and to mankind."[68] After rehearsing Sumner's political achievements through the war years and immediately afterward, Schurz discussed how Sumner had broken with Grant out of pure motives: disgust for corruption and true opposition to the annexation of Santo Domingo.[69] Schurz assured the Boston audience that Sumner had been fully willing to forgive the South, since, although he had despised the oppression of slavery, he had harbored no ill will toward the "former oppressor."[70] Schurz argued—in language that prefigured American imperialist rhetoric in decades to come—that Sumner's flag resolution was in no way an insult to "the soldiers who had spilled their blood in a war for human rights," but rather was a genuine attempt to re-create a sense of unbroken American nationalism.[71]

Schurz continued to rehearse how every "civilized nation" in history that had survived a civil conflict had the good sense to downplay its victories, and he gave examples from Irish, Scotch, Hungarian, French, and German history.[72] He imagined a reunited American military when he continued, "Should the Son of South Carolina, when at some future day defending the Republic against some foreign foe, be reminded, by an inscription on the colors floating over him, that under this flag the gun was fired that killed his father at Gettysburg?"[73] Schurz predicted the necessity for a reunited America to ready itself for fighting in foreign wars, as would be the case later in 1898 when Civil War memories would play a role in a narrative of reunification that pitted the United States against Spanish imperialism.[74]

Speaking rather frankly to his Boston audience, Schurz claimed that the Massachusetts censure of Sumner had been a wrongful and "bitter arrow in his heart."[75] Schurz counted it as fortunate that Sumner had lived to see the censure lifted, and he tried to turn the senator's death into a lesson about political integrity and independence.[76] He claimed that Sumner had used his "battle-axe" for righteous causes, though he had often been misunderstood.[77] Schurz surely sought to vindicate himself along with Sumner by emphasizing that it had been possible to oppose Grant and to advocate Southern forgiveness while still maintaining true Republican principles.

Indeed, Schurz made a connection between Sumner's flag resolution and his work for African American freedom, one that even Sumner himself had not made on the day he introduced both the Civil Rights Bill supplement and the flag resolution. Schurz argued that contention over names on army regimental battle flags was trivial, in the end, when real questions of African American rights were so much more important to public memory of the Civil War. Bostonians, indeed all Northerners, ought to be willing to obliterate the memories of their military gains as long as they could remember the progress made on behalf of Black men and women and that the union was preserved.

Schurz asked, "Do you want shining mementos of your victories? They are written upon the dusky brow of every freeman who was once a slave; they are written on the gate-posts of a restored Union; and the most shining of all will be written on the faces of a contented people, re-united in common national pride."[78] Schurz claimed that the accomplishments of the war should be enough to make its legacy meaningful: flags and relics were not useful. In this way, Sumner's memory could stand for reconciliation *and* for racial justice, but it required verbal acrobatics from Schurz.

African American Memory

Certainly, most of Sumner's African American mourners—and there were many—did not agree. Because of his tireless legislative efforts on their behalf, Black people all over the country felt Sumner's loss and worried about what

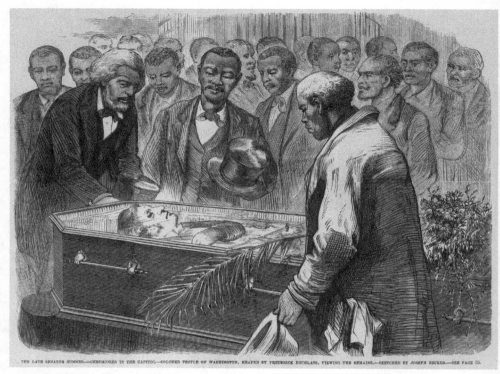

Joseph Becker, "The late Senator Sumner. Ceremonies in the Capitol—Colored People of Washington, Headed by Frederick Douglass, Viewing the Remains," *Frank Leslie's Illustrated Magazine*, March 28, 1874. Library of Congress, Prints and Photographs Division, LC-USZ62-139567.

it meant for the continuation of Reconstruction. African Americans convened special church and civic services to commemorate Sumner in Boston, Savannah, Little Rock, Pittsburgh, Davenport, Louisville, New York, Richmond, Wilmington, Chicago, Philadelphia, Portsmouth (Virginia), Toronto, and elsewhere.[79] While African American mourners might have agreed with Schurz's attempt to rehabilitate Sumner as a symbol of the fight for equality and freedom, they were not willing to use him as a symbol of Southern reconciliation. Blacks were willing to forgive the flag resolution, but they were not willing to endorse it as a way to forget Southern misdeeds.

Black orators, unlike Sumner, would not advocate forgetting the war—no matter how much national reconciliation might be needed. Though Sumner was a hero to many Black orators, they were quite willing to address his faults—including his 1872 support of Greeley and his flag resolution. Many African American leaders seemed to calculate that moving forward with the politics of racial reform would mean using Sumner as a symbol while also maintaining memories of the difficult past, a challenging rhetorical needle to thread.

South Carolina state legislator Robert Elliot delivered a tribute at Faneuil Hall at the Sumner Memorial that the "colored citizens of Boston" held on April 14 in which he claimed that the eulogy did not have to hold back all the faults of the great man. Elliot declared outright that he had differed from Sumner in the 1872 presidential race, but he did not believe that the senator's actions during and after the election had clouded his support for Black rights: "As his life was wholly consecrated to Duty, so his death was wanting in no element of moral grandeur. . . . He fell with armor on, with face still inflexibly turned towards present duties, fronting eternity with the simple trust which God gives to his faithful servant."[80]

Rev. Henry McNeal Turner told the huge audience of Sumner mourners at Savannah's St. Philip's African Methodist Episcopal Church that he had assured Sumner at their last meeting in 1873 "that I, like thousands of other colored men in the country, loved him, but could not endorse his rabid fight on the President." Despite this disagreement, Turner also praised Sumner as "Christ-like."[81] African American orators saw the senator's faults, but they could not afford to forget his advocacy and sacrifice on their behalf.

In this vein, Joshua B. Smith, a formerly enslaved man who was by the 1870s a successful Cambridge caterer and Massachusetts state legislator, stood out as one of the leading men who sought to preserve Sumner's memory.[82] Smith understood the power of interracial commemorative efforts, having been in 1865 the first to conceive of and begin fundraising for the Robert Gould Shaw memorial on the Boston Common. Smith had engaged Sumner to help lead the e. rt for a monument, and the two were longtime friends.[83] After the senator's c ath, Smith became what one newspaper called "one of the most thorough an reverential mourners for [Sumner] the great Massachusetts advocate of negro 1 3hts."[84] Smith knew all too well how controversial the senator had become in .vis final years of life, since he had introduced the resolution that had cleared Sumner's censure in the Massachusetts legislature and had hand delivered news of its passage to Washington, D.C., on the eve of Sumner's death. Smith had constantly attended to the senator during his last years of disfavor in Massachusetts, when Sumner felt that "little regard was paid to [his] public services."[85] Smith was unwilling to let the man whom he regarded as a great hero and a leader of the Black race fade in the public's mind.

Smith's purpose in holding on to Sumner as a strong symbol became clear in the eulogy he delivered at the city memorial in Faneuil Hall on the day Sumner's body arrived in Boston for his funeral. One newspaper reported that Smith "spoke with a genuine earnest feeling that captivated all hearts."[86] He worried that without Sumner, the fight for African American equality would be lost. He claimed that "our ship . . . which he has commanded is still adrift: we are standing out now in the open sea, with a great storm." Smith hoped for "a good man to take hold where he left off" to lead "those five millions of people of the United States" who were still too weak to lead themselves. He expressed a lack of confidence that any Black man could lead the cause as effectively as Sumner had. He continued, "We are not educated up to that point. . . . We cannot speak for ourselves; we must depend on others. . . . We can weep; but we must beg of you to give us a man who will still lead us forward."[87] While Sumner had sometimes seen his own relationship with African American leaders in paternalistic terms, Joshua Smith was the only Black orator who fully adopted that vocabulary when he argued, "We stand to-day like so many children whose parents have passed away. . . . We can weep; but we don't understand it."[88] Smith saw Sumner as key to the memory of emancipation and the continuance of the fight for Black rights.

Other African American leaders, although less enamored of Sumner's paternalism, also recognized the enormity of his lost leadership. The distinguished committee that had planned the celebration for Boston's "colored" population noted that "Mr. Sumner had been the life-long friend of the colored race, and had, more than any other man, helped to raise them, socially and politically, and to his memory they owed a debt of gratitude which could never be repaid."[89] In Savannah, Henry McNeal Turner wondered, "On whom shall Sumner's mantle fall?"[90]

Frederick Douglass, who eulogized Sumner in Washington, D.C., on the day of his burial, was alone among African American orators when he expressed confidence that the standard of Sumner's political leadership for Black rights would not disappear with his death. Douglass told his audience at the Sumner Memorial Hall: "The man is now living who will seize the banner laid down by Charles Sumner and lead us to higher plains of privilege." Douglass implied that either Wendell Phillips or someone else would be able to complete Sumner's work.[91] Douglass was certain, in his own career, that memory of Civil War military accomplishments would bolster the continued emancipationist cause, and he thought that Sumner would have to be replaced going forward.

Black orators who eulogized Sumner differed with Carl Schurz on the meaning of the Civil War. Schurz claimed that racial justice was the greatest legacy of the war, and that as long as "the faces of a contented people" showed happiness at a union restored and slavery ended, then Confederates could afford to be forgiven. Black orators disagreed that the work of the Civil War was over, however. Douglass certainly did not think the time had come for forgiving former slaveholders and Confederates.[92] Whether they had a new political leader in mind, as did Frederick Douglass, or they worried that no new white political leader would emerge, as did Joshua B. Smith, they knew that the fight for equal rights was not over. Of course, as David Blight has reminded us, Frederick Douglass was one of the strongest opponents of forgetting the Civil War, even as the fight for Black freedom continued: forgetting would only aid white supremacy.[93] Douglass was willing to use the emancipationist memory of Sumner's past to focus on the future work that was still needed to accomplish racial equality, even if Sumner himself had wrongly advocated forgetting the war.

Charles Sumner himself had pleaded that his colleagues should continue the work of equal rights on the very day he introduced the flag resolution into Congress. Although he wanted to obliterate Northern victories from the army register and from regimental flags, he was resolute that the battle for Black equality must continue. When Sumner introduced the supplementary Civil Rights Bill into the Senate, he said, "I, Sir, am anxious to see universal amnesty; but with it must be asserted also universal justice. . . . Our colored fellow-citizens must be admitted to complete equality before the law. . . . In other words, everywhere, in everything regulated by law, they must be equal with all their fellow-citizens."[94]

Sumner believed that war memory was separable from the continuing political battle for equal human rights: forgiveness and amnesty for the Confederate past, even forgetting the war, would be possible as long as the future fight on behalf of African Americans continued. But he was wrong. Black leaders were wise to worry, since it would be many decades before any white senator would take up the call for African American rights quite so vociferously. Sumner's Civil Rights Bill did not last long, and instead of full equality, Black Americans faced many more decades of legal segregation and racial injustice. After Sumner was gone, it was not the war that was forgotten in mainstream American culture, but rather much of the struggle against slavery and racial oppression.

The mourning for Charles Sumner in 1874 showed just how inseparable the two issues of war memory and equal rights were. It was not easy to celebrate Sumner as a martyr to liberty or as a symbol of the fight for African American freedom without acknowledging the political difficulties his flag resolution had caused. Sumner had strayed from the Republican fold in 1872, and he had misunderstood the extent to which the memory of Civil War battles *could* be forgotten. By the time voices for reconciliation between North and South became louder in the 1880s, they tended to tout the common sacrifices of white Civil War soldiers as the very thing worth remembering.[95] It was that potent social image that made it so hard for African American sacrifices and struggles to gain attention. Charles Sumner's own public memory—as the white freedom fighter or the opponent of Grant or the advocate of Black rights who was willing to forgive the South—was important but unstable.[96] Mourning for Sumner was unable to overcome the contradictions that would enable Reconstruction to unravel within just a few more years.

Joseph E. Johnston and Reconciliation

The year 1874 also saw a similar battle for historical reputation and memory by a figure who was the opposite of Charles Sumner in almost every conceivable way: Confederate general Joseph E. Johnston. In the year of Charles Sumner's death, Johnston published his *Narrative of Military Operations Directed during the Late War between the States*—one of the first military narratives by a Civil War officer and a book calculated to boost Johnston's command reputation, not the least by grinding an ax against former Confederate president Jefferson Davis. From 1874 until 1891, the year of his death, Johnston deeply engaged in public memories of the Civil War by writing, granting press interviews, attending veterans' events, unveiling monuments, and attending the public funerals of other Civil War officers, frequently serving as a pall-bearer. Johnston was Sumner's polar opposite: a Virginian, West Point graduate, U.S. Army quartermaster, and Confederate general. But when Johnston died in 1891, his funeral expressed in a similar manner to Sumner's just how contested Civil War memory, and forgetting, could get. Johnston also wanted to obliterate a key aspect of Civil War memory: his own. And, like Sumner, he failed.

Between 1874 and 1891, Johnston engaged in elaborate rituals of Civil War reunion and reconciliation, even as he clearly retained his identities as a Confederate and a white Southerner and remained active in Democratic politics. Johnston marched with and associated with Confederate veterans while he battled with Jefferson Davis and Confederate officers about memories of the war—particularly his own reputation as a commander. Johnston promoted the Lost Cause and publicly idolized its patron saint, Robert E. Lee, and prominent memorials to his memory, but Johnston also served as symbolic master of ceremonies at the 1876 Philadelphia Centennial Exposition, one of the strongest rituals of reunited U.S. nationalism. Johnston endorsed the Confederate battle flag (which he helped create) as a symbol of the South, but he also created public demonstrations of sectional reconciliation such as when he shook hands with General William T. Sherman at a national railroad convention in 1875. Johnston belonged to Civil War veterans' organizations, but he was also the only former Confederate officer ever to be offered an affiliate membership in the Grand Army of the Republic. Always keenly concerned to protect his own reputation and place in Civil War memory, Johnston seemed to accept every invitation that gave him a role in public commemoration in both the North and the South.

Johnston also played a huge role in public funerals and their connection to Civil War memory. Johnston, who retained good health into his eighties, had the chance to attend dozens of funerals for fellow officers during the 1880s, but his most famous role as a funeral mourner came not for his comrades in arms but for his former Civil War enemies. He especially distinguished himself as a public mourner and a pallbearer at the funerals of *Union* officers. During the 1880s, Johnston engaged in Civil War funeral rituals that seemed to cast him in a true light of sectional reconciliation—he was a public symbol who consistently posed as a Confederate mourner for great military men of the Union. Johnston was a pallbearer for former Union commander President Ulysses S. Grant, Gen. George B. McClellan, President Chester Arthur, Gen. Henry Jackson Hunt, Adm. David Porter, and Gen. William T. Sherman.

This constant participation in public Civil War funerals gave Johnston a unique understanding of how politicized such funerals really could be. That Johnston paid so much attention to how he, himself, should be mourned amply demonstrates that public funerals for Civil War figures had taken on an outsize importance. Although he seemed to accept the political tensions that came with the ebb and flow of Civil War memory in his last years, when it came to his own funeral, Johnston insisted on trying to silence Civil War memory. When he passed away in 1891, the man who had constantly fought to maintain his military reputation directed that his funeral should contain no military trappings whatsoever. Johnston mandated only the simplest form of funeral service and directed his heirs that he should be buried without military fanfare or symbols; he wished to be quietly interred with his wife in Baltimore. In what was perhaps the ultimate sign that reconciliation trumped the Lost Cause for Johnston, he sought to suppress the use of himself as a Southern symbol upon his death. Whether or not he entirely intended it, his request for a quiet, simple funeral constituted a direct mandate to forget the Civil War.

Former Confederates were distressed by his decision and fought to reclaim Johnston as a symbol against his wishes. They technically obeyed him regarding his funeral and burial—all the while complaining in meetings and in the press about his decision to rob them of his mourning rituals of Confederate memorialization. And they immediately moved to ritually commemorate Johnston against his wishes after the fact. Confederate veterans' organizations petitioned Johnston's heirs to move his remains to Hollywood Cemetery, the location of 18,000 Confederate graves and monuments to the Lost Cause.[97] And, although nothing eventually came of the movement to reinter General Johnston, Confederate veteran organizations dedicated Memorial Day ceremonies to his memory around the South in the month after his death.

Just as in the case of Charles Sumner, Johnston's funeral and public mourning proved that forgetting could not be mandated. Even if a prominent, symbolic figure wanted to bury the memory of the war, his supporters might express their sectional feelings as they buried him. Reconciliation and sectionalism found battlegrounds in the funerals for public heroes, be they politicians or generals, as the American national ritual of fighting over the memory of the war by contesting the funerals of great men continued.

Joseph E. Johnston and Civil War Memory

Joseph E. Johnston, a Virginian born to a Revolutionary War veteran and a niece of Patrick Henry, graduated from West Point in 1829 alongside fellow Virginian Robert E. Lee. He rose quickly in the U.S. Army, soon outranking Lee, served in the Second Seminole War and the Mexican-American War, and was promoted to brigadier general when he was appointed quartermaster general of the army in June 1860. Johnston had been wounded in battle and was experienced as an engineer, an artillery officer, and a cavalry officer.[98]

When Virginia seceded from the United States in April 1861, Johnston resigned from the U.S. Army and accepted a commission as brigadier general in the Confederate army. Although many saw Johnston as a talented commander, his later Civil War career was mostly characterized by a series of retreats, missed opportunities, and surrender—the interpretation of which he would fight over for the next thirty years as he battled Jefferson Davis. As commander of the Department of Northern Virginia in late 1861 and early 1862, Johnston opposed the slow advances of George B. McClellan toward the Confederate capital at Richmond, withdrawing from Bull Run and then from Yorktown. In May 1862, Johnston attacked McClellan at Fair Oaks (Seven Pines) and was wounded. Robert E. Lee assumed command of Johnston's army and drove McClellan away from Richmond in the Seven Days' Campaign.[99]

After recuperating, Johnston was appointed commander of the Confederate Department of the West, responsible for overseeing Braxton Bragg and John C. Pemberton. Johnston failed with troops under his personal command to relieve Pemberton, who was besieged at Vicksburg, Mississippi, in 1863, and after Vicksburg fell to Ulysses S. Grant in July, Johnston also lost Jackson, Mississippi, to Grant's subordinate Gen. William T. Sherman. Despite nearly constant arguments between the two men, President Davis put Johnston in charge of Braxton Bragg's Army of Tennessee after Bragg's defeat at Chattanooga in December 1863. Johnston effectively slowed Sherman's march through Georgia in the spring and summer of 1864, but Johnston stoked Davis's ire by his frequent withdrawals that eventually allowed Sherman to advance. Davis replaced Johnston with Gen. John Bell Hood in July 1864, only to reluctantly reappoint Johnston to command in February 1865 after Sherman had inflicted great damage on Confederates in the Carolinas. After Robert E. Lee surrendered to Grant at Appomattox Court House on April 9, Johnston negotiated with Sherman at the Bennett House near Durham Station, North Carolina, and surrendered his army to Sherman on April 26, 1865.[100]

After the war, Johnston took an interest in railroads and ran a Savannah insurance business before moving to Richmond, Virginia, in 1877. He petitioned the federal government for the removal of citizenship sanctions against him as a former Confederate in 1876. Johnston's disabilities under the Fourteenth Amendment were removed in 1877, just in time for him to be elected to Congress (as a Democrat) to represent Richmond in 1878. In 1885, he was appointed U.S. railroad commissioner, a position that took him cross-country annually inspecting railroads for the Department of the Interior, then headed by Lucius Q. Lamar, the same Southerner who had eulogized Sumner. Ignoring a personal plea from William Sherman that Johnston be retained, former Union general President Benjamin Harrison removed Johnston from his railroad commissioner position in 1889. Johnston lived in Washington, D.C., for the remaining two and half years of his life, traveling occasionally for veterans' reunions or to attend military funerals.

Most of the historiographical debate about Joseph E. Johnston has centered on whether or not he was an effective general, and scholars have paid only slight attention to his larger relationship to Civil War memory. Johnston's feud with Jefferson Davis occupies an important place in biographical and military assessments of both men, and their conflicts during the war have been framed as helping to fuel a postwar battle over each man's military reputation. Johnston biographer Craig Symonds notes that the wartime conflicts between Johnston and Davis blossomed into a postwar "Battle of the Books," which Symonds identifies as "Johnston's greatest defeat."[101] The print battle, conducted in magazine and newspaper articles as well as books, centered around issues of personal reputation and blame for the failure of the Confederacy.[102] It also became part of the larger battle over reconciliation and Civil War memory.

Johnston's book *Narrative of Military Operations* (1874) criticized Davis extensively for poor military management, for flawed strategic thinking, for removing Johnston from command, and for a host of other ills. Johnston's version of the Lost Cause was a tale of failed politics. Confederates were doomed not because the Confederate army could never have defeated Union troops who outnumbered them but because of "neglect on the part of the Confederate States to prepare for a great war before its actual commencement" and because the government failed to ever effectively finance the war.[103] Johnston's book did not sell well, and it was poorly reviewed, but the public took notice of his critique of Davis and Confederate politics, which was republished in both Northern and Southern newspapers.[104]

Gen. John Bell Hood argued against Johnston's criticisms of his Tennessee campaign in letters to the press (and later in his own 1879 book *Advance and Retreat*), but Johnston, likewise, fought back.[105] Davis responded with vitriolic criticism of Johnston in his book *The Rise and Fall of the Confederate Government* (1881), which portrayed Johnston as ineffective, timid, and borderline insubordinate at every turn.[106] Johnston fired back at Davis in press interviews, implying that he could still release damning evidence against Davis he had withheld from the 1874 book and accusing Davis of stealing Confederate gold reserves at the end of the war.[107]

Johnston battled in print to preserve his personal reputation, but all the books and articles played an important role in the overall rise of Civil War military memory in U.S. print culture at the end of the 1870s and beginning of the 1880s. The Johnston-Davis battle was part of the rising tide of books written by and about Civil War military men that came to dominate the literary marketplace for Civil War memory in those years, replacing popular histories with veterans' memories and a focus on battles. Alice Fahs and David Blight have identified this profusion of books as a key factor in the rise of a reconciliationist war memory that emphasized the common sacrifice of Civil War soldiers at the expense of the memory of the war as a larger social conflict.[108]

The Johnston-Davis dispute should remind us that there was still plenty of conflict in many of these publications: even if the overall effect of the print culture was to emphasize shared stories of sacrifice, the details and blame for that sacrifice continued to be negotiated. Johnston paid close attention to everything published about him and prepared careful rejoinders, lest his reputation be harmed.[109] In 1887, he told *Washington Post* editor W. A. Croffut in an interview: "I have been for many years misunderstood."[110] In the process of constantly trying to correct the record and raise his public reputation, Johnston also promoted a particular vision of Confederate military prowess and failures.

The rise of military memory in print culture reached new heights in the popular "Battles and Leaders" series published in *Century Magazine* between 1884 and 1887, and Johnston took his grievances against Davis straight into the pages of the magazine. David Blight stresses how the *Century Magazine* series de-emphasized ideology by featuring articles penned by both Northern and Southern officers, which were extremely popular both in the magazine and subsequently when published in book form.[111] But Johnston used his articles in *Century* to respond to Davis's memoir and to continue his own vision of the war and the Lost Cause; his 1884 article on the war titled

"Manassas to Seven Pines" was framed as "a reply to Jefferson Davis."[112] In the article, Johnston associated himself closely with Robert E. Lee, convincing the magazine's publishers to end his piece with a twinned portrait of the two generals taken after the war.[113] Johnston argued with *Century* editor Robert U. Johnston about the details of battle maps, proofreading, and other issues, but he accepted several $500 payments and continued to publish in the magazine over the next few years.[114]

Johnston's article "Opposing Sherman's Advance to Atlanta" (1887) continued to blast away at Davis for not sufficiently supporting the Confederate army and laid blame for Confederate defeat at the president's feet.[115] Although he had previously criticized Sherman in McClure's *Annals of the War* for being "extremely inaccurate" in his memoirs, in ? the *Century* Johnston cited "General Sherman's testimony" against Davis. Sherman's own article on the March to the Sea had appeared in the issue previous to Johnston's article.[116] The Johnston-Davis debate shows how contentious Civil War memory could be, even among those on the same side.

Surely, Johnston's personal bitterness and his vigorous, yearslong battle with Jefferson Davis form an important part of the larger outpouring of post-Reconstruction Civil War memory in print culture. But the Johnston-Davis clash in print formed only one aspect of each man's contribution to Civil War memory in that period. Scholars have made few connections between this print contest and the many other ways that Johnston contributed to Civil War memory in the aftermath of Reconstruction.

Johnston did more than write—he contributed to Civil War memory in many different forms. Johnston participated in the larger project of commemorating the Civil War and in the relationship of war memory to national identity. Besides his print war with Jefferson Davis, Johnston appeared in many other aspects of print culture related to the memory of the war, and he actively participated in a wide range of both Confederate rituals of commemoration and national pageants of reunion and reconciliation.

Johnston's high regard for his personal reputation and military memory certainly colored his participation in wider Civil War commemoration, but it cannot explain everything he did in the final seventeen years of his life. Ultimately, if all Johnston cared for were his military reputation, he never would have insisted on a small, quiet, civilian funeral for himself. Instead, Johnston's role in promoting the Lost Cause and his emphasis on national unity seem to have taught him a lesson about the fraught nature of Civil War memory that led him to ask the public to downplay his personal link to Confederate identity upon his death.

Johnston revered the Lost Cause, but he also sought reconciliation with the North, at times even on Northern terms as he participated in the U.S.

government and commemorated Sherman, Grant, and other Union officers. Johnston's position in the public fight for Civil War memory seemed fully able to contain both the Lost Cause and the Union Cause—he supported them both at different times, and he functioned as a symbol for both on the national stage. Johnston's public memory—and especially his funeral—show how his final decades contained both reconciliation and reunion, Lost Cause and Union Cause. Like American national identities themselves, Johnston was capable of containing contradictory ideas simultaneously.

Johnston's position as a promoter of the Lost Cause, who also engaged in rituals of reconciliation, put him in line with other former Confederates like John B. Gordon who, as Caroline Janney has argued, "believed they were free to observe, defend, and memorialize their cause when speaking to other white southerners" but would still engage in "gestures of reconciliation."[117] Where Johnston differed was in trying to tamp down the use of himself as a Lost Cause symbol upon his own death in March 1891. Johnston wished for a quiet burial with no Confederate symbolism, which would not create an opportunity for the Lost Cause to overwhelm the larger trend of reconciliation, unlike even Fitzhugh Lee, a former major general, who also mixed Lost Cause and reconciliationist memory but whose 1905 funeral turned into a post-Confederate commemoration that limited his memory as a national symbol.[118]

Johnston could not control memory, but his measured vision for his own funeral would have, if it had been pulled off, left him available as a national symbol. Nina Silber has argued that the complexity in national identity might best be appreciated if scholars move beyond the study of veterans, but Johnston shows that some veterans' public memories could absolutely feed the creation of a complex and contradictory national identity such as Silber describes.[119] Johnston simultaneously participated in the federal government and rituals of reunification and reconciliation while also being part of Lost Cause celebrations of the Confederacy—all of them serving different aspects of the "imaginative reconstitution" of the American nation.

Many average Confederate veterans revered Johnston. The praise Johnston lacked from some former Confederate politicians and commanders, he accepted from former enlisted men and civilians when he participated in Confederate commemorations and veterans' reunions. Between 1874 and 1891, Johnston helped to boost Lost Cause memories of the war, accepted public praise as a symbol of the Confederacy, and demonstrated that he felt a bond with his former soldiers. In return, he received public adulation from former Confederates. One veteran who invited Johnston to a reunion in Charleston in 1878 called him "the living Confederate Commander in whom the Southern people never lost confidence during the sadness and anguish of war, and for whom they cherish a love, which only grows stronger, as the years pass."[120]

When Johnston presented a student medal at Richmond College in 1877, a former Confederate captain presented him with a bouquet of magnolias as the "tribute of . . . esteem" from "a few of your friends—a thousand or more, and still a very few as compared with the whole number of those who love and honor you."[121] When he led the 1879 Decoration Day parade in Winchester, Virginia, to the unveiling of two Confederate monuments, Johnston was "repeatedly cheered along the line of march."[122] Johnston was lauded when he attended Confederate veterans' reunions, such as the large gathering in Atlanta in October 1880 and the Richmond reunion in October 1887.[123]

Although in failing health, Johnston returned to Atlanta for a veterans' reunion slated for the anniversary of his surrender to Sherman in 1890 because he desired "to meet my old companions, and I wished very much to see them."[124] Common veterans in Atlanta returned the sentiment when they shouted out for "Old Joe" in the streets, surrounded his carriage by the hundreds, and pulled it by hand along the parade route—moving Johnston to tears.[125] Johnston, who indeed had always been popular with his subordinates, could function as an effective object of Confederate veneration.

Johnston also lent his personal symbolic appeal to the dedication of many Confederate monuments, which were occasions for both elite and popular war memory to mix in a potent series of public rituals.[126] He became a visible presence at monument dedications, especially as these dedications became an important part of increasingly intense Confederate celebration from the 1870s onward.[127] In 1875, Johnston served as lead marshal for two huge parades at the dedication of memorials: the Confederate monument in Savannah, Georgia, and the statue of Stonewall Jackson in Richmond, Virginia.[128] He also attended the unveiling of the Stonewall Jackson monument in Nashville, Tennessee, in 1880.[129] Johnston sat on the platform at the dedication of the Confederate veterans' monument in Alexandria, Virginia, in May 1889.[130]

Most notably, Johnston played key roles related to the two most important monuments to Robert E. Lee and the Lost Cause: the sepulchral monument at Lee's grave at Washington College and the monumental equestrian statue in his honor in Richmond, Virginia. Johnston served as an officer of the Lee Monument Association that commissioned Edward Valentine to sculpt a funereal monument to Lee in 1871. Johnston was unable to attend the statue's unveiling in 1883 because of an illness, but the monument became a long-lasting highlight of many a Lost Cause pilgrimage to Lee's burial site in the college chapel.[131]

Johnston did not miss his chance to play a pivotal role in the unveiling of Lee's Richmond monument on May 29, 1890. The monument's dedication was likely the largest Confederate commemorative gathering up until that time, with as many as 150,000 people participating in the large parade and festival.

Johnston played one of the most dramatic roles in the entire ceremony, flanked by amputee veterans as he pulled the cord to release a cloth, unveiling the monument to the sound of deafening cheers that "almost drowned the boom of the cannon" firing a hundred-gun salute.[132] Johnston surely lent himself to the glorification of the Lost Cause.

What might be missed, however, by concentrating only on how Johnston contributed to Confederate Lost Cause memory, is that during the same years that he built up the Lost Cause he also performed important public rituals of reconciliation that worked to rebuild American national identity with a distinctly pro-Union flavor. The American public had frequent opportunity to read in the newspapers about Johnston's participation in commemorations as a model of the reconciling Confederate.

In popular culture, Johnston sometimes symbolized the reunification of the nation. At the national railroad convention in St. Louis in 1875, Johnston and Sherman shook hands on the speakers' platform as "gentlemen arose in their seats, waved their hats and cheered until exhausted."[133] The handshake (with nary a "bloody chasm" in sight) was widely commented on in the press, as was the chorus of objections that rang out from the same crowd when Jefferson Davis was invited to the dais.[134] Johnston was elected the ceremonial master of ceremonies at the opening of the Centennial Exposition in Philadelphia to celebrate the one hundredth anniversary of the nation in 1876.[135] He also participated at the national veterans' encampment at Marietta, Ohio, in September 1877.[136] It is perhaps not surprising that Johnston would play some role in rituals of unity, especially since he served in Congress and in other federal posts from 1878 until 1888, but service as a Democrat in the U.S. government did not mandate participation in rituals of union and reconciliation. Joseph E. Johnston chose to associate with Union memory to an unusual degree.

Johnston also received an unprecedented level of admiration from Northern veterans in 1888 when a Philadelphia post of the GAR voted to give him "honorary membership" in their organization. The many newspaper reports about the actions of the E. D. Baker Post noted that Johnston was "the only ex-Confederate soldier who has ever been received into the ranks of a Grand Army post," not surprising since the GAR was a pro-Union and Republican fraternal organization.[137]

The Baker post's move outraged some, who could not accept the notion of Johnston affiliating with the GAR and who would not stretch their memories of the Union Cause far enough to allow for praise for the former Confederate general. The lieutenant governor of New York objected to the Philadelphia post welcoming Johnston and insisted at a public dinner in Albany that only honorably discharged Union sailors and soldiers could enter the GAR on any terms.[138] The Stanton Post GAR in Los Angeles passed resolutions against the

Baker post's move to admit Johnston, declaring him "entirely unfit to become a member either honorary or otherwise."[139]

Johnston took to the papers to explain that the whole thing was a misunderstanding: he never meant to apply for honorary membership to the post, but actually wrote to it in order to donate ten dollars to the Baker Post's memorial efforts, an action that may have added him to the "contributing member" rolls.[140] Nonetheless, the Baker post was rebuked by Frank J. Magee, the Pennsylvania state commander of the GAR, for associating Johnston with the organization, and Magee pointed out that neither contributing nor honorary memberships were sanctioned by the GAR organization.[141] Regardless, the fact that Johnston contributed to the GAR and that he could even be talked about as an affiliate of any kind shows how he deeply he could be engaged as a symbol of reconciliation, even as he also supported the Lost Cause.

Although GAR members took part in reconciliationist Blue-Gray reunions, several scholars have noted that the GAR, overall, was one of the strongest bastions of sectional Union memory.[142] The notion of Johnston, as a former Confederate general, being associated in any way with the GAR showed him to be one of the former Confederates closest to the Union Cause in reconciliation memory. Not even James Longstreet, who, unlike Johnston, became a Republican and who even incurred post-Confederate ire by criticizing Robert E. Lee, ever became affiliated with the GAR.[143]

Johnston's most important role in reconciliationist war memory was his participation as a pallbearer at numerous funerals for important Union military officers between 1885 and 1891, a practice that ended just weeks before his own funeral. Johnston may have been solicited by the Baker post as friendly to Union memory in the first place because he had forged a reputation as a public symbol of reconciliation through a very high-profile presence as a pallbearer at important public funerals for Union officers. One Atchison, Kansas, newspaper noted in 1891 that "Gen. Joseph E. Johnston has a record as a pall bearer that is unparalleled."[144]

Even as he paid homage to the Lost Cause in other ways, Johnston did not take a central role at major Confederate funerals. Johnston did not attend Robert E. Lee's funeral in 1870, although he did deliver a eulogy in Savannah at the commemoration of Lee's death there, and he became the president of the Lee Memorial Association.[145] Nor did Johnston attend any of the elaborate 1889 funeral ceremonies for his old nemesis, Confederate president Jefferson Davis.[146]

Beginning with the massive funeral for Ulysses S. Grant in 1885, however, Johnston became a regular pallbearer at ceremonial funerals for Union officers, and his presence at these rituals functioned publicly as a symbol of Confederate reconciliation. Johnston acted as a visible sign of Confederate reconciliation by paying tribute to Grant and playing a key role in the huge national pageant of mourning in his honor. Joan Waugh has shown how Grant's massive funeral in New York City, attended by more than a million people and accompanied by additional ceremonies around the country, was a "benchmark event for sectional reconciliation" albeit with an emphasis on Union victory.[147]

As a symbol of reconciliation, President Cleveland appointed Johnston and fellow former Confederate general Simon Buckner to be pallbearers at Grant's funeral alongside Union generals William T. Sherman and Philip Sheridan.[148] Upon Grant's death in July 1885, Northern newspapers reported "southern sympathy" for his passing by quoting comments Johnston made about Grant's command bringing "the Civil War to a close sooner than it otherwise could have been accomplished" and Johnston's view that "the Southern people feel kindly and have always felt kindly towards Gen. Grant."[149]

On August 8, Johnston marched with Grant's casket through New York City streets thronged with viewers for the miles-long funeral procession, which included thousands of Union veterans, but also four companies of Confederate veterans marching in the parade line.[150] The papers reported that Generals Johnston and Buckner "clasped hands over the blue-covered coffin" with Generals Sherman and Sheridan: "Here were Sherman and Johnston the two great enemies who closed the war" clasping hands in peace over the body of Grant.[151] Charles Sumner's worry that Grant would serve as a permanently divisive "flag of war" was proved at least partially wrong as his funeral included scenes of exactly the kind of reconciliation Sumner would have approved of. The papers also widely reported that after the funeral was over, Johnston spent hours at the Fifth Avenue Hotel with General Sheridan and other Union and Confederate officers "talking over the war and the life and character of Gen. Grant."[152]

Over the next few years, Johnston often played a similarly prominent role in the public mourning for his other former military foes. Just a few months after Grant's funeral, Johnston reprised his role as pallbearer when former U.S. general George McClellan passed away. McClellan requested a quiet, civilian funeral at New York's Madison Avenue Presbyterian Church before being buried in Trenton, New Jersey. Although McClellan's funeral was far less elaborate and ceremonial than Grant's, the press still reported on every detail for public consumption—including the consolation telegram Johnston sent to Mrs. McClellan and her selection of Johnston as one of the pallbearers.[153] Unlike at Grant's funeral, Johnston was the only Confederate to be afforded a public role at McClellan's service. All the other pallbearers were U.S. military men, and the papers made no distinction between them and Johnston in the list of attendants.

Coming right in the middle of his 1885 print feud with Jefferson Davis, it seemed Johnston was more willing to be aligned with the memory of his old Union opponent than with the Confederate president. Just over a year later, when Johnston attended the funeral of former U.S. president Chester Arthur, the papers noted that he stayed on the same hotel floor as Sherman, giving them a chance to renew their fellowship.[154] In February 1889, Johnston served as an honorary pallbearer for Gen. Henry Jackson Hunt, the former chief artillery officer of the Army of the Potomac, and Johnston helped to spearhead a fundraising appeal for Hunt's widow.[155]

In the last few months of his own life in 1891, Johnston intensified his public identification with Union military funerals by serving within the same week as a high-profile pallbearer both for William T. Sherman and for Adm. David Porter. When Sherman died in New York on February 14, 1891, the papers immediately reprinted Johnston's condolences to Sherman's family.[156] Admiral Porter, who died the day before, was laid to rest in Washington, D.C., on February 17, as the Sherman family was waiting for William's son Thomas to arrive from England before conducting his funeral. A longtime friend of his nemesis in the Vicksburg campaign, Johnston acted as a pallbearer for Porter's public funeral in Washington, D.C., the only former Confederate given a public role at the ceremony.[157] Johnston served as a pallbearer for Sherman's large ceremonial funeral in New York City two days later on February 19, and he accompanied Sherman's funeral party on the long train ride to St. Louis for the funeral celebration and burial there.[158]

Johnston's role as Sherman's pallbearer stood out as an especially strong symbol of national reunion and reconciliation in the press. The *Topeka Weekly Capital* editorialized after Sherman's burial that "nothing could illustrate . . . the disposition of the heroes of the war to forget their mutual animosities and contradictory purposes" better than the image of Johnston serving as a pallbearer for Sherman.[159]

Several times since 1865, Sherman and Johnston had symbolized reconciliation at ceremonial occasions, and Sherman wrote to Johnston just a month before his death that "you and I became reconciled in April 1865; have remained so ever since with no apologies or concealments."[160] The *New York Times* sought to reassure its readers that although it might seem odd to have Johnston as Sherman's pallbearer because, unlike all the others, "he fought on the Southern side in the war of the rebellion," it was fine because Johnston was such a regular presence at important Union funerals: "At Gen. Grant's funeral he rode in the same carriage with Gen. Sherman."[161] The editors of the Democratic *New York Age* were not so sure, noting their surprise to see Johnston as a pallbearer for Sherman, since Johnston was just the kind of enemy Sherman had pledged to kill or remove from the country in 1862.[162]

The *Chicago Daily Tribune* simply noted that "Johnston and other military dignitaries" paid respect to Sherman's remains, without noting that Johnston stood out among the "dignitaries" as the only former Confederate.[163]

Johnston's identification with Union funerals indicated how sectional feeling could weave in and out of strong expressions of both reunion and reconciliation. Johnston simultaneously embraced the Lost Cause and served as a tangible symbol of reconciliation. Northern observers could, therefore, see in Johnston's public mourning career evidence of Southern capitulation, while still finding in him something to be admired as a sentimental Southern hero. Upon Johnston's death in 1891, for example, the *Nation* magazine likened him to Robert E. Lee in that "he put the war utterly behind him and used his great influence with the Southern people to renew the national allegiance in good faith. . . . Each so honestly helped to rebuild the new nationality on freedom and brotherhood that the whole nation has joined in rehabilitating them, and we bury them as honored fellow-citizens."[164] Of course, it helped Johnston's own reputation if officers like Sherman and McClellan, who had beaten him, were seen as towering military talents. If his foes were heroic and worthy, it was less humiliating to have succumbed to them.

Mourning Johnston

Johnston's own funeral in March 1891 demonstrated that it was impossible for any Civil War figure to completely control how he or she was remembered. After almost two decades of participating in seemingly contradictory Civil War commemorations, it is not surprising that Johnston's own public funeral contained huge contradictions of Civil War memory. Just like Charles Sumner, Johnston could not be used as a straightforward symbol for his side's cause.

Unlike Charles Sumner, however, Johnston applied the mandate to forget the Civil War to himself. Perhaps Johnston's final and greatest embrace of reconciliationist memory was to call for a quiet civilian funeral for himself and thereby to deny the kind of public display of Confederate memory that composed such a large part of the Lost Cause by 1891. Just like Sumner, Johnston could not control his own reputation or how it interacted with the Civil War memories he had helped to create, and he could not mandate the suppression of Civil War memory. Confederate veterans mourned him in ceremonies of Lost Cause memory that contradicted his own wishes.

The national press in 1891, along with many subsequent historians, emphasized that Johnston's embrace of reconciliation materially contributed to his death. Journalists and historians alike have maintained that Johnston was killed by a cold he contracted while performing his duty and catching a chill as a pallbearer at Sherman's burial, ignoring the facts that he had been in poor health for more than a year and that the common cold is caused by a nonlethal virus. Gen. Oliver Otis Howard, who superintended Sherman's St. Louis funeral, wrote a colorful version of the story in his 1908 memoir. Howard claimed that as the pallbearers stood outside Sherman's home with heads uncovered one onlooker told Johnston, "General, put your hat on, you will take cold." But Johnston refused, saying, "If I were in his place and he standing here in mine he would not put on his hat." Howard interpreted the move as signifying Johnston's "deep regard for Sherman. . . . In fact, these two, after their campaign was over, behaved toward each other as brothers."[165]

Howard's assertion, which dramatically reinforced that Johnston's reconciliation with Sherman killed him, has been repeated by every one of Johnston's modern biographers. But no evidence beyond Howard's memoir supports the story. Johnston's contemporaries did not report Johnston refusing to cover his head, even when they embraced the irony of his dying so soon after, perhaps because of, paying his respects to Sherman. Ken Burns featured Johnston's exposure at Sherman's funeral as a poignant moment in the final episode of his epic Civil War documentary series. The historians who repeat Howard's story all ignore the facts that Johnston could not have caught a cold by standing bareheaded, and, even if he could have, it would not have killed him.[166] Nevertheless, at least since 1908, the public has relished the story that Johnston was killed by his reconciling regard for Sherman. The story of reconciliation at Sherman's funeral has continued to shape public memory.

Johnston did not want to become a public symbol upon his own death. As someone who had taken a huge role in public mourning, he forbade any of his own. Johnston had expressed strong wishes to his friends and relatives that no military ceremony was to accompany his funeral, and they took pains to see that his wishes were enforced, even though these wishes silenced Confederate efforts to venerate his remains.

Because Johnston had no children, and his wife, Lydia McLane Johnston, had died in 1887, funeral arrangements were made by his brother-in-law, former Maryland governor Robert McLane, along with Johnston's great-nephew George Johnston, a Richmond physician. They arranged for St. John's Episcopal Church in Washington, D.C., Johnston's parish, to be the site of the service and for Johnston's remains to be unceremoniously transferred to Green Mount Cemetery in Baltimore for burial in the family plot. After Johnston's death was announced, only one simple black draping decorated his house in Washington, D.C., where he lay in an upstairs bedroom "attired in an ordinary civilian's suit of plain black and placed in a casket devoid of ornaments" awaiting burial. The family chose Confederate veterans residing in Washington, D.C., who had served under Johnston, as his active pallbearers and a mix of U.S. politicians and U.S. and Confederate military men as honorary pallbearers, but requested that all appear only in civilian dress.[167] A Baltimore Confederate veterans' association led by Gen. Bradley T. Johnson voted to attend Johnston's D.C. funeral and ceremonially accompany the body to Baltimore for burial, but Johnston's family refused them. They also declined the offer of Virginia's Governor McKinney to attend the funeral with a military escort.[168]

Despite pressure from several Confederate veterans' groups, Johnston's wishes for civilian honors were followed at his March 24 funeral service, transportation to Baltimore, and burial. The plainness of the funeral was remarkable, even more than for other former Civil War officers who had expressed wishes for simple burial rites. The *New York Times*, just like papers all over the country, told its readers that "all the ceremonies will be simple and devoid of display, this being the express wish of the dead man and his relatives."[169] Johnston's oft-repeated wish for a simple service took effect: "Though the church was filled with battle-scarred veterans, there was not a uniform visible to announce the fact." St. John's was decorated with only one wreath of immortelle flowers on the plain coffin, and the Episcopal service with no sermon moved the "imminent men" and old veterans, both Confederate and Union, to tears.[170] As one paper remarked, "There was nothing to distinguish the funeral from a private interment beyond the large attendance of distinguished persons."[171] Oliver O. Howard remarked that Johnston "had a military escort of Confederate friends but without arms," as all the "veteran soldiers" obeyed Johnston's final order that he be treated as a civilian.[172] One Minnesota newspaper declared that Johnston's funeral was an excellent sign that the war had ended, at last.[173]

The extreme lack of ceremony for Johnston stood in stark contrast to every other ceremonial funeral procession for a major Civil War figure, including Charles Sumner. No pomp and ceremony was allowed to follow his body. His remains were placed on the regular 12:10 P.M. train to Baltimore—housed in a pine box in the baggage car—with the honorary pallbearers following on a later train.[174] At the Baltimore station, when train workers and undertakers' assistants unceremoniously placed the box containing Johnston's coffin on a cart to move it to the hearse, Maryland Confederate veterans standing by were offended and "stepped forward, uninvited" to carry it to the hearse.[175] Confederate veterans of Baltimore who had served under Johnston wanted to parade his remains from the train station to his grave, but because, as the *New Orleans Daily Picayune* put it "they obeyed his command" for simplicity, they restricted themselves to standing in the train station with uncovered heads.[176] The procession from Baltimore's Union Station to Johnston's grave site at Green Mount Cemetery contained just the hearse and two carriages.[177] Johnston's last wish for a simple funeral—one without symbols of Confederate memory or any military symbols whatsoever—was observed.

But that did not mean that Confederate veterans' organizations and other keepers of Lost Cause memory were happy about it or willing to cede Johnston as a Confederate symbol. Alabama congressman Joseph Wheeler, himself a former Confederate officer, wrote to Johnston just a few days before his death, urging the general: "Take good care of yourself, for there are few men whom the old Confederates need as much and who are regarded with as much respect and affection as yourself."[178] Confederate veterans seemed to need Johnston just as much after death, and many organized mourning ceremonies to correspond with his funeral and burial.

Despite Johnston's wishes, former Confederates immediately began to commemorate him. The Confederate Veterans' Associations of North Carolina, the Maryland Confederate Society, the M. B. Forrest Camp of Confederate Veterans in Chattanooga, and veterans in Savannah, New Orleans, and New York City all expressed public mourning upon the announcement of Johnston's death.[179] During Johnston's funeral, flags on government buildings in Montgomery, Alabama, flew at half-staff as artillery fired a ceremonial salute, and the Arkansas legislature adjourned in Johnston's honor.[180]

Beyond just expressing their own sense of grief, veterans in Baltimore publicly protested the choice to bury Johnston without any military honors or memory. The *Washington Post* reported the day after Johnston's burial that ex-Confederates in Baltimore "were roused to a high pitch of indignation on account of the simplicity and apparent disrespectful manner in which the burial of Joseph E. Johnston was conducted. . . . To say that the ex-Confederates were angry at being deprived of the opportunity of paying the last sad tribute to the Southern chieftain would be putting it mildly." The Baltimore Confederate Society held a public meeting after Johnston's burial, and "speeches were made severely criticizing the manner in which the Johnston funeral had been conducted in this city."[181] Confederate veterans in Baltimore sniped at Johnston's relatives for following his own burial wishes.

The Robert E. Lee Camp No. 1, Confederate Veterans, the veterans' group in Richmond that was playing a pivotal role that same year in the creation of the national Sons of Confederate Veterans organization, took the most aggressive action to reclaim Johnston's memory from his own wishes for silence. Upon hearing of Johnston's death, the Lee Camp draped its hall in Richmond in mourning cloth, and members encouraged Richmond city officials to endorse resolutions and fire mourning guns honoring the dead general.[182] Members of the Lee Camp quietly attended Johnston's service in Washington, D.C., without wearing Confederate uniforms or making outward demonstrations of Confederate memory. But in the week after his burial, the Lee Camp renewed its attentions to Johnston's memory and decided to take more direct action: they proposed that Sunday, April 26 (the twenty-sixth anniversary of his surrender to Sherman), should be declared as a special memorial day on which Southerners, and especially veterans, would commemorate Joseph E. Johnston.[183] An illustrious Confederate general, no matter how controversial his command decisions may have been, could not be allowed to perish without public ceremony.

The Lee Camp also did not consider Johnston's burial a finished matter, and it sought to bring him to Richmond, hoping to further its growing civic identity as the resting place of Confederate memory. On April 2, the Lee Camp convened a civic meeting at the Richmond chamber of commerce, presided over by the city's mayor, at which those present resolved that Virginia had special claim to mourn General Johnston and proposed to reinter his remains in Richmond.[184] Nine days later, Johnston's executor, James L. McLane, communicated to the Richmond authorities that if "the united voice of his comrades in the armies of the South . . . demand that his body be entrusted to their keeping and placed with appropriate honors in his native State, near the capital of the late Confederacy," he and the rest of Johnston's family would consider the reinterment, even though it directly countered Johnston's will.[185] Burying Johnston at Hollywood Cemetery would include him in the highly visible pantheon of Southern heroes. Johnston's body was never moved to Richmond. Perhaps as a substitute relic, his great-nephew did donate his war-torn saddle and some other items to the Confederate Memorial Literary Society, an offshoot of the Ladies' Hollywood Memorial Association, for the new museum it was establishing in the old Davis executive mansion at Richmond.[186]

Meanwhile, on April 26, veterans' organizations around the South sponsored commemorative exercises for Johnston, as requested by the Lee Camp. The Raleigh newspaper bade its readers to gather at the Metropolitan Hall for services: "Let us come from our homes this evening and unite in a solemn service in commemoration of this great Southern captain who has so lately passed away."[187] The Richmond memorial service included veterans arrayed in Confederate uniform gathered to hear Rev. S. A. Goodwin especially praise in his oration the bravery of the men who followed Johnston.[188] Services in Johnston's honor were also held on that day in New Orleans; Charleston; Shreveport; and West Point, Mississippi.[189] Washington, D.C., veterans followed with another Johnston memorial service in mid-May.[190] Baltimore veterans also placed special floral tributes upon Johnston's grave in June during their regular Memorial Day ceremonies in that city.[191] Publications also spread the assertive Lost Cause memorialization of Johnston, allowing Southerners to read about commemorations and sermons in his honor. The *Southern Historical Papers* published a long story about the Richmond funeral commemoration sponsored by the Lee Camp and included lengthy biographical reminiscences in Johnston's honor.[192]

By holding up Johnston after his death as a paragon of the Lost Cause, even in contradiction to his express wishes, former Confederates tied themselves to a Southern version of American national identity that made room for memories of Confederate glory even as they acknowledged that the war was lost and the country reunited. Former Confederates could not allow Johnston to merely be buried quietly because they needed him as a public symbol of Confederate heroism, and public mourning was an essential part of creating him as a hero.

Anthony Toomer Porter, a former Confederate chaplain and prominent Charleston, South Carolina, Episcopal minister, exemplified this combination of nationalism and Lost Cause ideology in a sermon preached to a veterans' organization in honor of Johnston during the April 26 Memorial Day celebration in that city. Porter framed his praise of Johnston as "an incentive to our rising generation to emulate his heroic virtue" and noted that Southerners only worshipped heroes who were truly men of merit, such as Johnston and Robert E. Lee.[193] Porter denounced the "money loving . . . spirit of the age" and prescribed the memory of tragic heroes of the Confederacy as an antidote to the spirit of modernity that would sap the vital manhood of the rising generation.[194] Porter claimed Johnston as a noble, though doomed, Confederate whose memory would embolden younger men—all in a hail of Lost Cause images that ennobled the nostalgic Confederate past.

But Porter also recognized that praising Johnston was a way for former Confederates to connect themselves to a reunited United States. He framed the Lost Cause as an essential part of the greatness of America—as exemplified by Joseph E. Johnston's "admiration of the bravery of his opponents." When "a great people rose to assert their independence" but failed, men like Johnston knew how to reunite respectfully with Northerners while retaining the noble cause of Southern heroism. Porter recognized that by acting as a pallbearer for Ulysses S. Grant, Johnston "consented to be a citizen of this country," and that Johnston further proved his admiration for the United States by attending Sherman's body at his funeral. Porter called Johnston's pallbearing for Sherman "the crowning act of a great life" and urged his fellow former Confederates to take Johnston's example of how to live in peace in a post-Reconstruction United States.[195]

Porter's mourning for Joseph E. Johnston reconciled the Lost Cause with U.S. national identity by giving the South a special role in the peaceful, reunited nation. Porter was able to integrate the seemingly contradictory strands of Civil War memory that flowed from Johnston's reputation more smoothly than the general himself had anticipated. Johnston created Lost Cause memory but also embraced reconciliation in a way that suggested to him that his own funeral should be silent and lack the trappings of Confederate symbolism. Organizations that would soon become among the most important promoters of the Lost Cause into the twentieth century—the Lee Camp, the Southern Historical Papers, and the Confederate Memorial Literary Society—objected and loudly claimed Johnston as a Confederate symbol. They wanted to promote a version of American national identity that had a large space for heroes of the Lost Cause and for a South steeped in Confederate memory.

Both Charles Sumner and Joseph E. Johnston wanted to publicly forget parts of the Civil War in the interest of sectional reconciliation and to save their own reputations. But their funerals show how their sectional partisans could not afford to let them lie in peace. Even as prominent and powerful men, neither Sumner nor Johnston could control which parts of the past would be forgotten or remembered. Their own symbolic actions and the fights over the meanings of their deaths all contributed to the imagined reconstitution of the nation—a nation that strained to contain reconciliation, reunion, and continued tensions over race and section. Public mourning showed how national identity was sometimes composed of contradiction itself.

Chapter 5

Extraordinary Demonstrations of Respect

Frederick Douglass, Winnie Davis, and
Standards of Public Grief

After Frederick Douglass died on February 20, 1895, the *American Missionary* magazine noted the unprecedented nature of the public mourning offered to the formerly enslaved abolitionist, political activist, U.S. government official, orator, and writer: "The unexpected and sudden death of Mr. Douglass has awakened a sense of profound sympathy never before expressed toward a person identified with the negro race, and seldom toward one of the white race." The Congregationalist magazine that had supported abolitionism and many of the other causes championed by Douglass expressed no shock that Black Americans expressed "profound respect and sorrow" at Douglass's death, but the editors were pleasantly surprised "that the white race has shown almost equal regard for his memory, by their attendance when he lay in state in Washington, and when his body was interred in Rochester. The press has voiced the sentiment of the nation in the full and eulogistic notices of his life."[1]

Within hours of Frederick Douglass's sudden death from a heart attack, he was the subject of a huge outpouring of public grief—the type of which had never been lavished upon a Black man before in the United States but which was very familiar to those who had mourned great white men.[2] Days after Douglass's death, businesses and schools in Washington, D.C., closed as crowds thronged the Metropolitan African Methodist Episcopal (AME) church for his public funeral—an hours-long service attended by thousands of dignitaries. Douglass's body was then processed through the streets and transported via train to Rochester, New York, his home before the Civil War. In Rochester, Douglass lay in state at City Hall before another large funeral at the Presbyterian Central Church. Douglass's remains were then paraded to Rochester's Mount Hope Cemetery, where his first wife would also be reinterred next to him. A Rochester memorial association immediately formed and began planning to construct a monument to Douglass—also a first for a Black American.[3]

Mourning Douglass was a national effort: obituaries appeared in newspapers across the country, and within weeks public civic and religious services were held in his honor, accompanied by speeches and memorial resolutions, in more than twenty cities from Boston, Massachusetts, to Oskaloosa, Iowa, from Richmond, Virginia, to Tacoma, Washington. Black citizens mourned Douglass to celebrate racial uplift, and they were joined by many sympathetic white mourners. Even in the South and among Democrats and whites who were not sympathetic to Black rights, there was grudging respect for Douglass and an admission that his death was noteworthy.

Public mourning for Frederick Douglass was extremely significant in 1895, and his stands as one of the most important public funerals in the aftermath of the Civil War. The very fact that Douglass qualified as enough of a national hero to receive an outpouring of public grief signified that emancipationist memory of the Civil War had not faded away in 1895 and that the national identities created by public funerals had expanded enough to include an African American subject. Paradoxically, Douglass's funeral commemorations would also prove that the cultural force of reconciliationist white supremacy was very strong—his memory was contested, and funeral rites provided a chance for racists to voice their versions of Civil War memory and national identity, as well. But even the racist backlash provided evidence of the extreme national importance of public mourning for Frederick Douglass.

Anyone who had participated in one of the large festivals of mourning over the previous forty-five years, or really anyone who regularly read the newspaper, would have recognized the funerals and mourning rites that were lavished upon Frederick Douglass. There was a sameness to the public rituals for Douglass, who received all the hallmarks of public mourning that funerals for great men before him had established as proper: eulogies, floral tributes, special train travel, crowds observing the body, and more. But there was a radicalism in the sameness of Douglass's funeral and mourning—bestowing upon a formerly enslaved Black man the forms of public grief and national memory that statesmen, heroes, and even presidents had demanded for decades.

The funerals and mourning for Frederick Douglass in 1895 marked a radical departure in the politics of public grief, even though the forms of public commemoration for Douglass were nationally familiar, and the function remained tied to the "imagined reconstitution of the nation." Funeral ceremonies that had defined great, white heroes for decades took on new meaning as they were used for Douglass—a Black man, a hero of his race. Much has been written about Douglass, about his abolitionism, his philosophy and politics, his oratory and activism. Putting a close focus on his funeral rites, which have received much less scholarly attention, allows us to capture the moments when Douglass fully ascended into the pantheon of national heroes—albeit not without a fight from white supremacists who did not want to see men like him there.[4]

Just three years later, another unprecedented funeral that also displayed the familiar tropes of public mourning in new ways took place, the 1898 pub-

N. Clark Smithe, "Frederick Douglass Funeral March," 1895. Library of Congress, Rare Book and Special Collections Division, Alfred Whital Stern Collection of Lincolniana.

lic tributes to Varina "Winnie" Davis. Davis, the youngest daughter of Confederate president Jefferson Davis and first lady Varina Davis, was born in Richmond in 1864 in the Confederate "White House" and was known as "the Daughter of the Confederacy" because of her frequent appearances with her father at veterans' events and celebrations. Winnie Davis served as a feminine embodiment of Lost Cause ideology, and her 1898 death occasioned elaborate public funeral rites. Winnie Davis received the largest public funeral for a woman associated with the Civil War—and likely for any American woman—up until the twentieth century. After having her remains moved cross-country on a special train for funeral services in Richmond, Davis was buried in Hollywood Cemetery with full military honors, which was, as one newspaper put it, "a rare thing for a woman to have."[5]

It was, in fact, unheard of for any American woman to receive public mourning that included such lavish ceremony, complete with mourning rituals across several states, a miles-long funeral procession in Richmond, the formation of a monument society, and countrywide news coverage. The Washington, D.C., *Evening Star* claimed in the run-up to Winnie Davis's Richmond ceremony: "It will be one of the most remarkable funerals ever held in Richmond, where so many elaborate ceremonies of the kind have taken place."[6] Another Tennessee newspaper noted that Winnie Davis's funeral "was one of the most remarkable ceremonies of the kind ever seen in the south."[7] Commenting on the unprecedented nature of Davis's public funeral, Confederate general John B. Gordon in his role as commander in chief of the United Confederate Veterans said that the "ovations" that greeted her from Southern veterans all over "were such as have rarely been accorded any woman."[8]

Gordon's statement, speaking as a Confederate veteran on behalf of the mourning conducted by Confederate veterans, emphasized that a process of contested reconciliation analogous to what was taking place in the public funerals for Frederick Douglass was also at work in the rituals in honor of Winnie Davis. The pageantry of mourning for Winnie Davis in 1898 also showed how funeral rites prompted the expression of competing national narratives about Civil War memory. Gordon, the former Confederate veteran who had named Winnie Davis the Daughter of the Confederacy during her 1886 public tour of Georgia and Alabama, was among the most vocal proponents of the Lost Cause, but he also sometimes publicly mixed expressions of Lost Cause Southern exceptionalism with expressions of U.S. national pride when it suited his purpose.[9]

The same mixture was evident in the public mourning for Davis. Her funeral provided a massive opportunity for Lost Cause pageantry, but it also sometimes clothed that pro-Confederate memory in the language of national reconciliation. Confederate battle flags were plastered all over Winnie Davis's casket and displayed proudly during her funeral rituals, which featured strong themes of defiant Lost Cause memory, but mourning for her also allowed the Lost Cause to mix with notes of reconciliation.[10] Elvira Sydnor Miller wrote in her *Louisville Times* column about the funeral that it was wondrous Davis had "lived to see a reunited people" even as "the South bowed under a sorrow too eloquent for speech and too deep for tears."[11] Newspaper coverage of condolences to Varina Davis emphasized that messages flooded in "from all parts of the country."[12] The *Confederate Veteran* magazine wrote that "the press of the country teems with patriotic expressions because of the death of Miss Winnie Davis."[13] In this case, "patriotic" might mean both pro-Confederate and pro–United States.

This chapter analyzes the funerals and public mourning for Frederick Douglass and Winnie Davis to show how rituals of national grief opened up to include new kinds of people in the pantheon of national heroes. Since the 1850s, funerals had established public rituals of national grief that linked national memory, Civil War memory, and the creation of national identities. Now, at the turn of the twentieth century, public mourning rituals gave, for the first time, a Black man and a white woman power as national symbols. National reconciliation featured as a theme in mourning for both figures.

But the public recognition of the national importance of Frederick Douglass and Winnie Davis is certainly not a story of unalloyed inclusivity, and in each case reconciliation was also highly contested. The creation of national identities out of rituals of memory, the imagined reconstitution of the nation, expressed contradictory themes simultaneously: reconciliation and sectional defiance, Black pride and white supremacy. Douglass's public mourning occasioned several all-out fights over the meaning and terms of reconciliation and foreshadowed future battles about racialized Civil War memory. Douglass's funeral rites praised Black achievement and emancipationist Civil War memory, but his mourning was also appropriated by white supremacists who argued for their own version of reconciliation and even used Douglass backlash to promote Confederate commemoration. Winnie Davis's funeral showed signs of national reconciliation in the months after the conclusion of the Spanish-American War, but her rituals also emphasized that many former Confederates viewed national reconciliation as compatible with the Lost Cause and Southern exceptionalism. American national identity was forged in the simultaneous construction of and competition between often completely opposed ideals.

Mourning in Our National Capital

In 1895, huge public funerals for a great man still had the power to communicate national values, but they acquired a distinctive twist when used to commemorate Frederick Douglass, a figure of Black greatness. David Blight has shown us that Douglass himself was a "creature of memory" who "embodied the idea that history mattered," especially to the Black community.[14] Douglass's funeral commemorations gave those who praised him a chance to revere his embodiment of history and to express their hopes and expectation that he could continue as a potent symbol of Black liberty, long after death. They also argued that African Americans played a central role in the American nation itself. Douglass's mourning proved that Civil War memory created circumstances for African Americans to participate in national identity, but, unfortunately, backlash also showed how unstable that participation was.

For more than forty years, Frederick Douglass himself had engaged in the politics of public mourning, criticizing it when lavished on any public figure who supported the institution of slavery and participating in it when public grief could be mobilized for the antislavery cause or for the advancement of Black people. Before the Civil War, Douglass critiqued Henry Clay's massive public funeral rituals, noting that Clay's frequent compromises prolonged and spread the institution of slavery. Douglass had also called the outpouring of post-Confederate grief for Robert E. Lee "crocodile tears" that symbolized an excess of white supremacist nostalgia. On the other hand, Douglass publicly eulogized both Abraham Lincoln and Charles Sumner, giving speeches to help publicize and prolong his own emancipationist vision of the Civil War.[15] Douglass absolutely understood the political use of public grief, which continued in the 1890s. His own mourning rituals dramatized power struggles over race during a decade that historian Thomas A. Upchurch reminds us was when white prejudice fell "like a biblical plague upon the already downtrodden race."[16]

Although it was radical that such mourning was heaped upon Douglass, it made sense that if *any* Black figure could qualify for such public grief, it was him. Douglass had worked to create himself as a public symbol of Black freedom and achievement since the 1840s, when he began using his personal experiences as the cornerstone of his abolitionist writing and speaking. Over a fifty-year period, Douglass became the most famous representative of Black manhood and achievement: going on a public journey that took him from enslavement to abolition to Civil War advocate, to diplomat and politician, to activist for racial uplift. He argued tirelessly for equality—for African Americans and for all women—and he never shied away from making himself an example.[17]

The public recognized him as a symbolic man, referring to him as a "statesman" for the African American race. Immediately after his heart stopped, newspapers were filled with reports that "the great ex-slave statesman was dead."[18] Lamenting the loss of Douglass meant not just mourning for him, as a revered figure, but mourning for the loss of a great symbolic African American who could find a white audience for arguments about freedom. In a large memorial meeting of the Dallas Black community, educator J. W. Ray claimed that Douglass was exceptional because "he was a statesman whose voice was heard from the silver shores of the Atlantic to the golden shores of the Pacific."[19] Even some southern and Democratic papers that were directly unsympathetic to the cause of Black freedom reported on Douglass's death as the passing of "the greatest colored orator and statesman."[20]

Douglass's post–Civil War career had made him one of the most influential African American men in public life. Although he never served in elective office, Douglass had built on his reputation as an abolitionist and informal adviser to President Lincoln to emerge as one of the most prominent Black figures after the Civil War. After the war, Douglass moved from his home of more than twenty years in Rochester, New York, to Washington, D.C., where he edited the *New National Era* newspaper, which provided him a platform to comment on Reconstruction, politics, and continued struggles in race relations. In 1871, he served as assistant secretary of President Grant's Santo Domingo Commission, and he was elected as a trustee of Howard University. In 1874, he served for a time as the president of the Freedman's Savings Bank.

In 1877, he settled in Anacostia in southeast D.C.—in a stately home, Cedar Hill, overlooking the Anacostia River. He filled several federal appointments as marshal of the District of Columbia and as the district's recorder of deeds. After marrying Helen Pitts, a white woman who worked with him at the deeds office, in 1884, Douglass traveled with her in Europe and Africa. In 1889, Douglass was appointed as U.S. minister to Haiti (a high-profile, racially charged, and somewhat unsuccessful term, due to Haitian resistance to American expansionism). After returning from Haiti in 1891, he continued to write and speak, denouncing Jim Crow laws and lynching. Appointed as the Haitian representative to the 1893 World's Columbian Exposition, Douglass joined Ida B. Wells in the fair's Haitian pavilion to distribute her pamphlet *The Reason Why the Colored American Is Not in the World's Columbian Exposition*, to which he wrote an introduction decrying continued discrimination and racial injustice.[21]

Throughout Douglass's postwar career, he contributed to the "imagined reconstitution of the nation" by continually upholding an emancipationist memory of the Civil War and arguing that the work of Reconstruction and post-Reconstruction America should be shaped by remembering the Civil War as a struggle to rid the country of the scourge of slavery. His strong stance put him at odds with many white Southerners and white supremacists—some of whom would push back against his posthumous veneration as a symbol of racial uplift. By the 1890s, Douglass's legacy was also challenged—albeit in milder and friendlier terms—by Black activists like Booker T. Washington who did not wish to dwell on the past. In some respects—even as he was clearly venerated as a great man—contests over Frederick Douglass's memorialization would become a contest over the memory of abolition and racial uplift themselves. This dialogue was participated in by a hugely diverse public: white and Black, intellectuals and schoolchildren, politicians and mail carriers, men and women. It was clear the public mourned a great man when they mourned Frederick Douglass, but was he a figure of the fractured past or an example for the national future?

Douglass was a national figure and a fixture in the nation's capital when he suddenly died on February 20, 1895, in between speaking engagements. It became clear after his death that public mourning for Douglass would be necessary and important to Washington's civic life. As Helen Pitts Douglass absorbed her husband's death, she wished to hold off on making full arrangements until Douglass's children could all be consulted. Nine years earlier, Helen Pitts had married Frederick Douglass, making them the most high-profile, and therefore controversial, interracial married couple in the country. Frederick Douglass's four adult children had reacted badly to the marriage, only partly because of her race, and they were somewhat estranged from their stepmother. Despite the tensions, it took only four days after Frederick's death for Helen Pitts Douglass to consult with them, and Frederick's sons Lewis and Charles played an especially visible role in the public ceremonies of mourning that followed.[22]

The family really had no choice but to put aside any potential personal animosity because Douglass's funeral was a matter of national interest. His memory belonged to the public in the way that was expected of great and heroic men. A Chicago paper noted, "His funeral is expected to be one of the largest and most remarkable affairs of the kind, ever witnessed at the capital."[23] It was, in fact, similar to many other funerals for great men in Washington, D.C., but it was also remarkable because this time the great man was Black.

Frederick Douglass's funeral was, as the mayor of Rochester, New York, put it, "of national importance," and Black leaders especially wanted to be sure he was accorded the highest level of national respect.[24] At first, it seemed possible that Congress would recognize Douglass's greatness by including him in the select pantheon of those chosen to lie in state in the rotunda of the U.S. Capitol. But that was a step too far for Southerners in Congress, who may have rightly feared that honoring Douglass in such a manor would severely challenge white supremacy. In the House of Representatives, the last remaining African American congressman, George Washington Murray of South Carolina, tried to move that Douglass should lie in state in the rotunda of the U.S. Capitol, but Speaker Thomas Brackett Reed did not allow the motion to come forward. Senator Richard Pettigrew, a Republican from South Dakota, moved in the U.S. Senate that by unanimous consent Douglass be allowed to lie in state in the rotunda, but Democrat Arthur Gorman, who represented Douglass's native Maryland, objected, and the motion failed to be considered.[25]

It is remarkable that Douglass was even considered to lie in state, an honor bestowed before his time on select elected officials and presidents only. No African American would have their remains honored in the U.S. Capitol rotunda until more than a hundred years later. Representative John Lewis (2020) was the first Black person to lie in state in the Capitol rotunda, and only two African Americans, capitol police officer Jacob J. Chestnut (1998) and civil rights icon Rosa Parks (2005), have lain in honor in the Capitol rotunda. Congressman Elijah Cummings (2019) also lay in state in the Capitol, but he was placed in the Statuary Hall. Frederick Douglass's exceptional funeral set the pattern for national mourning of Black political heroes, but that pattern included some racially imposed limits.[26]

Although Congress fell short of according Douglass the highest national honor of allowing him to lie in state in the Capitol, plans developed for abundant rituals of public mourning that would mix national tribute with special attention from the local Washington, D.C., community, one-third of which was composed of African Americans.[27] Douglass was Washington's greatest Black celebrity, and he had marveled at how the work of Black people had transformed the city since the end of the Civil War, even as he had lamented the rise of corruption in politics and the regeneration of the Democratic Party.[28] The scale and national interest in his Washington funeral placed Douglass in the first rank of public figures and certainly exceeded any previous public tribute for a Black person. As one Pennsylvania newspaper noted: "His obsequies at Washington were attended by extraordinary demonstrations of respect."[29] African Americans, especially, took the opportunity to prepare for Douglass's funeral as a public ritual for the man whom the *New York Times* called "the representative man of his race."[30]

Public mourning for Frederick Douglass presented an opportunity—in the midst of a crisis of lynching and calculated violence against African American men and women—to capture public attention for a Black body not as the object of horror, violence, disgust, or pity but as a venerated sign of greatness. As part of his widespread work against lynching, Douglass wrote in 1892, the year he met Ida B. Wells, that a lynch mob "comes to its work in a storm of passion and thirsting for human blood, ready to shoot, stab, or burn its victim, who is denied a word of entreaty or explanation."[31] Douglass's own death spurred the opposite kind of crowd action: a spontaneous expression of grief over a distinguished Black man who was said to typify the best qualities of his race and of America. Instead of gawking white spectators staring at a dead Black man hanged on a tree, Douglass's dead body would inspire Black pride and expressions of respect from both Black and white observers.[32]

Despite segregation, Washington, D.C., was what Kate Masur has called "a hub of African American activism," and Black citizens were not about to let Douglass's death pass without their participation in the mourning, even if white citizens also participated. Since he was not placed in the U.S. Capitol, the family opened Douglass's Anacostia home, Cedar Hill, to the hundreds who flocked to view his embalmed body lying in honor.[33] The *Washington Post* took special care to note that white and Black people "of all conditions of life" came to pay their respects.[34]

The public ceremonies in D.C. took place at Metropolitan AME Church, the worship home since 1886 of many of the most prominent Black residents of the city, including Douglass. The church was housed in a large and impressive building on M Street near Georgetown.[35] Just over a year before, Douglass had delivered a fiery speech against lynching in the same location, and now his own remains would be the subject of public veneration in one of the most impressive integrated spaces in the city.[36] The Union League in D.C. voted that all African Americans should wear a mourning emblem in honor of Douglass for twenty days after his death.[37]

African American citizens were, to be sure, not the only ones who participated in public mourning for Douglass, but many deemed it especially important to connect themselves to his memory and to show themselves playing an important part in the tribute of the larger community. Douglass's funeral was a major national point of visibility for emancipationist memory of the Civil War, which African Americans especially needed to continue. Many newspapers noted that Douglass's funeral was the largest public showing of ritualized mourning from the African American community in Washington, D.C., since Lincoln's.[38]

On February 25, five days after his death, much of D.C. society turned out for the public funeral celebration for Frederick Douglass. That morning, an honor guard from a "colored" camp of the Sons of Union Veterans accompanied the body from Anacostia to the church, where the body was available for four hours of public viewing. Douglass was placed before the altar, and "A great crowd passed in and out and, while colored persons predominated, among the waiting multitude here were hundreds of white people."[39] When the viewing was stopped at 1:30 P.M., there were still thousands of people outside the church who had not yet gained admittance to see the body, and most of them waited outside as the services got underway.[40]

The church itself was filled with more than 2,000 people who had been granted tickets to participate in the service. The large sanctuary was packed, and hundreds more waited outside. The faculty of Howard University attended en masse. The notably mixed crowd included white and Black politicians, business owners, and social activists.[41]

Newspapers all over the country noted, especially, the huge number of beautiful floral tributes crowded around the altar—a key sign of public admiration whose meanings would have been carefully parsed by late nineteenth-century readers schooled in the language of flowers. Douglass's massive oak casket was decorated simply with lilacs, but floral arrangements overflowed the altar and filled the front of the church behind him.

Opposing commemorative forces of radical Black emancipation and of Southern post-Confederate reconciliation vied for public attention, albeit peacefully, in Douglass's floral tributes. The largest flower arrangement was "a magnificent shield composed of roses, orchids, and palms" from the Haitian government and Haitian minister Clément Haentjens. The Black republic paid due respects to Douglass as a Black hero, setting aside his somewhat tumultuous stint as a U.S. diplomat there. The only arrangement that came close to capturing as much of the crowd's attention was an arrangement sent by Baltimore police captain B. F. Auld, the nephew of Thomas Auld, Douglass's former owner. In his later years, Douglass had corresponded with and visited Thomas Auld, mostly to try to find out details of his childhood, but the press now made a show of Auld's floral tribute as a symbol of reconciliation between the slave-owning family and the formerly rebellious man who had escaped them.[42] The Haitian and Auld family flowers sitting side by side typified the contested reconciliation that ran throughout public mourning for Douglass: depending on which details the viewers honed in on, they might see bold statements of Black resistance and freedom, or they might see tokens of reconciling sentimentalism.

The nearly three-hour funeral service paid tribute to Douglass the formerly enslaved man and the great Black icon. It began at 2:00 P.M. with a funeral procession featuring the Douglass family, Black and white ministers, women's rights activists (including Susan B. Anthony, May Wright Sewall, and Rev. Anna Shaw), Supreme Court justice John Marshall Harlan, Senators John Sherman and George Frisbie Hoar, other government officials from the United States and Haiti, and many more. Douglass's coffin was guarded by Black Civil War veterans, and the honorary pallbearers included Black politicians George W. Murray (the congressman who had unsuccessfully tried to get Douglass to lie in state in the rotunda), Blanche K. Bruce, P. B. S. Pinchback, John R. Lynch, and others.

The rostrum was filled with Black leaders and white reformers. Pastor of the Metropolitan congregation Rev. J. G. Jenifer conducted the service, which included eulogies from AME bishop Alexander Walker Wayman, Rev. H. E. Stevenson of Anacostia, and Rev. J. E. Rankin, the president of Howard University. A member of the Haitian delegation to the United States (described in the press as a tall "very black" man) delivered a eulogy in French that was translated by

John S. Durham, who had succeeded Douglass as U.S. minister to Haiti. The last surviving member of the abolitionist Hutchinson Family Singers, John Hutchinson, spoke and sang two songs in honor of Douglass. Susan B. Anthony spoke and read a letter from Elizabeth Cady Stanton. May Wright Sewall praised Douglass for opening the way for the emancipation of African Americans and women, and Rev. Anna Shaw offered one of the closing prayers.[43]

In his eulogy for Douglass at the church, Howard University president J. E. Rankin claimed that the nation would feel Douglass's absence "as though a mountain peak had been removed from our moral horizon." He emphasized that Douglass had played a role that no one else could have, "for he was great, in a period of great men," and stood out, even among notables of the Civil War era. Rankin argued that Douglass was the central figure of the antislavery movement and "of the civil war and the reconstruction period, he was a man to whom Presidents and Senators, to whom millions of enfranchised people looked for counsel. He taught the Senators wisdom."[44] The D.C. ceremony contained lessons for the whole nation.

After the service, the symbolic honors continued, as Douglass's remains moved through the city. His body was borne by "eight colored letter carriers" to the hearse that carried the coffin to the train station as part of a long procession. Since Douglass could not be accompanied by military honors, the uniformed postal workers functioned, in the minds of some onlookers, "to link the memory of the man to the government of the nation."[45] Dignitaries and the Douglass family, all in carriages, were accompanied to the train station by military cadets and delegations from several posts of the GAR and other veterans' organizations. The streets were lined with "people who had tried in vain to get into the church and had waited four hours," and as the hearse moved through the streets, "a large proportion of the multitude crowded on after it."[46]

Douglass was closely associated with presidential memory and treated as the Black equivalent of the greatest white political leaders. Many newspapers and mourners likened the mourning for Douglass to that for Abraham Lincoln thirty years earlier—not because their deaths remotely resembled one another but because the association indicated the level of public respect and ceremony due to Douglass.[47] J. E. Rankin claimed in a speech to the New York Lyceum after Douglass's burial that he was "the typical man to the Afro-American, as Washington, as Lincoln, to the Anglo-American; the man that never dies. There can be no other Frederick Douglass."[48]

Upon the news of Douglass's death, the mayor and aldermen of New York City agreed with the request from "a delegation of colored men" to make arrangements for him to lie in state in City Hall there—presuming incorrectly that the body would, of course, stop on its way to Rochester. They wanted Douglass to rest " on the very spot where thousands paid their respects to

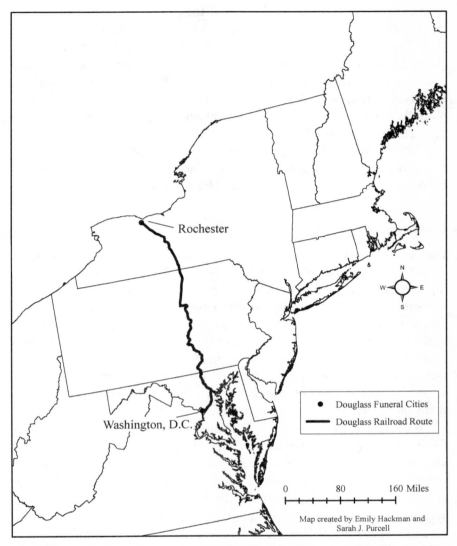

Frederick Douglass funeral route, 1895. Data from IPUMS, National Historical Geographic Information System; Jeremy Atack, "Historical Geographic Information Systems (GIS) database of U.S. Railroads for 1898 (May 2016)." Map by Sarah J. Purcell and Emily Hackman.

Ulysses S. Grant . . . directly below where the casket containing the body of President Lincoln rested in April, 1865."[49] The Black dignitaries from New York City attended Douglass's service in Washington, D.C., but were disappointed that no similar ceremony would take place in New York City. Douglass's funeral party traveled directly overnight to Rochester, stopping only for quiet train transfers inside the stations.[50] Douglass's tributes did not, in fact, reach the heights attained by Abraham Lincoln, but the comparisons between them remained nonetheless significant, and New York City residents held several tributes to Douglass's memory in the days that followed—even without his body present.[51] Douglass stood out as he seemed to merit—to some—presidential-level mourning, unheard of for any African American.

Exceptional Mourning in Rochester

Despite the quiet train transfers, more exceptional public mourning awaited. After passing through New York City, Douglass's remains and the party of dignitaries accompanying them traveled overnight to Rochester, New York, his home during the antebellum abolition fight and the publication site of his first newspaper, the *North Star*. Douglass and his first wife, Anna, had lived in Rochester for almost thirty years starting in 1847, and it was there that his career as an abolitionist, publisher, orator, and reformer blossomed. In Rochester, a hotbed of reform efforts born out of earlier nineteenth-century revivalism and economic modernization, Douglass had built a strong network with many of the century's most prominent activists, and he attended and organized numerous conventions of abolitionists and Black leaders, even while fighting public prejudice and segregation within the city. The Douglass family also helped harbor in their Rochester home more than 400 fugitives from enslavement who made their way to Canada. Although Douglass had left Rochester in 1872 when his house was destroyed in a suspicious fire, he was still associated with the city in the public mind.[52] After an enormous public funeral, Douglass would become the most famous resident of Mount Hope, Rochester's proud exemplar of the rural cemetery movement.[53]

The city of Rochester invested considerable civic attention in the Douglass mourning rituals. The *Rochester Democrat* reported that "all the bunting in Rochester was afloat . . . and all the flags were at half mast" on February 26 when Douglass's body reached the city on the morning train. The station was "filled with a surging mass of people," young and old, waiting for Douglass to arrive on the Northern Central line from D.C.[54] One man in the crowd commented to a reporter that he was glad to see parents bringing their children to "give them an historical memory of the event" just as he had been taken to "look upon the face of Lincoln" when he was a boy.[55]

After being removed from the train, Douglass's casket was placed in a hearse and ceremonially processed through the streets of Rochester to City Hall, accompanied by his family and local and national dignitaries and preceded by a regimental band and an honor guard. Immense crowds filled the streets and fell in behind the procession, as people made their way to city hall to "look upon the face of the dead" as Douglass lay in state. City hall was draped heavily in mourning, and the casket surrounded by flowers and palms, with a decorative bald eagle and a draped American flag hanging over the casket.[56] The line to pay respects to Douglass still stretched as far as the eye could see when the body had to be removed from City Hall to the church at three o'clock in the afternoon.[57]

Douglass's funeral in Rochester was held in the Central Church because the city's Common Council thought no other church would be large enough to accommodate the mourners, and indeed the people of Rochester filled the streets to capacity and crowded around the church during the ceremony.[58] The church was so full that many people stood through the hours-long service. The honorary pallbearers included prominent white and Black politicians who had come from D.C. such as Sen. John Sherman and former Louisiana governor P. B. S. Pinchback, while the physical pallbearers were chosen by Rochester's postmaster "from the colored letter carriers of the district."[59] The funeral showcased Black politics and the uplift of Black labor.

Rochester congratulated itself on the civic outpouring for one of its most famous ex-citizens. The composition of the mourners was a point of civic pride, as the *Rochester Democrat* reported that the crowds were "representative in the highest sense . . . [including] the leading business and professional men of the community; gray-haired citizens, whose life in Rochester dates to the older time which Douglass was here; white and colored children of the present time, and all the classes that intervene in age and character."[60] Public schools dismissed at 10:00 A.M. so that children could pay their respects, which was fitting because, as one paper reported, Douglass had protested in 1857 to integrate Rochester public schools in order for his own children to attend.[61]

The newspapers stressed racial progress and a unified spirit of grief. The Rochester *Chronicle* noted that the streets were lined with hundreds of people, young and old, Black and white, who could not fit into the church.[62] The funeral service itself in Rochester followed a similar pattern to the one in D.C., albeit without quite as many national political luminaries in attendance.

Rev. William Taylor, pastor of the Brick Church in Rochester, opened the service with prayer, and Rochester friends of Douglass followed with a poetic tribute and the recitation of his biography. After music, the Unitarian minister and abolitionist William Channing Gannett delivered the main eulogy, which noted that the occasion was exceptional because so many white people had joined with African Americans to publicly laud a Black man. He hoped that Douglass's funeral marked a celebration of the nation's emancipation from slavery "and also its emancipation from the slavery of prejudice and from the slavery of caste and color."[63] The service concluded with prayers.

Immediately following the service, the crowds parted as Douglass's remains—escorted by police, militia, and a band—were processed through the city's streets to Mount Hope Cemetery. The streets were lined with "great crowds of people" arrayed in solemn mourning as Douglass's remains passed. At Mount Hope, short prayers were read in the chapel before Douglass's body was deposited in a vault, to await burial when the ground thawed in summer.[64]

Heroic Statue for a Distinguished Fellow Citizen

Although no monument to a Black person had ever been built in the United States before, the "national" importance of Douglass became clear when a movement to memorialize him grew immediately from the public mourning rituals. Douglass became part of the larger landscape of Civil War memory in Rochester, although he retained most importance to the Black community. Douglass's grave in Mount Hope would become, over the next few years, a site of pilgrimage for social reformers and former abolitionists, but it was not the only site in Rochester to mark his physical presence and political inspiration. Even while Rochester was preparing to host Douglass's funeral rites, prominent African Americans in town, led by John W. Thompson, gathered to form the Douglass Monument Committee. The committee was determined, as part of the public mourning for Douglass, to raise funds to construct "a life size or heroic statue of the distinguished fellow citizen, whose death is so generally deplored, but whose memory we will ever honor."[65]

The committee adapted plans it had started the prior year to build a statue in honor of African American Civil War soldiers and sailors, a project Douglass had personally supported. In commemorating Douglass, the monument committee made a seamless transition, deciding that it could honor the Black soldiers and sailors on the shaft of the monument and place a bronze statue of Douglass on its top, which they desired to reflect Douglass's actual appearance as a person of African descent.[66]

The unprecedented nature of the monument project emphasized both how exceptional the mourning for Douglass was and how difficult it was to raise any Black hero to the pinnacle of national praise. The pioneering nature of building a public monument to a famous Black man, even someone as locally beloved and nationally renowned as Frederick Douglass, meant that the project faced obstacles. The committee had some trouble collecting enough funds from Rochester residents, both Black and white, to erect the monument, and spent several years petitioning New York state agencies for help.[67] The New York State Finance Committee appropriated $3,000 (as matching funds for donations) for the project in 1897, to which the government of Haiti added $1,000. Thompson and the other committee members raised over $2,000 from Black and white contributors (including Black schoolchildren), and in 1898 work on the monument began with a Masonic cornerstone laying ceremony.[68]

The monument sought to link Douglass to a decidedly emancipationist vision of Civil War memory in Rochester. At the cornerstone laying, Congressman John Van Voorhis, a Republican who represented Rochester, declared Douglass "pre-eminently our first citizen" who deserved to be memorialized for his successful "mission to emancipate millions of slaves."[69] The Rochester park commissioner declared that it was important for Douglass to be memorialized in a public Rochester park, stating, "Our great Civil War must ever remain as one of the most notable events of all time. I do not refer to the stupendous volunteering defense of the country, but rather to the emancipation of the slave."[70]

The Frederick Douglass monument project sought to extend the political influence of Douglass, transforming the civic memory and veneration of his remains in his Rochester funeral into veneration of his body in monumental form. Surely, erecting a monument to Douglass would help the cause of Black rights. At a public festival in honor of the monument in 1898, Ida B. Wells said that she came "as a pilgrim to Mecca" to pay tribute to Douglass's memory and noted that proper memory of Douglass should spur people to work for "anti-lynch law" and against the "hydra-headed monster of prejudice."[71] Financial struggles and production delays postponed the installation of the statue until the following year, but even as the Douglass Monument Committee sometimes struggled to raise enough funds to complete the project, the commemorative intentions were never far out of sight.

The effort to mark Frederick Douglass as a great public man culminated when his monument was unveiled and dedicated to national notice on June 9, 1899.[72] The statue, sculpted by Sidney Edwards, depicted Douglass in the act of giving an oration in Cincinnati just before the passage of the Fifteenth Amendment.[73] The Douglass monument was markedly different than other public emancipation monuments, most of which depicted humbled, anonymous freed people alongside (and subservient to) Abraham Lincoln. His statue depicted a besuited Douglass in a powerful oratorical stance, commanding the attention of all who looked at it. In honoring Douglass as an individual, who also functioned as a symbol of Black liberation, the monument also stood in stark contrast to efforts underway in several Southern states to memorialize supposedly loyal enslaved people—or the project promoted by the United Daughters of the Confederacy to erect a monument to "mammy" in every state.[74]

Frederick Douglass monument, Rochester, New York, 2010. Photo by the author.

Douglass's monument continued themes of racial uplift begun in his au-
tobiographies and continued in his public mourning. The dedication ceremony in 1899 drew 10,000 people to Douglass Park, public space set aside to
enshrine him as one of Rochester's foremost former citizens. New York governor Theodore Roosevelt delivered the main dedicatory oration to the
large crowd that came to see the statue unveiled. Roosevelt called Frederick
Douglass "a representative of his race" and "a worthy representative of the
American nation," and he linked emancipation to the Union Cause by praising Civil War veterans in the crowd "who fought for four years for the free-

dom of that race to which Frederick Douglass belonged, and in order that there might be an undivided and indissoluble Union."[75]

As opposed to Ida B. Wells in her speech the previous year, however, Roosevelt did not translate his praise for Douglass into an unequivocal statement against current-day racial prejudice and lynching. He ended his speech on a sour mixed note, cautioning the crowd that "the worst enemy of the colored race is the colored man who commits some hideous wrong, especially if that be the worst of all crimes, rape." And, even though he also decried in more elliptical terms the white man "who avenges that crime" by lynching, Roosevelt's speech seemed to lend credence to the idea that lynching was a punishment for real Black crime, rather than admitting that such rapes were just imaginary justification for racial oppression, as Douglass himself had argued in the last years of his life.[76] The Douglass monument itself stood as a marker of unprecedented adulation for a Black hero, but the struggle to get it built and Roosevelt's racist dedication showed the fragility and instability of Douglass as a great, national symbol.

Greatest Black Man

The conflicting strains in Theodore Roosevelt's speech honoring Frederick Douglass—calling him a representative of the "colored race" and a great American while simultaneously fueling the racist rage that drove lynching—typified many of the contradictions in public memory of Douglass upon his death and immediately thereafter. In 1895, Douglass was memorialized as a great man and afforded public mourning fit for a national hero and statesman, but turning Frederick Douglass into the subject of collective grief and praise, bestowing on him funerals that emphasized him as a fighter for emancipation, and making him the subject of a monument also drew criticism and backlash.

Douglass's death in 1895 coincided with the intensification of Jim Crow segregation in the South and of severe discrimination against African Americans all over the country. The 1890s was a difficult decade for unalloyed tributes to Black heroism. In 1896 the *Plessy v. Ferguson* ruling paved the way for the solidification and expansion of legal segregation across the country.[77]

National praise for Douglass upon his death allowed many Americans to express unabashed reverence for Black achievement and the fight for equality, but the funeral and monumental pageantry also emphasized that he was dead and gone. Now that Douglass was deceased and would have no more say in shaping his legacy as a symbol, contests over that legacy—many of which continue into the present day—began in earnest. Eulogizing Douglass provided the opportunity to claim him as a great Black man, but arguments ensued over just what that meant: Was he exceptional or emblematic? What part of Civil War memory did Douglass exemplify? Would Douglass inspire continued struggle for equality, or was his a story of self-improvement that could be fit into a narrative of racial uplift alongside accommodation to segregation? Was Douglass a great man because he was Black, or in spite of that fact? Was it possible, even, that Douglass's white ancestry contributed to his greatness? What did Douglass's death mean for the nation?

All these questions were present when, the moment that Frederick Douglass died, the battle over his memory intensified. The battle over Douglass's memory, then, also became part of both the struggle by mainstream American white culture to define African Americans and the struggle among African Americans to define their own identities in relation to the nation, what scholar Mitch Kachun has called the debate over "who held the power to define black identity and black culture."[78] The year of Frederick Douglass's death, 1895, was also the year that Booker T. Washington claimed national attention for his Atlanta Compromise, a starkly different vision of the Black future based more on education, accommodation, and uplift rather than remembering the past and struggling for political liberty.[79]

In 1895, emancipationist memory mattered. Those who claimed Douglass as a pillar of the emancipation struggle often linked him to the necessity to continue remembering the Civil War as a fight for freedom, noting the importance of remembering Douglass *and* his work as part of the national story. As Professor W. H. H. Hart argued to the students of Howard University Law School in a March 1895 eulogy, "The simple facts of the great anti-slavery crusade of which Frederick Douglass was the central and colossal figure, and which culminated in the civil war and the freedom and enfranchisement of the former slaves, surpass and dwarf any and every single achievement of moral and political reformation recorded in human history."[80] The formerly enslaved poet Josephine D. H. Heard wrote a collection of poems honoring Douglass upon his death, one of which stressed how the "seas of human blood" poured out in the war had caused slavery to "sink beneath the gory flood," noting that Douglass's memory would preserve the sanctity of slavery's eradication.[81] According to Hart and Heard, emancipationist political and military memory was absolutely necessary to the continuation of Black freedom.

The role of Douglass in Civil War memory served as the backdrop to an even larger discussion of how Douglass himself stood as the representative man of his race. The *Baltimore World* noted that "the death of Frederick Douglass has called forth much discussion of the question of the possible extent of the intellectual development of the negro," showing that there is "scarcely any limit to be placed to the progress of the race in that direction."[82] The former editor of the *Philadelphia Inquirer* claimed that in Douglass he saw "more than the champion of his race. He is representative of its possibilities of achievement—the bright particular star of a people once abject and still hedged about by unequal conditions."[83] Abolitionist Theodore Tilton noted in a memorial poem to Douglass that he was among "the noblest giants of my day . . . strong amid the strong."[84] In Douglass's reputation and memory, the Black community could claim global attention and a hero worthy of emulation.

Many Douglass eulogies claimed that he was one of the greatest Americans, of any race.[85] The Indianapolis *Sentinel* noted that Douglass's early accomplishments in life were "more creditable than those of white men who have arisen from lowly position" because he faced legal and racial prejudice in addition to poverty.[86] Omaha Black leader Dr. Matthew Oliver Ricketts echoed a similar sentiment in his eulogy for Douglass in that city.[87] The Rev. W. B. Derrick eulogized Douglass in the Washington, D.C., funeral ceremony by noting that the New York press had presented him as "a fit example for all conditions and classes of people, be they Black or white."[88] J. E. Rankin, the president of Howard University, who spoke at Douglass's D.C. funeral, proclaimed, "Here is thy greatest son, my Maryland! Rise up to greet him as he passes through. . . . Seventy-seven years ago thou gavest him the birth of the bondman. . . . But thou hast lost him. . . . The nation has claimed him, the wide world."[89] Rankin noted that Douglass's importance exceeded U.S. boundaries.

Other eulogists argued that Douglass's past actions presented an international example of American greatness. One Harrisburg, Pennsylvania, newspaper wrote that Douglass was so great that "no one thought of his color" when "well known men and women" honored him upon his death and that "nevertheless in Europe he would have been more honored than here. . . . Racial equality is not altogether a myth in Europe."[90] One Baptist minister preached that Douglass's death, by exposing the public to a constant stream of praise for him, "had done more against race caste and prejudice than any act in his life."[91] It was not just that Douglass was great himself, but that he provided an example of Black achievement that must not ever be forgotten for the good of the greater community.

Important to this conception of Douglass's greatness was the fact that he had risen above slavery but also the fact that racial oppression continued in the present. Many newspaper eulogies recounted Douglass's responses to racial prejudice such as being "thrust out of" a seat on a railway car or being denied a seat at a Benjamin Franklin memorial banquet "on account of race and color" as means to show that he overcame segregation and prejudice of the sort that any Black person might still experience in 1895.[92] Remembering the past was presented as a concrete guide to present-day action, even after the demise of slavery. Douglass offered a pathway for Black activism and resistance.

But setting up Douglass as a Black man worthy of political emulation also had pitfalls. Some eulogists, notably in Black-owned papers, worried that Douglass was *too* exceptional, essentially arguing that no one could ever succeed him as an important symbol and leader in the cause of Black equality.[93] Some African American leaders feared that by making Douglass too much into the exemplar of Black excellence, many other Black accomplishments and heroes would be overlooked. One group of Black ministers in Richmond, Virginia, publicly worried that Douglass memorials would divert attention from the many Black "men of genius" who were still alive and who went unrecognized.[94] Was it actually dangerous to praise the dead hero to the detriment of the living struggle?

The Richmond ministers had cause to worry. Some white editorial writers turned this argument on its head, trying to mollify African Americans with the thought that Douglass would need no successor, since he was the product of "times which, happily, are forever past."[95] Racial problems were framed as dead, just like Douglass. Even if they were willing to admit that racial inequality was still an issue, other editorialists felt that Douglass had established a standard for African American leadership that could not be equaled. The *New York World* called Douglass "leader of his race" and said that he exercised leadership "to which few men can aspire."[96] The *New York Tribune* claimed in Douglass's eulogy that even if no one could equal his leadership, his fame was "the heritage of millions of negroes who, little by little, and hand over hand, are struggling to work out their destiny, and to justify their emancipation as the crowning result of the fratricidal war of which slavery was the cause."[97]

The fact that white eulogists could use Douglass's legacy to note the difficulty of Black struggle (whether in sympathetic or unsympathetic terms) made it that much more important for some in the Black community to claim Douglass's memory for a stronger version of community progress and justice, based on Black action. The notable Black preacher Francis Grimké argued in a Douglass eulogy in Washington, D.C., that the Republican Party and the federal government were "ready to sacrifice the negro, to trample him in the dust, to put him aside, out of deference to popular prejudice," and advocated using Douglass's memory to continue spurring political action among the Black community.[98] Grimké argued that Douglass's actual past of abolitionist leadership required continued political resistance to present slights, even if no leader emerged who could replace Douglass.

Some Black leaders, alternatively, used Douglass as an example of racial uplift that fit with Booker T. Washington's new vision of Black progress through education, economic achievement, and the de-emphasis of politics. Douglass's life story gave them narrative material to work with. Douglass had been an advocate of Black industrial education and integration, and his auto-biographies stressed self-fashioning.[99] John W. Thompson, the prime mover behind the movement to build the Douglass monument in Rochester, declared that public veneration of Douglass told "our boys that the humbleness of birth is no insurmountable barrier to eminence, that all doors swing open to those who keep their hearts right, and give themselves with unremitting toil and high purpose to the work which lies before them."[100] Some newspapers framed Douglass as a modern self-made man.[101] Organizers of a Douglass memorial meeting of Black Philadelphians in 1896 distributed portraits of Douglass to the crowd and urged those in attendance to "hang up pictures of their own great men in their homes along with the white Abolition heroes." The event stressed "self-dependence" and held up Douglass as an example of divinely inspired racial uplift, as John Stephens Durham, who had succeeded Doug-lass as U.S. minister to Haiti, reminded the gathering: "God helps them who help themselves."[102]

Surely, Douglass would have agreed, but he also would have continued to hold the powers of structural inequality to account if he had lived longer.[103] He would have fought to keep the struggle for Black equality at the center of the national story and the center of Civil War memory.

Great White Man?

The debate over how best to consider Frederick Douglass as an example of Black greatness was not the only debate about race and identity inspired by his death and funeral. White supremacy proved resilient, even in public mourning for and commemorations of Frederick Douglass. Douglass's open-ness about his mixed-race heritage and his embrace of integration, even to the degree of marrying Helen Pitts, a white woman, also opened the door to an opposite point of view. White supremacy in 1895, newly buoyed by the de-velopment of social Darwinism and scientific racism, also informed some public appreciations of Douglass's greatness.[104] The acceptance of theories of racial hierarchy by intellectuals in the North and South dovetailed with pub-lic mourning for Douglass and surfaced in the discussion of what made him a great man (and for whom).[105] Some eulogists wanted to positively frame Douglass as an example of the progressive possibilities of racial mixing, but an emphasis on his "mixed blood" pushed beyond just framing him as an ex-ceptional Black leader into praise of his "whiteness."

In a significant and strange twist, some sought to frame Frederick Doug-lass as a great white man. The theme was first opened up by Douglass advo-cates, who wanted to frame him as a symbol of racial harmony. But it was soon seized upon by white supremacists—in both South and North—who took the opportunity to downplay Douglass's significance and to smear African American achievement and rights.

Emphasizing Douglass's status as a mixed-race person, even if it was intended to broaden his universal appeal as a great man, entailed risk. May Wright Sewall spoke at Douglass's D.C. funeral and stated,

> Many times during these solemn services, Frederick Douglass has been referred to as the 'hero of a race' with the evident restriction of the word "race" to the colored people. . . . His record is a glory to the colored race, but it must not at this hour be forgotten that through his veins there flowed a mingled strain of blood. . . . The white race as well as the Black has been uplifted by his career. . . . It is the whole race *human*, not the fractional race *African*, to which he belonged, and the annals of which will be illuminated by the splendid record of his life.[106]

In a bid to make Douglass a universal hero, rather than just a Black one, Sewall relied on his white ancestry, a fact that many more racist commentators would take in a whole new direction.

Other eulogists also tried to show Douglass as the positive outcome of racial mixing. The *Brooklyn Eagle* proclaimed that Douglass had Indian, white, and Black blood, making him "thrice an American."[107] The Brooklyn paper was, perhaps, echoing the tone of the eulogy given for Douglass in the AME church in that city by Dr. Louis Albert Banks, who claimed of Douglass that "in such a man the kinship of all races is demonstrated."[108]

But these bids to demonstrate Douglass as a positive example of racial amalgamation—to set him up as a universal standard, not as a great Black hero—lost ground to other commentators who rushed to identify which "great" characteristics in the man were inherent to which part of his racial heredity. The 1890s saw an increasing popularity of scientific theories, articulated by Joseph-Arthur de Gobineau and others, that denoted the white or "Aryan" race as "the only one capable of creative thinking and civilization building."[109] Adherents of scientific racism put their ideas to work assessing Frederick Douglass upon his death, and his death gave them a chance to publicize their views.

Frederick Douglass would have rebelled against any social Darwinist reading of his heritage, but he could not contribute to the discourse that his own death occasioned. The idea that Douglass's white heritage made him great exploded into public view when a Boston newspaper asked the governor of Massachusetts, moderate Republican Frederic Greenhalge, for a comment on Douglass the day after he died. The governor, influenced by scientific race theory, attributed Douglass's greatness to his white "blood," inherited from his father. Governor Greenhalge expressed regret at the death of the great "self-made man" to a reporter. But, the governor continued, "He represented the collation of two bloods, and represented the Anglo-American spirit of justice and liberty of all humanity. . . . In spite of his blood, everyone would say he was a white man in the full spirit of Americanism."[110] To the Massachusetts governor, and others who agreed, it was Douglass's white parentage that explained his achievement over and above the supposed more limited abilities of the Black race.

It was notable that Greenhalge, a northern Republican, was the first to make such racialized claims about Douglass's whiteness. Other white supremacists picked up on the governor's theme and ran with it, eager to explain Douglass's greatness (however much they disliked admitting it) with reference to his white "blood." Mixing admiration of Frederick Douglass with white supremacist ideology contradicted the Black arguments about why Douglass should be admired and remembered that had figured so loudly in his funeral commemorations. But the idea that Douglass was in some sense a "great white man" was also a way for white supremacists to admire him, explaining why he merited so much unprecedented public attention but still carried forth their racist ideologies. Paradoxically, because Douglass had qualified for public admiration, public funerals, and eulogies—things never before available to a Black man—he also qualified in some sense as a symbol of white supremacy.

Framing Douglass as a great white man took some level of mental gymnastics, but it was not impossible. For example, popular writer Frederic May Holland, who had published a biography of Douglass, *The Colored Orator*, in 1891 and who firmly advocated for Douglass's reputation, wrote extensively in a white supremacist manner about Douglass upon his death. When the Chicago scientific magazine *Open Court* asked Holland to write an obituary of Douglass, Holland wrote that Douglass "was the foremost man of the colored race; and the only question is, how much of his greatness was due to his white blood? I think the present Governor of Massachusetts is right in calling him a white American. . . . He belonged, both mentally and morally, to the race which founded our nation and keeps it free." Holland continued, calling Douglass an unoriginal thinker but admitting he was a capable leader. Holland lamented: "It is a pity that his social position was so largely determined by the darkness of his skin, instead of the whiteness of his intellect."[111] Holland, like Governor Greenhalge, thought that Douglass might better be thought of as a great white American.

Funeral celebrations for Douglass provided direct opportunity for Holland to spread his white supremacist ideas about Douglass. He capitalized upon Douglass's death by rushing out a second edition of his book in 1895, which continued the praise for Douglass's whiteness. May wrote that Douglass had "a white man's independence and originality of intellect. He was whiter than those who despised him on account of the color of his skin . . . it is easy to see that he had the best traits of the Anglo-Saxon race. . . . He was born to be a great leader."[112] Holland's estimation of Douglass's talents as attributable to his "white intellect" played in to the social Darwinist idea circulating widely in 1895 that African Americans were inferior not because they were dangerous but because they were childlike and naive: according to Holland, Douglass overcame the Black part of himself to become a great American.[113]

Holland's assessment of Douglass's whiteness was doubly dangerous, since Holland claimed to have the approval of the Douglass family and that he had prepared the book on Douglass's orations in consultation with Frederick Douglass and his sons. Frederick Douglass probably did provide Holland with some limited cooperation in the original book about his oratory, but Douglass also completely rejected the kind of scientific racial hierarchy advanced by Holland in 1895.[114] Douglass identified as Black and thought of himself "simply as an American citizen."[115]

Surely, Douglass would have denounced the view of himself as a great white man. According to Robert S. Levine, in 1893 Douglass had "remarked that he wished the famous scientist Benjamin Banneker had been 'entirely black' so that his intelligence would not be credited to his white blood."[116] While the comment may have revealed some ambivalence in Douglass about his own mixed heritage, it—along with his lifelong crusades against racial prejudice—surely meant that he would have countered anyone who wanted to claim that white ancestry formed his own greatness. Douglass understood how that sort of thinking sapped power from the symbolic figure of the revered Black man and perpetuated racism that hurt all African Americans.

Indeed, many southern and Democratic newspapers commented on Douglass's mixed-race heritage in crudely racist terms—taking the opportunity to belittle Douglass upon the occasion of his death. The *New Orleans Picayune* called attention to Douglass's Anglo-Saxon blood and derisively called him "a half-breed, his father having been a white man, he cannot be accepted as a real example of the development to which the negro is capable."[117] The *Minneapolis Tribune* was a bit more laudatory but carried a similar message, reminding readers that they should call Douglass "Afro-American" rather than Black because "his father was a white man, and the stamp of his intellect was in probability given him by his sire."[118] The *Memphis Commercial* newspaper quipped bitterly, "He accomplished much as the champion of the negro race, but he had very little negro blood in his veins. . . . He was almost a white man."[119] The *Kansas City Star* admitted that Douglass was Black but called him "the one great man produced by the African race in America."[120] A New York paper claimed that although Douglass was a great leader and a man of "genius," he did not actually lead the "rank-and-file" of African Americans, "who have not mastered the fine art of following anybody."[121] The science of racial hierarchy, therefore, allowed Southerners and Democrats to simultaneously smear Douglass and all the African Americans he stood for.

Other newspapers tried to push back. The Boston *Post* editorialized that it formed a bitter irony that so many wished to take note of Douglass's white blood now that he was dead, arguing that he presented himself to the world as a Black man, showing the greatest possibility of achievement of "the colored race."[122] And the Boston *Herald* reminded readers that although Douglass had a "full half of white blood in his veins," he was "thoroughly identified with the colored race in the public estimation."[123] Editors also noted that "he did wonderfully well for a man of any color."[124] When Rev. Francis Grimké eulogized Douglass in Washington, D.C., on March 10, 1895, he stated emphatically (likely in part as a retort to those who wanted to claim white blood for Douglass), "He was born a colored man. . . . He was identified with a despised race,—a race which had no rights white men were bound to respect."[125]

The task of these commentators, who wanted to remind the public firmly of Douglass's greatness as a Black man despite any racial mixing, was not helped by additional press coverage of Douglass's own mixed marriage. Frederick Douglass insisted that his interracial marriage to Helen Pitts was perfectly acceptable, but it provided further fuel for racists upon his death. The disapproval of Helen Pitts Douglass by the Douglass children, and the suspicion of the marriage by some within the Black community, did not help.[126]

White supremacist eulogies portrayed the Douglass marriage as a problem. During the period of public mourning, many newspapers noted alongside Douglass's obituary, in a move intended to shock readers, that he was "MARRIED TO A WHITE WIFE."[127] The *Atlanta Constitution* claimed that Douglass was "not in favor with his people" during the final years of his life because he married a white woman.[128] In fact, more than one newspaper correspondent used the occasion of Douglass's death to warn against racial intermarriage, noting that "his eminence as a man, as a statesman and a leader . . . only makes the step more appalling in its nature and effects."[129] Even many papers that posed Douglass as a hero worthy of emulation by African Americans took great pains to note that his second wife was white.[130] Many papers also tried to besmirch Douglass's memory by covering in salacious terms conflicts between Helen Pitts Douglass and her stepchildren over Frederick's estate.[131]

Some newspaper editors commented on Douglass's interracial marriage as a way to discuss directly what his death meant for segregation and continuing fights over race. The *New York Times* editorialized that "blacks" considered Douglass's marriage to a white woman "treason" that threatened to overshadow his legacy as a benevolent Black hero. The *Times* argued that because

Douglass was so advanced and so much greater than the average Black man meant that his memory could not solve "the race question" because Douglass "differed from his race for the better" and was isolated as a result.[132]

All of this racism, paradoxically, confirms the superadded national importance of public mourning for Frederick Douglass. Even white supremacists agreed that Frederick Douglass, in death, was a symbol worth fighting for. The fact that Douglass merited public funeral commemorations meant that most everyone in the national conversation about race in 1895 had something to say about him. According to the editors of *Public Opinion* magazine, Douglass was "a character who belongs to the preceding rather than to the present generation. . . . His death has afforded the text for considerable discussions of the relations between the two races."[133] Douglass could be used as a symbol of Black achievement and a symbol of white achievement—both the blessings and the dangers of racial amalgamation. But *everyone* agreed that his memory was vitally important. When people fought over Frederick Douglass, they seemed to be fighting for their own version of the United States and its racial order.

Douglass Mourning in Post-Confederate North Carolina

The stakes in this memory battle were high: the treatment of Douglass's death and mourning by the North Carolina legislature shows how such battles entailed consequences not only for culture, race, and society but also for the political order. Arguments over the meaning of Frederick Douglass, white supremacy, and how to recognize Douglass as a great American had the ability to alter power relations. The debate about how to properly commemorate Douglass and whether he merited the same treatment as great white heroes got entangled with post-Reconstruction politics in some unexpected ways. In North Carolina, Douglass's legacy ended up being indelibly tied to Confederate memory and efforts to "redeem" the state for the Democratic Party.

On February 21, 1895, the day after Douglass's death, Rep. William H. Crews, an African American legislator from Granville County, introduced a motion in the North Carolina House of Representatives to pay respects to Frederick Douglass. The motion, which would soon be misinterpreted as a motion to have the legislature adjourn in honor and observance of Frederick Douglass's death, passed on a party vote of 34 to 20.[134] Crews was a member of the "Fusion Party," a coalition of Republicans and Populists that just the year before had taken decisive control of the legislature from Democrats who were openly hostile to Black North Carolinians.

Even though it passed, the Douglass resolution immediately seemed to stress the fragile racial coalition among the Fusionists. Some papers reported that white members of the Fusion Party coalition were uncomfortable with the Douglass motion but that they seemed "paralyzed" at first to disagree with their Black colleagues. Ultimately, white Fusionists—as one Democratic journalist reported in highly racialized terms—went along with the resolution "almost under the lash."[135] The stress may have been more imagined than real, but it provided red meat to the Democratic opposition, nonetheless.

Since the legislature was actually past its usual time of adjournment for the day on February 21, the vote was largely ceremonial, but the move became an immediate political football. Newspapers from south to north noted—erroneously—that the legislature had failed to adjourn in honor of Robert E. Lee's birthday just a few days earlier and that it had also ignored George Washington's birthday which fell on the following day. The North Carolina House had, in fact, adjourned in honor of Lee's birthday and had observed Washington's birthday as usual on a Saturday, but Democrats lied about the commemorations of the white heroes to pump up outrage over the offer of honor to a Black man. That the North Carolina legislature would supposedly honor Douglass while ignoring Lee and Washington set off a firestorm of controversy. As the *Philadelphia Inquirer* noted, "This action causes great indignation."[136]

The outraged language was explicitly linked to racial grievance. White supremacist Democrats argued that it was outrageous that "a Negro had been honored while Washington and Lee had Been ignored."[137] The Columbus, Georgia, *Herald* picked up the theme and thundered that the actions of the North Carolina legislature made "the blood of every true Southerner boil with righteous indignation. It disgusts every self-respecting white man, whether he fought as a Union soldier or followed the flag of Lee."[138] The Douglass tribute was framed as an outrage against Southern white pride, proper Lost Cause memory, and unified white cross-sectional solidarity. The Democrats framed the Douglass tribute as part of a dangerous bid by the Fusionists to grant equal rights to North Carolina African Americans and to approve of racial mixing, a clear attempt to drive a racialized wedge into the Fusion Party's fragile interracial coalition.[139]

The outcry fueled not only racist outrage but also a pro-Democratic political strategy that made the violation of "proper" Civil War memory the basis for action against Fusionist legislative control. The Raleigh *News and Observer*—the capital's standard-bearer for white supremacy—marshaled Democratic outrage under the headline "Miscegenation Legislature Adjourns in Loving Memory of Fred Douglass" and reported, "The affair created a sensation in the whole city and will be a vital blow in the State at the fusionists, who knew this when they dared not step aside from the trap set for them by the negro . . . citizens of all classes are simply astounded at the colossal impudence of the whole affair."[140] The claim that North Carolina had improperly mourned

Douglass was repeated in papers around the South, where Democrats seemed outraged that the legislature would honor Douglass while supposedly slighting Washington and Lee—heroes of the United States and the Confederacy.

Some Northern papers editorialized against the Fusionists and the supposed slight against Washington and Lee, with even the until recently Republican *New York Times* calling Douglass "the miscegenation leader" and claiming that "this action, more correctly than any other official proceeding of this Legislature, shows the spirit of this body. . . . Fusion is a marriage of two parties having no principles in common."[141] Douglass's death allowed some of his former allies to turn against his radical Republican principles.

Other Northerners either ignored the use of the Douglass adjournment as a political critique or misunderstood the nature of controversy altogether. Some Northerners were simply astounded that North Carolina would praise Douglass at all, as one Minnesota newspaper commented, "A generation ago the state which now does Douglass honor would have lashed him as a runaway slave."[142] The *Democrat and Chronicle* in Rochester, New York, framed the North Carolina resolution as a sign of progress, noting that Douglass was "greater than Spartacus, greater than any slave in all history," and that the North Carolina House did itself honor by honoring his greatness.[143]

After the controversy simmered for a few days, Rochester editors realized their mistake and praised the North Carolina Fusionists for honoring Douglass and refusing to honor Lee, since "the name Douglass stands for freedom. . . . The name of Lee stands for a great rebellion, designed to disrupt this republic for the purpose of perpetuating and extending the system of slavery."[144] Not every editor was so clear-eyed. Another northern paper emphasized reconciliation and noted that "the legislature of North Carolina did itself great honor in adjourning upon the motion of a negro member, as a mark of respect to the memory of Frederick Douglass. . . . This shows that the spirit of a new and more liberal South is really gaining strength in North Carolina."[145] That judgment proved premature and overly optimistic. Northerners who overlooked the backlash against the Douglass adjournment to view North Carolina's resolution as a sign of progress did not recognize how fragile the Fusionist control of politics was, nor the strength of the white supremacy that countermanded it.

A few days after the controversy had exploded in papers all over the country, the North Carolina legislature was embroiled in controversy over just what had happened. Virgil Lusk, a former Confederate cavalry officer turned Republican who supported African American rights and the Fusion Party in the legislature, introduced a resolution stating that the entire episode was manufactured by Democratic newspapers that "willfully and maliciously" invented the entire controversy. Lusk explained that the legislature had, in fact, adjourned in respect of George Washington's birthday and that the resolution in honor of Frederick Douglass had not actually amounted to an adjournment in his honor. Lusk railed that the Democratic newspapers had twisted the facts with "unjust, untrue, misleading, malicious, and libelous" versions of the legislative action, since nothing in the tribute to Douglass removed any tribute to Washington. Democratic papers, however, countered that their version of events had been correct and that the North Carolina House journals had been "altered" to cover up the Republican Fusion Party actions.[146]

Douglass's death and the controversy over honoring him in the North Carolina legislature provided the opportunity for what Jane Turner Censer has called "race baiting" in that state. The idea of honoring a Black man's memory was so radical that it was perceived in and of itself as a threat to white supremacist memory, as it related both to U.S. patriotism and to the Lost Cause. The controversy opened the Fusion Party to political critique, and its fragile balance would last only three more years. The Frederick Douglass controversy still echoed in the 1898 campaign that saw the Democrats' return to power.[147]

Even beyond party politics, the controversy over honoring Frederick Douglass's memory in the North Carolina legislature also directly affected larger contests over Civil War memory and Confederate commemoration in the state. Honoring Douglass in North Carolina not only threatened white public memory but also added fuel to the fire of white Southern Confederate commemoration—aimed at countering public esteem for Black men like Douglass. The men and women of the North Carolina Monumental Association (NCMA) seized upon the Douglass resolution controversy to renew their efforts to erect a state Confederate monument in front of the state capitol in Raleigh. The NCMA grew out of the previous efforts of the Ladies' Memorial Association of North Carolina and started working to build a state Confederate monument in 1892, before the Fusionists had gained legislative control. But the NCMA was not able to finish the project until it capitalized upon the furor over commemorating Douglass's death to demand a Confederate commemoration as a counterweight.

North Carolina state politics had halted progress on the Confederate monument, and the NCMA seized the controversy over legislators' actions on Douglass to bring momentum back to their cause. The monument cornerstone was laid in 1894, but once the Fusionists came to power, they refused to grant any state funds to the project, preferring to prioritize education spending, and construction had stalled. The NCMA, finding itself $10,000 short of the funds necessary to begin construction, openly criticized the legislature for honoring Douglass while refusing to grant or lend the needed funds for a Confederate memorial (funds were rejected again two days after the Douglass motion).[148]

Carol M. Highsmith, "Confederate Monument on the State Capitol Grounds in Raleigh, North Carolina," photograph, 2017. Library of Congress, Prints and Photographs Division, Photograph by Carol M. Highsmith, LC-DIG-highsm-43739.

The Democratic press helped the NCMA to explicitly link the supposed disgrace of commemorating Douglass to the need for greater governmental support for Confederate commemoration. The *News and Observer* lashed out at the legislature for its willingness to honor Douglass while the Confederate monument went unfinished, calling for "all patriotic men [to] stand together to preserve the Anglo Saxon civilization" instead of commemorating a Black hero like Douglass.[149] The paper also published a cartoon showing white legislators weeping over Douglass's grave while desperate white women—members of the Ladies Monument Association—plead for them to help from in front of the incomplete monument "to the Confederate Dead." Catherine Bishir has argued that the "hints of black dominance and white subjugation" in the cartoon and in the controversy as a whole pushed the legislature to immediately appropriate funds for the Confederate monument "as an antidote to the Douglass problem."[150]

The *Boston Globe* was not wrong to headline an article about the controversy "FUSIONISTS CAUGHT IN A TRAP."[151] Paying respect to the memory of Black freedom and achievement in a mild tribute to Frederick Douglass was such a hot potato that the Fusionists ended up having to approve funding for the Confederate monument, a representation of Confederate memory that bolstered their Democratic opponents. On March 7, 1895, the legislature appropriated an additional $10,000 to finish the monument in a dramatic vote with some Republicans changing to support the monument during the last moments of debate.[152] To white supremacists in North Carolina, public mourning for Frederick Douglass proved so dangerous and unusual that they were able to shift both commemoration and politics back in a Democratic post-Confederate direction by drumming up public outrage. The North Carolina Confederate monument was unveiled on May 20, 1895, a white supremacist answer back to the funeral commemoration of Frederick Douglass as a Black hero.[153]

Reconciliation and "the Daughter of the Confederacy"

Three years later, a group of veterans who had served in Union regiments from Connecticut, Rhode Island, and Massachusetts arrived in southern Rhode Island at Narragansett Pier on September 22, 1898, to do their duty as honor guard and pallbearers for a famous woman with strong connections to the Civil War. She was an accomplished author and a society beauty who attended seasonal social functions in New York, New England, and Europe and whose poise and bearing were the subjects of wide commentary.[154] She died of malarial gastritis, just in her thirties. The old soldiers, members of the Sedgwick Post of the Grand Army of the Republic (GAR) in Wakefield, Rhode Island, accompanied her remains along with her mother from the Rockingham Hotel at Narragansett Pier to a waiting hearse and then to the train station, where they boarded a special train to New York City. Newspapers and magazines covered the old veterans, perhaps in part because Kate Pulitzer and her son, Joseph Pulitzer Jr., scions of the New York and St. Louis newspaper family, were members of the funeral party, riding on the train with the woman's remains as they traveled south.[155]

The scene of GAR veterans paying funeral honors to a woman whose memory was associated with the Civil War, concluded just over thirty years earlier, was not shocking; the GAR frequently took part in public and private funeral tributes as part of its mission of preserving Civil War memory.[156] What was remarkable was the identity of the dead woman: she was Varina Anne "Winnie" Davis, the Daughter of the Confederacy. To many, Winnie Davis personified the Confederate cause—seemingly at complete odds with the goals of the GAR, the fraternal group of Northern Civil War veterans, who often espoused "the Union Cause" as the foundation of public memory and national patriotism.[157]

But, in 1898, public mourning for Winnie Davis would strike a strong theme of reconciliation between North and South, albeit with some sectional twists. One of the GAR veterans who attended Winnie Davis's body wrote to *Confederate Veteran* magazine about why the men decided to offer their services as Winnie Davis began her 550-mile journey to be buried in Richmond, Virginia. He wrote: "It affords us great pleasure to perform such duty, thereby evidencing the fact that with us, old soldiers and citizens of the North, the sectional feeling between those who wore the blue and gray is wiped out." Winnie's mother, Varina Davis, also wrote to the magazine: "The offer of an escort from the Grand Army Post of Wakefield was especially grateful to my feelings, and I hope they will know how sincerely our whole family appreciate the delicately conceived compliment.... They proved my husband's theory: that the men who fought the war on neither side are the irreconcilables."[158] Both the GAR vets from Wakefield and Varina Davis herself saw their participation in Winnie's funeral as a sign of reconciliation between North and South. Several southern newspapers also reported on the GAR escort as a sign of reconciliation, and possibly with a note of triumph that the GAR would pay tribute to a Confederate figure.[159] Some Southerners relished the sign of GAR approval for the Confederacy; as one Tennessee newspaper put it, "Great pleasure was expressed by the citizens of Richmond over this spontaneous tribute of the men in blue."[160]

That Winnie Davis's public funeral could contain such a sign of reconciliation was ironic given her status as the Daughter of the Confederacy—a symbol of the Lost Cause that resisted reconciliation. In the last thirteen years of her life, Winnie Davis had become, as Cita Cook has argued, a "saintly model of the most awe-inspiring qualities of elite white southern womanhood, Davis became a personification of Confederate patriotism similar to the feminized symbol of Liberty. . . . many men thought of her as a central figure in an Arthurian legend in which she made every Confederate veteran her champion."[161] In 1886, when Winnie accompanied her ailing father on a tour of veterans' events in Alabama and Georgia, her rapport with the crowds led Gen. John B. Gordon to refer to her as the Daughter of the Confederacy, and the moniker had stuck. Winnie Davis had attended Southern veterans' events in the last decade of her life, even as she lived in the North, was engaged to a New Yorker, and published novels and wrote for Northern newspapers.

Winnie Davis was an honorary member of Confederate veterans' organizations and was held up as an ideal by many women who were in the process of forming chapters of the United Daughters of the Confederacy (UDC), an organization named after Winnie's honorific that would influence and promote Lost Cause memory for decades to come.[162] Davis also joined the New York City chapter of the UDC. Confederate veterans, UDC members, and journalists agreed that Winnie Davis was "an ideal American woman, both in appearance and in character."[163] The gendered nature of her public mourning mirrored the highly feminized role she played in Confederate memory.

In death, as in life, Winnie Davis as the Daughter of the Confederacy was a symbol of white, Southern womanhood and devoted memory to the Lost Cause of the Confederacy—the embodiment and celebration of Confederate values and memory. But, as indicated by the accompaniment of her body by devoted Union veterans in the GAR, her function as a Confederate symbol was also more complex.

Winnie Davis's funeral contained contradictory elements—reconciliation and the Lost Cause—which each helped contribute to American national identities in 1898. Even as it was newly crafted for a female subject, the public mourning in her honor shows that public funerals had proved durable forms of political expression throughout the second half of the nineteenth century. Union and Confederate memories had woven together by the turn of the twentieth century in some unpredictable ways. Reconciliation themes and Civil War memories that resisted them, like the Lost Cause, coexisted in the national rituals of mourning for Winnie Davis. As with Frederick Douglass's funerals, unexpected things happened when public mourning expanded to include subjects other than great, white men.

Davis's funeral also showed, just three years after the public mourning for Frederick Douglass had introduced the idea, that standards of public grief had become more malleable since the 1850s. Funerals were still a way to construct a vision of American national identity by focusing attention on the death of a beloved figure, but the standards of who qualified for such attention had broadened to include a woman. Women had long played important roles in the politics of public memory as organizers, mothers, spouses, writers, and monument builders.[164] But Davis was the first woman who was, herself, so widely and publicly mourned as the embodiment of Southern (or American) public memory. Winnie Davis's funeral was a national event.

Each part of the journey of her remains from Rhode Island to Richmond, where they were buried next to those of her father in Hollywood Cemetery, was accompanied by high ceremony and followed closely in the press—where the curious public could read about the flowers, the veterans' tributes, and the efforts to construct a marble monument over her grave. Winnie Davis's death severed, as the *Richmond Dispatch* put it, "a living link, binding us [Southerners] to heroic days and sacred memories," but her funeral allowed those memories to be expressed in important and new ways that would carry Civil War memory and its role in U.S. nationalism into the twentieth century.[165]

Southerners, especially, made themselves visible along the journey of Winnie Davis's remains. When the funeral train arrived in New York, it was met by white Southerners residing in that city, who heaped floral tributes on the casket before it departed for points farther south.[166] The train continued to Washington, D.C., and on to Richmond, where Winnie's body arrived on the morning of September 23. Her train was met by a committee of Confederate veterans (in a reverse of the scene from Rhode Island) and by a committee of the Ladies Confederate Memorial Association before her remains were processed through the streets "witnessed by immense throngs" who gathered to pay their respects.[167] Bells tolled in her honor and flags flew at half-staff across the South from Baltimore to Atlanta to Mobile.[168] The *Richmond Dispatch* noted that "the funeral procession may be said to have extended from Narragansett Pier to Richmond, with delegations from the South joining it here."[169]

The prominent Lee Camp chapter of the Sons of Confederate Veterans— of which Winnie was an honorary member—took the lead in planning the funeral procession through Richmond and coordinating the tributes from SCV and UDC chapters all over the region.[170] Although the Confederate Memorial Literary Society, an all-female offshoot of the Hollywood Memorial Association, wished for her body to lie in honor at its Confederate Museum located in the former "Confederate White House," Davis's remains were instead viewed in the "lecture room" at St. Paul's Episcopal Church before her funeral service in the sanctuary.[171] The service at St. Paul's featured prayers, sermons, and hymns (including favorites of Jefferson Davis and Robert E. Lee) sung by the hundreds of veterans and dignitaries from around the South who formed the congregation.[172]

The forms of mourning were familiar to those who had been in Richmond for the funeral tributes to previous Confederate heroes like Stonewall Jackson and Robert E. Lee. After the service, Winnie's funeral procession moved through Richmond streets "between dense lines of humanity" several miles

Varina "Winnie" Davis funeral route, 1898. Data from IPUMS, National Historical Geographic Information System; Jeremy Atack, "Historical Geographic Information Systems (GIS) database of U.S. Railroads for 1898 (May 2016)." Map by Sarah J. Purcell and Emily Hackman.

to Hollywood Cemetery.[173] Another "enormous throng" of people crowded the half mile of pathways leading from the cemetery gates to the Davis family grave site, and "tens of thousands" looked on from surrounding hillsides.[174] One Richmond newspaper noted that both Jefferson Davis's grave and Winnie's burial site were covered with floral tributes and wreaths, "and the occasion might well have been one of national pride rather than of funeral rite."[175] After a short graveside service and some hymns sung by a Methodist choir, Winnie's mother and sister kissed her for the last time, her casket was closed, and the "sorrowing crowd dispersed."[176]

Certainly, many of the symbols used in Winnie Davis's funeral ceremonies, once her body reached Richmond, confirmed her association with the Lost Cause and with Confederate memory. Beneath stained glass windows that honored Robert E. Lee and Jefferson Davis, Winnie Davis's casket rested on a catafalque covered by a Confederate flag during the service in St. Paul's, and several floral tributes also displayed Confederate emblems and the battle flag.[177] Within a week of the funeral services, photographic prints of her grave site, souvenirs suitable for home display, were advertised for sale at the Confederate Museum, which had been draped in black and white crepe in her honor.[178] The general order of the Sons of Confederate Veterans issued in Winnie's memory at the organization's headquarters in Charleston, South Carolina, noted that veterans had "learned to esteem and love her for her . . . devotion to the cause of the survivors of the confederacy."[179]

Hundreds of tributes to Davis from SCV and UDC chapters emphasized that her name would "be forever associated" with the Lost Cause and Confederate memory.[180] At a memorial service held for Winnie Davis in Nashville, Presbyterian minister and former Confederate chaplain James Hugh McNeilly preached that mourners were drawn to her "by our devotion to a glorious past" because she "stood sponsor for the purity of our purpose, the justice of our cause, the courage of our people, the honor of our conduct in the great war which we waged for the independence of the south."[181] Katie Cabell Currie, president of the UDC, ordered that members of each chapter should plan to honor Winnie Davis and should wear mourning badges for thirty days.[182]

But in 1898, Winnie Davis was mourned as more than just a symbol of the Lost Cause; she was also seen as a symbol of national reconciliation. Nina Silber has argued that the Spanish-American War in 1898 necessitated a spirit of Northern forgiveness and hastened a culture of martial reconciliation in both sections, and Winnie's funeral, which took place less than one month after the end of that war, confirms that idea as it coincided with the need to see Southern men as true "Americans."[183] The New York World, Joseph Pulitzer's paper for which Winnie Davis and her mother, Varina, wrote and which was itself involved in ginning up the war with Spain, published an obituary for Winnie touting the power of her memory to unite "men born under the palmetto and men born under the pine." The *World* opined that Davis was "beloved of all southerners, as a woman peculiarly representing their region, its civilization and its culture," but also noted that Northerners who knew her loved her equally. The paper continued, arguing that the name of Winnie Davis "had come to represent the restoration, the good will, the truly national feeling which in this new war of ours has found so fitting an expression in the fighting of southerner and northerner side by side."[184]

Other newspapers agreed that a nation newly united by the Spanish-American War would join in grief for Winnie Davis. The *Chicago Tribune* editors wished that her death would help the sections to put aside their differences and forget the Civil War in the interest of national action in the present. They wrote: "The sooner the veil of oblivion is drawn over the whole matter of the Southern rebellion against the American union the better and wiser for all concerned. . . . The Spanish war should be allowed to cover the last of the old enmities and war talk out of sight and hearing."[185] The *Atlanta Constitution* editor claimed on the same day, "The war with Spain has demonstrated the fact that the citizens of the United States are one people—no more sectionalism."[186] In the press coverage of Winnie Davis's funeral, reconciliation was a central factor in a renewed vision of American national identity.

As with so many public funerals in the past, the press framed mourning for Winnie Davis as capable of doing the work of holding the nation together. Newspapers, both Northern and Southern, stressed that she could serve as a symbol of reconciliation—even as Richmonders closely associated her with the Lost Cause. The *Atlanta Constitution* noted the fact that Davis died in Narragansett was "peculiarly suggestive of restored peace and good will between the sections. . . . In many respects Miss Winnie Davis was identified with the old South and with sectional memories, but this was due rather to the surroundings of her birth and to the homage of which she was made the recipient on the part of the old soldiers than to any absence of national spirit in her allegiance."[187] The *New York Times* claimed that Winnie Davis "had almost as many, if not more, friends among Northerners as in the Southland."[188] Charles M. Robinson of Rochester, New York, published a poem in the *Chicago Tribune* entitled "Winnie Davis" that posed her as an absolute symbol of reconciliation, buried "Under the Stars and Stripes." Robinson imagined that even though Davis was a true symbol of the Lost Cause for Confederates, both "Gray coats and blue" would pay her tribute:

"Our daughter," say the gray;
"Yours and ours: One, today."
Whisper the blue.[189]

Robinson's vision represented well the fact that Winnie Davis was praised in both North and South upon the occasion of her death and funeral. But his depiction of her lying beneath the Stars and Stripes went too far, probably evincing a hoped-for unity instead of any power that Davis possessed to truly instill full reconciliation. Confederate flags, the Stars and Bars not the Stars and Stripes, flew over Winnie Davis's grave and that of her father, located just next to her. Mourning Winnie Davis represented hoped-for reconciliation but still showed how potent the Lost Cause could be.

Within a year of her death, the Richmond UDC chapter raised money to erect a marble monument over Winnie Davis's grave. The monument, designed by George Julian Zolnay, "the Sculptor of the Confederacy," and carved in Italy of Carrara marble, was a seven-foot-high depiction of the "Angel of Grief."[190] The marble angel, who presides over the whole Davis family grave site by bending to place poppies on Winnie Davis's grave, emphasizes personal grief and mourning in the visual language of funerary sculpture popular at the end of the 1890s.[191] At the memorial's unveiling in November 1899, the program described it as the work of "friends and admirers [from] both North and South."[192] The monument was framed as a tribute from the reconciled nation.

But the UDC members who funded and erected the monument seldom promoted this tone of absolute reconciliation. The UDC favored Southern dominance in culture and memory.[193] In 1898, there were more than 14,000 UDC members, the most powerful of whom resisted complete reconciliation and, as Joan Cashin has argued, "embraced the Lost Cause as a secular religion" that should be taught in public schools and emphasized in Southern civic culture.[194] The UDC was frequently at odds with Winnie's mother, Varina, viewing her as a traitor to the Southern cause and disapproving of her residence in New York City and her friendship with Julia Grant, among other things.[195] Despite their enmity toward Varina Davis, the UDC embraced Winnie as a usable symbol. Many UDC members who contributed funds for Winnie's graveside monument did so out of their sorrow and their sense of her value as the Daughter of the Confederacy, and they viewed their monetary contributions as an extension of the "self-denial" they showed in the war itself.[196]

Members of the UDC, by and large, framed Winnie Davis as an embodiment of Southern sacrifice in the Civil War that should never be forgotten and which put a spin on the spirit of reconciliation in 1898. Members of the UDC were willing to see Winnie Davis, her death in the North, and the tributes paid to her by Northerners and Southerners alike as a "token of our reunited country." But, simultaneously and even more strenuously, they emphasized that she stood for the Confederate cause, truly glorious, even in defeat.

Winnie Davis memorial, Hollywood Cemetery, Richmond, Virginia, c. 1908,
Detroit Publishing Co. Library of Congress, Prints and Photographs Division,
LC-DIG-det-4a23050.

Rev. James I. Vance reminded the UDC women who gathered for a memorial service in Nashville, Tennessee, that a true Southern woman "prefers to lose everything rather than sacrifice honor. . . . God keep the South true to this mighty sentiment of the past, and may the shaft which rises above the grave of the Daughter of the Confederacy be another sentinel pointing the faith of the people upward to that which may be intangible, but is eternal!"[197] The "Angel of Grief" (the actual monument that replaced the simple shaft imagined by Reverend Vance) associated Winnie Davis with the ideal of Southern womanhood that bolstered the Lost Cause in its essence. This Lost Cause, presiding over the grave of the Daughter of the Confederacy, could allow reconciliation but only on limited and Southern terms.

Winnie Davis's funeral, her burial, and the monument erected over her grave show how public funerals enabled Americans to envision sometimes conflicting notions of American national identity—a process that had persisted for almost fifty years since the death of Henry Clay in 1852. Visions of the meaning of the union itself were tied to memorial practices over and over again. Aspects of the funeral and mourning rituals were familiar. Davis's body traveled like Henry Clay's. Mourning rituals for Winnie Davis lauded the common white, male sacrifice of Civil War soldiers, praise that began during funerals for Elmer Ellsworth and Stonewall Jackson. Richmond's role in Davis's funeral and her burial in the Hollywood Cemetery echoed themes from the fights over civic pride in that city since the funerals of Stonewall Jackson and Robert E. Lee. Using Davis as a symbol of needed unity during a time of international conflict echoed the transatlantic funeral of George Peabody. The ways that the UDC used Winnie Davis as a symbol, sometimes at odds with her own embrace of the North, showed that fragile mixture of memory and forgetting, such huge themes in the funerals of Charles Sumner and Joseph E. Johnston, were still operating. Like Frederick Douglass, Winnie Davis showed that public mourning could stretch in new ways, but only so far.

Ultimately, Winnie Davis's funeral and public mourning show the complexity and considerable irony of Civil War memory and its place in U.S. national identity. Reconciliation between North and South was definitely underway when Winnie Davis died at the turn of the twentieth century. But her death shows that reconciliation simultaneously meant different things to different people, even as they engaged in the reunification process together. David Blight maintains that "reconciliation joined arms with white supremacy in Civil War memory" because many Northerners agreed to accede to the Lost Cause memory of Southern heroism while forgetting Black sacrifice and the ties between war and emancipation.[198] Winnie Davis's death and commemoration certainly boosted this version of Lost Cause reconciliation, emphasizing feminine sacrifice and the strength of Confederate memory.

Other scholars argue that Union veterans, particularly, resisted the reconciliation narrative, emphasizing instead a more limited reunion that neither forgot slavery nor de-emphasized the Union Cause.[199] Northern newspapers mourned for Winnie Davis as a symbol of reunion, especially a reunion needed for the Spanish-American War. But, even as they constantly worked to remember the Union Cause, at least some Northern veterans—from the Wakefield, Rhode Island, GAR—were also willing to participate in her funeral rituals, as steeped in Lost Cause mythology as they were. Notably, no African Americans publicly mourned the Daughter of the Confederacy, whose memory was not open enough to encompass any emancipationist vision of the past. When it came to reconciliation, some white northerners, however, seemed willing to mourn Winnie Davis, even on Southern terms.

American national identities in the second half of the nineteenth century were fashioned out of this kind of contest between versions of Civil War memory. When we try to determine the role that Civil War memory played in the reconstitution of U.S. national identity at the turn of the twentieth century, we would be well advised not to be too absolute in any of our statements. Distinct strains of memory mattered, and they all overlapped: Winnie Davis was a symbol of the Lost Cause, and she was a symbol of reconciliation. U.S. national identity was not only made up of the remnants of the Union Cause or symbolism (whether or not influenced by the Lost Cause). Some forms of U.S. national identity were reconstituted out of strands of Union and Confederate memory. Mourning for Winnie Davis shows how reconciliation and the Lost Cause could work together.

The same contested reconciliation was present in public mourning for Frederick Douglass. The Douglass monument in Rochester, New York, and the North Carolina Confederate monument in Raleigh represented diametrically opposed strands of Civil War memory. But *both* were symbols of the power of public grief and admiration. Douglass commanded attention, respect, and reaction—standing as a great inspiration to those who would admire Black people, and to those who would repress them.

Frederick Douglass's funerals, and the mourning and monuments in their aftermath, show how standards of national grief had shifted by the 1890s to include Black heroism and accomplishment—even as white supremacy also proved resilient. Traditional public funeral forms paid public respect to Douglass, and his Black body was memorialized as none other in American history. But the stakes of public mourning were so high that white supremacists could not be content with Douglass being praised as a dead hero. American identity, as created by the memory of great men like Douglass, was open enough to include him in the pantheon of mourned heroes, but post-Confederate racists fought back, challenging both the focus on Douglass and any excess of public grief spent on him and not on white Southerners. The conflicts emphasized that Douglass's fight for Black freedom and equality would have to go on without him.

The public grief for Winnie Davis, in both the North and the South, continued the enduring cultural power of Confederate images: monuments, flags, poetry, and print culture. That power would change and grow in the twentieth century and would haunt the American nation into the twenty-first century. The struggle with public grief and divided American identities long outlived the Daughter of the Confederacy herself. A national identity that made room for the Lost Cause alongside the Union Cause would have enduring consequences, and it has not yet been buried.

Conclusion

On July 26, 2020, civil rights icon Congressman John Lewis took his last trip across the Edmund Pettus Bridge in Selma, Alabama, in a casket flanked by weeping, singing, and cheering admirers. A stately horse-drawn carriage transported Lewis's flag-draped coffin over a pathway of rose petals, with red roses on the south side of the bridge, where Lewis had been beaten by state and local police during the "Bloody Sunday" voting rights march fifty-five years earlier. In 2020, when Lewis reached the far side of the bridge, instead of beating him, Alabama state troopers saluted. Many mourners wore shirts or carried signs that linked Congressman Lewis's legacy to the Black Lives Matter movement and the ongoing protests for racial justice that swept the United States in the summer of 2020. National television stations provided live coverage of Congressman Lewis's remains crossing the bridge, and hundreds of thousands of viewers watched the scene on television, YouTube, and other internet live feeds. Hundreds of thousands also immediately signed petitions and endorsed a movement that had picked up steam in 2020 to rename the bridge after Lewis, a proposed reversal of the 1940 naming of the bridge in honor of Pettus, a Confederate general and Alabama Ku Klux Klan leader.[1]

Congressman Lewis's extensive funeral honors proved that public funerals still have power to hold Americans in thrall and to inspire political expression about what the nation should stand for. The fact that many Americans were also having to limit or forgo family funerals as the COVID-19 pandemic killed hundreds of thousands also may have magnified collective public expressions of grief for John Lewis. The trip across the Edmund Pettus Bridge followed funeral services in Representative Lewis's hometown of Troy and in Selma, and it began his journey to lie in repose at the Alabama state capitol in Montgomery. The next day, July 27, John Lewis lay in state in the rotunda of the U.S. Capitol, the first Black person ever to receive this state honor, and thousands paid their respects as the congressman rested on Abraham Lincoln's catafalque. His remains were then transported to Atlanta for a private funeral at the historic Ebenezer Baptist Church and burial at South-View Cemetery.[2] Public attention and news coverage followed Congressman Lewis's funerals at every turn, especially as Lewis's civil rights legacy amplified the renewed calls for civil rights in the wake of the May 25, 2020, police killing of George Floyd in Minneapolis and so many other recent incidents of police violence against Black people.

It was no coincidence that Lewis's public funeral also showed the continued historical echo of Civil War memories, which retain considerable power as politicized symbols in U.S. culture. Lost on no one was the irony of Lewis receiving funeral honors on a bridge named for a Confederate hero, where Lewis had his skull broken by hostile law enforcement officers during a civil rights protest, to which he had returned many times for symbolic anniversary marches over the decades. Mourner Ralph Williams, who traveled from his home in Jasper, Alabama, to pay his respects to Lewis during the funeral procession at the bridge, told the *New York Times* that the events there in 1965 were "as significant as the battle of Gettysburg in the history of this country," using the public funeral for Lewis as a connection between the Civil War, the civil rights movement, and the events of the summer of 2020.[3] John Lewis's public funeral commemorated the struggle for Black equality as the struggle continued.

Many of the elements in Lewis's public funerals—lying in state, crowds praising the deceased as his remains traveled past in a carriage, church services, meaningful political eulogies—will feel familiar to readers of this book. Public funerals, especially those for nationally important politicians like John Lewis, retain many of the same formal elements established in the nineteenth century. Public interest in the rituals of grief can spread faster in the twenty-first century via social media, internet, and television, but the rituals of mourning retain remarkable echoes of funerals of Henry Clay or Frederick Douglass or Elmer Ellsworth.

John Lewis's public funeral also retained the essential function of allowing mourners to imagine how the memory of the deceased hero could reinforce their ideas about the American nation. Former president Barack Obama said in his eulogy for Lewis at the Ebenezer Baptist Church that he had come to praise "an American whose faith was tested again and again to produce a man of pure joy and unbreakable perseverance—John Robert Lewis. . . . Now, this great country is a work in progress. . . . We were born with instructions: to form a more perfect union . . . that what gives each new generation purpose is to take up the unfinished work of the last and carry it further than anyone might have thought possible."[4] Many public mourners, political candidates, and social justice activists took up John Lewis's call to create "good trouble" to help "perfect" the United States in the wake of his death and mourning.

The larger commemorative landscape that grew up around the rituals of mourning in post–Civil War America explored in this book—monuments, holidays, rituals of remembrance—are changing, especially the clash between

Confederate symbols (and their white supremacist associations) and the ongoing movements for racial justice. Civil War commemoration continues to be a part of current-day political struggles in the United States, as people fight over the present using the symbols of the past. In recent years, long-standing calls to remove Confederate memorials from public spaces all over the country have accelerated, especially after the 2015 murder of nine Black worshippers in the Mother Emanuel AME Church in Charleston, South Carolina, and the deadly 2017 clash between white supremacists and social justice activists around the Robert E. Lee memorial in Charlottesville, Virginia.[5]

In the context of recent challenges to Confederate commemoration, several of the commemorations and monuments in these chapters, intended by mourners in the nineteenth century to be permanent, have been changed or removed. Henry Clay's grave and monument in the Lexington Cemetery, paradoxically, have recently been surrounded by large Confederate memorials removed by the city of Lexington, Kentucky, from downtown public areas and relocated to the cemetery.[6] Amid civic reexamination of the use of Confederate symbols in Alexandria, Virginia, the United Daughters of the Confederacy-sponsored plaque on the former Marshall House Hotel commemorating the "murder" of James W. Jackson by Col. Elmer Ellsworth and his men was removed after the Marriott corporation purchased the hotel on the site in 2016.[7]

Even some of the most prominent Confederate memorials chronicled in this book have been recently removed. City officials in Richmond, Virginia, removed the Stonewall Jackson memorial (among others) from Monument Avenue on July 1, 2020.[8] Robert E. Lee's is the only major Confederate memorial still standing on Monument Avenue, and it has since been painted over and transformed as a site of antiracist speeches, performances, and rallies.[9] The recumbent Lee sculpture over his grave in the Washington and Lee University chapel is still there, but no Confederate flags adorn the space.[10]

Perhaps not surprisingly in a time when racial justice has been the subject of a renewed round of roiling debates, the monuments associated with Frederick Douglass discussed in chapter 5 of this book have all changed in recent years. After years of resisting change, the North Carolina Confederate memorial in front of the state capitol at Raleigh, erected in 1895 in the backlash against the state legislature marking the death of Frederick Douglass, was removed in June 2020.[11] Meanwhile, the memorial to Frederick Douglass conceived of immediately after his 1895 death has been moved twice in Rochester, New York, to give it a more prominent public position, and his grave in Mount Hope Cemetery is often visited by people who pay respects and leave behind coins and flowers.[12] Douglass still has the power to provoke racist backlash, however, and one of several smaller memorials to him that have been placed around Rochester in his honor in recent years was ripped from its base and defaced on July 4, 2020, as a rebuke to the summer's protests against racism.[13] The Metropolitan AME Church in Washington, D.C., where Douglass's massive funeral service took place in 1895, is suing the white supremacist Proud Boys group and one of its founders, Enrique Tarrio, for stealing and defacing a "Black Lives Matter" sign hung outside the church in December 2020.[14]

Even though Douglass's church was attacked by white supremacists, for the most part commemorations in cemeteries have been left untouched, with even Confederate symbols there protected by their association with graves and a less public display. Winnie Davis's "Angel of Grief" statue still oversees the Davis family grave site in Richmond's Hollywood Cemetery, although the cemetery has downplayed the display of Confederate battle flags and Jefferson Davis's Monument Avenue statue was toppled by protesters and removed by the city.[15] Although the city of Lexington, Virginia, features far fewer Confederate flags and emblems in public than it used to, and even the statue of Stonewall Jackson on the VMI campus has been removed, Jackson's grave is still a noted pilgrimage site in the town.[16]

In the summer of 2020, as the commemorations of Rep. John Lewis reminded us, public funerals still retained the power to communicate loud messages about contemporary politics and national identities, tinged with memories and legacies of the U.S. Civil War that haunt us still. Death continues to frame politicized fights over the Lost Cause, the Union Cause, emancipationist memory, and the future of the United States. History seems relevant in both expected and unexpected ways.[17] As a global pandemic raged, the past year has seen both massive nationwide protests in favor of racial equality and the angry display of the Confederate battle flag in the U.S. Capitol, carried by white supremacists protesting and seeking to stop the certification of the 2020 Electoral College vote.[18] In a new time of mass death, when the legacies of the U.S. Civil War are far from over and its memory is not entirely faded, we have not finished the work of using funerals to imagine contested meanings of the American nation itself.

Notes

Abbreviations

ALPLM	Abraham Lincoln Presidential Library and Museum, Springfield, MA
FDP	Frederick Douglass Papers, Library of Congress
FDSB I	Frederick Douglass Obituaries, Accounts of His Funeral and Other Material, Scrapbook, Monroe County (NY) Public Library Special Collections, Rochester, NY
Hoar File, AAS	George Frisbie Hoar File, American Antiquarian Society, Worcester, MA
LOC	Library of Congress, Washington, DC
MCL Papers	Mary Custis Lee Papers, Virginia Historical Society, Richmond, VA
MHS	Massachusetts Historical Society, Boston, MA
Newberry Scrapbook	"Sumner Newspapers Articles," General Collection, Newberry Library, Chicago, IL
Peabody DBS	Peabody Death and Burial Scrapbook, Peabody Institute Library and Archives, Peabody, MA
Peabody FCS	Peabody Funeral Correspondence Scrapbook, Peabody Institute Library and Archives, Peabody, MA

Introduction

1. Matt Morgan, "Charles Sumner," *Frank Leslie's Illustrated Newspaper*, March 28, 1874. On Morgan and the support of the Liberal Republicans by *Frank Leslie's*, see Kent, "War Cartooned/Cartoon War."

2. "A Nation's Honor," *Inter-Ocean*, March 14, 1874.

3. See the AP dispatch in *Hartford Daily Courant*, March 14, 1874, and *New York Times*, March 14, 1874; the *Philadelphia Inquirer*, the *Chicago Daily Tribune*, the *Little Rock Daily Republican*, and the *Sioux City Daily Journal* also gave special notice to the presence of African American mourners at the Capitol, in their issues dated March 14, 1874; Mattie, "Why Lamar Eulogized Sumner."

4. Douglass, "Eulogy for Charles Sumner," 397, 398, 399.

5. Silber, "Reunion and Reconciliation," 61.

6. To understand the trajectory of scholarship on Civil War memory, see: Silber, *Romance of Reunion*; Silber, *This War Ain't Over*; Silber, "Reunion and Reconciliation"; Blight, *Race and Reunion*; Blight, *American Oracle*; Gannon, *Won Cause*; Gannon, *Americans Remember*; Janney, *Remembering the Civil War*; Cook, *Civil War Memories*; Harris, *Across the Bloody Chasm*; Fahs and Waugh, *Memory of the Civil War*.

7. For a similar argument that Northern and Southern identities mutually constituted one another, see Cobb, *Away Down South*. Important works on nationalism that relate

include Rable, *Confederate Republic*; Faust, *Creation of Confederate Nationalism*; Rubin, *Shattered Nation*; Gallagher, *Becoming Confederates*; Bonner, *Colors and Blood*; Lawson, *Patriot Fires*; Parish, *North and the Nation*; Clarke, *War Stories*.

8. McIvor, *Mourning in America*, 66; Rollins, "Ethics of Epedeictic Rhetoric."

9. Anderson, *Imagined Communities*. Some of the most influential texts on collective memory and commemoration are Halbwachs, *On Collective Memory*; Nora, *Realms of Memory*; Rosenzweig and Thelen, *Presence of the Past*; Gillis, *Commemorations*; Kammen, *Mystic Chords of Memory*; Gobel and Rossell, *Commemoration*. On nineteenth-century Americans' penchant for spectacle, see Tenneriello, *Spectacle Culture*; Greiman, *Democracy's Spectacle*; Oriard, *Reading Football*.

10. On collective memory and national identity, see Halbwachs, *On Collective Memory*; Purcell, *Sealed with Blood*; Schwartz, *Abraham Lincoln and the Forge*; Thelen, *Memory and American History*; Gillis, *Commemorations*; Hobsbawm and Ranger, *Invention of Tradition*; Silber, *This War Ain't Over*.

11. Brown, "Civil War Remembrance as Reconstruction," 206–36.

12. Important works on the earlier periods of mourning that influenced the funerals discussed in this book include Laderman, *Sacred Remains*; Lepore, *Mansion of Happiness*; Isenberg and Burstein, *Mortal Remains*; Purcell, *Sealed with Blood*.

13. Hacker, "Has the Demographic Impact," 456; see also Hacker, "A Census-Based Count."

14. Faust, *This Republic of Suffering*; Schantz, *Awaiting the Heavenly Country*; Janney, *Burying the Dead*; Neff, *Honoring*; Blair, *Cities of the Dead*.

15. Garlick, *Final Curtain*; Gordon and Marshall, *Place of the Dead*; Sinnema, *Wake of Wellington*; Geary, *Living with the Dead*; Reis, *Death Is a Festival*; Standaert, *Interweaving of Rituals*; Meyer-Fong, *What Remains*.

16. Seeman, *Death in the New World*; Seeman, *Huron-Wendat Feast*; Bullock, *Tea Sets*; Meyer, *Cemeteries and Gravemarkers*; Yalom, *American Resting Place*; Giguere, *Characteristically American*; Farrell, "Dying of Death"; Huntington, *Celebrations of Death*; Tharp, "'Preserving Their Form and Features.'"

17. Puckle, *Funeral Customs*; Curl, *Celebration of Death*; Hertz, *Death and the Right Hand*; Sharp, *Bodies*; Koslofsky, *Reformation of the Dead*; Armour and Williams, "Image Making"; DiGirolamo, "Newsboy Funerals"; Jumonville, "Wastebasket"; Wilson, "Southern Funeral Director."

18. Laqueur, *Work*, 1; see also Craughwell, *Stealing Lincoln's Body*; Schwartz, *Dead Matter*; Flood, "Contemplating Corpses"; Porter, *Flesh in the Age of Reason*.

19. Goodheart, *1861*; Randall, *Colonel Elmer Ellsworth*; Janney, *Remembering the Civil War*, 140–43; Parker, "Funeral of George Peabody"; Welch, "George Peabody's Funeral."

20. For examples, see Heidler and Heidler, *Henry Clay*; Korda, *Clouds of Glory*.

21. Fox, *Lincoln's Body*; Hodes, *Mourning Lincoln*; Peterson, *Lincoln in American Memory*; Waugh, *U.S. Grant*; Collins, *Death and Resurrection*.

Chapter One

1. "A Beautiful and Affecting Scene," *Pittsfield Sun*, July 22, 1852. Small portions of this chapter, in different form, appear in Purcell, "All That Remains of Henry Clay," and are used here by permission.

2. *Louisville Daily Times*, July 10, 1852.

3. *Cincinnati Gazette* quoted in *Louisville Daily Times*, July 14, 1852; "Reception in Cincinnati" and "A Beautiful and Affecting Scene," *New York Times*, July 17, 1852.

4. "Cortege Down the River," *Louisville Evening Bulletin*, July 9, 1852; see also *(Boston) Daily Atlas*, July 23, 1852. The women of Sharpsburg, Kentucky, put on a similar display in that town's Fourth of July parade; "Celebrated in Sharpsburg," *Kentucky Whig*, July 9, 1852.

5. *Cincinnati Gazette* quoted in *Louisville Daily Times*, July 14, 1852. Thirty-one women of Hudson, New York, also dressed in mourning to represent an allegory of the states mourning; see *Report of the Committee of Arrangements*, 53.

6. On women's participation in Whig politics, see Varon, *We Mean to Be Counted*.

7. "Hon. Henry Clay's Remains from Cincinnati to Louisville," *Louisville Evening Bulletin*, July 9, 1852; "Reception in Cincinnati," *New York Times*, July 17, 1852; "Latest Intelligence . . . Mr. Clay's Remains in Louisville," *New York Times*, July 10, 1852; Coleman, *Last Days*, 11.

8. "Cortege Down the River," *Louisville Evening Bulletin*, July 9, 1852; Purcell, "Henry Clay's Coffin."

9. Laderman, *Sacred Remains*, 17; Kahler, *Long Farewell*.

10. Costello, *Property of the Nation*, 36.

11. While many of the early hagiographic biographies of Clay devoted considerable attention to his funeral as a means to praise him, not many contemporary biographers have commented extensively on the huge funeral celebrations, and even scholars who have studied, for example, his eulogies, have not connected them to the tour of his body or the widespread national ritual. See Sargent, *Life and Public Services of Henry Clay*, 367–423; Colton, *Last Seven Years*; Schurz, *Life of Henry Clay* 2:405–6; Remini, *Henry Clay*, 780–86; Heidler and Heidler, *Henry Clay*, 492; Apple, *Family Legacy of Henry Clay*, 94–95.

12. On Clay's role in the Compromise of 1850, see Hamilton, *Prologue to Conflict*; Bordewich, *America's Great Debate*; Baptist, *The Half Has Never Been Told*, 337–42; Potter, *Impending Crisis*, 90–120; Holt, *Political Crisis of the 1850s*, 81–86; Remini, *Henry Clay*, 730–61; Heidler and Heidler, *Henry Clay*, 458–75.

13. *New York Times*, July 1, 1852; *Report of the Committee of Arrangements*, 10; Coleman, *Last Days*, 1.

14. Cass, Houston, Jones, and Stockton were Democrats; Underwood and Fish were Whigs; Senate Historical Office and House of Representatives Historical Office, *Biographical Directory of the United States Congress*.

15. *Eulogies Delivered in the Senate and House*, 2:8; for reprints, see, for example, "The Memory of Mr. Clay," *Weekly Crescent*, July 10, 1852; "Eulogies of Mr. Clay in Congress," *Baltimore Weekly Sun*, July 3, 1852; "Henry Clay—Living and Dead, Mr. Seward's Remarks," *New York Times*, July 2, 1852.

16. Butler, "Sermon, Delivered in the Senate Chamber," 492.

17. On mourning for previous politicians and heroes, see Purcell, *Sealed with Blood*; Laderman, *Sacred Remains*; Isenberg and Burstein, *Mortal Remains*; Kammen, *Digging Up the Dead*; Zboray and Zboray, *Voices without Votes*, 169–70, 174–78. Clay's funerals bore some remarkable similarities to the funeral honoring the Duke of Wellington in England in November 1852; see Sinnema, *Wake of Wellington*.

18. Brooke, "To Be 'Read by the Whole People'"; Applegate, *Most Famous Man in America*, 236.

19. On Taylor's funerals, see Bauer, *Zachary Taylor*, 316–19; Smith, *Presidencies of Zachary Taylor and Millard Fillmore*, 156–58; Dyer, *Zachary Taylor*, 406–10; Hamilton, *Zachary Taylor*, 2:393–400; Greenberg, "Ohioans vs. Georgians," 575–98; Hodges, *New York City Cartmen*, 171. A story circulated that Clay had refused to eulogize Zachary Taylor; see "Mr. Clay's Quarrel with General Taylor," *National Era*, November 10, 1859.

20. *Louisville Daily Times*, July 10, 1852.

21. "Cortege Down the River," *Louisville Evening Bulletin*, July 9, 1852.

22. "Funeral of Henry Clay," *(Trenton) State Gazette*, July 2, 1852. Several papers noted the "telegraphic despatches conveying the intelligence of the death of Mr. Clay"; see "Death of Hon. Henry Clay," *Barre Gazette*, July 2, 1852; "From the Memphis Whig Extra," *Mississippi Palladium*, July 1, 1852; "The Obsequies of the Honorable Henry Clay," *Bangor Daily Whig and Courier*, July 5, 1852; *Baltimore Weekly Sun*, July 10, 1852. On the feeling of technological change in the 1850s and its impact on popular and political culture, see Neely, *Boundaries of American Political Culture*; Lehuu, *Carnival on the Page*. Telegraphic communication had also played a role in the coordination of mourning for John Quincy Adams; see Parsons, "The 'Splendid Pageant,'" 465. On the telegraph, see Hindle, *Emulation and Invention*, 85–107.

23. Varon, *Disunion!*, 248.

24. Holt, *Rise and Fall*, 725.

25. Henry Clay quoted in Remini, *Henry Clay*, 740; on Clay and union, see Varon, *Disunion!*, 12, 46–47, 212–13.

26. Verdery, *Political Lives of Dead Bodies*, 1; Johnson, "Why Dead Bodies Talk," 1–26.

27. Koudounaris, *Heavenly Bodies*; Ken, *Christian Mummification*; Kleinberg, *Flesh Made Word*, 34–43.

28. On the similar treatment of Lincoln, see Fox, *Lincoln's Body*, 61–64.

29. "Henry Clay," *National Era*, July 8, 1852, 110. The *Richmond Examiner* also called Clay seemingly "inexhaustible"; see "From the Richmond Examiner," *Georgia Telegraph*, July 13, 1852. On the connection between the state of bodies and politics in the mid-nineteenth century, see Rice, "Picturing Bodies," 213–35.

30. Neely, *Boundaries of American Political Culture*, 14–17. On Clay's "magnetism" as part of the combination of his body and personality, see Brown, "Henry Clay and the Politics of Consensus," in *Politics and Statesmanship*, 117–19.

31. Heidler and Heidler, *Henry Clay*, 24, 71; see "Death and Obsequies of Henry Clay," *New York Daily Times*, July 3, 1852.

32. Wheeler, *Phrenological Characters*, 3.

33. Magoon, *Living Orators*, 153.

34. Brown, *Eulogy on the Life and Character of Henry Clay*, 29. In another eulogy, Henry Tator praised Clay's "personal appearance," voice, and gesture, comparing him to both oak and pine trees; Tator, *Eulogy Commemorative of the Character of Hon. Henry Clay*, 14; see also "Henry Clay," *National Era*, July 8, 1852, 110; "From the Richmond Examiner, Henry Clay," *Macon Weekly Telegraph*, July 13, 1852; Anderson, *Funeral Oration*, 30; Briggs, *Lincoln's Speeches Reconsidered*, 114–16. Clay himself also sometimes employed bodily metaphors in his speeches; see Watson, *Liberty and Power*, 244.

35. "The Clay Statue. A Model of a Man."

36. Heidler and Heidler, *Henry Clay*, 482–83.

37. Heidler and Heidler, *Henry Clay*, 487. In fact, newspapers reported on Clay's failing health as early as 1848; see *National Era*, November 23, 1848; see also "The Wife of Henry Clay," *Farmer's Cabinet*, June 3, 1852.

38. "Clay, Calhoun, and Webster," *Arkansas Whig*, June 3, 1852.

39. "Henry Clay," *Pennsylvania Freeman*, quoted in *Frederick Douglass' Paper*, January 15, 1852.

40. "Party Bitterness," *Daily Alabama Journal*, June 4, 1852; see also "From Philadelphia," *Kentucky Whig*, July 9, 1852; "Disgusting," *Daily Picayune*, May 11, 1852; "Speech of Hon. H. Marshall, of Kentucky," *Daily Globe*, May 28, 1852.

41. See "Latest Intelligence . . . The Death of Henry Clay," *New York Daily Times*, June 30, 1852, on Clay's instructions to his son. Because Clay's oldest son, Theodore, was emotionally troubled and led a dissipated life, Clay's second son, Thomas, became his chief confidant; see Apple, *Family Legacy of Henry Clay*.

42. Morrison, "American Reaction," 115; Johnson and Johnson, "Funeral Pageantry," 144–51; Parsons, "The 'Splendid Pageant.'" John Quincy Adams's body was also followed by the press as it was moved via train to Boston for burial. Adams received four large funeral ceremonies in northern cities. But Clay's tour was much longer, with many more stops, and the outpouring of public grief was an order of magnitude larger.

43. United States House of Representatives: History, Art & Archives, "Individuals Who Have Lain in State or in Honor," https://history.house.gov/Institution/Lie-In-State/Lie-In -State-Honor/, accessed June 19, 2019; *New York Weekly Tribune*, July 10, 1852. John Lutz, who laid out the Lexington Cemetery, gave Clay four plots in the parklike burial ground in 1850; Heidler and Heidler, *Henry Clay*, 483.

44. Butler, "The Strong Staff Broken," 246. Upon learning of Clay's death, newspapers immediately spread the news of municipalities lowering their flags and beginning to drape public spaces in mourning; see, for example, "Special Telegraphic Correspondence," *North American and United States Gazette*, June 30, 1852; "Death of Mr. Clay," *Daily Atlas*, June 30, 1852. Henry Clay's Death," *New York Daily Times*, June 30, 1852, reports on reactions in Newburyport, Poughkeepsie, Rochester, Albany, Buffalo, Harrisburg, Philadelphia, and Baltimore.

45. Remini, *Henry Clay*, 136–37; Baxter, *Henry Clay*, 208–9.

46. Many articles note how people gathered to see Clay as he traveled on trains and boats. See, for example, "Remains of Henry Clay," *New York Observer and Chronicle*, July 15, 1852; *Gleason's Pictorial Drawing-Room Companion*, July 31, 1852, 76, and August 14, 1852, 104; "Funeral Obsequies of Henry Clay," *Buffalo Morning Express*, July 7, 1852; "Henry Clay," *Volksblatt*, July 9, 1852; "Transit of Mr. Clay's Remains," *Baltimore Weekly Sun*, July 10, 1852. For descriptions of train car decor, see *Cleveland Plain Dealer*, July 7, 1852; "The Remains of Henry Clay," (Rochester, NY) *Daily Advertiser*, July 7, 1852. The *New York Observer* commented on the pride the directors of the New York and Erie Railroad could take in transporting Clay's body; "Mr. Clay's Remains," *New York Weekly Tribune*, July 3, 1852.

47. "The Route of Procession, Incidents," *Baltimore Weekly Sun*, July 3, 1852; "Meeting in Baltimore in Reference to the Death of Henry Clay," *State Gazette*, July 1, 1852; "Mr. Clay's Death—Proceedings in Baltimore," *New York Daily Times*, July 1, 1852. It was important in the mid-nineteenth century for Americans to view their dead loved ones, and they reacted similarly to Clay's death with an urge to view his face; see Laderman, *Sacred Remains*, 75.

48. "Transit of Mr. Clay's Remains," *Baltimore Weekly Sun*, July 10, 1852.

49. "The Funeral Scene in Philadelphia," *New York Daily Times*, July 3, 1852.

50. "The Funeral Scene in Philadelphia," *New York Daily Times*, July 3, 1852; "Arrival of Mr. Clay's Remains at Philadelphia," *Baltimore Weekly Sun*, July 10, 1852; "A Funeral Procession at Night. The Body of Mr. Clay," *Natchez Weekly Courier*, July 21, 1852; "Reception of Henry Clay's Funeral Cortege in Philadelphia," *New York Times*, July 1, 1852; "Funeral of Henry Clay," *State Gazette*, July 2, 1852; "The Body of Henry Clay," *State Gazette*, July 3, 1852; "Reception of the Remains . . . ," *Farmer's Cabinet*, July 8, 1852. On the place of Philadelphia fire companies in civic culture and its resemblance to their violent rioting, see Caric, "From Ordered Buckets," 139–41.

51. "The Remains on the Route," *Baltimore Weekly Sun*, July 10, 1852.

52. "Henry Clay—Departure of Remains from Philadelphia," *New York Times*, July 5, 1852; "Ceremonies in Honor of Henry Clay," *Newark Daily Advertiser*, July 3, 1852.

53. *New York Weekly Tribune*, July 10, 1852; "Honors to the Illustrious Dead," *Tri-Weekly Commercial*, July 8, 1852; see the report on the Jersey City celebration, "Obsequies of Henry Clay," *New York Times*, July 3, 1852.

54. "Reception of Henry Clay's Remains in New York," *Savannah Daily News*, July 8, 1852; "The Funeral Obsequies of Henry Clay," *National Police Gazette*, July 24, 1852; "New York—July 3," *Farmer's Cabinet*, July 8, 1857. New York's Common Council held a second, elaborate funeral for Clay on July 20; "Programme of Arrangements . . . ," *New York Times*, July 19, 1852; on New York support for Clay, see Remini, *Henry Clay*, 773–74, 779.

55. "The Relics of the Dead," *New York Daily Times*, July 3, 1852.

56. "Henry Clay's Remains," *New York Times*, July 5, 1852; see Benjamin Wiser, "Heat-Struck, July 1852," *New York Times*, July 28, 2013. By the time Clay's remains reached Kentucky, the temperature was as high as 101 degrees; "Letter from Cincinnati," *National Era*, August 5, 1852.

57. "Letter from Cincinnati," *National Era*, August 5, 1852; *Gleason's Pictorial Drawing-Room Companion*, July 31, 1852.

58. "The Pulpit. Sermons on the Fourth of July and the Death of Henry Clay," *New York Times*, July 5, 1852; "Marks and Remarks," *Literary World*, July 17, 1852.

59. "Obsequies of Henry Clay," *New York Times*, July 7, 1852; *Report of the Committee of Arrangements*, 47–48.

60. *Report of the Committee of Arrangements*, 52.

61. *Report of the Committee of Arrangements*, 52.

62. "Remains of Henry Clay," *State Gazette*, July 8, 1852; "Arrival of the Remains at Poughkeepsie," *Weekly Herald*, July 10, 1852; "Funeral Obsequies of Henry Clay," *Buffalo Morning Express*, July 7, 1852; "Funeral Honors to Clay at Buffalo," *New York Times*, July 8, 1852.

63. *Newark Daily Advertiser*, July 9, 1852; "Remains of Henry Clay. Reception in Cincinnati," *Daily Cincinnati Gazette*, July 9, 1852.

64. "Funeral Honors at Cincinnati," *Sun*, July 10, 1852; "Mr. Clay's Remains in Cincinnati," *New York Times*, July 9, 1852.

65. "Mr. Clay's Burial," *Kentucky Whig*, July 16, 1852.

66. "The Funeral of Henry Clay," *Frankfort Commonwealth*, July 13, 1852. The *Kentucky Whig* estimated 40,000; "Mr. Clay's Burial," July 16, 1852; the *Tri-Weekly Maysville Eagle* estimated 50,000, "Funeral of Henry Clay at Lexington," July 17, 1852; James B. Clay to Sarah Clay, July 11, 1852, Henry Clay Family Papers, Library of Congress, Box II, Folder 42.

Probably the closest competitor for the largest public celebration in Lexington before 1852 was that surrounding the visit of the Marquis de Lafayette, who came to Lexington in May 1825 as part of his triumphal tour of the United States; see Purcell, *Sealed with Blood*, 180; Wright, *Lexington*.

67. Skinner, *Clay Memorial*, 53. For the coffin advertising, see "Fisk's Metallic Burial Cases," *(Trenton) State Gazette*, June 27 and July 20, 1853; "A. Barnes & Son, Are the Only Agents in Berkshire Country for the Sale of Fisk's Patent Metallic Burial Cases," *Pittsfield Sun*, September 1, December 1 and 15, 1853 (the same ad appeared fourteen times in 1854 and fifteen times in 1855 in the *Pittsfield Sun*). Fisk & Raymond, *Fisk's Patent Metallic Burial Cases*, the trade catalog is in the collection of the American Antiquarian Society.

68. *Report of the Committee of Arrangements*, 134; also quoted in Coleman, *Last Days*, 15–16. On the advertising campaign for the Fisk's coffin, see Purcell, "Henry Clay's Coffin."

69. "The Funeral of Henry Clay," *Frankfort Commonwealth*, July 13, 1852.

70. "The Washington Correspondence of the *Philadelphia Ledger*," *Buffalo Morning Express*, July 19. 1852.

71. "Funeral of Henry Clay at Lexington," *Tri-Weekly Maysville Eagle*, July 17, 1852.

72. "The Death of Henry Clay," *New York Daily Times*, July 1, 1852.

73. "Arrangements for Mr. Clay's Funeral," *Charleston Courier*, July 2, 1852; see also "Death of Henry Clay," *Tri-Weekly Maysville Eagle*, July 1, 1852; "Respect to Mr. Clay," *Tri-Weekly Maysville Eagle*, July 8, 1852. F. R. Anspach compared Clay's funerals to the mourning for Washington in a eulogy he presented in Hagerstown, Maryland; Anspach, *Discourse Pronounced on Sabbath Evening*, 5.

74. "Reception of Mr. Clay's Remains at Lexington," *Frankfort Commonwealth*, July 20, 1852.

75. Purcell, *Sealed with Blood*, 171–209; Somkin, *Unquiet Eagle*; Kramer, *Lafayette in Two Worlds*.

76. Green, "On Tour with President Andrew Jackson," 209–28; Moats, *Celebrating the Republic*; Pluta, "Presidential Politics on Tour," 335–61.

77. This sum was arrived at by adding together Clay funeral expenses identified in *Contingent Expenses of the House of Representatives* (1852) and *Report of the Secretary of the Senate Showing the Payments Made from the Contingent Fund of the Senate for the Year Ending December 4, 1852*.

78. The Adams cost was arrived at by adding together expenses noted in *Contingent Expenses of the House of Representatives* (1848) and *Report of the Secretary of the Senate of Expenditures from the Contingent Fund of the Senate*. On Harrison, see *Funeral Expenses of William Henry Harrison*. The value of 1852 expenditures in 2013 dollars was calculated using tools on the MeasuringWorth Foundation's *Measuring Worth* site (http://www.measuringworth.com/ppowerus/).

79. See, for example, expenses for Sen. John C. Calhoun and Sen. F. H. Elmore in *Report of the Secretary of the Senate with a Statement of the Payments from the Contingent Fund of the Senate*.

80. *Contingent Expenses of the House of Representatives* (1852) and *Report of the Secretary of the Senate Showing the Payments Made from the Contingent Fund of the Senate for the Year Ending December 4, 1852*; on railroad donation from the New York and Erie, see "Mr. Clay's Remains," *New York Weekly Tribune*, July 10, 1852; on the metallic burial case donation, see *New York Weekly Tribune*, July 3, 1852.

81. "The Herald," *New York Daily Times*, July 17, 1852. The accusation should not surprise anyone familiar with the New York City Common Council in 1852, whose members were frequently accused of graft and who were linked to the notorious "Forty Thieves"; Spann, *New Metropolis*, 304–7; Burrows and Wallace, *Gotham*, 822–26.

82. Lehuu, *Carnival on the Page*, 36–58.

83. "'Querist' Is Respectfully Informed," *New York Daily Times*, July 1, 1852.

84. Lehuu, *Carnival on the Page*, 16.

85. Anderson, *Imagined Communities*; Redfield, "Imagi-nation"; Nord, *Communities of Journalism*, 199–224. Newspapers as far away as Honolulu reported on Clay's death; "Death of Henry Clay," *Friend*, September 15, 1852; Southard, *Sermon on the Life and Death of Henry Clay*, 9; Smith, *Eulogy upon the Life*, 5.

86. 1850 Census Data, Inter-University Consortium for Social and Political Research; Justin Erickson (Grinnell '10) performed statistical analysis on the counties that Clay traversed using ArcGIS software as part of a Mentored Advanced Project at Grinnell College in the fall of 2009.

87. Otey, *Funeral Address*; Foster, *Funeral Oration*; Capers, *Eulogy on the Life and Public Services of the Hon. Henry Clay*; Chadbourne, *Mortal and the Immortal*; Jenkins, *Eulogy on the Life and Services of Henry Clay*; Smith, *Eulogy upon the Life, Character, and Services of Henry Clay*; Anspach, *Discourse Pronounced on Sabbath Evening*; Morse, *An Address on the Life, Character and Public Services of Henry Clay*; "Obsequies of Mr. Clay in Norfolk," *Sun*, July 22, 1852; "There Was a Large Funeral Procession at Petersburg," *Sun*, July 23, 1852; Brooke, *Eulogy on the Life and Services of Henry Clay*; "Honors to Mr. Clay," *Sun*, July 14, 1852; Hilliard, "Life and Character"; "Funeral Obsequies to Mr. Clay," *Daily Alabama Journal*, July 5, 1852; "Obsequies of Henry Clay," *Daily Alabama Journal*, September 1, 1852; Richardson, *National Bereavements*; "Obsequies of Henry Clay, Proceedings in Chillicothe, Ohio," Henry Clay Family Papers, Library of Congress, Box II, Folder 40; Upfold, *Funeral Discourse*; "Honors to Henry Clay," *Sunday Morning Republican*, July 11, 1852; "Honors to the Memory of Henry Clay," *Daily Missouri Republican*, July 12, 1852; "Clay Obsequies in St. Louis," *(Trenton) State Gazette*, July 17, 1852; "The Day in Boston," *Liberator*, July 9, 1852; Brown, *Eulogy on the Life and Character of Henry Clay*; "Obsequies of Mr. Clay," *(Baltimore) Sun*, July 27, 1852; Elsegood, *Death of Henry Clay*; Krauth, *Discourse on the Life and Character of Hon. Henry Clay*. Pittsburgh, Dover, Boston, and New Orleans are reported upon in *Weekly Herald*, July 10, 1852; "Remarkable Circumstance," *New-England Historical and Genealogical Register* 12 (October 1858): 330; "Preparations for the Funeral Obsequies of Henry Clay," *Placer Times and Transcript*, August 4, 1852; "The Funeral Procession at Mokelumne Hill," *Placer Times and Transcript*, August 16, 1852; "Philadelphia," *Pittsfield Sun*, July 15, 1852; "Obsequies of Mr. Clay," *New York Daily Times*, July 10, 1852; Baldwin, *Discourse on Henry Clay*; Lakin, *Sermon on the Death of Henry Clay*; M'Jilton, *God's Footsteps*; Anderson, *Funeral Oration*; Lord, *Our Strong Rods*; "Funeral Obsequies in Newark, N.J.," *New York Daily Times*, July 14, 1852; "Mr. Crittenden's Eulogy on Henry Clay," *New York Daily Times*, October 5, 1852; "Henry Clay. Eulogy Delivered by Hon. Theodore Frelinghuysen, at Newark, on the 13th of July," *New York Daily Times*, July 15, 1852; Southard, *Sermon on the Life and Death of Henry Clay*.

88. Schantz, *Awaiting the Heavenly Country*, 9, 19, 27–30; Walker, *Oration*. For some of the ways middle-class material culture incorporated death, see Ames, *Death in the Dining Room*.

89. One of the best pieces of evidence of the frank commercialization of mourning was the range of goods offered at the Philadelphia Mourning Store in 1851; Besson and Son, "Spring & Summer Circular"; Schantz, *Awaiting the Heavenly Country*, 75; Woods, *Emotional and Sectional Conflict*, 211–12. On a similar trend in Europe, see Laqueur and Cody, "Birth and Death," 53–56.

90. Peter, *History of Fayette County*, 285. On cemeteries, see Cothran and Danylchak, *Grave Landscapes*; Smith, *Rural Cemetery Movement*.

91. "The Funeral Ceremonies at the National Capital," *State Gazette*, July 2, 1852.

92. "Funeral Obsequies of Henry Clay," *Daily Ohio Statesman*, July 2, 1852.

93. "Funeral of Henry Clay," *New York Daily Times*, July 2, 1852.

94. "The Funeral of Henry Clay," *Daily Atlas*, July 2, 1852.

95. Winterer, "From Royal to Republican." The Duke of Wellington's elaborate funeral car was, by contrast, criticized by some for being gaudy and old-fashioned; see Sinnema, *Wake of Wellington*, 76.

96. Waterman, *Flora's Lexicon*; Goody, *Culture of Flowers*, 280; Mancoff, *Flora Symbolica*.

97. "A Beautiful Incident," *(Amherst, NH) Farmer's Cabinet*, July 29, 1852.

98. "Remains of Henry Clay," *(Trenton) State Gazette*, July 8, 1852; on Anne Stephens, see Library Company of Philadelphia, "Portraits of American Women Writers," accessed February 24, 2015, https://librarycompany.org/women/portraits/stephens_ann.htm.

99. Marler-Kennedy, "Immortelles."

100. See Coleman, *Last Days*, 15.

101. Tenneriello, *Spectacle Culture*, 129–30.

102. "Authentic Print of Henry Clay," *New York Daily Times*, July 7, 1852; Library Company of Philadelphia, "Marcus Aurelius Root."

103. "The Life of Henry Clay," *National Era*, September 9 and 16, 1852.

104. *Contingent Expenses of the House of Representatives* (1852), 157, 163; *Report of the Secretary of the Senate Showing the Payments Made from the Contingent Fund of the Senate for the Year Ending December 4, 1852*, 102, 122.

105. "List of Acts. Passed 1st Session Thirty-Second Congress," *National Era* 6 (September 23, 1852): 153; United States House of Representatives: History, Art & Archives, "Speaker Portrait Collection," accessed February 19, 2015, https://history.house .gov/Exhibitions-and-Publications/Capitol/Speaker-Portrait-Collection/. George Lambert also advertised oil paintings of Clay in the years to follow; "Paintings," *National Era*, September 4, 1856.

106. "The Annual State Fair," *Sacramento Daily Union*, August 27, 1858; "Ladies' Department," *Indiana Farmer*, November 1, 1852.

107. Clarence Cook, "The Fine Arts," *Independent*, January 4, 1855; on Cook, see Georgi, *Critical Shift*; on purchases of Clay busts, see "The Gentlemen of the Bar of New York," *Rochester Daily Advertiser*, July 5, 1852.

108. "Death of Henry Clay," *Newark Daily Advertiser*, June 29, 1852.

109. Baker, *Rescue of Joshua Glover*, 52–54; Maltz, *Fugitive Slave on Trial*, 30–36; Lubet, *Fugitive Justice*.

110. "Eulogy Delivered by Hon. Theodore Frelinghuysen, at Newark, on the 13th of July," *New York Daily Times*, July 15, 1852.

111. Octavia Le Vert, "A Letter to the Honorable Henry Clay, Sunday, May 10, 1850," quoted in Argo, "Madame Octavia Levert's Tribute to Henry Clay," 633; on Le Vert, see

Harriet E. Amos Doss and Sara Frear, "Octavia Walton Le Vert," *Encyclopedia of Alabama,* accessed May 12, 2015, http://encyclopediaofalabama.org/article/h-2355.

112. "Death of Mr. Clay" and "English Judgment of Henry Clay," *New York Daily Times,* July 2, 1852.

113. Mayoralty of New Orleans to Lucretia Clay, July 3, 1852, Henry Clay Family Papers, Library of Congress, Box II, Folder 40.

114. A.S.A., "Reflections on Witnessing the Funeral of Henry Clay," *Christian Recorder,* July 17, 1852, 113.

115. "Disgusting," *(New Orleans) Daily Picayune,* May 11, 1852.

116. "Sketch of the Life of Henry Clay," *Kentucky New Era,* July 13, 1852.

117. Archer et al., *Historical Atlas of U.S. Presidential Elections,* maps 15, 16, 17.

118. "Clay Festival Association," *New York Daily Times,* July 1, 1852. One paper reported that "banners of the various Clay Clubs draped with crape" decorated the city during Clay's second funeral procession there on July 20; see "The Clay Obsequies in New York," *State Gazette,* July 21, 1852.

119. "The Funeral Scene in Philadelphia," *New York Daily Times,* July 3, 1852.

120. "Obsequies of Henry Clay," *New York Daily Times,* July 19, 1852.

121. "Funeral of Henry Clay," *New York Daily Times,* July 2, 1852; the same article is reproduced in the *(Trenton) State Gazette,* July 3, 1852. Other papers noted Scott's presence among other unnamed military officers; see "The Funeral of Henry Clay," *Daily Atlas,* July 2, 1852; "Funeral Obsequies of Henry Clay," *Daily Ohio Statesman,* July 2, 1852; "Death and Obsequies of Henry Clay," *New York Daily Times,* July 3, 1852; "The Obsequies of the Honorable Henry Clay," *Bangor Daily Whig and Courier,* July 5, 1852; "Funeral of Henry Clay," *Constitution,* July 7, 1852.

122. "Death of Henry Clay," *American Baptist,* quoted in *Frederick Douglass' Paper,* July 16, 1852.

123. Smith, *Presidencies of Zachary Taylor and Millard Fillmore,* 243.

124. Smith, *Presidencies of Zachary Taylor and Millard Fillmore,* 246; Potter, *Impending Crisis,* 233.

125. "Whig State Convention" and "Obsequies to Honor Henry Clay," *(Montgomery) Daily Alabama Journal,* August 30, 1852. The *Journal* later claimed the Whig convention planners were unaware of the coinciding dates, but the events nonetheless shared public space on that day; "Erratum," *Daily Alabama Journal,* September 1, 1852.

126. "Death of Henry Clay," *Illinois Daily Journal,* July 2, 1852; "Whig State Convention," *Illinois Daily Journal,* July 6, 1852.

127. "Mr. Clay's Vacancy in the Senate," *Louisville Journal,* quoted in *New York Daily Times,* July 8, 1852.

128. "The Vacant Senatorship," *New York Daily Times,* July 3, 1852.

129. *Charleston Daily Courier,* July 7, 1852; "Hon. Henry Clay," *Independent Democrat,* July 8, 1852; "Death of Henry Clay," *New Hampshire Patriot and State Gazette,* July 7, 1852; "Speeches and Letters of General Franklin Pierce," *Weekly Herald,* October 30, 1852.

130. "Obsequies of Henry Clay, The City Shrouded in Mourning," *New York Daily Times,* July 21, 1852.

131. "The Granite Club—Organization of the San Francisco Democracy" and "Preparations for the Funeral Obsequies of Henry Clay," *Placer Times and Transcript,* August 4, 1852.

132. "Notice to Cartmen," *New York Daily Times*, July 15, 1852; Hodges, *New York City Cartmen*.

133. "Native American Convention," *New York Daily Times*, July 2, 1852.

134. "Death of Henry Clay," *Burlington Sentinel*, July 1, 1852.

135. "From the Independent—Letter from Mrs. Harriet Beecher Stowe," *Frederick Douglass' Paper*, July 30, 1852.

136. "The Late Henry Clay," *Rochester Daily Advertiser*, July 10, 1852.

137. "The Dead Patriot and the Living Hero," *Rochester Daily Advertiser*, July 14, 1852; see also "From the Richmond Examiner. Henry Clay," *Macon Weekly Telegraph*, July 13, 1852. Frederick Douglass's newspaper claimed that Horace Greeley accused the Democrats of "play[ing] crocodile" at Clay's funeral solemnities in an article chiding the Whigs for being more conservative than the Liberty Party; "The Sexton," *Frederick Douglass' Paper*, July 16, 1852.

138. "Sketch of the Life of Henry Clay," *Kentucky New Era*, July 13, 1852.

139. "From the Richmond Examiner, Henry Clay," *Georgia Telegraph*, July 13, 1852.

140. *Louisville Daily Times*, July 10, 1852.

141. Potter, *Impending Crisis*, 234–35; Brown, *Politics and Statesmanship*, 219.

142. Landis, *Northern Men*, 75

143. "Henry Clay," *Pennsylvania Freeman*, quoted in *Frederick Douglass' Paper*, January 15, 1852.

144. Blight, *Race and Reunion*.

145. "Kossuth and Mr. Clay," *National Era* 6 (March 25, 1852): 50.

146. Lincoln, "Eulogy on Henry Clay," 2:121–32; Neely, "American Nationalism in the Image of Henry Clay," 57–58.

147. "The Late Henry Clay," *Christian Recorder*, July 24, 1852; see the language repeated in "Henry Clay's Late Will," *Frederick Douglass' Paper*, July 30, 1852.

148. "The Reception of the Intelligence of Mr. Clay's Death at Ashland," *Weekly Herald*, July 10, 1852.

149. Skinner, *Clay Memorial*, 52.

150. Blight, "For Something beyond the Battlefield."

151. Yung, Chang, and Lai, *Chinese American Voices*, 9.

152. "Preparations for the Funeral Obsequies of Henry Clay," *Placer Times and Transcript*, August 7, 1852.

153. Norman Asing, letter to the *Daily Alta California*, May 5, 1852, quoted in Yung, Chang, and Lai, *Chinese American Voices*, 10.

154. "From California," *Pittsfield Sun*, September 9, 1852; "California," *New York Evangelist*, September 9, 1852. The news of the Chinese participation circulated widely; a notice from a New Orleans newspaper about the San Francisco parade appeared in the *State Gazette*, September 6, 1852.

155. *Boston Commonwealth*, quoted in *Springfield (IL) Daily Republican*, July 5, 1852.

156. "Dear Gray," *Cleveland Plain Dealer*, July 7, 1852.

157. "Colored Hotel—Mrs. Stowe with the Colonizationists," *(Toronto) Provincial Freeman*, September 2, 1854.

158. "Funeral Honors," *Pennsylvania Freeman*, July 10, 1852.

159. "From Our Brooklyn Correspondent," *Frederick Douglass' Paper*, July 30, 1852.

160. "The Honors Paid to Henry Clay," *Liberator*, July 9, 1852.

161. William C. Nell was the secretary of the meeting; "Anti-Colonization Meeting," *Liberator*, August 27, 1852; also reported in "Anti-Colonization Meeting," *Frederick Douglass' Paper*, August 27, 1852.

162. J.T., "The Jerry Rescue Celebration at Syracuse," *Frederick Douglass' Paper*, October 8, 1852.

163. "Gibbon," "The Fourth in Jefferson," *Cleveland Daily Plain Dealer*, July 7, 1852.

164. I find no mention of Clay's funeral in any of the major literature on Douglass's speech; Blassingame, *Frederick Douglass Papers*, 5:359; Foner, *Life and Writings of Frederick Douglass*, 2:181–204; McFeely, *Frederick Douglass*; Blight, *Frederick Douglass: Prophet of Freedom*; Blight, *Frederick Douglass's Civil War*; Deacon, "Navigating 'The Storm, the Whirlwind, and the Earthquake,'" 65–83; McClure, "Frederick Douglass's Use of Comparison," 425–44. Shelly Fisher Fishkin and Clara L. Peterson discuss Douglass's 1847 open letter to Clay but make no mention of Clay's funeral; Fishkin and Peterson, "We Hold These Truths to Be Self-Evident," 197–98. In his book on the relationship between Lincoln and Douglass, James Oakes briefly discusses Lincoln's eulogy of Clay but makes no mention of Douglass's attention to Clay's demise; Oakes, *Radical and the Republican*, 51.

165. "Henry Clay Is Dead," *Frederick Douglass' Paper*, July 1, 1852. Wilbur M. Hayward compared Clay and Douglass as America's greatest orators; "American Eloquence," *Frederick Douglass' Paper*, September 3, 1852; on the preparation of Douglass's speech, see Colaiaco, *Frederick Douglass and the Fourth of July*. Douglass had considered Clay to be a "man-stealer," since the time of Clay's work with the American Colonization Society; Blight, *Frederick Douglass: Prophet of Freedom*; see also Frederick Douglass, "Letter to Henry Clay, The North Star," December 3, 1847, Frederick Douglass Papers, Library of Congress (hereafter FDP), accessed October 9, 2015, http://hdl.loc.gov/loc.mss/mfd.21008.

166. Frederick Douglass, "What to the Slave Is the Fourth of July?," in Blassingame, *Frederick Douglass Papers*, 2:375.

167. "What Were Caesar's or Napoleon's Triumphs to This?," *Frederick Douglass' Paper*, July 16, 1852.

168. "The Will of Henry Clay," *National Era*, August 5, 1852.

169. "Summary," *National Era*, August 18, 1853; "Ashland," *Frederick Douglass' Paper*, September 2, 1853.

170. Apple, *Family Legacy of Henry Clay*, 101.

171. "Politeness of a Councilman," *Frederick Douglass' Paper*, November 5, 1852.

172. "Henry Clay," *National Era*, July 8, 1852.

173. *Report of the Committee of Arrangements*, 19.

174. Hilliard, "Life and Character of Henry Clay," in *Monument to the Memory of Henry Clay*, 462, 461.

175. *Eulogies Delivered in the Senate and House*, 21, 37, 40, 62, 95.

176. *Farmer's Cabinet*, June 3, 1852.

177. Paulus, "America's Long Eulogy for Compromise"; see the Clay envelopes in the collections of the American Antiquarian Society.

178. The statue and crypt were not finished until 1859, but the crypt was ready for the cornerstone ceremony in 1857; Clay Monumental Association, *Articles for the Government*; "Henry Clay Monument, &c.," *(Washington, DC) Daily National Intelligencer*, December 8, 1852, July 9, 1857. Katherine Verdery notes that memorial statues relate directly to the dead bodies of politicians, becoming the person's new body, arresting decay, and "bringing

him into the realm of the timeless"; Verdery, *Political Lives of Dead Bodies*, 5. Monuments to Clay were constructed in Lexington, Kentucky; Richmond, Virginia; Pottsville, Pennsylvania; and New Orleans, Louisiana; see Brown, *Civil War Monuments*, 145. A statue of Clay is one of two that represent the state of Kentucky in the U.S. Capitol Statuary Hall; "Monument to Henry Clay," *Gleason's Pictorial Drawing Room* 4 (January 8, 1853): 32. A marble sarcophagus was added in 1859; see "A Sarcophagus for Henry Clay," *Charleston (SC) Mercury*, September 7, 1859; *Macon (GA) Weekly Telegraph*, September 13, 1859.

179. Clay Monument Association, *Ceremonies*; "Monument to Henry Clay," *Pittsfield Sun*, July 30, 1857; "Monumental," *Charleston Mercury*, September 20, 1859; quotation from "A Visit to the Tomb of Henry Clay," *Philadelphia Inquirer*, February 12, 1862.

180. See Marshall, *Creating a Confederate Kentucky*, 83–85, Harlow, *Religion, Race, and the Making of Confederate Kentucky*.

Chapter Two

1. "Assassination of Col. Ellsworth," *New York Herald*, May 25, 1861; "Assassination of Col. Ellsworth," *Liberator*, May 31, 1861; McKay, *Henry Wilson*. On the *Herald* changing its views on Lincoln and gearing up for the Civil War, see Crouthamel, *Bennett's New York Herald*, 117–21; Fermer, *James Gordon Bennett*, 178–89. Portions of this chapter, in different form, have appeared in Purcell, "Martyred Blood and Avenging Spirits," 280–93; and Purcell, "Seeing Martyrdom," 51–67, and are used here by permission.

2. "Assassination of Col. Ellsworth," *New York Herald*, May 25, 1861, and quoted in "Items Pertaining to the Massacre of Col. Ellsworth," *Wisconsin Patriot*, June 1, 1861. The *Herald* and the Wisconsin paper rendered Lincoln's quotation as "I will take no apology," but from the context "make" is probably correct, and some reprints of the story changed the quotation to "make"; "The Assassination of Col. Ellsworth," *Independent*, May 30, 1861; Randall, *Colonel Elmer Ellsworth*, 262. Harold Holzer calls Ellsworth one of Lincoln's "loyal, young acolytes"; Holzer, *Lincoln*, 420. C. A. Tripp included a chapter on Lincoln's relationship with Ellsworth in his psychological and sexual investigation of Lincoln; Tripp, *Intimate World of Abraham Lincoln*, 109–24. For a catalog of some of the most important of the many times Lincoln teared up in public, see Shutes, "Tears of Lincoln," 20–31. Tears continue to be controversial for politicians and candidates, and although the meanings are radically transformed in the twenty-first century, there are some similarities in reactions to the "unusual spectacle" of a crying man; see Gesualdi, "Man Tears and Masculinities," 304–21; Harris, "'In My Day It Used to Be Called a Limp Wrist,'" 278–95.

3. William Nelson Pendleton to Anzolette Elizabeth Page Pendleton, June 1, 1863, in Lee, *Memoirs of William Nelson Pendleton*, 274.

4. On the ideals of manhood that mixed together in Civil War America, see Foote, *Gentlemen and the Roughs*.

5. Ellsworth himself recalled that he *had* been given a commission to West Point, but he had to decline it; Elmer Ellsworth, Autobiographical Manuscript, 1861, Miscellaneous Manuscript Collection, Library of Congress.

6. "Our Military Guests," *New York Herald*, July 18, 1860; "The Chicago Zouave Cadets," *New York Herald*, July 30, 1860; "Items Pertaining to the Massacre of Col. Ellsworth," *Wisconsin Patriot*, June 1, 1861. In New Orleans, his "Chicago Zouave notoriety" was taken note of when news of his death made the papers; "General Butler Noticed," *Lowell Daily*

Citizen and News, June 6, 1861; Winter, "Zouaves Take St. Louis," 20–29; Renner, "Ye Kort Martial," 376–86.

7. "The Zouaves. Their Drill at the Academy of Music," *New York Times*, July 20, 1860.

8. Fahs, *Imagined Civil War*, 84.

9. Abraham Lincoln to Simon Cameron, March 5, 1861, in Basler, *Collected Works of Abraham Lincoln*, 4:273; on New York fire volunteers' reputation, see Anbinder, *Five Points*, 183; Jones, "Mose the Bowery B'hoy," 170–81.

10. "Late Headquarters of Colonel Ellsworth" and "The New York Fire Zouaves Quartered in the House of Representatives," *Harper's Weekly*, May 25, 1861, 333; "Camp of Colonel Ellsworth's Zouaves . . . ," *New York Illustrated News*, June 1, 1861.

11. *Life of James W. Jackson*, 12–14, 22; "Jackson . . . ," *Lowell Daily Citizen and News*, May 28, 1861.

12. Diary of Judith B. McGuire, May 4, 1861, quoted in Leepson, "The First Civil War Martyr," 3; *Life of James W. Jackson*, 12.

13. "The Late James W. Jackson—His Antecedents," *Daily Register*, 1 June 1861. One of Ellsworth's aides commented to the *New York Times* that Jackson had "flaunted out a secession flag" to attract the ire of Union troops; quoted in "The Death of Col. Ellsworth—Further Particulars," *Wisconsin Patriot*, June 1, 1861.

14. *Life of James W. Jackson*, 28.

15. Randall, *Colonel Elmer Ellsworth*, 257.

16. Some of the most important considerations of Ellsworth include Goodheart, *1861*, 278–92; Randall, *Colonel Elmer Ellsworth*; Ingraham, *Elmer E. Ellsworth*; Dirck, *Black Heavens*, 57–75. Few scholars have really considered Jackson's martyrdom in any careful way, with an exception being Bonner, *Colors and Blood*, 65–75; on political martyrdom, see Soboul, "Religious Feeling and Popular Cults," 217–32; for the religious background of martyrdom, see Cormack, *Sacrificing the Self*.

17. Frank E. Brownell to John Powers, May 24, 1878, Abraham Lincoln Presidential Library and Museum (hereafter ALPLM), SC 194; "Third Dispatch," *(Philadelphia) Press*, May 25, 1861.

18. "The Remains of Col. Ellsworth," *Hartford Daily Courant*, May 27, 1861; Randall, *Colonel Elmer Ellsworth*, 263; Thomas W. Sherman Letters, May 24, 1861, ALPLM, SC 1381.

19. "The Hero of Alexandria," *Philadelphia Inquirer*, May 30, 1861.

20. See White House Historical Association, "Presidential Funerals," accessed April 20, 2015, https://www.whitehousehistory.org/presidential-funerals.

21. Waud, "Funeral Service over Col. Ellsworth at the White House East Room." The White House funeral scene does not appear in the *Illustrated News*, but that paper did carry several other Ellsworth portraits and scenes of his Zouaves in action; Ray, *"Our Special Artist,"* 14–15. One newspaper described the scene in a way that echoes Waud's drawing; "Washington Correspondence," *(Philadelphia) Press*, May 27, 1861.

22. "The Hero of Alexandria," *Philadelphia Inquirer*, May 30, 1861; E.R.L., "Letter from Washington," *Hartford Daily Courant*, May 28, 1861; "Van," "From Washington," *Springfield (MA) Republican*, June 1, 1861; Andrews, *To Tell a Free Story*, 80.

23. On the train route, see "Obsequies of Col. Ellsworth," *New York Herald*, May 27, 1861.

24. "Col. Ellsworth's Remains," *New York Times*, May 25, 1861.

25. W. H. Wickham quoted in Moran, "'The Star Spangled Banner,'" 58.

26. "The Pro-slavery Rebellion," *Independent*, May 30, 1861; "Testimonials to the Lamented Dead," *Philadelphia Inquirer*, May 27, 1861.

27. "Obsequies of Col. Ellsworth," *New York Times*, May 27, 1861.

28. Shea, *Fallen Brave*, 22.

29. "Reception of Col. Ellsworth's Remains at New York," *(Baltimore) Sun*, May 27, 1861; "Assassination of Col. Ellsworth," *Liberator*, 31 May 1861.

30. "How Col. Ellsworth's Death Is Noticed," *New York Times*, May 26, 1861; "The Death of Col. Ellsworth," *Philadelphia Inquirer*, May 25, 1861; "Honors to Colonel Ellsworth," *New York Herald*, May 26, 1861; "Notes of the Rebellion," *New York Times*, June 1, 1861; "Late News," *Saturday Evening Post*, June 1, 1861; "At Half-Mast" and "Flags at Half-Mast," *San Francisco Bulletin*, June 6, 1861; "Chicago's Illustrious Dead," *New York Evangelist*, June 13, 1861.

31. "Obsequies of Col. Ellsworth," *New York Times*, May 27, 1861. In most contemporary sources, the name of Ellsworth's town was rendered as "Mechanicsville," although it is now known as "Mechanicville." I have not corrected the spelling in primary sources, but I use the contemporary spelling myself.

32. *Frank Leslie's Illustrated Newspaper*, June 1, 1861, 40–41.

33. *Harper's Weekly*, June 8, 1861, 354–55; June 15, 1861, 369.

34. *New York Illustrated News*, June 1, 8, 1861.

35. Henry B. Whittington, Diary, May 24, 1861, quoted in Marc Leepson, "The First Union Civil War Martyr," *Alexandria Chronicle*, accessed June 9, 2012, https://alexandriahistorical.org/wp-content/uploads/2018/05/2011_Fall_Chronicle.pdf.

36. "From Washington," *Hartford Daily Courant*, May 27, 1861. McKenna, identifies Jackson's undertaker, *Four Assassins*, 23.

37. Leepson, *Flag*, 110; Wolcott and Temple, "Col. Ellsworth Patriotic Stationery," 136–40; Boyd, *Patriotic Envelopes*, 90–93; "Opera House" and "Amusements," *Daily Evening Bulletin*, August 23, 24, 1861; "Bust of the Late Col. Ellsworth," *New York Times*, June 11, 1861; "The Academy of Music," *Milwaukee Daily Sentinel*, May 16, 1864. The American Antiquarian Society holds a large number of Ellsworth envelopes, prints, and other ephemera.

38. "Death of James W. Jackson," *Macon Daily Telegraph*, July 1, 1861.

39. Fahs, *Imagined Civil War*, 84–88.

40. For an examination of Nathaniel Bowditch as Union martyr, a symbol who served similar purposes to Ellsworth, see Clarke, *War Stories*, 28–50; on the power of martyrs in previous wars, see Purcell, *Sealed with Blood*, 12–31; Conway, "Heroes," 158–61; on mobilization, see Mitchell, *Civil War Soldiers*, 1–36; McPherson, *For Cause and Comrades*.

41. Laderman, *Sacred Remains*, 128–30.

42. "Obsequies of Col. Ellsworth," *New York Herald*, May 27, 1861.

43. "A Speedy Retribution," *Philadelphia Inquirer*, May 25, 1861.

44. "The Assassination," *Philadelphia Inquirer*, May 27, 1861.

45. John Hay, "Ellsworth," *Atlantic Monthly* 8 (July 1861): 122, 120; on Ellsworth's physical vigor, see also Abraham Lincoln to Ephraim D. and Phoebe Ellsworth, May 25, 1861, in Basler, *Collected Works of Abraham Lincoln*, 4:385; John May, "Col. Ellsworth as His Friends Knew Him," *Philadelphia Inquirer*, May 29, 1861.

46. *Daily Commercial Register*, May 25, 1861.

47. "The Late Col. Ellsworth," *Lowell Daily Citizen and News*, May 27, 1861.

48. Faust, *This Republic of Suffering*, 94; *(Madison) Wisconsin Patriot*, June 1, 1861.

49. "The Hero of Alexandria," *Philadelphia Inquirer,* May 30, 1861; *(Philadelphia) Press,* May 24, 1861; "Obsequies of Col. Ellsworth," *New York Times,* May 27, 1861. The *Milwaukee Morning Sentinel* claimed that an attempted death mask of Ellsworth failed because "death had so changed the features" of his face; "Col. Ellsworth," June 4, 1861.

50. "Funeral Obsequies of Col. Ellsworth at His Native Place," *Weekly Champion and Press,* June 8, 1861.

51. *Newark Daily Advertiser,* May 25, 1861.

52. *Illinois State Journal,* May 27, 1861.

53. Currier and Ives, "Death of Col. Ellsworth"; Neely and Holzer, *Union Image,* 28–30; LeBeau, *Currier and Ives,* 76.

54. Truesdell, *Catalog Raisonné*; Neely and Holzer, *Union Image,* 22; on the geographic reach of sales, see "Lithograph of Col. Ellsworth," *Daily Evening Bulletin,* June 8, 1861. Collections of considerable numbers of Ellsworth portraits can be seen in the archives of the Kenosha (WI) Civil War Museum and the American Antiquarian Society.

55. *In Memory of Col. Ellsworth.*

56. "Colonel Ellsworth," *Newark Daily Advertiser,* May 25, 1861.

57. Dytch, "'Remember Ellsworth!,'" 25.

58. "July 4th '76–'61" (n.p.: n.p., [1861]), Archive of Americana Database.

59. Purcell, *Sealed with Blood,* 18–19, 32–38; Purcell, "Martyred Blood and Avenging Spirits."

60. McPherson, *This Mighty Scourge,* 10; Parish, *North and the Nation,* 71–91.

61. Ellsworth, *Zouave Drill,* vi.

62. *Atlantic Democrat,* May 25, 1861; see also *Newark Daily Advertiser,* May 25, 1861.

63. *Daily Commercial Register,* May 25, 1861.

64. George William Curtis as "The Lounger," "Ellsworth," *Harper's Weekly,* June 8, 1861, 354.

65. "Our Troops at Federal Hill, Letter from a Volunteer," *Philadelphia Inquirer,* May 28, 1861; See also "Excitement in West Chester," *Philadelphia Inquirer,* May 27, 1861.

66. Burke, *Eyewitnessing,* 50–51.

67. *New Testament of Our Lord and Savior Jesus Christ*; on the importance of Ellsworth cartes de visite, see Andrea l. Volpe, "The Cartes de Visite Craze," *New York Times,* August 6, 2013.

68. Neely and Holzer, *Union Image,* 29.

69. Bellanta, "His Two Mates Around Him Were Crying," 489.

70. "Highly Important News!," *Daily True Delta,* May 25, 1861; "The Death of Col. Ellsworth," *Philadelphia Inquirer,* May 25, 1861; for a similar sentiment, see "The War Begins," *Spirit of the Times* 31 (June 1, 1861): 260.

71. "Vengeance! Vengeance!!," *Wisconsin Patriot,* June 1, 1861.

72. "Assassination of Col. Ellsworth," *Milwaukee Morning Sentinel,* May 25, 1861; similar sentiments are expressed in "A Fire Zouave," *Hartford Daily Courant,* June 6, 1861.

73. "The News of Col. Ellsworth's Assignation," *Milwaukee Morning Sentinel,* May 25, 1861; "Death of Col. Ellsworth," *Milwaukee Morning Sentinel,* May 27, 1861. In a separate article, the paper claimed that Ellsworth's Zouaves were threatening to burn Alexandria to the ground; "Special Dispatches to the Daily Sentinel," *Milwaukee Morning Sentinel,* May 27, 1861; *Atlantic Journal,* May 31, 1861; see also "Death of Col. Ellsworth," *Springfield (MA) Republican,* June 1, 1861.

74. "How the Death of Ellsworth Was Received at His Home," *(Baltimore) Sun*, May 27, 1861.

75. "Chicago's Illustrious Dead," *New York Evangelist*, June 13, 1861.

76. The *Macon Daily Telegraph* celebrated the Fire Zouaves' disbandment; "Last of the Fire Zouaves," June 4, 1862. It was not unusual for companies composed of New York firemen to experience enlistment issues, in part because many were Democrats; Gilmore, "New York Target Companies," 61–63.

77. Hudson, "Ellsworth's Avengers!" (Baltimore: Doyle, [1861]); Hudson, "Ellsworth's Avengers! (New York: H. DeMarsan, [1861]). The *Daily True Delta* reported that other regiments were being recruited in New York "to raise men who are to swear to avenge the death of Col. Ellsworth"; "War Movements," June 5, 1861; see "Honor to Col. Ellsworth," *New York Times*, July 16, 1861; "An Ellsworth Regiment," *New Hampshire Sentinel*, August 1, 1861. Another song was dubbed "Ellsworth. Zouave Battle Cry," in *A Collection of Songs*; John Hay, "Washington Correspondence," *Missouri Republican*, October 31, 1861, in Burlingame, *At Lincoln's Side*, 260.

78. "Excitement in West Chester," *Philadelphia Inquirer*, May 27, 1861.

79. Burlingame, *Abraham Lincoln*, 2:178.

80. See "Mary B.," "In Memory of Col. Elmer Ellsworth," *Scioto Gazette*, July 23, 1861; Rose Terry, "Murdered by a Traitor at Alexandria," *Scioto Gazette*, June 4, 1861, *Ripley Bee*, June 20, 1861; Heldrick, "A Voice from Ellsworth!"; Hudson, "Ellsworth's Avengers, Song and Chorus."

81. *Milwaukee Morning Sentinel*, June 3, 1861.

82. "The Effect of Col. Ellsworth's Murder," *Jamestown Journal*, June 7, 1861.

83. "The Butchery of Jackson," *Charleston Tri-Weekly Mercury*, May 30, 1861.

84. "The Death of Ellsworth," *Daily Constitutionalist*, May 30, 1861.

85. Woods, *Emotional and Sectional Conflict*, 218–29.

86. *(Savannah) Daily Morning News*, June 24, 1861; "News from the South," *(Baltimore) Sun*, June 4, 1861; "The Southerners . . . ," *Milwaukee Morning Sentinel*, June 10, 1861; *Portland Daily Advertiser*, July 4, 1861. By November, the *Lowell (MA) Daily Citizen and News* claimed that collections had reached $30,000; "Multiple News Items," November 22, 1861.

87. *Kentucky Statesman* quoted in Carl Sandburg, "Darling of Destiny," *Redbook* 68 (December 1936): 71.

88. Quoted in "James W. Jackson," *Richmond Enquirer*, March 30, 1863.

89. *Richmond Daily Whig*, May 30, 1861.

90. "The Killing of Ellsworth by Jackson," *(Savannah) Daily Morning News*, May 29, 1861; *Richmond Daily Whig*, May 28, 1861.

91. House's account is reprinted in "The Murder of Colonel Ellsworth," *Harper's Weekly*, June 8, 1861, 357; "Account of Ellsworth's Death by an Eyewitness," *New York Tribune*, reproduced in Ingraham, *Elmer E. Ellsworth*, 153.

92. "Particulars of Ellsworth's Death," *Boston Daily Advertiser*, May 25, 1861; "Highly Important News—Occupation of Alexandria—Death of Col. Ellsworth," *Lowell Daily Citizen and News*, May 25, 1861.

93. Observation of the bloodstained clothes by Sarah Summers Clarke biographer Ralph W. Milliken quoted in Netherton et al., *Fairfax County Virginia*, 317.

94. "Death of Col. Ellsworth," *Macon Daily Telegraph*, May 25, 1861; see also "Sandy," "Camp Lee," *Macon Daily Telegraph*, May 31, 1861.

95. "The Butchery of Jackson," *Charleston Tri-Weekly Mercury*, May 30, 1861; see also "Liberty or Death!," *Richmond Daily Whig*, May 28, 1861; "The Killing of Ellsworth by Jackson," *Daily Morning News*, May 29, 1861; *Weekly Raleigh Register*, May 29, 1861; on the relationship of the Confederate flag to Confederate nationalism, see Bonner, *Colors and Blood*; Faust, *Creation of Confederate Nationalism*, 8; for similar language about invading "ruffians," see Gallagher, *Becoming Confederate*, 26–27.

96. "The First Rebel Yell," *San Francisco Evening Bulletin*, May 23, 1891; Bonner, *Colors and Blood*, 71–72.

97. "The Marshall House," *Philadelphia Inquirer*, June 10, 1861.

98. "News Items," *Saturday Evening Post*, June 22, 1861; "The Marshall House at Alexandria," *Lowell Daily Citizen and News*, June 7, 1861; see also *Life of James W. Jackson*, 38.

99. Elijah S. Brown letter quoted in Zeller, *Second Vermont Volunteer Infantry Regiment*, 21.

100. "From Washington," *Hartford Daily Courant*, May 28, 1861.

101. "The Marshall House at Alexandria," *Lowell Daily Citizen and News*, June 7, 1861. Pennsylvanian David Wise preserved vials of blood of both Ellsworth and Jackson that were displayed at Michigan State Normal College (now Eastern Michigan University) until they were destroyed in a fire in 1989; see Bien, "The Mystery of Civil War Blood Vials," *Ypsilanti Gleanings,* accessed April 6, 2015, https://aadl.org/ypsigleanings/89913.

102. "The Landlord of the Marshall House," *Lowell Daily Citizen and News*, August 24, 1867; "The Marshall House in Alexandria," *Daily Constitution*, December 13, 1872. The *Worcester Daily Spy* reported in 1886 upon a cane owned by Robert Yale of Norwich, New York, that featured relics "taken from many historical points," including a piece of "the stairway where Col. Ellsworth was shot in Alexandria, Va.," February 18, 1886. One newspaper had mocked the ridiculous excess of Ellsworth relics by pointing out that one man claimed to have saved a piece of cheese from the hero's haversack; "News Items," *Saturday Evening Post*, June 22, 1861; on relics, see Kleinberg, *Flesh Made Word*, 25–33.

103. *Hartford Daily Courant*, May 28, 1861.

104. Silber, "Colliding and Collaborating," 3.

105. Andrews, *To Tell a Free Story*.

106. "From Washington," *Hartford Daily Courant*, May 28, 1861. Enslaved people also began to escape and seek protection with Union forces in Alexandria; "The Latest from Alexandria," *Philadelphia Inquirer*, June 10, 1861. One Charleston newspaper claimed that the day after the invasion, the whites of Alexandria were entirely quiet, while only a few "negroes" stood in public "talking in low tones to each other"; "Affairs in Alexandria," *Charleston Tri-Weekly Mercury*, June 1, 1861.

107. Blight, *Race and Reunion*, 189.

108. "Col. Elmer E. Ellsworth . . . ," *Bangor Daily Whig and Courier*, June 1, 1861; "Col. Ellsworth's Last Letter," *Freedom's Champion*, June 8, 1861.

109. "The Late Col. E. E. Ellsworth," *Atlantic Democrat*, June 1, 1861; on secession, see "The Lounger," *Harper's Weekly*, June 8, 1861, 354.

110. "Revenge in Warfare," *Springfield Republican*, June 1, 1861.

111. "Obsequies of Col. Ellsworth," *New York Times*, May 26, 1861.

112. "Revenge in Warfare," *Springfield Republican*, June 1, 1861.

113. "The First Martyr," *Richmond Daily Whig*, May 27, 1861; T. F., "Jackson Our First Martyr," in *Life of James W. Jackson*, 47; see other examples of Jackson as martyr in poetry in Fahs, *Imagined Civil War*, 88.

114. *Richmond Examiner* quoted in "Threatenings from Virginia," *Liberator*, June 14, 1861.

115. *Richmond Examiner* quoted in "The Other Side," *Lowell Daily Citizen and News*, May 31, 1861.

116. *Richmond Enquirer* quoted in "The Other Side," *Lowell Daily Citizen and News*, May 31, 1861; on the place of "home" in Confederate nationalism and war motivation, see Sheehan-Dean, *Why Confederates Fought*; Faust, *Mothers of Invention*; Bonner, *Colors and Blood*, 73.

117. *Daily True Delta*, June 6, 1861.

118. "The Invaders," *Richmond Daily Whig*, May 25, 1861.

119. *Life of James W. Jackson*, 9.

120. John Hay, "Ellsworth," *Atlantic Monthly* 8 (July 1861): 125. W. Burns Jones Jr. echoed Hay when he called Ellsworth and Jackson "reciprocal images of each other"; Burns, "Marshall House Incident," 8. The only other primary source that makes such a clear argument about the twinned martyrdom appeared in the *Southern Bivouac* magazine in 1883; the author notes that "in the South, Jackson was the noble Roman, and Ellsworth, the savage chief of Chicago ruffians. In the North, an opposite opinion prevailed; "The Jackson-Ellsworth Tragedy," *Southern Bivouac* 2 (1883–84): 312.

121. Finkelman, "Manufacturing Martyrdom," 41–66; "Relics," *Annals of Iowa* 11 (1873): 386.

122. Sánchez-Eppler, *Touching Liberty*; on the fine line between acceptable and unacceptable masculine emotion and the public reaction that tears demanded, see Shamir and Travis, *Boys Don't Cry?*, 1–19; Hendler, *Public Sentiments*.

123. "Assassination of Col. Ellsworth," *New York Herald*, May 25, 1861. The Washington correspondent of the *(Philadelphia) Press* also noted that the president might be unhappy at the reports of his emotional response, but the correspondent argued that manly emotion was cathartic; "A Scene in the White House," May 27, 1861. On the connection between tears, emotion, and the nation in Civil War America, see Travis, "Soldier's Heart," 23–50.

124. Chapman and Handler, "Annals of Blubbering," 1–16; Kimmel, "Masculinity as Homophobia," 86–88; Howard, "What Is Sentimentality?," 63–81; Garton, "Scales of Suffering," 40–58. Clyde Griffen called the Civil War "a major turning point for middle-class attitudes toward masculinity" in "Reconstructing Masculinity," 191; Rotundo, *American Manhood*, 232–33.

125. John Hay, "A Young Hero. Personal Reminiscences of Colonel E. E. Ellsworth," *McClure's Magazine* 6 (March 1896): 361.

126. "The Assassination of Col. Ellsworth," *Independent*, May 30, 1861; Dirck, *Black Heavens*.

127. "Assassination of the Late Col. Ellsworth," *New York Illustrated News*, June 8, 1861, 74.

128. See Hodes, *Mourning Lincoln*, 68–69.

129. "The News of Colonel Ellsworth's Death," *Daily Gazette and Reporter*, May 27, 1861; see also "Affecting Incident," *Lowell Daily Citizen and News*, May 28, 1861; *Bangor Daily Whig and Courier*, June 1, 1861; "Assassination of the Late Col. Ellsworth," *New York Illustrated News*, June 8, 1861, 74.

130. "Fourth Dispatch," *(Philadelphia) Dispatch*, May 24, 1861.

131. Nicolay wrote that "I had been with him daily—almost hourly for six months past," to the father of Ellsworth's fiancée; quoted in Ingraham, *Elmer E. Ellsworth*, 149.

132. John G. Nicolay to Therena Bates, May 25, 1861, in Burlingame, *With Lincoln in the White House*, 43. Helen Nicolay, John G. Nicolay's daughter, included a snippet of the same letter in her biography of her father, but she notably omitted the line about him feeling "weak and womanish"; Nicolay, *Lincoln's Secretary*, 104.

133. Nelson, *Ruin Nation*, 184–86; Clinton and Silber, *Battle Scars*; Clarke, *War Stories*; Miller, "Traumatized Manhood," 25–44; Miller, *Empty Sleeves*.

134. *Life of James W. Jackson*, 34, 36. The author of this work identified himself only as "Capt.—" but dedicated the volume to Henry W. Thomas, who was married to James W. Jackson's sister; Thomas was a member of the Confederate Congress, and he also acted as agent for the funds contributed for the Jackson family by Southerners; see "The Widow of the Late James W. Jackson," *(Savannah) Daily Morning News*, June 24, 1861.

135. Illinois, *New York Examiner*, May 30, 1861, quoted in Burlingame, *Dispatches from Lincoln's White House*, 7.

136. Walt Whitman quoted in Anbinder, *Five Points*, 183.

137. "Col. Ellsworth Murdered. His Assassin Killed! Great Excitement!," *Newark Daily Advertiser*, May 24, 1861.

138. Ellsworth, *Zouave Drill*, v–vi; see also Burns, *Patriot's Offering*, 13.

139. "Camp of Colonel Ellsworth's Zouaves," *New York Illustrated News*, June 1, 1861; "Colonel Ellsworth Was a Man of Exemplary Moral Habits," *Christian Recorder*, June 8, 1861; "Ellsworth's Early Character and Training," *Christian Recorder*, September 14, 1861; Ellsworth, *Zouave Drill*, v–vi; Foote, *Gentlemen and the Roughs*, 41–92.

140. "Col. Ellsworth," *Hartford Daily Courant*, May 28, 1861. Mary S. Robinson called Ellsworth the truest "specimen of a Christian American," in an 1866 children's book, *Brother Soldiers*, 75. Lincoln admired his strength, military "taste," modesty, and deference in his last letter to Ellsworth's parents; Lincoln to Ephraim D. and Phoebe Ellsworth, May 25, 1861, in Basler, *Collected Works of Abraham Lincoln*, 4:385.

141. "Camp of Colonel Ellsworth's Zouaves," *New York Illustrated News*, June 1, 1861; Cole, *Exercises Connected*, 64.

142. John Hay, April 21, 1861, in Burlingame and Ettlinger, *Inside Lincoln's White House*, 5; Neely, "Apotheosis of a Ruffian," 59.

143. *Charleston Tri-Weekly Mercury*, May 25, 1861; "Washington Items," *Alexandria Gazette and Virginia Advertiser*, May 23, 1861;

144. "The First Martyr," *Richmond Daily Whig*, May 27, 1861.

145. "Reminiscences of an Officer of Zouaves," *DeBow's Review* 5 (May/June 1861): 659.

146. "Camp of Colonel Ellsworth's Zouaves," *New York Illustrated News*, June 1, 1861; on the fire at the Willard Hotel see *New York Illustrated News*, May 25, 1861; Gifford, "The Celebrated World of Currier and Ives," 348–65; Butsch, "Bowery B'hoys and Matinee Ladies," 374–405.

147. "Account," *Daily Constitutionalist*, May 30, 1861.

148. *Life of James W. Jackson*, 44.

149. Kasson, *Rudeness and Civility*, 123; Adams, *Bowery Boys*, xvi–xvii.

150. Jefferson Davis to Robert E. Lee, May 11, 1863, in Crist, Dix, and Williams, *Papers of Jefferson Davis*, 9:179; Royster, "Death of Stonewall," 193–231.

151. "General Orders No. 61," Mary Custis Lee Papers, Virginia Historical Society, see Virginia Museum of History and Culture, accessed September 11, 2018, https://virginiahistory .org/learn/historical-book/general-orders-no-61; Lively, *Calamity at Chancellorsville*, 126.

152. Douglas, *I Rode with Stonewall*, 228; see Miller, *Empty Sleeves*, 64. Lee told Lt. Gen. John Bell Hood that "we must endeavor to follow the unselfish, devoted, and intrepid course" Jackson had pursued; see Chambers, *Stonewall Jackson*, 2:448.

153. Nolan, "Anatomy of the Myth," 18–19, 17.

154. Gwynne, *Rebel Yell*, 556, 557; Dabney, *Life and Campaigns*, 731. Here, Gwynne's attitude resembles that of Robertson, observed by Nolan; "Anatomy of the Myth," 18.

155. Anderson, *Blood Image*, 1–16; Avirett, *Memoirs of General Turnery Ashby*, 223–43; "The Last Day of Gen. Ashby," *Selma Daily Reporter*, June 17, 1862; Janney, *Burying the Dead*, 34–35.

156. Gwynne, *Rebel Yell*, 557.

157. See Bohland, "Look Away, Look Away," 268.

158. Preston, *Life and Letters*, 164. Jackson was also seen as a fearsome disciplinarian; Carmichael, "So Far from God," 33–66; Robertson, *Stonewall Jackson*.

159. Alexander, *Lost Victories*, 302–15; Krick, *Smoothbore Volley*, 17–24. A very clear narrative of Jackson's movements and wounding can be found in Farwell, *Stonewall*.

160. National Park Service, "Ellwood Manor," accessed September 15, 2018, https://www .nps.gov/frsp/learn/historyculture/ellwood.htm; "The Curious Fate of Stonewall Jackson's Arm," *NPR Morning Edition*, June 28, 2012.

161. Richenbacher, "Demise of Stonewall Jackson," 635–55; Rozear and Greenfield, "'Let Us Cross over the River,'" 2, 29–46; Krick, "Smoothbore Volley," Gallagher, ed., *Chancellorsville*, 133.

162. "Stonewall Jackson," *Macon Telegraph*, May 7, 1863; "The War News," *(Baltimore) Sun*, May 13, 1863; "The Battles of the Rappahannock," *Richmond Enquirer*, May 15, 1863; McGuire, *Diary of a Southern Refugee*, 209; "Particulars of the Wounding and Death of Gen. 'Stonewall' Jackson," *Alexandria Gazette*, May 18, 1863; "Death of Stonewall Jackson," *Nashville Daily Union*, May 21, 1863; "From Washington," *Detroit Free Press*, May 13, 1863; Royster, "Death of Stonewall," 211.

163. Vandiver, *Mighty Stonewall*, 478–94.

164. *Richmond Enquirer* quoted in "The Wounds of Stonewall Jackson," *New York Times*, May 13, 1863; also in *Chicago Tribune*, May 15, 1863; for the opposing view, see "Death of Stonewall Jackson, Circumstances of His Death," *Chicago Tribune*, May 15, 1863; see Gallagher, "The Making of a Hero," 101–17; Wilson, *Baptized in Blood*, 25; Kaufman, *Civil War in American Culture*, 48–55.

165. Nolan, "Anatomy of the Myth," 14.

166. "Latest from the Army," *New York Times*, May 13, 1863; "Stonewall Jackson's Death," *New York Times*, May 13, 1863.

167. Colson quoted in Robertson, *Stonewall Jackson*, 755.

168. Ash, *Rebel Richmond*, 219–21.

169. On dislocation of the Southern population, see Ash, *When the Yankees Came*; Berlin et al., *Wartime Genesis of Free Labor*.

170. McGuire, *Diary of a Southern Refugee*, 202–3; McCurry, *Confederate Reckoning*, 184–91; Martinez, *Virginia at War*, 44–45; Chesson, "Harlots or Heroines?," 131–75; Clinton, "'Public Women' and Sexual Politics," 126–27.

171. Douglas, *I Rode with Stonewall*, 228.

172. Lee, *Memoirs of William Nelson Pendleton*, 270.

173. Douglas, *I Rode with Stonewall*, 229.

174. McGuire, *Diary of a Southern Refugee*, 212; Douglas, *I Rode with Stonewall*, 29; "Arrival of Jackson's Remains," *(New York) World*, May 16, 1863.

175. "Stonewall Jackson, from the *Richmond Examiner*," *New York Times*, May 20, 1863.

176. Faust, *Creation of Confederate Nationalism*, 7; on doomed heroism, see Nolan, "Anatomy of the Myth."

177. "The Funeral Ceremonies," *Richmond Daily Dispatch*, May 12, 1863.

178. Jones, *Rebel War Clerk's Diary*, 1:392; "City Council," *Richmond Examiner*, May 12, 1863.

179. "The Funeral Ceremonies," *Richmond Daily Dispatch*, May 12, 1863.

180. Preston, *Life and Letters*, 166; "Reception of the Remains of General T. J. Jackson," *Richmond Examiner*, May 12, 1863; Cooke, *Stonewall Jackson*, 446; Coski, *Confederate Battle Flag*, 17; John M. Coski, "The Birth of the 'Stainless Banner,'" *New York Times*, May 13, 2013.

181. Bonner, *Colors and Blood*, 95, 115.

182. "The Funeral in Richmond," *Charleston Mercury*, May 16, 1863. The horse was not Jackson's famous steed Little Sorrel, which bolted at Chancellorsville after Jackson was shot; Faust, "Equine Relics," 38. On Jim Lewis, see Schmitz, "At the Stonewall Jackson Shrine," 23–24; National Park Service, "Jim Lewis," accessed September 15, 2018, https://www.nps.gov/frsp/learn/historyculture/jim-lewis.htm.

183. "Reception of the Remains of General T. J. Jackson," *Richmond Examiner*, May 13, 1863.

184. Cooke, *Stonewall Jackson*, 447.

185. "The Funeral Ceremonies," *Richmond Daily Dispatch*, May 12, 1863; "Funeral Procession in Honor of Lieut. Gen. Thos. J. Jackson," *Richmond Daily Dispatch*, May 13, 1863; Douglas, *I Rode with Stonewall*, 229; Chambers, *Stonewall Jackson*, 2:452; Robertson neatly summarizes the debate over when Jackson was embalmed; Robertson, *Stonewall Jackson*, 922.

186. "From the *Richmond Enquirer*, May 13, the Funeral of Jackson," *New York Times*, May 16, 1863; "The Wounding, Death and Funeral of Stonewall Jackson," *Boston Herald*, May 18, 1863; "Funeral Procession in Honor of Lieut. Gen. Thos. J. Jackson," *Richmond Daily Dispatch*, May 13, 1863; on the turnout, see "Arrival of Gen. Jackson's Remains in Richmond," *Alexandria Gazette*, May 15, 1863; "From the *Richmond Enquirer*, May 13, the Funeral of Jackson," *New York Times*, May 16, 1863; "The Funeral Ceremonies, from the *Richmond Dispatch*," *Times Picayune*, May 22, 1863.

187. McGuire, *Diary of a Southern Refugee*, 212.

188. Jones, *Rebel War Clerk's Diary*, 1:392.

189. Jefferson Davis to Robert E. Lee, May 11, 1863, in Crist, Dix, and Williams, *Papers of Jefferson Davis*, 9:180.

190. Jones, *A Rebel War Clerk's Diary*, 329.

191. Jackson, *Memoirs of Stonewall Jackson*, 461–62.

192. Jackson, *Memoirs of Stonewall Jackson*, 463.

193. Jackson, *Life and Letters*, 477; Lively, *Calamity at Chancellorsville*, 130.

194. VMI General Orders . . . , May 1863, Stonewall Jackson Death and Funeral, VMI, accessed June 26, 2019, https://archivesspace.vmi.edu/repositories/3/digital_objects/168;

May 14–15, 1863, Charles T. Haigh Notebook-Diary, Stonewall Jackson Death and Funeral, VMI, accessed June 26, 2019, https://vmi.contentdm.oclc.org/digital/collection/p15821coll11/id/563/; "All That Was Mortal," *Lexington Gazette*, May 20, 1863; "Honors to Jackson," *Richmond Enquirer*, May 22, 1863.

195. Samuel Baldwin Hannah to Mary Elizabeth Richardson Hannah, May 17, 1863, Hannah Family Papers, 1760–1967, Charlotte County, Virginia; also Arkansas and Mississippi, Mss1H1956a, Virginia Historical Society, ProQuest History Vault, accessed June 26, 2018, https://congressional.proquest.com/histvault?q=002477-027-0152&accountid=7379.

196. "All That Was Mortal," *Lexington Gazette*, May 20, 1863; Lee, *Memoirs of William Nelson Pendleton*, 270.

197. Preston, *Life and Letters*, 166; "The Funeral of Lieutenant General T. J. Jackson (Stonewall) from the *Richmond Whig*," *New York Herald*, May 27, 1863; Klein, "Wielding the Pen," 227; Robertson, *Stonewall Jackson*, 761.

198. Stowell, "Stonewall Jackson and the Providence of God," 187–207.

199. Preston, *Life and Letters*, 166; Chambers, *Stonewall Jackson*, 458.

200. Preston, *Life and Letters*, 166.

201. Binnington, *Confederate Visions*, 116.

202. McGuire, *Diary of a Southern Refugee*, 211–12.

203. Jones, *A Rebel War Clerk's Diary*, 392.

204. Stowell, *Rebuilding Zion*, 5.

205. Dabney, *Life and Campaigns*, 727.

206. Preston, *Life and Letters*, 165.

207. "Funeral Procession in Honor of Lieut. Gen. Thos. J. Jackson," *Richmond Daily Dispatch*, May 13, 1863. John Esten Cooke recorded in his biography of Jackson, written in 1863, that Jackson's body was accompanied by "tears not only of women but of bearded men"; *Stonewall Jackson*, 448.

208. Jackson, *Life and Letters*, 476.

209. Meier, *Nature's Civil War*, 7; Cashin, "Hungry People," 160–75; Miller, *Empty Sleeves*.

210. Hacker, "A Census-Based Count," 313.

211. "From the Knoxville Register," *Richmond Daily Dispatch*, May 15, 1863.

212. Judicial proclamation of the Hustings Court quoted in "The Courts," *Richmond Examiner*, May 13, 1863.

213. "Funeral Procession in Honor of Lieut. Gen. Thos. J. Jackson," *Richmond Daily Dispatch*, May 13, 1863.

214. *Charleston Courier* quoted in *(Baltimore) Sun*, May 15, 1863.

215. "Reception of the Remains of General T. J. Jackson," *Richmond Examiner*, May 12, 1863.

216. "The Funeral Ceremonies," *Richmond Daily Dispatch*, May 12, 1863.

217. "The Death of Gen. Jackson," *Richmond Daily Dispatch*, May 15, 1863.

218. "Death of General Jackson," *Lancaster Ledger*, May 20, 1863.

219. Royster, "Death of Stonewall," 211.

220. *Whig* obituary quoted in "The Death of Stonewall Jackson," *New York Times*, May 15, 1863; "Our Dead Hero," *(New York) World*, May 16, 1863; "Our Dead Hero," *Detroit Free Press*, May 19, 1863; "Death of Stonewall Jackson," *Goodhue Volunteer*, May 20, 1863; "'Stonewall' Jackson," *New York Observer and Chronicle*, May 21, 1863; "Stonewall Jackson's Death," *Cincinnati Daily Commercial*, September 8, 1865.

221. "Jackson's Last Hours," *Macon Telegraph*, May 21, 1863.

222. Jones, *A Rebel War Clerk's Diary*, 329.

223. Rice, "An Account of the Battle of Fredericksburg," 41.

224. McCabe, *Life of Thomas J. Jackson*, 124.

225. Douglas, *I Rode with Stonewall*, 230.

226. "'Stonewall' Jackson," *Times Picayune*, May 20, 1863.

227. John T. Norton to Morgan Norton, May 23, 1863, Death and Funeral of Stonewall Jackson, VMI Special Collections, accessed June 26, 2019, http://digitalcollections.vmi.edu /digital/collection/p15821coll11/id/1750.

228. "From Fortress Monroe," *Hartford Daily Courant*, May 14, 1863; "From the Rappahannock," *New York Times*, May 14, 1863; "From Richmond," *Detroit Free Press*, May 14, 1863; "Death of Stonewall Jackson," *Chicago Tribune*, May 15, 1863; "The Wounding, Death and Funeral of Stonewall Jackson," *Boston Herald*, May 18, 1863; "News from the Southwest via Richmond," *Maine Farmer*, May 21, 1863; "Death of Stonewall Jackson," *Cass County Republican*, May 21, 1863.

229. "Gen. Stonewall Jackson," *Harper's Weekly*, May 30, 1863, 349; "Notes on Current Events, the Military Situation," *Knickerbocker Monthly* 61 (June 1863): 572.

230. "Virtues of Patriotism," *Nassau Literary Magazine* 24 (October 1863): 88.

231. "The Death of Stonewall Jackson," *Providence Daily Journal*, [1863], Newberry Library Collection.

232. Hettle, *Inventing Stonewall Jackson*, 21–22; Hettle, "Mary Johnston and 'Stonewall' Jackson," 34–35.

233. Royster, "Death of Stonewall," 213.

234. "The News," *Chicago Tribune*, May 14, 1865. Two days later, the *Tribune* offered a more positive view of Jackson; "The Late Stonewall Jackson," May 16, 1863.

235. "Stonewall Jackson," *Chicago Tribune*, May 16, 1863.

236. "The Death of Stonewall Jackson," *New York Times*, May 14, 1863. The *Times* obituary was reprinted in the *Chicago Tribune*, May 14, 1863. One of the war correspondents pronounced Jackson a "gallant foe" several days later; *New York Times*, May 22, 1863.

237. "War Sketches . . . Guinney's Station," *Detroit Free Press*, June 9, 1863. In 1865, the *Hartford Daily Courant* compared Jackson to Benedict Arnold; "Possibly," September 8, 1863.

238. "Stonewall Jackson," *Vanity Fair* 7 (June 13, 1863): 166.

239. "Stonewall Jackson," *Sacramento Daily Union*, May 15, 1863.

240. "From the New York World," *Louisville Daily Democrat*, May 21, 1863; "Death of Stonewall Jackson," *Patriot*, May 21, 1863.

241. "'Stonewall' Jackson," *New York Observer and Chronicle*, May 21, 1863; "The Death of Stonewall Jackson, from the Cincinnati Enquirer," *Detroit Free Press*, May 15, 1863; "Current Events," *New York Evangelist*, May 21, 1863.

242. *New York World* quoted in "Gen. McClellan on Stonewall Jackson," *Cincinnati Commercial Tribune*, May 19, 1863.

243. "The Northern Press on the Death of Jackson," *Richmond Enquirer*, May 19, 1863, and *Macon Telegraph*, May 25, 1863; "Comments of the New York Herald on the Death of Gen. Jackson," *Camden Confederate*, May 29, 1863.

244. William Nelson Pendleton to Anzolette Elizabeth Page Pendleton, May 14, 1863, in Lee, *Memoirs of William Nelson Pendleton*, 272.

245. Carmichael, "'Oh for the Presence and Inspiration of Old Jack,'" 161–62; Nolan, "Anatomy of the Myth," 17.

246. Taylor, "Stonewall Jackson and the Valley Campaign," 261; see Wilson, *Baptized in Blood*, 18–36.

247. "Reception of the Remains of General T. J. Jackson," *Richmond Examiner*, May 12, 1863.

248. Dabney, *Life and Campaigns*, 732.

249. Hettle, *Inventing Stonewall Jackson*, 40.

250. "All the Poor Honors," *Richmond Examiner*, May 14, 1863; "Burial Place of General Jackson," *Charleston Mercury*, May 16, 1863;

251. *Richmond Enquirer* quoted in Addey, *Stonewall Jackson*, 226.

252. Gross, "United Daughters of the Confederacy," 182; Janney, *Burying the Dead*, 49–51; Smith, *Rural Cemetery Movement*, 5, 6; Mitchell, *Hollywood Cemetery*.

253. Janney, *Burying the Dead*, 44–60.

254. Janney, *Burying the Dead*, 58.

255. "General Observance of the Day," *Richmond Examiner*, May 10, 1866; see Blair, *Cities of the Dead*, 55–66.

256. *Lexington Gazette* quoted in *Richmond Examiner*, May 10, 1866.

257. "General Observance of the Day," *Richmond Examiner*, May 10, 1866. The same newspaper issue also printed a biography of Jackson and a recounting of his death and Lexington funeral.

258. Blight, *Race and Reunion*, 65.

259. *Richmond Examiner*, May 10, 1866.

260. Richmond *Times* quoted in "The Memory of Stonewall Jackson," *Macon Weekly Telegraph*, May 17, 1866.

261. "The Day in Raleigh," *Richmond Examiner*, May 10, 1866.

262. Kinney, "'If Vanquished I Am Still Victorious,'" 239; Gross, "United Daughters of the Confederacy," 183; Bishir, "Memorial Observances," 69. Blight provides a good guide to the different dates that were observed in the former Confederacy until after 1910; Blight, *Race and Reunion*, 77.

263. Blight, *Race and Reunion*, 171–253.

Chapter Three

1. "The Funeral of George Peabody," *(Baltimore) Sun*, February 1, 1870; "Special Notices," *(Baltimore) Sun*, November 9, 1869; *(Hartford) Daily Courant*, February 19, 1870; *Peabody Institute*, 39–40; "Both Branches," *Boston Daily Advertiser*, November 12, 1869; "Current Notices," *New York Times*, November 12, 1869; "Honors to the Late George Peabody," *Chicago Tribune*, December 25, 1869; "Maryland," *Philadelphia Inquirer*, February 9, 1870.

2. Wallis, *Discourse*, 15.

3. On Greeley's first use of the "clasp hands" metaphor, made on the day Lincoln was shot, see Williams, *Horace Greeley*, 266–67. Greeley was much more derided by radicals and lampooned by rival publications for his use of the metaphor "clasping hands over the bloody chasm" in the 1872 presidential election; on the British-American relationship during the war, see Foreman, *World on Fire*.

4. Wallis, *Discourse*, 57, 58, 59.

5. Robinson, *Union Indivisible*, 179.

6. Steiner, "Severn Teackle Wallis: First Paper," 58–74; Steiner, "Severn Teackle Wallis: Second Paper," 129; Barnhart, "Apostles of the Lost Cause," 407; on Reconstruction in Maryland, see Foner, *Reconstruction*, 40–41.

7. Blight, *Race and Reunion*; Janney, *Remembering the Civil War*. Works emphasizing reconciliation and the suppression of emancipationist memory include Cox, *Dixie's Daughters*; Silber, *Romance of Reunion*; works that emphasize sectionalism and reunion include Harris, *Across the Bloody Chasm*, and Gannon, *The Won Cause*. Several works also stress how Civil War memory, especially Confederate memory, worked as a spur to modernity; see Brown, *Civil War Canon*; Ring, *Problem South*. Good historiographical summaries can be found in Cook, *Civil War Memories*, and Gannon, *Americans Remember*.

8. Silber, "Reunion and Reconciliation," 83.

9. The best source on Peabody's business career, up to 1854, is Hidy, *George Peabody*; quotation about merchant banking is in Hidy, *George Peabody*, 186; for comment on Peabody's business dealings from 1854 to 1869, see Parker, *George Peabody*. The currency conversion across time was calculated using Edvinsson, "Historical Currency Converter."

10. "George Peabody's Birth-Place," *Harper's Weekly*, July 14, 1866, 438; on nineteenth-century philanthropy, see Chernow, *Titan*; Wall, *Andrew Carnegie*; on the British cultural importance of Peabody to British diplomacy, see Hall and Goldstein, "Writers, the Clergy," 127–54. Peabody's congressional gold medal is displayed in the main public reading room of the Peabody Institute Library in Peabody, Massachusetts; "Death of Mr. George Peabody," *Sheffield and Rotheram Independent*, November 6, 1869.

11. On Peabody's wartime attitudes and actions, see Parker, *George Peabody*, 110–23. An idea of his wartime activities can be gained from the George Peabody Papers, Mss 181, Phillips Library, Peabody Essex Museum, Rowley, MA.

12. Winthrop quoted in Conniff, *House of Lost Worlds*, 26; on Peabody's philanthropy, see also, Conniff, *House of Lost Worlds*, 36–37; Parker, *George Peabody*; Schaaf, "George Peabody," 269–85; Tapley, *Chronicles of Danvers*, 171; Hanaford, *George Peabody*; Baltzell, *Puritan Boston*, 276–77; "Mr. Peabody's Munificence in Aid of Southern Education," *Journal of Education of Upper Canada*, March 1, 1867; on segregation and the Peabody Trust, see Johnson, "Peabody Fund," 114; Vaughn, "Partners in Segregation"; "George Peabody, Another Gift," *New York Times*, August 17, 1869. On the 1869 value of the federal budget, see Wallis, "Table Ea636-643"; "Mr. Peabody's Gift to General Lee's College," *New York Times*, August 28, 1869.

13. Blight, *Race and Reunion*, 344–54; Silber, *Romance of Reunion*.

14. Hidy, *George Peabody*, 357–58.

15. George Peabody quoted in Sexton, *Debtor Diplomacy*, 103.

16. "The President Call on Geo. Peabody," *Weekly Alta California*, March 16, 1867.

17. George M. Brown to A. A. Abbott, January 5, 1870, Peabody Funeral Correspondence Scrapbook (hereafter Peabody FCS).

18. "Death of Geo. Peabody," *Chicago Republican*, November 5, 1869; "Foreign. Death of George Peabody," *Chicago Tribune*, November 5, 1869; "Death of Philanthropist, George Peabody," *New York Times*, November 5, 1869; "Death of George Peabody," *Times Picayune*, November 5, 1869; "Obituary. George Peabody," *New York Herald*, November 5, 1860;

"Transatlantic, Death of Mr. George Peabody" and "Obituary," *Philadelphia Inquirer*, November 5, 1869; "Death of George Peabody," *Hartford Daily Courant*, November 5, 1869.

19. "England," *New York Herald*, November 7, 1869; "Great Britain," *New York Times*, November 7, 1869.

20. Quotation from "Editorial Paragraphs," *Flake's Weekly Galveston Bulletin*, November 10, 1869; "The Late George Peabody," *Philadelphia Inquirer*, November 9, 1869; "The Late George Peabody," *(Baltimore) Sun*, November 6, 1869; "George Peabody," *Punch*, November 13, 1869, 189; "In Memoriam. George Peabody," *Fun*, November 13, 1869, 96.

21. "The Late Mr. Peabody," *(London) Times*, November 9, 1869; "From Europe, Honors to the Remains of George Peabody," *Times-Picayune*, November 10, 1869.

22. "Obsequies of the Late Geo. Peabody," *Peabody Press*, November 17, 1869; Evans, *Death of Kings*, 26–27.

23. "Funeral Obsequies of the Late George Peabody in London," *Chicago Tribune*, November 13, 1869; "Funeral of George Peabody at Westminster Abbey," *New York Times*, November 13, 1869; Westminster Abbey, "Lord John Thynne & Family," accessed December 27, 2016, https://www.westminster-abbey.org/abbey-commemorations/commemorations/lord-john-thynne-family.

24. Bishop of London quoted in "Late George Peabody," *Chicago Tribune*, November 15, 1869.

25. "George Peabody," *Macon Daily Telegraph*, November 19, 1869.

26. "Funeral of the Late George Peabody," *(Honolulu) Friend*, February 1, 1870, 12; "George Peabody, from Newman Hall's Funeral Discourse," *Vermont Watchman and State Journal*, December 22, 1869.

27. "The Remains of Mr. Peabody," *Daily National Intelligencer and Washington Express*, November 12, 1869; "World-Wide News Exhibit," *New York Herald*, November 12, 1869; "The Remains of Mr. Peabody," *(Wilmington, NC) Daily Journal*, November 13, 1869; "George Peabody," *Weekly Alta California*, November 13, 1869; "George Peabody and Queen Victoria," *(Baltimore) Sun*, November 13, 1869; "George Peabody," *Gentlemen's Journal*, December 1, 1869. See the sermon preached by Joseph Parrish Thompson at the Broadway Tabernacle in New York, in which he praised the "monarch's grief"; "The Dignity of Philanthropy," *New York Times*, January 10, 1870.

28. "The Peabody Obsequies in Westminster Abbey," *New York Herald*, November 14, 1869.

29. Quoted in "The Banquet of the Lord Mayor of London," *New York Times*, November 10, 1869; "By Telegraph," *Atlanta Constitution*, November 11, 1869.

30. "The English Premier and the Late George Peabody," *New York Times*, November 11, 1869.

31. Charles Pettit McIlvaine to William Carus, November 16, 1869, in Carus, *Memorials*, 294.

32. "The Funeral at Westminster Abbey, London—Observances in the United States," *New York Times*, November 12, 1869; "Boston," *Chicago Tribune*, November 13, 1869; "Respect to the Memory of George Peabody," *(Baltimore) Sun*, November 15, 1869.

33. "Mr. Peabody's Funeral," *Harper's Weekly*, December 18, 1869, 808–9; "Foreign News," *Harper's Weekly*, November 27, 1869, 755. See, for example, "Funeral of Geo. Peabody," *New-Orleans Commercial Bulletin*, November 16, 1869; "Funeral of George Peabody," *New Hampshire Patriot*, November 17, 1869; "The Funeral of Mr. Peabody," *New*

Hampshire Sentinel, November 18, 1869; "Funeral of George Peabody," *Daily Columbus En-quirer*, November 18, 1869; "George Peabody," *Weekly Georgia Telegraph*, November 19, 1869; "The Peabody Obsequies, the Funeral in Westminster Abbey," *(Baltimore) Sun*, November 25, 1869; "The Peabody Obsequies," *Chicago Tribune*, November 27, 1869; "Funeral of George Peabody," *Hawaiian Gazette*, December 15, 1869; "Funeral of the Late George Peabody," *Frank Leslie's Illustrated Newspaper*, December 18, 1869; "The Monument in Westminster Abbey to George Peabody," *Chicago Tribune*, January 3, 1870.

34. "George Peabody," *New York Herald*, November 18, 1869.

35. "Great Britain, the Remains of George Peabody," *Chicago Tribune*, November 12, 1869; "Royal Honors to Mr. Peabody's Remains," *New York Herald*, November 12, 1869; "A British Man-of-War to Convey the Body to the United States," *New York Times*, November 12, 1869. A few papers also claimed that a French warship would transport Peabody's remains; "New Arrangement for the Removal of Mr. Peabody's Remains," *New York Times*, November 17, 1869; "France Honoring the Memory of George Peabody," *New York Herald*, November 18, 1869.

36. "An American Man-of-War to Bring the Body to the United States," *New York Times*, November 13, 1869; "Our Washington Letter . . . George Peabody," *Atlanta Constitution*, November 17, 1869.

37. See correspondence and reports about the ships in De Meissner, *Old Naval Days*, 350–51; "The Peabody Obsequies in Westminster Abbey," *New York Herald*, November 14, 1869.

38. "George Peabody's Funeral—The War Ship Monarch," *New York Herald*, November 28, 1869; "The Late Mr. Peabody," *New York Times*, December 14, 1869; "George Peabody," *New York Times*, December 29, 1869; "George Peabody," *Philadelphia Inquirer*, December 30, 1869; "Foreign News," *Harper's Weekly*, January 1, 1870, 3.

39. "Foreign News," *Harper's Weekly*, 3; "From Europe," *Hartford Daily Courant*, November 17, 1869; "According to the New Arrangement," *Dubuque Daily Times*, November 18, 1869; "The Remains of George Peabody," *Chicago Tribune*, December 2, 1869; "Europe." *New York Times*, December 9, 1869; "Weekly Resume of Foreign Affairs," *Georgia Weekly Telegraph*, December 14, 1869; "The Late Mr. Peabody, The Reception of the Body on Board the Monarch," *Frank Leslie's Illustrated Newspaper*, January 15, 1870, 301–3.

40. "According to the New Arrangements," *Dubuque Daily Times*, November 18, 1869; "Postponed," *Dubuque Daily Times*, November 25, 1869; "The Remains of George Peabody," *Chicago Tribune*, December 4, 1869; "George Peabody's Funeral—The War Ship Monarch," *New York Herald*, November 28, 1869. The same description of the *Monarch* from the *Cork Constitution* can be found in *Chicago Tribune*, December 2, 1869; "George Peabody's Remains," *Daily Evening Bulletin*, December 28, 1869.

41. "The Remains of George Peabody," *New York Times*, November 22, 1869; "The Richmond, Transport to the Inconstant—Her History," *New York Times*, December 2, 1869.

42. "George Peabody. Preparations for the Removal to America of His Remains," *New York Times*, December 6, 1869; "Grand Naval Funeral Procession," *Chicago Tribune*, January 5, 1870.

43. "Army and Navy Journal" of February 19, 1870, quoted in *Correspondence Respecting the Visit of Her Majesty's Ship*, 3.

44. "Public Resolution—No. 6," *Bangor Daily Whig and Courier*, January 5 and January 8, 1870; Hanaford, *George Peabody*, 231.

45. Charles Sumner, then chair of the Senate Foreign Relations Committee, argued in 1869 that the British owed the United States $4 billion; Hackett, *Reminiscences*, 51; Whitridge, "The Alabama," 184–85.

46. Cook, *Alabama Claims*, 124–33.

47. "Practical Friendship Better Than a Policy of Settlement," *Pall Mall Gazette*, reprinted in *New York Times*, December 2, 1869, and *Chicago Tribune*, December 9, 1869.

48. "Associated Press Dispatches . . . Mr. Peabody's Remains," *Daily National Intelligencer and Washington Express*, December 8, 1869; on Grant's decision to calm tempers over the claims in late 1869, see Long, *In the Shadow*, 172–73.

49. "Congress," *New York Herald*, December 16, 1869; "America," *(London) Times*, December 16, 1869. A month later, he also offered a resolution, which passed, to authorize the president to prepare to receive the body in the United States; "Remains of George Peabody," *Chicago Tribune*, December 22, 1869; "America," *(London) Times*, December 23, 1869; on Grant's message, see Nevins, *Hamilton Fish*, 297–98.

50. Greenberg, "Ohioans vs. Georgians," 575–98.

51. On the controversy in Congress, see Welch, "George Peabody's Funeral," 126–28; *Congressional Globe*, 41st Cong., 2d Sess., Part I, House of Representatives, December 15 and 21, 1869. Just a few months later, Grant appointed Schenck to be the American high commissioner to the Geneva tribunal to settle the *Alabama* claims, indicating that Peabody's reputation did not actually smooth everything over; see Hackett, *Reminiscences*. In 1871 Grant appointed Schenck minister to Great Britain.

52. Welch, "George Peabody's Funeral," 116; Parker, "Funeral of George Peabody."

53. "The Peabody Pomp," *Chicago Tribune*, December 16, 1869.

54. Sexton, "Funded Loan," 449–78; Sexton, *Debtor Diplomacy*, 190–251.

55. "A Powerful Hint," *Mountaineer*, February 9, 1870.

56. "The Monitor Terror," *New York Times*, March 22, 1870, and *Milwaukee Daily Sentinel*, March 29, 1870.

57. "George Peabody, from Neman Hall's Funeral Discourse," *Vermont Watchman and State Journal*, December 22, 1869; see Lunt, *Threnody*.

58. "The *Monarch* . . . ," *Punch*, January 1, 1870, 262; Maryland Historical Society, *In Memory of George Peabody*, 5.

59. Foote, *Bountiful Return*, 16.

60. "Honors to Mr. Peabody," *Pittsfield Sun*, November 25, 1869. In France, Victor Hugo eulogized Peabody as a great transatlantic philanthropist; "Victor Hugo's Letter on George Peabody," *Boston Investigator*, January 12, 1870.

61. Commerell quoted in "The Late Mr. Peabody," *New York Times*, December 14, 1869.

62. "Preparations for the Obsequies in Boston and Peabody," *New York Herald*, January 19, 1870.

63. "Remains of George Peabody," *Chicago Tribune*, November 20, 1869; "The Remains of George Peabody," *Chicago Tribune*, December 18, 1869.

64. "The Remains of Mr. George Peabody," *New York Times*, December 19, 1869; "Preparations in Portland for the Reception of the Remains of George Peabody," *New York Herald*, December 19, 1869.

65. "Reception of the Remains of George Peabody," *New York Herald*, January 1, 1870; "The Remains of George Peabody," *New York Herald*, January 4, 1870; "Grand Naval Funeral Procession," *Chicago Tribune*, January 5, 1870; "The Funeral of George Peabody,"

New York Herald, January 6, 1870; "Reception of the Remains of Mr. Peabody," *New York Times*, January 6, 1870; "Two War Vessels Have Left New York," *Detroit Tribune*, January 6, 1870.

66. David Farragut to A. A. Abbot, January 7, 1870, Peabody FCS; Farragut chose six officers to accompany him, including Rear Admiral H. K. Thatcher (who had played a key role in the capture of Mobile during the war); "Naval Orders," *Chicago Tribune*, January 23, 1870; "The Staff of Admiral Farragut," *New York Times*, January 23, 1870.

67. "Latest News," *Lowell Daily Citizen and News*, January 6, 1870; quotation from *Peabody Press*, November 10, 1869, in Peabody Death and Burial Scrapbook (hereafter Peabody DBS).

68. "Preparations at Peabody for the Funeral Ceremonies," *Chicago Tribune*, December 20, 1869; "George Peabody," *New York Herald*, December 28, 1869.

69. "News from the Peabody Fleet," *New York Times*, January 17, 1870.

70. "The Late Mr. Peabody, the Reception of the Body on Board the Monarch," *Frank Leslie's Illustrated Newspaper*, January 15, 1870, 301–3; "From England to America," *Harper's Weekly*, January 15, 1870, 36–37.

71. See "From Maine," in Peabody DBS, 18; on the *Alabama* sinking of Maine ships and the political climate in the state during Reconstruction see *Maine History Online*, "1850–1870 The Civil War," accessed January 11, 2017, https://www.mainememory.net/sitebuilder/site/903/page/1314/display; Clark, *Maine*, 125.

72. "Posthumous Honors to George Peabody," *New York Herald*, January 11, 1870.

73. Joshua Chamberlain to David W. Lewis, December 2, 1869, in Goulka, *Grand Old Man of Maine*, 31; on Chamberlain's views of Reconstruction and African American rights, see Trulock, *In the Hands of Providence*, 334–42; Perry, *Conceived in Liberty*, 345–51; Smith, *Fanny and Joshua*, 194–95, 209.

74. Blight, *Race and Reunion*, 171–300.

75. "Letter from Portland, Arrangements for the Reception of the Remains of Mr. Peabody," *Boston Daily Advertiser*, January 1, 1870; "The Posthumous Honors to George Peabody," *New York Times*, January 10, 1870; "Honors to George Peabody," *New York Times*, December 24, 1869; "Honors to George Peabody," *Daily Evening Bulletin*, January 4, 1870; "Preparations for the Obsequies in Boston and Peabody," *New York Herald*, January 19, 1870; "Letter from Augusta," *Bangor Daily Whig and Courier*, January 22, 1870.

76. "Maine Legislature," *Bangor Daily Whig and Courier*, January 8, 1870; "George Peabody," *New York Herald*, January 8, 1870; "Albany . . . the Funeral of Mr. Peabody," *New York Times*, January 20, 1870; "Committee of the Maryland Legislature to Be Present," *Boston Daily Advertiser*, January 27, 1870.

77. "Official Honor to the Late George Peabody," *Boston Daily Advertiser*, January 7, 1870; "The Legislature and the Peabody Funeral," *Boston Daily Advertiser*, January 17, 1870; "Maine Legislature," *Bangor Daily Whig and Courier*, January 17, 1870; "Preparations for the Obsequies in Boston and Peabody," *New York Herald*, January 19, 1870; "Letter from Augusta," *Bangor Daily Whig and Courier*, January 22, 1870.

78. "Maine Legislature," *Bangor Daily Whig and Courier*, January 24, 1870; General McDowell also ordered the Fifth Battalion of Maine artillery to attend the funeral; "Maine," *Boston Daily Advertiser*, January 20, 1870; "The Reception of George Peabody's Remains," *New York Times*, January 20, 1870; *Chicago Tribune*, January 22, 1870; "Military Gossip," *New York Times*, January 23, 1870.

79. "The Maine Legislature Finally Vote to Attend," *New York Times*, January 23, 1870; "Maine Legislature," *Bangor Daily Whig and Courier*, January 26, 1870; "Maine," *Vermont Chronicle*, January 29, 1870; "Additional Intelligence," *(Baltimore) Sun*, January 27, 1870. Even after voting to attend, only some of the Maine legislators actually attended the ceremonies in Portland because of a delay in removing Peabody's remains from the *Monarch*; "Augusta," *Boston Daily Advertiser*, January 27, 1870.

80. On the *Miantonomoh* visit to England and its influence on the design of the *Monarch*, see Fuller, *Clad in Iron*, 273–79; "The Naval Ceremonies," *(Baltimore) Sun*, January 27, 1870; "Portland, the Funeral Fleet in the Harbor," *Boston Daily Advertiser*, January 27, 1870; "George Peabody . . . An Impatient Multitude in Small Boats," *New York Times*, January 28, 1870; Eastman, "Maine Fortifications," 366–67.

81. HMS *Monarch* log book; "Arriaal [*sic*] of the Peabody Fleet," *Lowell Daily Citizen and News*, January 26, 1870; "The Naval Ceremonies," *(Baltimore) Sun*, January 27, 1870; "Incidents," *New York Times*, January 29, 1870; "The Funeral of George Peabody," *(Baltimore) Sun*, February 1, 1870.

82. "The Monarch," *Boston Daily Advertiser*, January 26, 1870; "H. E. M. Steamer Monarch," *(Baltimore) Sun*, January 27, 1870; "The Chamber of Death," *Boston Daily Advertiser*, January 27, 1870.

83. "Funeral Procession from the Monarch to the City Hall," *Boston Daily Advertiser*, January 27, 1890; "George Peabody, the Funeral Fleet," *New York Times*, January 29, 1870; "The Remains of George Peabody at Portland, ME," *Frank Leslie's Illustrated Newspaper*, February 12, 1870, 367.

84. "The 'Monarch' in Portland Harbor," *Harper's Weekly*, February 12, 1870, 100; "The Procession of War Vessels, as Seen from Port Gorges," *Frank Leslie's Illustrated Newspaper*, February 12, 1870, 368; "The Peabody Funeral," *Frank Leslie's Illustrated Newspaper*, February 19, 1870, 385.

85. "The Remains of George Peabody," *New York Herald*, January 26, 1870.

86. "From Massachusetts," *North American and United States Gazette*, January 27, 1870.

87. "The Peabody Funeral," *Hartford Daily Courant*, January 27, 1870; "Order of the Funeral Procession," *Boston Daily Advertiser*, January 29, 1870; "George Peabody . . . Large Number of Distinguished Persons to Be Present," *New York Herald*, January 29, 1870; "George Peabody—Portland Full of Visitors," *New York Herald*, January 31, 1870.

88. "The Peabody Obsequies," *Hartford Daily Courant*, January 31, 1870; "General," *New York Times*, January 31, 1870; "George Peabody, The Ceremonies in Portland," *Bangor Daily Whig and Courier*, January 31, 1870; "From Maine," *North American and United States Gazette*, January 31, 1870; "Obsequies of Mr. Peabody," *Vermont Chronicle*, February 5, 1870; "George Peabody," *Chicago Tribune*, February 2, 1870.

89. "The Peabody Obsequies," *Hartford Daily Courant*, January 31, 1870.

90. "The Funeral Honors," *Lowell Daily Citizen and News*, January 31, 1870; "George Peabody . . . Our Special Correspondent," *New York Times*, January 31, 1870; "The Peabody Funeral Ceremonies at Portland," *Peabody Press*, February 2, 1870.

91. "The Peabody Obsequies," *New York Times*, February 1, 1870.

92. "George Peabody—Portland Full of Visitors," *New York Herald*, January 31, 1870.

93. "Peabody," *Lowell Daily Citizen and News*, February 2, 1870; "The Railroad Car," *Daily State Gazette*, January 8, 1870; "The Funeral of George Peabody," *New York Herald*, January 6, 1870; "George Peabody," *Philadelphia Inquirer*, February 1, 1870.

94. "The Peabody Funeral Car," *Harper's Weekly*, February 5, 1870, 87; "George Peabody, Preparation of a Funeral Train," *Chicago Tribune*, January 8, 1870; "George Peabody—The Departure from Portland," *Bangor Daily Whig and Courier*, February 2, 1870; "The Peabody Funeral Train," *New York Herald*, January 22, 1870.

95. "Telegraphic Summary," *New Hampshire Patriot*, February 2, 1870; "The Funeral of George Peabody," *Boston Daily Advertiser*, January 31, 1870; "The Special Train from Portland," *Lowell Daily Citizen and News*, February 1, 1870; "The Peabody Obsequies," *New York Times*, February 2, 1870; "The Remains of George Peabody," *New York Herald*, February 2, 1870.

96. "The Peabody Funeral Obsequies," *Boston Daily Advertiser*, February 2, 1870; "The Visitors to Peabody," *New York Times*, February 5, 1870. One Vermont paper reported that 6,677 people viewed the body at the institute; "Notes and Comments," *Vermont Watchman and State Journal*, February 9, 1870; "The Last Honors," *Harper's Weekly*, February 19, 1870.

97. "George Peabody," *New York Herald*, January 14, 1870; "The Peabody Obsequies," *New York Times*, January 15, 1870.

98. See Committee of Invitation to Stephen Salisbury, December 29, 1869, "The Funeral of the Late Mr. George Peabody," pasted inside the cover of Hanaford, *George Peabody*; "George Peabody," *Chicago Tribune*, February 9, 1870; "The Final Obsequies," *Vermont Chronicle*, February 12, 1870.

99. Winthrop, *Eulogy Pronounced at the Funeral of George Peabody*.

100. "The Funeral of Mr. Peabody," *Boston Daily Advertiser*, February 9, 1870; "The Last of George Peabody," *New York Herald*, February 9, 1870; "George Peabody—Late Rites over the Remains of the Illustrious Dead," *New York Herald*, February 9, 1870; "George Peabody—Final Funeral Ceremonies in Massachusetts," *New York Times*, February 9, 1870; "George Peabody's Funeral," *Chicago Tribune*, February 12, 1870; "Prince Arthur," *Vermont Chronicle*, February 12, 1870; "Mr. Peabody's Burial," *Congregationalist and Boston Recorder*, February 17, 1870; "Funeral of Mr. Peabody," *Daily Evening Bulletin*, February 18, 1870; "Funeral of the Late George Peabody," *Frank Leslie's Illustrated Newspaper*, February 26, 1870, 401.

101. *Correspondence Respecting the Visit of Her Majesty's Ship*.

102. "The Peabody Demonstration!!!" unidentified in Peabody DBS, 31.

103. "George Peabody—Scandalous Conduct over a Dead Man," *Daily Cleveland Herald*, February 12, 1870.

104. "New England News," *Boston Daily Advertiser*, March 5, 1870; second quotation from unidentified newspaper clipping, Peabody DBS, 32. Other press coverage, in contrast, emphasized the sincere mourning for Peabody by London's poor; "George Peabody's Monument," *Harper's Weekly*, December 11, 1869.

105. Winthrop, *Eulogy Pronounced at the Funeral of George Peabody*, 5.

106. Train quoted in Parker, "Funeral of George Peabody," 121.

107. William Lloyd Garrison, "Mr. Peabody and the South," *Independent*, August 16, 1869, reprinted in Merrill, "William Lloyd Garrison and George Peabody," 51–52.

108. William Lloyd Garrison, "Honored beyond His Deserts," *(New York) Independent*, February 10, 1870, reprinted in Merrill, "William Lloyd Garrison and George Peabody," 54.

109. Merrill, "William Lloyd Garrison and George Peabody," 55.

110. Merrill, "William Lloyd Garrison and George Peabody," 57, 58.

111. On Schenck's wartime defense of Black rights in Maryland, see Fields, *Slavery and Freedom*.

112. Janney, *Remembering the Civil War*, 103–31; Gannon, *Won Cause*; Harris, *Across the Bloody Chasm*.

113. Quoted in "The Late George Peabody—A Vindication of His Course during the War," *New York Times*, December 23, 1869. The Weed letter is also discussed and excerpted in "George Peabody and the Rebellion," *Daily Evening Bulletin*, December 21, 1869.

114. "The Question of George Peabody's Disloyalty," *Daily Cleveland Herald*, January 29, 1870; "Mr. Peabody's Patriotism," *Daily Cleveland Herald*, February 2, 1870; see also "Honors to George Peabody," *Vermont Watchman and State Journal*, February 2, 1870.

115. Robert E. Lee to George Peabody Russell quoted in *Salem Gazette*, November 30, 1869; see Parker, "George Peabody and Maryland," 48.

116. Nevins, *Hamilton Fish*, 293.

117. William Branch Giles quoted in Maryland Historical Society, *In Memory of George Peabody*, 19–20.

118. Augustus Bradford quoted in Maryland Historical Society, *In Memory of George Peabody*, 27.

119. "The Tennessee Legislature on George Peabody," *New York Times*, November 11, 1869; "Georgia News," *Atlanta Constitution*, November 18, 1869; Franklin Parker, "George Peabody and Maryland," 48; see also praise for Peabody in Charleston, South Carolina, *Memoir of George Peabody*, 7.

120. Review of "Discourse on the Life and Character of George Peabody," *Southern Review* 8 (1870): 241.

121. "George Peabody. The Philanthropist," *Philadelphia Inquirer*, November 6, 1869.

122. *London Times* quoted in "From Europe. The London Press on the Death of George Peabody," *Hartford Daily Courant*, November 6, 1869; "George Peabody's Name and Memory," *New York Herald*, November 6, 1869; "The London Press on the Life and Character of George Peabody," *Chicago Tribune*, November 6, 1869; "George Peabody," *New York Times*, November 6, 1869.

123. "Death of Mr. Peabody," *New-Orleans Commercial Bulletin*, November 6, 1869; "Obituary. George Peabody, from the New York Tribune," *Chicago Tribune*, November 8, 1869.

124. "The Late George Peabody," *Frank Leslie's Illustrated Newspaper*, November 20, 1869, 155; see "Letter from Greenbrier, West Virginia, Springs, Visitors—Gen. Lee—Mr. Peabody," *Weekly Georgia Telegraph*, September 3, 1869; "A Historic Group," *New York World*, September 14, 1869; "Virginia White Sulphur Springs," *Weekly Georgia Telegraph*, October 8, 1869; "Signed Photograph of Robert E. Lee and George Peabody (and others) at White Sulphur Springs, West Virginia, August 1869," *Broadus R. Littlejohn*, Book 313, accessed May 25, 2007, http://digitalcommons.wofford.edu/littlejohnmss/313; Parker, "Robert E. Lee, George Peabody," 94; on the social prominence and place of visits to White Sulphur Springs in Southern genteel culture, see Lewis, *Ladies and Gentlemen on Display*, 173–75.

125. Robert E. Lee to A. A. Abbott, January 7, 1870, Peabody FCS; Cyrus H. McCormick, Bolivar Christian, and Thomas I. Kirkpatrick to A. A. Abbott, January 26, 1870, Peabody FCS; Robert E. Lee to Nahum Capen, January 20, 1870 and Robert E. Lee to Sidney Root, January 21, 1870, Washington and Lee University Special Collections, accessed June 26, 2019, https://dspace.wlu.edu/handle/11021/19229; see also Flood, *Lee*, 215–16.

126. The portrait is still visible on the wall of Lee's office, which is preserved in the basement of Lee Chapel at Washington and Lee University, across the hall from Lee's burial crypt.

127. "General Lee and Mr. Peabody," *Chicago Tribune*, January 20, 1870; "Gen. R. E. Lee," *(Baltimore) Sun*, January 27, 1870; "General Lee," *Peabody Press*, January 19, 1870.

128. "Lee's Tribute to Peabody," *New York Times*, November 26, 1869, reprinted in *Daily Evening Bulletin*, December 9, 1869.

129. "We Learn . . . ," *Daily Arkansas Gazette*, February 1, 1870.

130. Lee to A. A. Abbott, January 7, 1870, Peabody FCS. Lee biographer Margaret Sanborn claims that Lee was displeased by the ostentation of mourning rituals for Peabody, which contrasted with his own "feelings of sorrow & resignation," but she offers no evidence for the claim; Sanborn, *Robert E. Lee*, 384.

131. Winthrop to John Pendleton Kennedy, February 2, 1870, quoted in Parker, "Funeral of George Peabody," 125.

132. Miller, *John Bell Hood*, 198.

133. Barnhart, "Apostles of the Lost Cause," 371–72; Foster, *Ghosts of the Confederacy*.

134. Ayers, "Not Forgotten," 12; Fellman, "Robert E. Lee," 185–204.

135. William R. Black, "Untangling the Lost Cause Myth from the American Story Will Be Hard," *Washington Post*, August 25, 2017,

136. The best treatments of the rise of Lee as a national hero by the turn of the twentieth century are Connelly, *Marble Man*, 99–122, and Silber, *Romance of Reunion*, 173–78, 195. David Blight tracks how the process mirrored the rise of Jim Crow in *Race and Reunion*, 266–71.

137. Reagan, *Baptized in Blood*.

138. Harsh, *Confederate Tide Rising*.

139. Biographies of Lee are numerous, to say the least. The most up-to-date interpretation is Pryor, *Reading the Man*; Thomas, *Robert E. Lee*, is also excellent and emerges from the extraordinary shadow cast by Douglas Southall Freeman's *R. E. Lee*, which perpetuated the Lost Cause and Lee's Southern demigod status; see also Flood, *Lee*; Nolan, *Lee Considered*; Reeves, *Lost Indictment of Robert E. Lee*.

140. Thomas, *Robert E. Lee*, 20; see Fishwick, *Lee after the War*; Connelly, *Marble Man*; Wert, "James Longstreet and the Lost Cause," 131–34; Foster, *Ghosts of the Confederacy*, 51–61; Nolan, "Anatomy of the Myth." An example of a book that participates in the cult of Lee is Meredith, *Face of Robert E. Lee*.

141. Among the few who emphasize this trend are Myers, "Southern Traitor or American Hero?," 211–21; Gallagher, *Lee and His Army*, 274–76; Janney, *Burying the Dead*, 106.

142. "From the New York Herald, General Robert E. Lee," *(Richmond) Daily Dispatch*, October 1, 1870.

143. Frederick Douglass, quoted in Gallagher, *Lee and His Army*, 275; same quotation in Blight, *Race and Reunion*, 270.

144. Frederick Douglass, 1870, quoted in Wilson, "Foreword," vii.

145. Bostwick, *Memorializing Robert E. Lee*, 7.

146. See Thomas, *Robert E. Lee*, 398–409; O'Brien, "Brady and Lee," 6–8.

147. Rozear et al., "R. E. Lee's Stroke," 291–308.

148. William Nalle to Mrs. Thomas Botts Nalle, October 16, 1870, VMI Archives Digital Collections, accessed December 1, 2017, https://vmi.contentdm.oclc.org/digital

/collection/p15821coll11/id/1559/; "The Death of General Lee," *Lynchburg Virginian*, October 15, 1870. The funeral was further simplified, probably, by the weather; for example, the local supply of refined coffins was lost in flooding, and a delegation had to appropriate a coffin for Lee that had washed up on an island downriver several miles from Lexington; Chittum, *Story of Finding the Coffin*; Freeman, *R. E. Lee*, 4:527.

149. See Lawton, "Constructing the Cause," 12; Foster, *Ghosts of the Confederacy*, 52; Goldfield, *Still Fighting the Civil War*, 29–30; Mary Custis Lee to Joseph Johnston, November 14, 1870, Custis-Lee Family Papers, Library of Congress.

150. Wilson, "Death of Southern Heroes," 4–5.

151. William Nalle letter; Wilson, *Baptized in Blood*, 122.

152. "Lee's Funeral," *New York Herald*, October 16, 1870.

153. *Funeral Obsequies, October 15, 1870.*

154. William Nalle letter; "The Funeral at Lexington," *(Baltimore) Sun*, October 17, 1870.

155. "The Late Robert E. Lee," *New York Times*, October 15, 1870; see Bostwick, *Memorializing Robert E. Lee*, 41–48; Thomas, *Robert E. Lee*, 416; see Lee, *Memoirs of William Nelson Pendleton*, 453–54. Lee's beloved horse, Traveller, would later be buried just outside the chapel; Faust, "Equine Relics," 23–49.

156. *Santa Fe Post* quoted in "Robert E. Lee Is Dead," *Weekly Arizona Miner*, November 19, 1870.

157. "From the Petersburg Index, the Death of General Lee," *(Richmond) Daily Dispatch*, October 14, 1870.

158. "Death of Gen. Robert E. Lee," *Weekly Arizona Miner*, November 5, 1870.

159. "Gen. Robert Edmund Lee," *(New York) Sun*, October 13, 1870.

160. *New York Herald*, October 13, 1870; "From the *New York Herald*," *(Richmond) Daily Dispatch*, October 15, 1870.

161. "General R. E. Lee," *Frank Leslie's Illustrated Newspaper*, October 29, 1870, 101.

162. "At the Memorial Service," *Bangor Daily Whig and Courier*, October 26, 1870; Cooke, *Life of Gen. Robert E. Lee*, 564; "Meeting in New York to Honor General Lee's Memory," *(Richmond) Daily Dispatch*, October 24, 1870; for Lincoln's 1859 address, see "Cooper Union Address," *Abraham Lincoln Online*, accessed February 9, 2017, http://www .abrahamlincolnonline.org/lincoln/speeches/cooper.htm.

163. "Robert Edmund Lee," *Newark Daily Advertiser*, October 13, 1870. The *Chicago Republican* noted that even those who thought of Lee as a criminal would remember him for his magnanimity; "Obituary, Robert E. Lee," October 13, 1870.

164. Jones, *Washington Family Relics*, 6. Similar sentiments were expressed by the editors of the *Philadelphia Press*, in "The Southern Papers," October 18, 1870.

165. Citizens of Louisville, *Robert E. Lee*, 9; Cooke, *Life of Gen. Robert E. Lee*, 507–12; "The Late General Lee. The Louisville Meeting," *(Richmond) Daily Dispatch*, October 20, 1870.

166. Citizens of Louisville, *Robert E. Lee*, 13; "General Lee, Louisville," *Daily Evening Bulletin*, October 17, 1870.

167. "Discourse of Rev. W. H. Pratt," in Citizens of Louisville, *Robert E. Lee*, 37.

168. University of Louisville, "Reconstruction/Readjustment: Side 2," accessed October 26, 2017, https://louisville.edu/freedompark/historical-obelisks/reconstruction-readjustment.

169. Janney, *Remembering the Civil War*, 140; on the tensions between "war powers and the return to civil authority" in national politics and during the phase-out of military occupation, see Downs, *After Appomattox*, 213–36.

170. Ross, "The Commemoration," 135–50; "New Orleans, Oct. 13," *(Richmond) Daily Dispatch*, October 14, 1870; *Lynchburg Daily Virginian*, October 15, 1870; K. C. Stiles to Mary Randolph Custis Lee, December 12, 1870, Mary Custis Lee Papers, 1694–1917 (Mss1 L5144 a), Virginia Historical Society, Richmond, VA (hereafter MCL Papers); see also Ross, *Great New Orleans Kidnapping Case*, 12.

171. "Charlottesville, October 13, 1870," *Richmond Daily Whig*, October 15, 1870; "Robert Edmund Lee. Public Meetings in Virginia," *Richmond Daily Whig*, October 17, 1870; "Los Angeles Matters," *Daily Evening Bulletin*, October 15, 1870.

172. "Death of Gen. Robert E. Lee, Meeting at Mercantile Library Hall," *Missouri Republican*, October 15, 1870; "Lee's Memory Honored at St. Louis," *Daily Evening Bulletin*, October 15, 1870

173. "Atlanta," *Chicago Republican*, October 13, 1870; "Robert E. Lee," *New York Times*, October 14, 1870; Cooke, *Life of Gen. Robert E. Lee*, 513–16; "Atlanta, Ga," *Daily Dispatch*, October 17, 1870; "Atlanta's Honor to the Memory of General Robert E. Lee," *Atlanta Constitution*, October 18, 1870.

174. "Robert E. Lee," *New York Times*, October 14, 1870; "Selma, ALA, Oct. 13," *Daily Dispatch*, October 14, 1870; "Selma, Ala., Oct. 13," *Lynchburg Daily Virginian*, October 14, 1870.

175. Cooke, *Life of Gen. Robert E. Lee*, 545; "Remarks of General Wade Hampton on the Death of General Lee," *Daily Dispatch*, October 17, 1870; Lesesne quoted in "Charleston's Tribute to Gen. Lee," *Charleston Courier, Tri-Weekly*, October 18, 1870.

176. "Chattanooga, Tenn. October 14," *Richmond Daily Whig*, October 15, 1870. Brown was elected governor just a few weeks later; Elliott, *John C. Brown of Tennessee*, 179.

177. Cooke, *Life of Gen. Robert E. Lee*, 545–49; "The Memory of Gen. Lee in Baltimore," *Daily Dispatch*, October 18, 1870; "Great Demonstration in Baltimore," *Richmond Daily Whig*, October 17, 1870.

178. Cooke, *Life of Gen. Robert E. Lee*, 557.

179. "Public Meeting," *Spirit of Jefferson*, October 18, 1870; on Hawks's devotion to Lee, see Robert E. Lee to W. I. Hawks, January 8, 1866, Washington and Lee Manuscript Collections, accessed October 28, 2017, https://dspace.wlu.edu/bitstream/handle/11021/20754/WLUcoll0170_b01_f014_001.jpg?sequence=10&isAllowed=y.

180. "Lee Memorial Meeting in Kansas City," *Spirit of Jefferson*, November 8, 1870; see "The Last Roll: Henry M. Withers," *Confederate Veteran* 17 (February 1909): 88.

181. Blight, *Race and Reunion*.

182. Reverdy Johnson quoted in Cooke, *Life of Gen. Robert E. Lee*, 551. Johnson's eulogy was followed by a laudatory speech from former Baltimore mayor George William Brown, who had been imprisoned by the Union military for nearly the entire Civil War due to his Confederate sympathies, in which Brown assured hearers that Northerners and Southerners would worship Lee's grave as they did the grave of George Washington; Cooke, *Life of Gen. Robert E. Lee*, 556.

183. "General Robert E. Lee Dead," *Atlanta Constitution*, October 13, 1870; for similar rhetoric see Virginia Dialectic Society to Mary Randolph Custis Lee, [October 1870], MCL Papers.

184. Cooke, *Life of Gen. Robert E. Lee*, 538; "The Memorial Meeting in Richmond," *Spirit of Jefferson*, November 15, 1870.

185. *Flake's Semi-Weekly Galveston Bulletin*, October 19, 1870.

186. "Flags at Half Mast," *Flake's Semi-Weekly Galveston Bulletin*, October 19, 1870; "Washington, Oct. 13," *Daily Dispatch*, October 14, 1870. The incident resembled some of the flap over public signs of mourning during the reburial of Confederate general Albert Sidney Johnston in Texas in 1867; Thompson, "When General Albert Sidney Johnston Came Home."

187. "General Lee and History," *Daily Dispatch*, October 24, 1870.

188. "Death of Gen. Lee," *Flake's Semi-Weekly Galveston Bulletin*, October 22, 1870.

189. "The Harvest of Death," *Boston Daily Advertiser*, October 14, 1870; see also "General Robert E. Lee Died," *Boston Daily Advertiser*, October 13, 1870.

190. "Death of General Robert E. Lee," *Daily Cleveland Herald*, October 13, 1870.

191. "The Portland, Me., Argus," *Wilmington Journal*, October 28, 1870.

192. "Mourning Lee in Indiana," *Galveston Tri-Weekly News*, October 17, 1870.

193. For a consideration of both positive and negative qualities, see "The Death of General Lee," *(Philadelphia) Press*, October 19, 1870.

194. "Robert Edmund Lee," *Chicago Republican*, October 13, 1870. The eulogy was reprinted in the *Yankton Press*, October 19, 1870.

195. "The Raleigh Standard, an Extremely Bitter Republican Paper," *Alexandria Gazette and Virginia Advertiser*, October 14, 1870.

196. "Death of General Robert E. Lee," *North American and United States Gazette*, October 13, 1870. A similar, if milder, sentiment is expressed in *Lowell Daily Citizen and News*, October 14, 1870.

197. "Death of General Robert E. Lee," *Daily Evening Bulletin*, October 13, 1870.

198. "The Death of General Lee," *Weekly Alta California*, October 22, 1870.

199. "The Late General Robert E. Lee," *Bangor Daily Whig and Courier*, October 14, 1870.

200. George Alfred Townsend, "Lee's Greatest Campaign," *Hinds County Gazette*, November 16, 1870.

201. "From the Lynchburg Virginian. Robert Edmund Lee," *Daily Dispatch*, October 14, 1870.

202. Cooke, *Life of Gen. Robert E. Lee*, 1.

203. "Robert E. Lee," *Spirit of Jefferson*, October 18, 1870.

204. "General Robert E. Lee Is Dead," *Charleston Courier, Tri-Weekly*, October 22, 1870.

205. "Memorial Resolutions," *Lynchburg Virginian*, October 14, 1870.

206. "General Lee," *New York Herald*, October 13, 1870; "Very Small Indeed," *New York Herald*, October 14, 1870.

207. "Obituary, Robert E. Lee," *New York Times*, October 13, 1870.

208. See "The Northern Press on General Lee," *Richmond Daily Whig*, October 15, 1870; *Daily Dispatch*, October 15, 1870; *Lynchburg Daily Virginian*, October 18, 1870; "Philadelphia on Lee," *Wilmington Journal*, October 28, 1870; "The Death of General Lee. Comments from the Northern Press," *Spirit of Jefferson*, October 25, 1870; "Robert E. Lee," *Charleston Courier, Tri-Weekly*, October 18, 1870.

209. *Lynchburg Daily Virginian*, October 18, 1870; *Richmond Whig* quoted in *(Philadelphia) Press*, October 18, 1870; "General Robert E. Lee, A Nation's Tribute," *Charleston Courier*, October 18, 1870; "R. E. Lee, A Nation's Tribute," *Charleston Courier, Tri-Weekly*, October 20, 1870;

210. "Meeting in New York to Honor General Lee's Memory," *Daily Dispatch*, October 26, 1870.

211. "Robert E. Lee, Personal Reminiscences and Anecdotes," *Newark Advocate*, November 18, 1870.

212. Mary Meade to Mary Randolph Custis Lee, October 19, 1870, MCL Papers.

213. "By Associated Press," *Daily Dispatch*, October 14, 1870.

214. "Letter from Lexington," *Wilmington Journal*, October 28, 1870.

215. "Carry W. Styles," *Atlanta Constitution*, October 15, 1870.

216. Images of postwar Black loyalty to the Union played a huge role in debates over civil rights and images of loyal slaves or obedient servants who venerated the Confederacy fed the Lost Cause; see Mathisen, *Loyal Republic*; Wallace-Sanders, *Mammy*; Blight, *Race and Reunion*, 286–88.

217. Mary Randolph Custis Lee quoted in Pryor, *Reading the Man*, 464.

218. Faust, *Mothers of Invention*.

219. On Southern women's role in the creation of memory, see Clinton, *Civil War Stories*, 83–111; Faust, *Mothers of Invention*, 188–89; Blight, *Race and Reunion*, 273–84; Janney, *Remembering the Civil War*, 232–64; Gross, "United Daughters of the Confederacy," 180–200.

220. Pryor, *Reading the Man*, 448.

221. On widowhood, see Janney, *Burying the Dead*; Faust, *This Republic of Suffering*; Faust, *Mothers of Invention*.

222. Corporation Court of the City of Alexandria, October 17, 1870, MCL Papers. Hundreds of letters of consolation, both public and private (and mixed), are collected in the MCL Papers.

223. Citizens of Graham, North Carolina, October 18, 1870, MCL Papers; Citizens of St. Louis, Missouri, October 17, 1870, MCL Papers; see also Council of the City of Columbia, Georgia, October 15, 1870, MCL Papers.

224. University of Nashville, Tennessee, [October 1870], MCL Papers.

225. Proceedings of the Mayor and City Council of Nashville, Tennessee, October 13, 1870, MCL Papers.

226. Blight, *Race and Reunion*, 180–82.

227. Bowdon College Institution, Carroll County, Georgia, October 17, 1870, MCL Papers; see also Theological Seminar, Columbia, South Carolina, October 15, 1870, MCL Papers.

228. Citizens of Columbia, South Carolina, October 22, 1870, MCL Papers; see also "Tribute to the Memory of General Lee—At a Meeting Held at Columbia," *Charleston Courier, Tri-Weekly*, October 18, 1870.

229. Citizens of Covington, Kentucky, October 15, 1870, MCL Papers; Citizens of Orangeburg County, South Carolina, November 3, 1870, MCL Papers.

230. Robert E. Lee Base Ball Club, New Orleans, Louisiana, October 20, 1870, MCL Papers.

231. Southern University, Greensboro, Alabama, October 1870, MCL Papers; Officers and Soldiers of the (Late) Confederate Army, Hampton, Virginia, October 26, 1870, MCL Papers.

232. Charles Wesley Andrews to Mary Randolph Custis Lee, November 10, 1870, MCL Papers; Pierre Gustave Toutant Beauregard to Mary Custis Lee, October 14, 1870, MCL Papers.

233. W. C. Brantley to Mary Randolph Custis Lee, November 17, 1870, MCL Papers. Correspondents also discussed public eulogies and print culture in Lee's honor; L. M. Burwell to Mary Custis Lee, November 9, 1870, MCL Papers. Mary T. Gaillard commented on mourning in Athens, Georgia, in a letter to Mary Randolph Custis Lee, October 24, 1870,

MCL Papers; Lavinia Fauntleroy to Mary Randolph Custis Lee, October 25, 1870, MCL Papers; G. Mason Graham to Mary Randolph Custis Lee, October 24, 1870, MCL Papers. Letters also came from Europe and Canada; George A. Magruder to Mary Randolph Custis Lee, October 28, 1870, MCL Papers; Bessie Lee Cooper to Mary Custis Lee, October 22, 1870, MCL Papers; Matilda Seton to Mary Custis Lee, October 16, 1870, MCL Papers.

234. Jubal Early to Mary Randolph Custis Lee, February 18, 1871, MCL Papers; Harry St. John Dixon to Mary Randolph Custis Lee, October 24, 1870, MCL Papers; Fitz-John Porter to Mary Randolph Custis Lee, October 12, 1870, MCL Papers.

235. Mrs. E. G. Johnston to Mary Randolph Custis Lee, October 28, 1870, MCL Papers; Julia Johns to Mary Randolph Custis Lee, October 12, 1870, MCL Papers.

236. Mary C. S. Lee to Mary Randolph Custis Lee, October 16, 1870, MCL Papers.

237. Ash, *Rebel Richmond*, 224.

238. Rachleff, *Black Labor in the South*, 13–14.

239. "Robert E. Lee," *New York Times*, October 14, 1870; "Robert E. Lee," *Daily Cleveland Herald*, October 14, 1870.

240. McCarthy, *Walks about Richmond*, 140–42. McCarthy took his description, almost verbatim, from "The Death of Gen'l. Lee. A Day of Mourning in Richmond," *Daily Dispatch*, October 14, 1870; see also "Richmond, Oct. 13," *Lynchburg Daily Virginian*, October 14, 1870.

241. "The City. General R. E. Lee. Richmond in Mourning," *Richmond Daily Whig*, October 14, 1870; Takagi, *"Rearing Wolves to Our Own Destruction,"* 145–46; "The City Draped in Mourning," *Richmond Daily Whig*, October 15, 1870; Ezekiel and Lichtenstein, *History of the Jews of Richmond*, 154. Richmond's Jewish community maintained close ties with and reverence for Robert E. Lee; see Berman, *Richmond's Jewry*, 176–203.

242. "The City. General R. E. Lee. Richmond in Mourning," *Richmond Daily Whig*, October 14, 1870.

243. "Expressions of Public Grief," *Daily Dispatch*, October 13, 1870.

244. "The Dead Chieftain," *New York World*, October 14, 1870; "Virginia," *Atlanta Constitution*, October 15, 1870; "General Lee's Funeral," *New York Herald*, October 17, 1870.

245. Janney, *Burying the Dead*, 101; Brown, *Civil War Monuments*, 203–4; "Personal," (St. Louis) *Missouri Republican*, October 14, 1870; Mitchell, *Hollywood Cemetery*, 78–79, 72–74.

246. "The Death of Gen'l. Lee. A Day of Mourning in Richmond" and "Proceedings of the City Council," *Daily Dispatch*, October 14, 1870.

247. "Death of Gen. R. E. Lee!" *Richmond Daily Whig*, October 13, 1870.

248. Citizens of Richmond, VA, to Mary Randolph Custis Lee, October 13, 1870, MCL Papers; E. H. Brown to Mary Randolph Custis Lee, October 26, 1870, MCL Papers; "The Obsequies," *Daily Dispatch*, October 14, 1870.

249. "From Richmond," *Lynchburg Daily Virginian*, October 15, 1870; "Is General Lee to Be Buried at Hollywood?," *Richmond Daily Whig*, October 15, 1870.

250. Lee, *Memoirs of William Nelson Pendleton*, 453.

251. *Daily Dispatch*, October 20, 21, 1870; Janney, *Burying the Dead*, 108.

252. "Meeting of the Soldiers and Officers of the Army of Northern Virginia," *Daily Dispatch*, October 28, 1870. M. Keith Harris contends that Lee's death precipitated the formal organizing of larger numbers of groups of Confederate veterans; Harris, *Across the Bloody Chasm*, 19.

253. See Foster, *Ghosts of the Confederacy*, 52–53; Piston, *Lee's Tarnished Lieutenant*.

254. Levin, "William Mahone," 378–412; Janney, *Burying the Dead*, 110–12; Reeves, *Lost Indictment of Robert E. Lee*, 194.

255. "A Westminster Abbey for Virginia," *Alexandria Gazette and Virginia Advertiser*, October 20, 1870.

256. Jubal Early to Mary Randolph Custis Lee, February 18, 1871, MCL Papers; Janney, *Burying the Dead*, 113–17; see Gallagher, "Jubal A. Early," 199–226.

257. Mitchell, *Hollywood Cemetery*, 79.

Chapter Four

1. *Congressional Globe*, 42d Cong., 3d Sess., December 2, 1872, 2. Portions of this chapter were previously published as Purcell, "Mourning Charles Sumner" and are used by permission.

2. Blight, *Race and Reunion*.

3. Silber, "Reunion and Reconciliation," 78–83. One influential idea about the importance of collective forgetting is Klein, *History of Forgetting*.

4. Taylor, *Young Charles Sumner*, 81.

5. "Infamous Coalition," *Floridian and Journal*, January 25, 1851.

6. Hoffer, *Caning of Charles Sumner*; Donald, *Charles Sumner and the Coming of the Civil War*, 290–301; Benson, *Caning of Senator Sumner*.

7. On the previous resolutions, see Pierce, *Memoir and Letters of Charles Sumner*, 4:550.

8. See Slap, *Doom of Reconstruction*.

9. Charles Sumner quoted in Donald, *Charles Sumner and the Rights of Man*, 564; on Sumner's opposition to Grant, see Waugh, *U.S. Grant*, 143.

10. *Congressional Globe*, 42d Cong., 3rd Sess., December 16, 1872, 221, 235.

11. Dearing, *Veterans in Politics*, 175–76.

12. Dearing, *Veterans in Politics*, 207–8.

13. Blue, *Charles Sumner*, 205; Pierce, *Memoir and Letters of Charles Sumner*, 4:551–52; see *Hartford Daily Courant*, December 19, 1872, and *Hartford Daily Courant*, February 27, 1873.

14. Pierce, *Memoir and Letters of Charles Sumner*, 4:589; *Trenton State Gazette*, February 13, 1874; *San Francisco Bulletin*, February 20, 1874; Holmes, "Whittier and Sumner," 71; Gannon, *Won Cause*.

15. See Blight, *Race and Reunion*; Wilson, *Baptized in Blood*; Grow, "Shadow of the Civil War," 77–103; Clarke, *War Stories*; Gannon, *Won Cause*; Janney, *Remembering the Civil War*.

16. Charles Sumner to Willard P. Phillips, December 21, 1872, in Palmer, *Selected Letters of Charles Sumner*, 2:614; see Papers Concerning the 1872 Resolution of Condemnation against Charles Sumner, Harvard University Houghton Library. On reactions to war memory during the election of 1872, see Blight, *Race and Reunion*, 128; Gallman, "Is the War Ended?," 154–79.

17. *Idaho Statesman*, April 3, 1873. The Baltimore *Sun* noted that Sumner was "very unpopular" in Massachusetts just after the censure; November 17, 1873.

18. Thomas Nast, "Let Us Have Complete Restoration, While You Are About It," *Harper's Weekly*, December 28, 1872, 1021.

19. Wyatt-Brown, "Civil Rights Act of 1875," 769–70.

20. Sinha, "Caning of Charles Sumner," 233–62.

21. Both doctors and newspapers described Sumner as suffering from angina pectoris; C. E. Brown-Séquard to John Collins Warren, March 21, 1874, John Collins Warren Papers, 1738–1926 (Ms. N-1731), Massachusetts Historical Society, Boston (hereafter MHS); see, for example, *Chicago Daily Tribune*, March 12, 1874.

22. "By Telegraph, Charles Sumner," *Sioux City Daily Journal*, March 14, 1874. A large folio scrapbook held by the Newberry Library contains hundreds of newspaper articles about Sumner's illness and death. No record exists of who assembled the book or donated it to the Newberry, but the collector obviously followed news of his death extremely closely; "Sumner. Newspaper Articles," General Collection Newberry Library (hereafter Newberry Scrapbook). The other U.S. senator from Massachusetts, George Frisbie Hoar, also assembled a file of article clippings about Sumner's death and funerals, now in the collection of the American Antiquarian Society (hereafter Hoar File, AAS). A good range of newspaper quotations is reproduced in Lester, *Life and Public Service of Charles Sumner*, 517–59; on Pinchback's defense of Sumner, see Angell, "Black Minister," 44.

23. See "The Dead Statesman," *San Francisco Bulletin*, March 14, 1874; "Our Honored Dead," *Chicago Daily Tribune*, March 13, 1874; "The Memory of Mr. Sumner" and "The Late Senator Sumner," *New York Times*, March 13, 1874; "Obsequies of Mr. Sumner," *New York Times*, March 14, 1874; "Congressional Tributes to the Dead," *(Baltimore) Sun*, March 13, 1874; "The DEATH of SENATOR SUMNER," *Daily Evening Traveller*, March 12, 1874 (Newberry Scrapbook); "The Sumner Obsequies," *Philadelphia Inquirer*, March 14, 1874; *Memorial of Charles Sumner*, 67.

24. "General Grief at Boston," *Springfield Daily Republican*, March 12, 1874; "Boston's Tributes to the Distinguished Dead," *Springfield Daily Republican*, March 13, 1874; "Sorrow for Sumner in Boston," *Macon Weekly Telegraph*, March 17, 1874.

25. Nason, *Life and Times of Charles Sumner*, 339–40.

26. "The Dead Senator," *Springfield Daily Republican*, March 16, 1874.

27. Nason, *Life and Times of Charles Sumner*, 340.

28. "The Dead Statesman," *Springfield Daily Republican*, March 16, 1874.

29. "The Dead Statesman," *Little Rock Daily Republican*, March 17, 1874; *Memorial of Charles Sumner*, 69; "Lying in State," *(Boston) Daily Advertiser*, March 16, 1874, Hoar File, AAS.

30. See the ticket "Funeral Services over the Remains of Charles Sumner," MHS; "Scenes and Incidents" *Springfield Daily Republican*, March 17, 1874," Hoar File, AAS.

31. "The Dead Statesman," *Little Rock Daily Republican*, March 17, 1874; "Funeral of Charles Sumner," *(Baltimore) Sun*, March 17, 1874; Linden, *Silent City on a Hill*, 238–39; Kendrick, *Lively Place*, 123–26.

32. Pierce, *Memoir and Letters of Charles Sumner*, 604–5.

33. *Memorial of Charles Sumner*, 73–79.

34. Schurz, *Eulogy on Charles Sumner*; "Extracts from the Eulogy Pronounced by Carl Schurz on Charles Sumner," *Advocate of Peace* 5 (June 1874): 47–48; *Memorial Addresses on the Life and Character*. Eulogies delivered in New Orleans, Kalamazoo, Savannah, Little Rock, Washington, DC, Chicago, New York, and many other cities were published in pamphlet form and in newspapers for months after Sumner's death.

35. "Death of Charles Sumner," *(New York) World*, March 12, 1874 (Newberry Scrapbook).

36. Heroic obituaries, which especially focus on his caning, include "Charles Sumner," *New York Times*, March 12, 1874.

37. "Death of Charles Sumner," *(New York) World*, March 12, 1874 (Newberry Scrapbook).

38. "Death of Charles Sumner," *(New York) World*, March 12, 1874 (Newberry Scrapbook).

39. On the tradition of political mourning, see Burstein, "Immortalizing the Founding Fathers," 91–107; Purcell, *Sealed with Blood*.

40. Sumner quoted in Blue, *Charles Sumner*, 208.

41. First quotation in John Greenleaf Whittier to Willard Peele Phillips, February 10, 1873, in Pickard, *Letters of John Greenleaf Whittier*, 3:288; second and third quotations in John Greenleaf Whittier to Henry Wilson, March 11, 1874, in Pickard, *Letters of John Greenleaf Whittier*, 3:315.

42. First quotation in John Greenleaf Whittier to Charles Sumner, February 17, 1874, in Pickard, *Letters of John Greenleaf Whittier*, 3:314; second quotation in John Greenleaf Whittier to Henry Wilson, March 11, 1874, in Pickard, *Letters of John Greenleaf Whittier*, 3:315.

43. "Charles Sumner, Sudden Death of the Distinguished Statesman," *Chicago Daily Tribune*, March 12, 1874.

44. "Death of Senator Sumner," *New York Times*, March 12, 1874.

45. "Dead. Hon. Charles Sumner Expired . . . ," *Inter-Ocean*, March 12, 1874.

46. "Death of Charles Sumner," *New Hampshire Sentinel*, March 19, 1874; *(Baltimore) Sun*, March 12, 1874.

47. Kenneth Allen Diary, March 12, 1874, AAS. Allen incorrectly noted that the censure was lifted "a month or two ago."

48. Russell, *Remarks*, 7.

49. Bradlee, *Death and the Resurrection*, 13; see also Johnson, *Memorial of Charles Sumner*, 4.

50. "The Late Senator Sumner," *New York Times*, March 13, 1874.

51. "The Massachusetts Historical Society," *Chicago Daily Tribune*, March 13, 1874; on Winthrop's reconciliation with Sumner, see Donald, *Charles Sumner and the Rights of Man*, 573.

52. "Massachusetts Historical Society," *Boston Evening Journal*, March 12, 1874 (Newberry Scrapbook).

53. "Mr. Sumner's Faneuil Hall Speech, Boston Times," *Richmond Enquirer*, January 17, 1851.

54. "Charles Sumner," *Boston Statesman and Weekly Post*, March 13, 1874 (Newberry Scrapbook).

55. See the Thomas Nast cartoon "Let Us Clasp Hands over the Bloody Chasm," which lampooned Greeley's statement and also became fodder for his critics, in *Harper's Weekly*, September 21, 1872, HarpWeek, accessed February 23, 2013, https://www.harpweek.com /09Cartoon/BrowseByDateCartoon.asp?Month=September&Date=2.

56. Blight, *Race and Reunion*, 122–26; Slap, *Doom of Reconstruction*.

57. "Obituary. Charles Sumner," *Daily Constitution*, March 13, 1874.

58. *(New Orleans) Picayune* quoted in Chaplin and Chaplin, *Life of Charles Sumner*, 445.

59. "Mr. Sumner and the South," *New York Times*, March 13, 1874.

60. Lucius Q. Lamar quoted in Lamar to Clay, September 5, 1874, in Russell, "Why Lamar Eulogized Sumner," 377, 376; on other uses of similar imagery by Lamar, see Brown, "Monumental Legacy of Calhoun," 147. Lamar's eulogy of Sumner was one of the reasons John F. Kennedy Jr. included Lamar in *Profiles in Courage*, 152–77.

61. *Chicago Daily Tribune*, April 28, 1874. Georgian Robert Toombs bitterly criticized Lamar for his eulogy of Sumner and reportedly threatened to fight Lamar; "Personal," *Harper's Weekly*, June 13, 1874, 495.

62. Lucius Q. C. Lamar, "Eulogy on Sumner," in Mayes, *Lucius Q. Lamar*, 186.

63. Charles Sumner to Willard P. Phillips, March 16, 1873, in Palmer, *Selected Letters of Charles Sumner*, 2:618.

64. Bonner, *Colors and Blood*, 76. Bonner was referring to Confederate soldiers' attachment to their regimental flags, but the same can be said of Union veterans; GAR posts revered both regimental flags and the U.S. flag as symbols of their Civil War service; McConnell, *Glorious Contentment*, 224–31; see also Madaus and Zeitlin, *Flags of the Iron Brigade*; Harris, *Across the Bloody Chasm*.

65. George William Curtis, "Charles Sumner: A Eulogy," *Harper's Weekly Supplement*, June 20, 1874, 531.

66. "The Sumner Battle Flag Resolution," *Chicago Daily Tribune*, March 13, 1874.

67. "The Homage Due Sumner," *Chicago Daily Tribune*, March 14, 1874.

68. Carl Schurz, "The Oration," in Cornell, *Charles Sumner*, 105.

69. Schurz, 140–41.

70. Schurz, 149.

71. Schurz, 150. Nina Silber discusses how such language about emancipation was used to establish a "moral framework for U.S. imperialism" by 1890 in "Reunion and Reconciliation," 74.

72. Schurz, "The Oration," 150–51.

73. Schurz, "The Oration," 151.

74. Silber, *Romance of Reunion*, 178–85.

75. Schurz, "The Oration," 152–53.

76. Schurz, 153–55.

77. Schurz, 159.

78. Schurz, 152. On Schurz's opinion about the limits of the fight for Black rights, see Foner, *Reconstruction*, 498.

79. "Colored People's Wishes," *Iowa State Register*, March 12, 1874; "Meeting of Our Colored Citizens," *Little Rock Daily Republican*, March 13, 1874; "Pittsburgh," *Sioux City Journal*, March 14, 1874; "The Colored People at Davenport," *Chicago Daily Tribune*, March 15, 1874; "Memorial Services and Meetings in Other Places," *New York Times*, March 17, 1874; "Eulogy on Sumner," *New York Times*, May 18, 1874.

80. Elliott, *Oration of Hon. Robert B. Elliott*, 18.

81. Turner quoted in Angell, "Black Minister," 49, 51.

82. See "A Colored Man's Veneration for Charles Sumner," *San Francisco Bulletin*, January 22, 1875; "Boston. The Legislature and Senator Sumner," *Hartford Daily Courant*, March 1, 1873.

83. Interestingly, Smith thought the memorial should take the form of a traditional statue of the dead, heroic commander; Savage, *Standing Soldiers*, 196–97.

84. "A Colored Man's Veneration for Charles Sumner," *San Francisco Bulletin*, January 22, 1875.

85. Sumner made the remark to George Washington Warren, who also noted that Smith was consoling Sumner with gifts of fruit during his distress. Warren praised "the bountiful caterer" for "tendering his homage and aid to the one to whom he reverently looked up as the special friend and elevator of his race." See "Sumner, Chase, and Agassiz," *San Francisco Bulletin*, April 15, 1874; the article was a reprint from Warren's reminiscence of Sumner published in the *Bunker Hill Times*.

86. "Boston Correspondence . . . The Sumner Obsequies," *Hartford Daily Courant*, March 21, 1874.

87. Smith's eulogy quoted in Nason, *Life and Times of Charles Sumner*, 341.

88. Smith quoted in Nason, *Life and Times of Charles Sumner,* 341; on Sumner's paternalism, see Angell, "Black Minister," 32.

89. Elliott, *Oration of Hon. Robert B. Elliott*, 3.

90. Henry McNeal Turner, "The Conflict for Civil Rights," quoted in Angell, "Black Minister," 54.

91. Douglass, "Eulogy for Charles Sumner," 4:398.

92. See Blight, "For Something beyond the Battlefield," 93–119.

93. Blight, *Race and Reunion*, 316–19; Blight, *Frederick Douglass: Prophet of Freedom*, 530.

94. "The Supplementary Civil Rights Bill Again . . . Remarks in the Senate," in Sumner, *Works of Charles Sumner*, 15:290.

95. Silber, *Romance of Reunion*, 96–123.

96. Sumner's memory continued to be most potent in Massachusetts. The most significant, lasting public tribute to him was the statue in his honor in Boston sculpted by Thomas Ball; see Thomas Ball Letters, 1869–1882 (Ms. S-275), MHS.

97. Mitchell, *Hollywood Cemetery*; Janney, *Burying the Dead*.

98. On Johnston, see Symonds, *Joseph E. Johnston*; Govan and Livingood, *Different Valor*; Johnson, *Memoirs of the Life*.

99. See Downs, "'The Responsibility Is Great,'" 29–70.

100. Shea and Winschel, *Vicksburg Is the Key*; Jones, "Vicksburg Campaign"; Williams, "Lost Chance to Save Vicksburg"; Bradley, *This Astounding Close*.

101. Symonds, *Joseph E. Johnston*, 359; see also Moore, "Civil War Feud," 72–81.

102. On Johnston's reputation, see Frank E. Vandiver's introduction to the reprint of Johnston's *Narrative of Military Operations*, vii–xxxi; Symonds, *Joseph E. Johnston*, 383–86. Gary Gallagher contrasts Lee's reputation as an "audacious commander" to Johnston's status as an "arch-retreater," as one diarist called him, in *Lee and His Generals in War and Memory*, 16–17; Jeffrey Lash excoriates Johnston in *Destroyer of the Iron Horse*; Stephen H. Newton makes a positive assessment of Johnston's command in Virginia early in the war in *Joseph E. Johnston and the Defense of Richmond*; on the battle between Davis and Johnston see Downs, "'The Responsibility Is Great,'" 53–56, 62–63; Govan and Livingood, *Different Valor*, 377–93. Confederates were not alone, in these years, in battling over military reputation in the pages of memoirs and magazines. Sherman, Chamberlain, and Grant also published memoirs and articles that offered their versions of events; see Cushman, *Belligerent Muse*, 69–114, 147–64; Samet, "Adding to My Book."

103. Johnston, *Narrative*, 70, 421–70.

104. Symonds, *Joseph E. Johnston*, 364–65; Account Book, 1873–1875, Letter Book, 1874–1875, Joseph E. Johnston Papers, Mss. 39.1 J63, item 7, item 8, William and Mary Earl Gregg Swem Library; *Little Rock Republican*, April 8, 1874; "What Might Have Been," *Galveston Daily News*, May 4, 1874. Excerpts of Johnston's chapter "Why the South Failed" were republished widely; *North American and United States Gazette*, April 7, 1874; *Georgia Weekly Telegraph and Georgia Journal and Messenger*, April 7, 1874; *Daily Evening Bulletin*, April 9, 1874.

105. "General J. B. Hood . . . ," *Galveston Daily News*, May 12, 1874; "The Johnston-Hood Controversy," *Galveston Daily News*, May 24, 1874; "Gen. Joseph E. Johnston's Letter," *Georgia Weekly Telegraph and Georgia Journal and Messenger*, August 14, 1874; *Galveston Daily News*, August 20, 1874; "In General," *Boston Daily Advertiser*, August 24, 1874; *Inter Ocean*, August 25, 1874; *Hinds County Gazette*, September 2, 1874; Hood, *Advance and Retreat*; Samuel G. French to Joseph E. Johnston, July 7, 1874, and Daniel C. Govan to Joseph E. Johnston, July 16, 1874, Joseph E. Johnston Papers, Mss. 39.1 J63, Box 2, Folder 1, item 11, item 13, William and Mary Earl Gregg Swem Library; J. William Jones to Joseph E. Johnston, June 24, 1885, Robert Morton Hughes Papers, General Joseph E. Johnston, Collection No. MG 7, Series X, Subseries K, Box 27, Folder 2, Old Dominion University Libraries, Special Collections and University Archives, Patricia W. and J. Douglas Perry Library; Miller, *John Bell Hood*, 200–214.

106. Davis, *Rise and Fall*.

107. *Daily Inter Ocean*, February 16, 1881; *Daily Evening Bulletin*, March 22, 1881; "Gen. Joe Johnston Scores Jeff. Davis," *St. Louis Globe-Democrat*, June 12, 1881; "Joe Johnston's Vindication," *Washington Post*, June 13, 1881; "J. Davis: His Book," *North American*, June 16, 1881; "The Volume Which Jeff Davis Is Now Writing," *Inter Ocean*, February 16, 1881; "Joe Johnston's Reply to Jeff. Davis," *Galveston Daily News*, June 16, 1881; "Johnston and Davis," *St. Louis Globe-Democrat*, June 21, 1881; "Gen. Joe Johnston," *Daily Arkansas Gazette*, June 23, 1881; "A Georgia Contemporary Says," *Lynchburg Virginian*, June 25, 1881; "Jefferson Davis," *Frank Leslie's Illustrated Newspaper*, July 9, 1881; "A Startling Story," *St. Louis Globe-Democrat*, December 18, 1881; the story about the gold was republished in the *Milwaukee Sentinel*, December 22, 1881; *Daily Inter Ocean*, December 22, 1881; *Daily Evening Bulletin*, December 22, 1881; see also "Denying That Jeff Davis Stole the Silver," *Georgia Weekly Telegraph and Journal and Messenger*, December 30, 1881.

108. Fahs, "Market Value of Memory," 133; Fahs, "Feminized Civil War," 1485; Fahs, *Imagined Civil War*, 314; Blight, *Race and Reunion*, 160–64.

109. Robert Morton Hughes Papers, Joseph Johnston Collection, Old Dominion University Libraries, Special Collections and University Archives, Patricia W. and J. Douglas Perry Library. Craig Symonds judges Johnston harshly for continuing the battle over his reputation in the *Century* magazine, *Joseph E. Johnston*, 367–71.

110. W. A. Croffut, "Two Brave Men," *Milwaukee Sentinel*, December 11, 1887.

111. Blight, *Race and Reunion*, 173–84; see also Caron, "'How Changeable Are the Events of the War,'" 151–71.

112. Joseph E. Johnston, "From Manassas to Seven Pines," *Century* 30 (May 1885): 99.

113. Joseph E. Johnston, "From Manassas to Seven Pines," *Century* 30 (May 1885): 121.

114. "What the Literary Generals Get," *Daily Evening Bulletin*, March 10, 1885. Letters between Johnston and the *Century* editors can be found in two collections: New York Public Library, Archives and Manuscripts Division, Century Company Papers, Series II,

MssColl 504; Robert Morton Hughes Papers, General Joseph E. Johnston, Collection No. MG 7, Series X, Subseries K, Box 27, Folder 6-7; see also John, *Best Years of the Century*, 128.

115. Joseph E. Johnston, "Opposing Sherman's Advance to Atlanta," *Century* 34 (August 1887): 585–96.

116. Blight discusses Johnston's *McClure's* article in *Race and Reunion*, 165; Joseph E. Johnston, "Opposing Sherman's Advance to Atlanta," *Century* 34 (August 1887): 596; William T. Sherman, "General Sherman's March to the Sea," *Century* 34 (July 1887): 464–65.

117. Janney, *Remembering the Civil War*, 191.

118. Baker, "American Hero, Confederate Idol," 44, 56–63.

119. Silber, "Reunion and Reconciliation," 74–79, 82–83.

120. Rudolph Siegling to Joseph E. Johnston, February 7, 1878, in Robert Morton Hughes Papers, General Joseph E. Johnston, Collection No. MG 7, Series X, Subseries K, Box 27, Folder 1.

121. "A Tribute to General Joseph E. Johnston," *Georgia Weekly Telegraph and Georgia Journal and Messenger*, July 3, 1877.

122. "The Graves of the Gray," *St. Louis Globe-Democrat*, June 7, 1879.

123. "The Atlanta Reunion," *Daily Inter Ocean*, October 21, 1880; "The Richmond (Va.) Celebration," *St. Louis Globe-Democrat*, October 27, 1887.

124. "Joseph E. Johnston," *News and Observer*, April 27, 1890. April 26, the date of Johnston's surrender, was a popular day for decorating Confederate graves in some Deep South communities in the late 1860s; Foster, *Ghosts of the Confederacy*, 42.

125. *Atlanta Constitution*, April 25–27, 1890; Symonds, *Joseph E. Johnston*, 380.

126. On the mix of popular and elite sentiment in monuments, see Savage, *Standing Soldiers*, 7.

127. Foster, *Ghosts of the Confederacy*, 88.

128. "Confederate Monument Unvailed [*sic*] at Savannah, Ga," *Frank Leslie's Illustrated Newspaper*, June 19, 1875, 233; "Statue to Stonewall Jackson, " *Inter Ocean*, October 27, 1875; "Stonewall Jackson," *Boston Daily Advertiser*, October 27, 1875, and *Milwaukee Daily Sentinel*, October 28, 1875; "By Telegraph," *Georgia Weekly Telegraph and Georgia Journal and Messenger*, November 2, 1875.

129. "Unveiled," *St. Louis Globe-Democrat*, May 21, 1880.

130. "Honor for Brave Men," *Washington Post*, May 23, 1889.

131. Foster, *Ghosts of the Confederacy*, 88–89; "The Statue of Gen. Robert E. Lee," *Frank Leslie's Illustrated Newspaper*, June 23, 1883, 282; Wilson, *Baptized in Blood*, 158–59; "A Confederate Soldier," in *A Father's Talks with His Children*; Lawton, "Constructing the Cause."

132. The amputees are noted in "R. E. Lee's Statue," *St. Paul Daily News*, May 29, 1890; "Gray and Blue," *Wisconsin State Register*, May 31, 1890; cannon quotations from "Unveiling the Monument," *Milwaukee Daily Journal*, May 29, 1890, and "In Lee's Memory," *Milwaukee Sentinel*, May 30, 1890; see also "The Lee Statue Dedication," *Frank Leslie's Illustrated Newspaper*, June 14, 1890, 400; "Loyalty to the Union," June 2, 1890; "The Lee Monument," *News and Observer*, May 30, 1890. On the Lee monument unveiling, see Foster, *Ghosts of the Confederacy*, 101–3; Blight, *Race and Reunion*, 267–70; Janney, *Burying the Dead*, 141; Janney, *Remembering the Civil War*, 181–82; Savage, *Standing Soldiers*, 150–51; Symonds, *Joseph E. Johnston*, 380.

133. "Remarkable Instances," *Galveston Daily News*, November 30, 1875.

134. "Political and Personal," *Bangor Daily Whig and Courier*, December 1, 1875. Among the many articles on the meeting, see "Telegraphic Summary," *Sun*, November 24, 1875; "The National Railroad Convention at St. Louis," *Leavenworth Daily Times*, November 24, 1875; "St. Louis, November 23rd," *Salt Lake Weekly Tribune*, October 27, 1875.

135. See "The Coming Celebration," *Daily Arkansas Gazette*, May 23, 1875; "Notes on the Way," *Georgia Weekly Telegraph and Georgia Journal and Messenger*, June 8, 1875; "Centennial Programme," *Detroit Tribune*, May 27, 1875; "Fitting Round-Up of the Nation's Centennial Celebration," *Washington Post*, May 2, 1889.

136. "Soldiers' National Reunion," *Inter Ocean*, July 6, 1877.

137. "A Reconstructed Rebel," *Daily Inter Ocean*, April 29, 1888; "Gen. Johnston a Member," *Milwaukee Sentinel*, April 29, 1888; "Joined the G.A.R." *Atchison Daily Champion*, April 29, 1888; "A Noble Compliment" and "Blue and Gray," *Daily Picayune*, April 29, 1888; "General J. E. Johnston," *Atchison Daily Globe*, April 30, 1888.

138. "Latest Telegraph," *Daily Evening Bulletin*, May 4, 1888; see opposing opinions in "Many Contemporaries," *Daily Inter Ocean*, May 2, 1888; "Why 'Joe' Johnston Is Liked, from the Cincinnati Enquirer," *Washington Post*, May 9, 1888.

139. "Not for Joe," *Los Angeles Times*, May 5, 1888.

140. "Personal and General Notes," *Daily Picayune*, May 7, 1888; "Gen. Joseph E. Johnston," *Atchison Daily Globe*, May 10, 1888.

141. "Taken to Task," *Atchison Daily Champion*, May 19, 1888; "Grand Army Men Censured" and "Domestic," *(Chicago) Daily Inter Ocean*, May 19, 1888.

142. See Gannon, *Won Cause*; Harris, *Across the Bloody Chasm*.

143. Connelly and Bellows, *God and General Longstreet*, 34–37; Wert, "James Longstreet and the Lost Cause," 127–46; Piston, *Lee's Tarnished Lieutenant*. Piston incorrectly identifies Longstreet as the only former Confederate general willing to recognize Grant's military genius.

144. "Men of the Day," *Atchison Daily Globe*, April 3, 1891.

145. "In Memory of Gen. Lee," *(Baltimore) Sun*, October 14, 1870.

146. In *Death and Resurrection*, Donald E. Collins never mentions Johnston in any of the funeral celebrations for Davis.

147. Waugh, *U.S. Grant*, 218; for a good overview of primary sources on Grant's funeral, see Kelsey, *Ulysses S. Grant*.

148. "Selection of Pall-Bearers," *Milwaukee Daily Journal*, July 31, 1885; Waugh, *U.S. Grant*, 236; "Hero's Pall Bearers," *New York Times*, July 31, 1885.

149. See "Voice of the South," *Daily Evening Bulletin*; "Southern Sympathy," *St. Louis Globe-Democrat*, July 24, 1885; "Gen. Joseph E. Johnston," *Milwaukee Sentinel*, July 25, 1885; "The Burial at Riverside," *North American*, August 1, 1885; "Grant's Love for the South," *Milwaukee Sentinel*, August 8, 1885; "More Southern Tributes," *Boston Daily Advertiser*, August 8, 1885.

150. On Southern presence at the funeral and expressions of grief for Grant, see Waugh, *U.S. Grant*, 237–41; "The People Pay Homage," *New York Times*, August 7, 1885; "A Nation at the Tomb," *New York Times*, August 8, 1885; "The Last Days of General Grant," *Harper's Weekly* 29 (August 15, 1885): 538; Cyrus Bussey to William S. Hancock, July 26, 1885, "Copies of Communications Relating to the Funeral of General Grant," National Archives, RG 393, Pt. 1, Entry 1471, Vol. 1.

151. "The Pall Bearers," *Atchison Daily Globe*, August 14, 1885; "Old Men of the War," *St. Louis Globe-Democrat*.

152. "Patriotic Utterances of Ex-Confederate Generals," *Boston Daily Advertiser*, August 11, 1885.

153. "The Dead General," *Galveston Daily News*, October 31, 1885; "Gen. M'Clellan," *Daily Evening Bulletin*, October 30, 1885; "The Dead General," *Boston Daily Advertiser*, October 31, 1885; "Gen. McClellan's Funeral," *Washington Post*, October 31, 1885; "M'Clellan's Funeral," *Atchison Daily Globe*, November 3, 1885.

154. "Many Noted Men," *Milwaukee Sentinel*, November 22, 1886.

155. "Near Gen. Logan's Tomb, The Remains of Gen. Hunt Interred," *Washington Post*, February 15, 1889; "A Soldier Laid to Rest," *Macon Telegraph*, February 15, 1889; "In Honor of a Dead Hero," *Washington Post*, March 5, 1889.

156. "Messages of Sympathy," *(Baltimore) Sun*, February 16, 1891; "Words of Tender Sympathy," *New York Times*, February 16, 1891; "Mourning for Sherman," *Chicago Daily Tribune*, February 16, 1891; "Honors to Sherman," *Philadelphia Inquirer*, February 16, 1891.

157. "Honors Paid to a Dead Hero," *Milwaukee Journal*, February 17, 1891; "The Dead Admiral," *New York Times*, February 16, 1891; "Naval Hero Buried," *Philadelphia Inquirer*, February 18, 1891; "State Funerals," *Huntsville Gazette*, February 21, 1891.

158. On Sherman's funerals, see Marszalek, *Sherman*, 492–99; Lewis, *Sherman*, 650–53; "A Grand Funeral Pageant," *New York Times*, February 18, 1891; "Along the Line of March," *New York Times*, February 20, 1891; "Sherman's Funeral," *Harper's Weekly* 35 (February 28, 1891): 154; "The Funeral Train to St. Louis," *Harper's Weekly* 35 (March 7, 1891): 171; "Borne to the Tomb," *Weekly Inter Ocean*, February 24, 1891.

159. "Sherman and Johnston," *Topeka Weekly Capital*, February 26, 1891; see also "The Late General Johnston," *Washington Post*, March 22, 1891.

160. William T. Sherman to Joseph E. Johnston, January 5, 1891, quoted in Fellman, *Citizen Sherman*, 402; see "Personal," *Harper's Weekly* 35 (March 7, 1891): 167; "Men and Women," *San Francisco Evening Bulletin*, March 14, 1891.

161. "A Nation Is in Mourning," *New York Times*, February 16, 1891. New York City's Confederate veterans did also march in Sherman's funeral parade; "New York's Tribute," *Times Picayune*, February 20, 1891.

162. *New York Age*, February 21, 1891.

163. "Honors for a Dead Hero," *Chicago Daily Tribune*, February 20, 1891; see also "Sherman's Funeral," *(Baltimore) Sun*, February 20, 1891; *Wisconsin State Register*, March 28, 1891.

164. "General Johnston," *Nation* 52 (March 26, 1891): 257.

165. Howard, *Autobiography of Oliver Otis Howard*, 2:554.

166. Cold weather can make the cold virus easier to contract, but it does not cause colds, a fact that was not known in 1891 but has been known at least since the 1940s; Foxman et al., "Temperature-Dependent Innate Defense," 827–32. On Ken Burns's use of the anecdote, see Blight, "'What Will Peace among the Whites Bring?,'" 393. For reports that Johnston caught cold "soon after the Sherman funeral," see "Johnston Improving," *Macon Telegraph*, March 19, 1891; "Illness of Joseph E. Johnston," *Columbus Daily Enquirer*, March 19, 1891; *Omaha World Herald*, March 19, 1891; "Gen. Johnston," *Atchison Champion*, March 22, 1891; "Curtain Rung Down," *Dallas Morning News*, March 22, 1891; "Gen. Joe Johnston Dead," *New York Times*, March 22, 1891; "Gen. Jos. E. Johnston," *Washington*

Post, March 22, 1891; "Gen. Joe Johnston Dead," *Knoxville Journal*, March 22, 1891; "The Death of Johnston," *Daily Enquirer*, March 22, 1891; "Last of All, Save One," *Macon Telegraph*, March 22, 1891; "Death of General Johnston" and "Washington Gossip," *Philadelphia Inquirer*, March 22, 1891; Dead," *Chicago Daily Tribune*, March 22, 1891; "Following Close on the Death of General Sherman," *Vermont Watchman*, March 25, 1891; "General Joseph E. Johnston Dead," *Topeka Weekly Capital*, March 26, 1891; "Gen. Joe Johnston Dead," *Weekly Sentinel and Wisconsin Farm Journal*, March 26, 1891; "Another Hero Dead," *Huntsville Gazette*, March 28, 1891; "The Confederate Fabius," *Atchison Daily Globe*, April 2, 1891; Howard, *Autobiography of Oliver Otis Howard*, 2:554. Howard's story is routinely repeated without reference to the fact that he is the only one who phrased it as such in Symonds, *Joseph E. Johnston*, 380; Govan and Livingood, *Different Valor*, 389; Lewis, *Sherman*, 652. John Marszalek identifies Howard as the source of the quotation; Marszalek, *Sherman*, 496.

167. "The Dead Confederate General," *Columbus Daily Enquirer*, March 24, 1891; "No Military Display," *Rocky Mountain News*, March 24, 1891; "Simple Funeral Rites," *Washington Post*, March 23, 1891; "Gen. Johnston's Funeral," *Dallas Morning News*, March 23, 1891; "Will Be Buried Tuesday," *Knoxville Journal*, March 23, 1891; "The Soldier's Funeral," *Macon Telegraph*, March 23, 1891; "Gen. Johnston's Funeral," *Times Picayune*, March 23, 1891; "General Johnston," *Wheeling Register*, March 23, 1891; "Gen. Johnston's Funeral," *Atchison Daily Globe*, March 23, 1891; "General Johnston's Funeral," *Daily Inter Ocean*, March 23, 1891; "Gen. Johnston's Funeral," *Milwaukee Sentinel*, March 23, 1891; "The Dead Soldier," *San Francisco Evening Bulletin*, March 23, 1891; "Johnston Surrenders," *Aberdeen Daily News*, March 24, 1891.

168. "A Brave Soldier Gone," *(Baltimore) Sun*, March 23, 1891; "Simple Funeral Rites," *Washington Post*, March 23, 1891; "The Dead Chieftain," *State*, March 24, 1891; "The Dead Confederate General," *Columbus Daily Enquirer*, March 24, 1891; "Burial in Baltimore," *(Baltimore) Sun*, March 24, 1891; "Gen. Jos. E. Johnston," *(Baltimore) Sun*, March 24, 1891; "Desire No Show," *Knoxville Journal*, March 24, 1891; "General Johnston's Funeral," *Philadelphia Inquirer*, March 25, 1891; "General Joseph E. Johnston's Funeral," *Albuquerque Morning Democrat*, March 25, 1891.

169. "Gen. Johnston's Funeral," *New York Times*, March 23, 1891; for comparison to another "simple" officer's funeral that nonetheless had troops attending the body of Gen. Hancock, see "The Dead Soldier," *Kansas City Star*, February 10, 1886; "Gen. Johnston's Funeral," *Dallas Morning News*, March 25, 1891; "Gen. Johnston's Funeral," *Wheeling Register*, March 25, 1891; "Gen. Johnston's Funeral," *Times Picayune*, March 25, 1891; "General Johnston's Funeral," *Salt Lake Weekly Tribune*, March 26, 1891; "Gen. Johnston's Funeral," *Leavenworth Advocate*, March 28, 1891.

170. "Borne to the Tomb," *Emporia Daily Gazette*, March 25, 1891; "Honors to Johnston," *Rocky Mountain News*, March 25, 1891; "Gen. Johnston's Funeral," *New York Times*, March 25, 1891; "Funeral of Gen. Joseph E. Johnston," *Chicago Daily Tribune*, March 25, 1891; "Vale Johnston," *Omaha World Herald*, March 25, 1891; Johnson, *Memoirs of the Life*, 280–83.

171. "Joseph E. Johnston," *Galveston Daily News*, March 25, 1891; see also "Simple Funeral Rites," *Morning Oregonian*, March 25, 1891; "Gen. Johnston's Funeral," *Milwaukee Sentinel*, March 25, 1891.

172. Howard, *Autobiography of Oliver Otis Howard*, 2:554.

173. "The War Is Ended," *Duluth Tribune*, May 2, 1891.

174. "A Quiet Funeral," *News and Observer*, March 25, 1891; "Buried as a Civilian," *Washington Post*, March 25, 1891.

175. "Buried as a Civilian," *Washington Post*, March 25, 1891; "A Hero Laid to Rest," *(Baltimore) Sun*, March 25, 1891; for a more charitable version of what transpired in the Baltimore rail station see Johnson, *Memoirs of the Life*, 285.

176. "Gen. Johnston's Funeral," *Daily Picayune*, March 25, 1891.

177. "Funeral Services," *Boston Daily Advertiser*, March 25, 1891.

178. Joseph Wheeler to Joseph E. Johnston, March 18, 1891, Joseph E. Johnston Papers, William and Mary Swem Library, Box II, Folder 6. The day after Johnston died, a ceremony in his honor was held in Washington, DC, by the Southeastern Tariff Association, Livingston Mills, *Tribute to Jos. E. Johnston* (n.p.: n.p., [1891]), Graff 2182, Newberry Library Special Collections.

179. "In Honor of Johnston," *News and Observer*, March 26, 1891; "Ex-Confederates Indignant," *(Baltimore) Sun*, March 25, 1891; "Chattanooga, Tenn.," *New York Times*, March 25, 1891; "A Meeting in Savannah," *Macon Telegraph*, March 24, 1891; "Army of Northern Virginia, Resolutions Adopted," *Daily Picayune*, April 12, 1891; "Actions of the Southern Society, New York," *(Baltimore) Sun*, March 24, 1891.

180. "At Montgomery," *(Baltimore) Sun*, March 25, 1891; "Honored in Montgomery," *Washington Post*, March 25, 1891; "The Arkansas Legislature," *Galveston Daily News*, March 25, 1891.

181. "Ex-Confederates Indignant," *Washington Post*, March 25, 1891; Johnson, *Memoirs of the Life*, 272–73.

182. "Lee Camp at Richmond," *Knoxville Journal*, March 24, 1891; "The Richmond Resolutions," *Macon Telegraph*, March 24, 1891.

183. "Proposed Memorial Day" and "Proposed Memorial Day for General Johnston," *Daily Picayune*, April 9, 1891; "Since Our Last Issue," *Fayetteville Observer*, April 16, 1891; "Some Reminiscences," *News and Observer*, April 25, 1891; Johnson, *Memoirs of the Life*, 318–25; "In Memoriam," *Southern Historical Papers* 18 (1891): 158–71; on the Lee Camp's role in creating the SCV, see Foster, *Ghosts of the Confederacy*, 107–9; Records, United Confederate Veterans, Lee Camp No. 1, Mss3 G7628 a FA 1, Virginia Historical Society.

184. "Eulogizing Her Son," *Washington Post*, April 2, 1891.

185. "Gen. Johnston's Body," *Washington Post*, April 12, 1891; "Latest News Items," *Daily Evening Bulletin*, May 12, 1891.

186. "Gen Joseph E. Johnston's Saddle," *Washington Post*, May 15, 1891; "A Confederate Relic," *New York Times*, May 15, 1891; "People in General," *Washington Post*, May 16, 1891; Janney, *Burying the Dead*, 162.

187. "This Afternoon," *News and Observer*, April 26, 1891; "Memorial Services," *News and Observer*, April 26, 1891.

188. "Lee Camp and Pickett Corps," *Washington Post*, April 27, 1891.

189. "Army of Tennessee," *Daily Picayune*, April 15, 1891; "Personal and General Notes," *Daily Picayune*, April 25, 1891; "Confederate Veterans," *Galveston Daily News*, April 15, 1891; "West Point," *Daily Picayune*, April 25, 1891; "Memorial Services for General Johnston," *Daily Picayune*, April 26, 1891; "Memorial Services," *Daily Picayune*, April 27, 1891.

190. "In Memory of Gen. Joseph E. Johnston," *Washington Post*, May 10, 1891; "The Johnston Memorial," *Washington Post*, May 12, 1891; "In Johnston's Memory," *Washington*

Post, May 13, 1891. For a copy of the oration at the Washington service, see "General Joseph E. Johnston," *Southern Historical Papers* 19 (1891): 337–70.

191. "On Confederate Graves," *Washington Post*, June 7, 1891.

192. "In Memoriam," *Southern Historical Papers* 18 (1891): 158–217; "General Joseph E. Johnston," *Southern Historical Papers* 19 (1891): 337–70.

193. Porter, *In Memoriam*, 3, 11.

194. Porter, *In Memoriam*, 11.

195. Porter, *In Memoriam*, 26; on Porter, see Quintard, "I Was Elected Chaplain," 27.

Chapter Five

1. "Death of Frederick Douglass," *American Missionary* 49, no. 4 (April 1895): 121.

2. "Death of Fred Douglass," *New York Times*, February 21, 1895; "Fred Douglass Dead," *Washington Post*, February 21, 1895; "Fred Douglass Dead," *Boston Daily Globe*, February 21, 1895; "Frederick Douglass Dead," *Pennsylvania Grit*, [February 21, 1895], Frederick Douglass Obituaries, Accounts of His Funeral and Other Material, Scrapbook (hereafter FDSB I), Monroe County (NY) Public Library Special Collections, S. B. Division, Row 11, also digitized at http://www.libraryweb.org/~digitized/scrapbooks/rsc00001colorcover.pdf, accessed December 1, 2017.

3. "The Douglass Funeral," *Washington Post*, February 22, 1895.

4. On Douglass, see, among others, Blight, *Frederick Douglass: Prophet of Freedom*; Blight, *Frederick Douglass's Civil War*; Foner, *Life and Writings of Frederick Douglass*; Fought, *Women in the World of Frederick Douglass*; McFeeley, *Frederick Douglass*; Sundquist, *Frederick Douglass*; Sweeney, *Frederick Douglass and the Atlantic World*.

5. "Miss Davis's Funeral," *Richmond Dispatch*, September 24, 1898; on Davis as the feminized embodiment of the Lost Cause, see Cook, "Lost Cause Legend," 4; Drake, "Funerals of Winnie Davis and Varina Davis."

6. "Winnie Davis' Funeral," *Evening Star*, September 21, 1898. The Stanford, Kentucky, newspaper noted something similar about Richmond, "where so many illustrious dead have been laid to rest; "The Funeral of Miss Winnie Davis," *Semi-Weekly Interior Journal*, September 27, 1898.

7. "Body Rests in Hollywood," *Camden Chronicle*, September 30, 1898.

8. John B. Gordon quoted in "United Confederate Veterans," *Confederate Veteran* 6 (September 1898): 401; see also "To Confederate Veterans," *Semi-Weekly Messenger*, September 23, 1898, and *Alexandria Gazette*, September 20, 1898; "He Announces the Death of the Idolized Daughter," *(Savannah) Morning News*, September 20, 1898.

9. Gordon notably showed a mixture of the themes a few months before Davis's funeral in his address to the national encampment of the UCV in Atlanta; Venet, *Gone but Not Forgotten*, 52.

10. "The Funeral of Miss Winnie Davis," *Alexandria Gazette and Virginia Advertiser*, September 24, 1898.

11. Elvira Sydnor Miller quoted in "United Daughters of the Confederacy," *Confederate Veteran* 6 (September 1898): 402.

12. "Miss Davis' Funeral," *(Maysville, KY) Evening Bulletin*, September 20, 1898.

13. "United Daughters of the Confederacy," *Confederate Veteran* 6 (September 1898): 402.

14. Blight, *Frederick Douglass: Prophet of Freedom*, 531.

15. On Douglass and emancipationist memory, see Blight, *Race and Reunion*; Blight, *Frederick Douglass's Civil War*, 219–39.

16. Upchurch, *Legislating Racism*, 218; on Douglass's own understanding of mourning, see Stow, "Agonistic Homegoing," 681–89.

17. Moses, "Where Honor Is Due," 177–89; O'Neill, "Frederick Douglass," 118–53; Sweeney, *Frederick Douglass and the Atlantic World*, 188–91; Zafar, "Franklinian Douglass," 112–13.

18. "Fred Douglass Dead," *Idaho Daily Statesman*, February 21, 1895. W. E. B. DuBois defined Douglass as a "statesman" in his eulogy at a memorial service at Wilberforce University; Aptheker, "Dubois on Douglass," 265.

19. J. W. Ray quoted in "Frederick Douglass . . . The Colored Citizens," *Dallas Morning News*, February 28, 1895.

20. "Fred'k Douglass," *Richmond Planet*, February 23, 1895.

21. John Muller, "The Life and Times of Frederick Douglass," *Readex Report*, accessed May 24, 2018, https://www.readex.com/readex-report/issues/volume-9-issue-1/life-and-times-frederick-douglass-anacostia-washington-dc; Muller, *Frederick Douglass*; Brantley, "Black Diplomacy," 197–209; Paddon and Turner, "African Americans and the World's Columbian Exposition," 20–22; on the relationship between Douglass and Wells, see Schechter, *Ida B. Wells-Barnett*, 21–23; Love, *Race over Empire*, 16; Fought, *Women in the World of Frederick Douglass*, 277–90.

22. Blight, *Frederick Douglass: Prophet of Freedom*, 650–55, 753; Fought, *Women in the World of Frederick Douglass*, 229–31, 240–42.

23. "Sadness at the Capital," *(Chicago) News*, February 21, 1895.

24. "The Douglass Funeral," *(Rochester) Post*, February 25, 1895.

25. "His Body to Lie in State," *Washington Post*, n.d., FDP, vol. 15, reel 10; "All Speak Well of Him," *American*, February 22, 1895; "Senatorial Scraps," *Grand Forks Daily Herald*, February 24, 1895; "The Session of the Senate," *Idaho Daily Statesman*, February 24, 1895; "Honors Denied at the Capitol," *(Washington, DC) Evening Star*, February 26, 1895, FDP, vol. 16, reel 11; "Honors Denied at the Capitol," *Evening Star*, February 25, 1895.

26. Architect of the Capitol, "Lying in State or in Honor," accessed January 15, 2020, https://www.aoc.gov/what-we-do/programs-ceremonies/lying-in-state-honor; United States House of Representatives History, Art and Archives, "Individuals Who Have Lain in State or in Honor," accessed January 20, 2021, https://history.house.gov/Institution/Lie-In-State/Lie-In-State-Honor/; Clare Foran, "John Lewis Is First Black Lawmaker to Lie in State in US Capitol Rotunda," *CNN Politics*, July 27, 2020, https://www.cnn.com/2020/07/27/politics/john-lewis-lies-in-state-capitol/index.html.

27. Haines, Table Aa2868-2964, "District of Columbia Population," accessed March 19, 2019, https://hsus-cambridge-org.grinnell.idm.oclc.org/HSUSWeb/search/searchTable.do?id=Aa2868-2964.

28. See "Our National Capital" (1877), FDP, Digital Edition, Speech File, reel 15; Blight, *Frederick Douglass: Prophet of Freedom*, 588–91.

29. "Frederick Douglass," *Observer*, March 8, 1895.

30. "Fred Douglass," *New York Times*, February 23, 1895.

31. Frederick Douglass, "Lynch Law in the South," *North American Review* 155 (July 1892): 18.

32. On lynching and spectacle, see Holloway, *Passed On*, 57–79; Wood, *Lynching and Spectacle*; Mixon, "Shadow of Slavery," 247.

33. Masur, *Example for All the Land*, 261; *Post Express*, n.d., FDP, vol. 16, reel 11.

34. "Ready for the Tomb," *Washington Post*, February 25, 1895.

35. "Metropolitan African Methodist Episcopal Church," *Washington*, accessed April 6, 2018, https://www.metropolitaname.org/.

36. "The Grandest Effort of His Life," *Cleveland Gazette*, January 27, 1894.

37. "His Body to Lie in State," *Washington Post*, February 24, 1895; "The Body of Douglass," *Post Express*, February 25, 1895, FDP, vol. 15, reel 10.

38. "Great Gathering of Colored People at the Funeral in Washington," FDP, vol. 15, reel 10; "Last Tribute to Douglass," *Torchlight*, March [3], 1895, FDP, vol. 15, reel 10; "Said in His Honor," *Democrat and Chronicle*, February 26, 1895, FDSB I; Thompson, *Authentic History*, 17.

39. "Honor to Douglass," *Herald*, February 26, 1895; "Said in His Honor," *Democrat and Chronicle*, February 26, 1895, FDSB I.

40. "Said in His Honor," *Democrat and Chronicle*, February 26, 1895, FDSB I.

41. See Blight, *Frederick Douglass: Prophet of Freedom*, 753.

42. "Said in His Honor," *Democrat and Chronicle*, February 26, 1895, FDSB I; "Tributes of Two Races," *New York Times*, February 26, 1895; "Fred Douglass's Funeral," *Baltimore Sun* [n.d.], FDP, vol. 16, reel 11; on Douglass and Haitian memory, see Clavin, *Toussaint Louverture*, 181–82; on symbolic and real links between Douglass and Haiti, see Jackson and Bacon, *African Americans and the Haitian Revolution*, and Clavin, *Toussaint Louverture*; on Douglass's relationship to the Auld family, see Levine, "Frederick Douglass and Thomas Auld," 34–45.

43. "Rites over Douglass," *Washington Post*, February 26, 1895; "Said in His Honor," *Democrat and Chronicle*, February 26, 1895, FDSB I; "Tributes of Two Races," *New York Times*, February 26, 1895; "The Funeral Arrangements," *New York Times*, February 25, 1895; "All Paid Tribute," *Greencastle Democrat*, March 2, 1895; "The Burial of Douglass," *Los Angeles Herald*, February 26, 1895.

44. J. E. Rankin, quoted in Douglass, *In Memoriam*, 35.

45. R. B. Peters, "The Douglass Pall-Bearers," *Washington Post*, February 27, 1895.

46. "Taken to the Station," *Evening Star*, February 26, 1895, FDP, vol. 16, reel 11; "Said in His Honor," *Democrat and Chronicle*, February 26, 1895, FDSB I.

47. "Frederick Douglass," *Post Express*, February 25, 1895, FDP, vol. 15, reel 10.

48. J. E. Rankin quoted in Douglass, *In Memoriam*, 207; Rankin, *Frederick Douglass*, 12.

49. "To Lie in State in New York," *Washington Post*, February 24, 1895; "In State at Gotham," *(Pittsburgh) Dispatch*, February 24, 1895. David Blight claims that Douglass did lie in state inside the vestibule of New York's City Hall, but there is no evidence that the event took place, and the timing does not line up with the heavily documented ceremonies in Rochester; Blight says that the event took place "from 8:00 a.m. to 10:00 a.m." on February 26, but the train bearing Douglass's body actually arrived at the Rochester station at 9:40 A.M., and he lay in state in Rochester beginning at 1:30 P.M.—there was simply no way he could have also been in New York City that morning; Blight, *Frederick Douglass, Prophet of Freedom*, 754. Additionally, Helen Pitts Douglass makes no mention at all of any New York City Hall ceremony in her 1897 memorial volume that describes all the public mourning; Douglass, *In Memoriam*. The *New York Times* also makes no mention of

any City Hall ceremony for Douglass, although the paper did cover his full funeral in DC and Rochester. Newspaper searches confirm that although the Black delegation in New York received permission to hold a viewing of Frederick Douglass's remains in New York City, they were ultimately disappointed that it did not take place. On the train arrival times in Rochester, see *Rochester Democrat and Chronicle*, February 26, 1895; *Union and Advertiser*, [February 27, 1895], FDSB I.

50. The disappointment of the New York City delegation is directly addressed in "Taken to Rochester," *Evening Star*, February 27, 1895; on the quiet train transfers, see "En Route to Rochester," *Baltimore Sun*, February 26, 1895, FDP, vol. 16, reel 11.

51. "Eulogy on Frederick Douglass," *Post Intelligencer*, February 25, 1895, FDP, vol. 15, reel 10.

52. Thompson, *Authentic History*, 22; Hewitt, *Women's Activism*, 166–68, 173, 179, 192, 225; on the reform background of Rochester, see Johnson, *Shopkeeper's Millennium*.

53. Linden-Ward, "Strange but Genteel Pleasure Grounds," 293–328; O'Keefe, *Frederick and Anna Douglass in Rochester*, 101.

54. "Burial of Frederick Douglass," *New York Times*, February 27, 1895.

55. "Douglass Funeral," *New York Tribune*, [March 7], 1895, FDP, vol. 16, reel 11.

56. "The Last Honors," *Chronicle*, February 27, 1895, FDP, vol. 16, reel 11.

57. "The Last Honors," *Rochester Democrat*, February 27, 1895; "The Douglass Funeral," *(Rochester) Post*, February 25, 1895; "At His Old Home," *Evening Star*, February 5, 1895, FDP, vol. 15, reel 10.

58. "Douglass Funeral," *New York Tribune*, [March 7], 1895, FDP, vol. 16, reel 11.

59. *Post Express*, n.d., FDP, vol. 16, reel 11.

60. "The Last Honors," *Rochester Democrat*, February 27, 1895; "Fred. Douglass's Funeral," *Baltimore Sun*, February 26, 1895; on Rochester's civic identity, see McKelvey, *Rochester*.

61. "The Last Honors," *Rochester Democrat*, February 27, 1895; "Douglass Funeral," *New York Tribune*, March 1, 1895.

62. "The Last Honors," *Chronicle*, February 27, 1895, FDP, vol. 16, reel 11.

63. Gannett quoted in "The Last Honors," *Chronicle*, February 27, 1895, FDP, vol. 16, reel 11; "Interred at His Old Home," *Washington Post*, February 27, 1895.

64. "The Last Honors," *Chronicle*, February 27, 1895, FDP, vol. 16, reel 11; Gregory, *Frederick Douglass*, 270.

65. Thompson, *Authentic History*, 33; Brown, *Civil War Monuments*, 151–52.

66. Thompson, *Authentic History*, 39, 40.

67. Thompson, *Authentic History*, 41–44; "In Memory of Frederick Douglass," *Kansas City Star*, September 15, 1898; "Monument to Douglass," *Boston Daily Globe*, May 13, 1895.

68. Thompson, *Authentic History*, 46, 53, 62–69, 114; Shackel, *Memory in Black and White*, 141.

69. Thompson, *Authentic History*, 55.

70. Thompson, *Authentic History*, 59.

71. Thompson, *Authentic History*, 104.

72. "Monument to Frederick Douglass Unveiled," *Charlotte Daily Observer*, June 10, 1899.

73. Du Bois, *City of Frederick Douglass*, 32; Brown, *Civil War Monuments*, 151–52.

74. "The Dedication of a Monument to Frederick Douglass," *Kansas City Star*, June 10, 1899; Savage, *Standing Soldiers*; Blight, *Race and Reunion*, 288–89.

75. Roosevelt, "Address at Unveiling."

76. Thompson, *Authentic History*, 125–26; Theodore Roosevelt, "Address at Unveiling of Frederick Douglass Monument, at Rochester, June 10, 1899."

77. Shackel, *Memory in Black and White*, 14; see also Brands, *Reckless Decade*, 219–53.

78. Kachun, *Festivals of Freedom*, 13.

79. On Washington's rise in 1895, see Norrell, *Up from History*, 115–28; West, *Education of Booker T. Washington*, 57, 92–93, 135–36; Brands, *Reckless Decade*, 242–43.

80. "Address of Professor W. H. H. Hart," in Douglass, *In Memoriam*, 263. J. E. Rankin explicitly noted Douglass's role in recruiting Black troops was an important part of his war work; quoted in Douglass, *In Memoriam*, 204. Rev. Francis J. Grimké made a similar point in his memorial address about Douglass in Washington, DC, a few weeks later; see Douglass, *In Memoriam*, 188.

81. Josephine D. H. Heard, "In Memory of the Hon. Frederick Douglass, the Sage of Anacostia," *Chautauquan*, April 21, 1895.

82. "Some Learned Black Men," *Baltimore World*, February 23, 1895.

83. "By an Ex-Editor," *Philadelphia Inquirer*, February 22, 1895.

84. Tilton, "A Career Unique," 183.

85. "Frederick Douglass," *Washington Post*, February 22, 1895.

86. "Comments of the Indianapolis Press," *Freeman*, March 2, 1895; *Indianapolis Sentinel*, February 25, 1895, quoted in Douglass, *In Memoriam*, 295. The *Freeman* frequently held up Douglass as a great example of Black manhood and offered a portrait of Douglass as a premium with a three-month paid subscription; *Freeman*, March 30, 1895.

87. "Eulogy on Fred Douglass," *Omaha World Herald*, March 18, 1895.

88. W. B. Derrick, quoted in Douglass, *In Memoriam*, 41.

89. J. E. Rankin, "Frederick Douglass's Character and Career," April 1895, in *Douglass in His Own Time*, 175.

90. "Harrisburg, Pa.," February 27, 1895, FDP, vol. 14, reel 10; see also "Views of Colored Editors," *(Washington, DC) Star*, February 22, 1895.

91. "Greater in Death Than in Life," *Washington Post*, February March 4, 1895.

92. "In Memory of Fred. Douglass," *New York Times*, February 21, 1895; "Death of Frederick Douglass," *Union and Advertiser*, February 25, 1895.

93. "As to Douglass' Successor," *Freeman*, December 7, 1895.

94. *New York Tribune*, February 26, 1895.

95. "With the Death of Frederick Douglass," *Wilkes-Barre Times*, February 21, 1895.

96. Quoted in "Fred Douglass," *Daily Olympian*, April 1, 1895.

97. "A Precious Heritage," *New York Tribune*, February 22, 1895, in Douglass, *In Memoriam*, 295.

98. Francis Grimké, quoted in Douglass, *In Memoriam*, 190; "The Greatest Negro," *Washington Post*, March 11, 1895; see also Robert Reyburn, "In Memoriam—Frederick Douglass," *Washington Post*, February 24, 1895.

99. Clark, *Defining Moments*, 160; Norrell, *Up from History*, 85–86.

100. Thompson, *Authentic History*, 156.

101. "With the Death of Frederick Douglass," *Wilkes-Barre Times*, February 21, 1895; "Lived a Romance," *Boston Daily Globe*, February 25, 1895.

102. "Douglass Memorial," *Philadelphia Inquirer*, July 7, 1896. Durham had also spoken at the Philadelphia memorial meeting for Douglass just after his death; "Frederick Douglass,

Philadelphia's Colored Population Assemble to Honor His Memory," *Philadelphia Inquirer*, April 16, 1895; Wynes, "John Stephens Durham," 527–37; "A Worthy Colored Report," *Wilkes-Barre Times*, March 23, 1901.

103. For comparisons between Douglass and Booker T. Washington, see Blight, *Frederick Douglass: Prophet of Freedom*, 757–58; Moses, *Creative Conflict*.

104. Frederickson, *Black Image*, 231–32; Foner, *Forever Free*, 193.

105. Love, *Race over Empire*, 8–9.

106. May Wright Sewall, quoted in Douglass, *In Memoriam*, 46.

107. *Brooklyn Eagle*, February 21, 1895, in Douglass, *In Memoriam*, 286. Douglass may have had some Indian ancestors, and he at least entertained the possibility at several points in his life; Preston, *Young Frederick Douglass*, 9–10. For another claim that Douglass had Indian forebears, see "Frederick Douglass' Ancestry," *Washington Post*, January 8, 1900.

108. "An Extract from a Discourse by Rev. Dr. Louis Albert Banks," in Douglass, *In Memoriam*, 259; Louis Albert Banks, "A Warm Tribute," *Leslie's Weekly*, March 14, 1895, n.p., FDP, vol. 15, reel 10; see Bernasconi, "'Our Duty to Conserve,'" 519–40.

109. Jackson and Weidman, *Race, Racism, and Science*, 107.

110. "What the Governor Said of Douglass," *Mail*, February 23, 1895, FDP, vol. 16, reel 11.

111. F. M. Holland, "Frederick Douglass," *Open Court*, March 7, 1895; FDP, vol. 16, reel 11; on the scientific philosophical journal *Open Court*, see Meyer, "Paul Carus," 597–607.

112. Holland, *Frederick Douglass*, 410. Not much is known about Holland, but he claims to have prepared the biography in consultation with Douglass's sons; he is identified as an "American Unitarian divine and miscellaneous writer" in Warner, *Library of the World's Best Literature*, 270; see also Wilson and Fiske, *Appleton's Cyclopaedia of American Biography*, 234.

113. See Frederickson, *Black Image*, 286.

114. For the claim that Douglass himself worked with Holland, see McKivigan, *Frederick Douglass Papers*, xxiv. Booker T. Washington called Holland's book "an incredibly valuable biography"; Washington, *Frederick Douglass*, 204.

115. Douglass quoted in Washington, *Frederick Douglass*, 204.

116. Levine, *Martin Delaney*, 236.

117. "The Late Frederick Douglass, A Reminiscence by Rev. J. H. Hargis D.D.," in Douglass, *In Memoriam*, 329; "Frederick Douglass," *New Orleans Picayune*, quoted in *Public Opinion*, February 28, 1895, FDP, vol. 16, reel 11.

118. "Death of Frederick Douglass," *Minneapolis Tribune*, February 21, 1895.

119. Memphis *Commercial* quoted in "Fred Douglass," *Daily Olympian*, April 1, 1895; "The Late Frederick Douglass," *Knoxville Journal*, February 25, 1895; *Public Opinion*, February 28, 1895, FDP, Library of Congress, vol. 16, reel 11.

120. "Frederick Douglass," *Kansas City Star*, February 21, 1895. The same sentiment was expressed by the *Kansas City Journal*, quoted in "Fred Douglass," *Daily Olympian*, April 1, 1895.

121. "The Question of Race Leadership," *New York Age*, March 14, 1895; FDP, vol. 14, reel 10.

122. "Race and Heredity," *Boston Post*, February 24, 1895, in Douglass, *In Memoriam*, 303.

123. "Frederick Douglass," *Boston Herald*, quoted in *Public Opinion*, February 28, 1895, FDP, vol. 16, reel 11; see also *Christian Intelligencer*, February 27, 1895, FDP, vol. 15, reel 10.

124. Quoted in "Fred Douglass," *Daily Olympian*, April 1, 1895; "Death of Frederick Douglass," *Chicago Tribune*, February 22, 1895, quoted in Douglass, *In Memoriam*, 296–97.

125. Grimké quoted in Douglass, *In Memoriam*, 180.

126. On Helen Pitts Douglass—her marriage and efforts to preserve Frederick's memory—see Fought, *Women in the World of Frederick Douglass*, 229–304; "Mr. Douglass' Widow," *Washington Post*, May 30, 1897. Orlando Patterson was still criticizing Douglass's marriage to a white woman more than a hundred years later; Patterson, *Ordeal of Integration*, 104.

127. "Fred Douglass Dead," *(New York) Press*, February 21, 1895; "Frederick Douglass," *New Orleans Picayune*, quoted in *Public Opinion*, February 28, 1895, FDP, vol. 16, reel 11; *Independent*, March 7, 1895, FDP, vol. 15, reel 10.

128. "A Remarkable Life," *Atlanta Constitution*, quoted in *Public Opinion*, February 28, 1895, FDP, vol. 16, reel 11; "The Late Fred Douglass," *Atlanta Constitution*, February 22, 1895.

129. G.W.S., "The Late Frederick Douglass," in FDP, vol. 15, reel 10; "What Does It Mean?," *Atlanta Constitution*, February 28, 1895; "Letters from the People, the Douglass Incident," *Atlanta Constitution*, March 30, 1895; "What Mrs. McLendon Thinks about It," *Atlanta Constitution*, April 10, 1895.

130. "Frederick Douglass Is Gone," *Commercial Appeal*, February 21, 1895, FDP, vol. 15, reel 10; "Strange Career Closed," *Budget*, February 24, 1895, FDP, vol. 15, reel 10; "Death of Fred. Douglass," *(Worcester) Gazette*, February 21, 1895.

131. "Denied by the Two Sons," *Washington Post*, March 8, 1895; "To Contest Fred Douglass's Will," *New York Tribune*, [March 7, 1895], FDP, vol. 16, reel 11; "The Frederick Douglass Will," *Washington Post*, March 20, 1895; "Frederick Douglass' Estate," *Washington Post*, March 27, 1895; "A Good Share to the Widow," *Washington Post*, March 30, 1895; "Contest of the Douglass Will," *Washington Post*, March 31, 1895; "To Settle Their Differences," *Washington Post*, April 4, 1895; "Douglass Will Dispute," *Washington Post*, June 15, 1895; "Mr. Douglass' Widow Wins," *Washington Post*, April 14, 1895; "Frederick Douglass' Personal Estate," *Washington Post*, July 9, 1895; "Wants the Proceeds Divided," *Washington Post*, August 29, 1895.

132. "Fred Douglass," *New York Times*, February 23, 1895.

133. "Editorial Summary," *Public Opinion*, February 25, 1895.

134. "Douglass v. Washington," *State*, February 22, 1895; "Henry Romeike's Bureau of Press Cuttings," FDP, vol. 14, reel 10; "An Invidious Distinction," *New York Times*, February 22, 1895.

135. "Douglass v. Washington," *State*, February 22, 1895; "Henry Romeike's Bureau of Press Cuttings," FDP, vol. 14, reel 10; "An Invidious Distinction," *New York Times*, February 22, 1895; Anderson, *Race and Politics in North Carolina*, 223.

136. "Honored Douglass and Not Lee," *Philadelphia Inquirer*, February 22, 1895. David Blight claims that the U.S. Senate adjourned in honor of Douglass's death, but no record of the adjournment is found in the records of the Fifty-Third Congress; Blight, *Frederick Douglass, Prophet of Freedom*, 753.

137. *History of the General Assembly of 1895*, quoted in Edmonds, *Negro and Fusion Politics*, 42. Edmonds provides a careful account of the actual motions and the truth of the legislature's honoring Lee and Washington.

138. *Herald* quoted in "It Causes Ill Feeling," *(Mobile) Register*, February 27, 1895.

139. See Edmonds, *Negro and Fusion Politics*, 42–43.

140. *Raleigh News and Observer*, quoted in Bishir, "'A Strong Force of Ladies,'" 15; "The North Carolina House," *Columbus Daily Enquirer-Sun*, February 22, 1895; on the racial politics of the *News and Observer*, see Logan, *Negro in North Carolina*, 23; "Resent the Criticisms," *Atlanta Constitution*, February 26, 1895.

141. "An Invidious Distinction," *New York Times*, February 22, 1895.

142. "The Changes of Sentiment," *News-Tribune*, February 24, 1895; see also *Providence Journal*, quoted in *Public Opinion*, February 28, 1895, FDP, vol. 16, reel 11; "A Memorial Suggestion," *Star*, February 22, 1895; *(Saginaw) News*, February 23, 1895, FDP, vol. 15, reel 10.

143. "In Honor of Douglass," *Democrat and Chronicle*, n.d., FDSB I.

144. "Douglass and Lee," *Democrat and Chronicle*, February 26, 1895, FDSB I.

145. Unidentified newspaper clipping, FDP, vol. 16, reel 11; see also "Frederick Douglass and Robert E. Lee," (Boston, MA), n.t., February 28, 1895, FDP, vol. 15, reel 10; "All Speak Well of Him," *American*, February 22, 1895.

146. "A Red Hot Legislature," *Columbus Daily Enquirer*, February 26, 1895; on Lusk, see Nash, *Reconstruction's Ragged Edge*; Edmonds, *Negro and Fusion Politics*, 43.

147. Edmonds, *Negro and Fusion Politics*, 43; Domby, *False Cause*, 24–25.

148. Censer, *Reconstruction of White Southern Womanhood*, 201; "Confederate Monument, State Capitol, Raleigh," *Commemorative Landscapes of North Carolina*, accessed May 31, 2018, https://docsouth.unc.edu/commland/monument/106; on the racial and gendered dimensions of Confederate monument associations, see Brundage, "Women's Hand and Heart," 72.

149. *News and Observer*, quoted in Catherine Bishir, "North Carolina's Union Square," *Commemorative Landscapes of North Carolina*, accessed February 16, 2018, https://docsouth.unc.edu/commland/features/essays/bishir_two/.

150. Bishir, "'A Strong Force of Ladies,'" 15, 16.

151. "It Paralyzes Them," *Boston Daily Globe*, February 22, 1895; "They Are Indignant," *Atlanta Constitution*, March 5, 1895.

152. Domby, *False Cause*, 25.

153. "Confederate Monument, State Capitol, Raleigh," *Commemorative Landscapes of North Carolina*, accessed March 20, 2019, https://docsouth.unc.edu/commland/monument/106.

154. There were at least three Sedgwick Posts of the GAR in Rhode Island: South Kingston, Peace Dale/Wakefield, and Natick; see "Sons of the Union Veterans of the Civil War—Grand Army of the Republic (GAR)—Records Program, Rhode Island," accessed May 25, 2015, https://www.suvcw.org/garrecords/garcat/garcat-ri.htm.

155. "Miss Davis's Funeral," *New York Times*, September 23, 1898.

156. The best overall history of the GAR is McConnell, *Glorious Contentment*; important recent works include Gannon, *Won Cause*; Janney, *Remembering the Civil War*; and Harris, *Across the Bloody Chasm*.

157. Cook, "Lost Cause Legend," 1–17; Lee, *Winnie Davis*; see also Cashin, *First Lady*.

158. Both the veteran and Varina Davis quoted in "Grand Army Veterans Who Escorted Her Remains," *Confederate Veteran* 6 (November 1898): 508.

159. See "To Escort Miss Davis' Remains," *Bourbon News*, September 23, 1898; "Escorted to the Station by Union Veterans," *Richmond Dispatch*, September 23, 1898; "The Offer Accepted," *Bryan Morning Eagle*, September 23, 1898; "The Late Miss Winnie Da-

vis," *Alexandria Gazette*, September 22, 1898; "To Escort Miss Davis' Remains," *Daily Public Ledger*, September 22, 1898; "Escort of Grand Army Men," *Camden Chronicle*, September 30, 1898.

160. "Escort of Grand Army Men," *Camden Chronicle*, September 30, 1898.

161. Cook, "Lost Cause Legend," 4.

162. The UDC took on the name of Winnie Davis's honorific in 1895; "The Child of the Confederacy," *Chicago Daily Tribune*, November 6, 1886; Cook, "Women's Role," 144–60; Cox, *Dixie's Daughters*, 14–15; Lee, *Winnie Davis*, 161.

163. "At the Atlanta Reunion," *Richmond Dispatch*, September 20, 1898. *Harper's Weekly* said in Davis's obituary: "It is little wonder that a lady, so truly representative of what is best and most admired in the women of the South, and so identified with the last hours of the Confederacy, should have been the idol of Southern chivalry"; "Varina Anne Jefferson Davis," *Harper's Weekly* 10 (October 1, 1898): 974.

164. Silber, *Gender and the Sectional Conflict*; Clinton, *Civil War Stories*, 81–112; Faust, *Mothers of Invention*.

165. "Miss Winnie Davis Dead," *Richmond Dispatch*, September 20, 1898; see also *History of the Confederated Memorial Associations*, 192.

166. "Miss Davis's Funeral," *New York Times*, September 23, 1898; "Winnie Davis Is Dead," *Chicago Daily Tribune*, September 19, 1898; "Winnie Davis' Funeral," *Milwaukee Sentinel*, September 20, 1898.

167. Quotation from "Winnie Davis's Funeral," *New York Times*, September 24, 1898; "Honoring Her Memory," *Richmond Dispatch*, September 24, 1898.

168. "The Toll of Funeral Bells in Petersburg," *Richmond Dispatch*, September 24, 1898; "Bells Toll for Miss Winnie Davis," *Atlanta Constitution*, September 24, 1898; "General Flag-Raising at Atlanta," *Los Angeles Times*, September 24, 1898; "Maryland Veterans Mourn," *Richmond Dispatch*, September 21, 1898.

169. "Miss Davis's Funeral," *Richmond Dispatch*, September 24, 1898.

170. "Miss Winnie's Comrades," *Richmond Dispatch*, September 21, 1898; "Winnie Davis's Funeral," *Salt Lake Semi-Weekly Tribune*, September 23, 1898.

171. "Richmond, Va.," *New York Times*, September 21, 1898; "Winnie Davis's Funeral," *New York Times*, September 24, 1898.

172. "Men Who Wore Grey Honor the Memory of Winnie Davis," *Chicago Daily Tribune*, September 24, 1898.

173. "Men Who Wore Grey Honor the Memory of Winnie Davis," *Chicago Daily Tribune*, September 24, 1898; "Bands Played and Bells Tolled," *Richmond Dispatch*, September 24, 1898.

174. "Winnie Davis's Funeral," *New York Times*, September 24, 1898; "Miss Davis's Funeral," *Richmond Dispatch*, September 24, 1898.

175. "On the Left of Her Father," *Richmond Dispatch*, September 24, 1898.

176. "Winnie Davis's Funeral," *New York Times*, September 24, 1898.

177. Lee, *Winnie Davis*, 162; "The Floral Designs," *Richmond Dispatch*, September 24, 1898; St. Paul's Episcopal Church at Capitol Square, Richmond, VA, "A Walking Tour of St. Paul's."

178. "The Memorial Society Meets," *Richmond Dispatch*, September 29, 1898; "Will Be Laid to Rest in Richmond," *Atlanta Constitution*, September 24, 1898.

179. General Order No. 11 quoted in *Atlanta Constitution*, September 24, 1898.

180. Quotation from "Confederates of Lexington Kentucky," *Confederate Veteran* 6 (November 1898): 503. The pages of the *Confederate Veteran* for months after Winnie Davis's death were filled with tributes from SCV and especially UDC chapters.

181. McNeilly quoted in "Tributes to Miss Winnie Davis," *Confederate Veteran* 6 (October 1898): 467.

182. "Mrs. Currie Issues Orders," *Atlanta Constitution*, September 21, 1898; "United Daughters of the Confederacy," *Confederate Veteran* 6 (September 1898): 401–2.

183. Silber, *Romance of Reunion*, 178–85.

184. *New York World*, quoted in "Beloved in Both Sections," *Atlanta Constitution*, September 25, 1898; Cashin, *First Lady*, 274–75; Morris, *Pulitzer*, 338–44; Swanburg, *Pulitzer*.

185. "Let the Confederacy Rest," *Chicago Daily Tribune*, September 30, 1898; see also "Death of Winnie Davis," *Chicago Daily Tribune*, September 20, 1898.

186. "A Plea for the Old Soldiers," *Atlanta Constitution*, September 30, 1898.

187. *Atlanta Constitution*, quoted in "The South's Tribute to Winnie Davis," *Chicago Daily Tribune*, September 22, 1898.

188. "What Is Doing in Society," *New York Times*, September 30, 1898.

189. Charles M. Robinson, "Winnie Davis," *Chicago Daily Tribune*, October 9, 1898.

190. "Monument to Mark the Grave of Winnie Davis," *Chicago Daily Tribune*, March 13, 1899; Burkhardt, "Lost Cause Ideology," 16–25.

191. Fariello, "Personalizing the Political," 124.

192. Program quoted in Fariello, "Personalizing the Political," 124.

193. See Cox, *Dixie's Daughters*; Blight, *Race and Reunion*, 278–99.

194. Cashin, *First Lady*, 293.

195. Cashin, *First Lady*, 300–310.

196. "News from the Georgia Division of the UDC," *Confederate Veteran* 6 (October, 1898): 457.

197. "Address of Rev. James I. Vance," *Confederate Veteran* 6 (October 1898): 469.

198. Blight, *Race and Reunion*, 397.

199. See especially Gannon, *Won Cause*; Janney, *Remembering the Civil War*, and Harris, *Across the Bloody Chasm*.

Conclusion

1. "John Lewis Crosses Edmund Pettus Bridge in Selma for Final Time," *Guardian*, July 26, 2020; "Rep. John Lewis Crosses Edmund Pettus Bridge One Final Time," *NBC Nightly News*, YouTube, accessed January 24, 2021, https://youtu.be/_nX5fcynEcM; Rick Rojas, "Selma Helped Define John Lewis's Life. In Death, He Returned One Last Time," *New York Times*, July 26, 2020; "2020: The Year in Pictures, Selma, Ala., July 26," *New York Times*, https://www.nytimes.com/interactive/2020/world/year-in-pictures.html?searchResultPosition =2#june; Errin Whack, "Who Was Edmund Pettus?," *Smithsonian Magazine*, March 7, 2015, https://www.smithsonianmag.com/history/who-was-edmund-pettus-180954501/; Sydney Trent, "John Lewis Nearly Died on the Edmund Pettus Bridge. Now It May Be Renamed for Him," *Washington Post*, July 26, 2020. Some activists oppose the renaming, fearing that it will erase some of the civil rights history of the 1960s, and another group is proposing to rename the section of Interstate 80 that travels over the bridge after Lewis; Steve Cohen, "Bidding Farewell to My Friend and Colleague John Lewis," *States News Service*, July 31, 2020.

2. United States House of Representatives, History, Art & Archives, "Individuals Who Have Lain in State or in Honor," accessed January 24, 2021, https://history.house.gov /Institution/Lie-In-State/Lie-In-State-Honor/; Steve Cohen, "Bidding Farewell to My Friend and Colleague John Lewis," *States News Service*, July 31, 2020; Stephanie Toone, "What to Know about the Place Where John Lewis Will Be Buried," *Atlanta Journal-Constitution*, accessed January 29, 2021, https://www.ajc.com/news/what-to-know-about -the-place-where-john-lewis-will-be-buried/B5PFWUGC25C55I4EH7SKXO27BE/.

3. Williams quoted in Rojas, "Selma Helped Define John Lewis's Life."

4. Barack Obama, "Transcript: Barack Obama's Address at John Lewis' Funeral," Associated Press, July 30, 2020.

5. Cox, *No Common Ground*; see Hilary Green, *Confederate Monument Removal, 2015–2020, A Mapping Project*, accessed January 31, 2021, https://hgreen.people.ua.edu/csa -monument-mapping-project.html.

6. Karla Ward and Beth Musgrave, "Confederate Statues Quietly Moved to Lexington Cemetery," *Lexington Herald Leader*, July 24, 2018.

7. Rebecca Cooper, "Alexandria to Lose Two Kimptons as Hotels Are Sold," *Washington Business Journal*, December 13, 2016, https://www.bizjournals.com/washington /news/2016/12/13/alexandria-to-lose-two-kimptons-as-hotels-are.html; Andrew Beaujon, "Alexandria's Confederate Statue Has Been Removed," *Washingtonian*, June 2, 2020; the plaque was removed before November 2019.

8. Denise Lavoie and Alan Suderman, "Stonewall Jackson Removed from Richmond's Monument Avenue," *AP News*, July 1, 2020, https://apnews.com/article/b27b2bfce3ecefe13 c917a69a59cd9da.

9. Rebecca J. Ritzel, "In Richmond, Black Dance Claims a Space Near Robert E. Lee," *New York Times*, August 6, 2020; Azi Paybara, "Virginia Governor Can Remove Robert E. Lee Statue, But Not Yet, Judge Rules," *New York Times*, October 28, 2020; Cox, *No Common Ground*.

10. Washington and Lee University was pushed to remove Lee's name (and possibly Washington's also) from the name of the institution, but the Board of Trustees decided in June 2021 to retain both names; Susan Svrluga, "Faculty Resoundingly Votes to Change the Name of Washington and Lee," *Washington Post*, July 7, 2020; Annie Schroeder, "Debate Continues over the Fate of Washington and Lee's Name," *WSLS News*, January 28, 2021, https://www.wsls.com/news/local/2021/01/28/debate-continues-over-future-of-washington -and-lees-name/; Lilah Burke, "Retaining Its Name," *Inside Higher Ed*, June 7, 2021, https://www.insidehighered.com/news/2021/06/07/washington-and-lee-maintain-name -face-opposition.

11. Andrew Carter, "Witnessing a New History, Confederate Statue Comes Down in NC after 125 Years," *(Raleigh) News and Observer*, June 23, 2020.

12. "Original Frederick Douglass Statue Is on the Move," *Democrat and Chronicle*, October 21, 2019.

13. Gary Craig and Ryan Miller, "Frederick Douglass Statue Vandalized on the Anniversary of His Famous Fourth of July Rochester Speech," *Democrat and Chronicle*, July 5, 2020.

14. Allison Klein, "Historic D.C. Black Churches Attacked during Pro-Trump Rallies Saturday," *Washington Post*, December 13, 2020; Michelle Boorstein, "D.C. Houses of Worship Beef Up Security as Trump Defenders Descend on the Nation's Capital," *Washington Post*, January 4, 2021.

15. Rex Springston, "'A Symbolic Cacophony': As Monuments Come Down the Unraveling of the Rebel Flag Continues," *Virginia Mercury*, July 28, 2020, https://www.virginiamercury.com/2020/07/28/a-symbolic-cacophony-as-monuments-come-down-the-unraveling-of-the-rebel-flag-continues; Gregory S. Schneider, "Richmond's Mayor Took Down Confederate Monuments This Summer," *Washington Post*, November 7, 2020.

16. Ian Shapira, "VMI Commandant to Retire as Racial Reckoning Continues," *Washington Post*, January 23, 2021.

17. See Phillips, "Taking Things Seriously."

18. Spencer S. Hsu, Rachel Weiner, and Ann E. Marimow, "Retired Firefighter Accused of Attacking Police, Man Carrying Confederate Flag Charged in Capitol Riots, *Washington Post*, January 14, 2021.

Bibliography

Primary Sources

Manuscript Collections

Abraham Lincoln Presidential Library and Museum, Springfield, MA
  Elmer Ellsworth Papers
  Francis Edwin Brownell Small Collection
  Thomas W. Sherman Letters
Alexandria Library Local History/Special Collections Division, Alexandria, VA
  Henry B. Whittington Diary
  http://www.alexandria.lib.va.us/lhsc_online_exhibits/cwpix/cwpix.html
American Antiquarian Society, Worcester, MA
  Committee of Invitation to Stephen Salisbury, December 29, 1869, "The Funeral of the
    Late Mr. George Peabody"
  George Frisbie Hoar File
  Kenneth Allen Diary
College of William and Mary. Earl Gregg Swem Library
  Joseph E. Johnston Papers, Mss. 39.1 J63
Harvard University Houghton Library
  Papers Concerning the 1872 Resolution of Condemnation against Charles Sumner
Library of Congress
  Custis-Lee Family Papers
  Frederick Douglass Papers
  Henry Clay Family Papers
  Miscellaneous Manuscript Collection, Elmer Ellsworth, 1861, Autobiographical
    Manuscript
Massachusetts Historical Society
  "Funeral Services over the Remains of Charles Sumner," Boston: Committee of the
    Legislature, 1874
  John Collins Warren Papers, 1738–1926 (Ms. N-1731)
  Thomas Ball Letters, 1869–1882 (Ms. S-275)
Monroe County Public Library Special Collections, Rochester, NY
  Frederick Douglass Obituaries, Accounts of His Funeral and Other Material, Scrapbook
  Frederick Douglass Scrapbook
National Archives, Washington, DC
  Bussey, Cyrus, Cyrus Bussey to William S. Hancock, July 26, 1885, Copies of Communications
    Relating to the Funeral of General Grant, Record Group 393, part 1, entry 1471, vol. 1

Newberry Library, Chicago, IL
　"Sumner. Newspaper Articles," General Collection
　Tribute to Jos. E. Johnston (n.p.: n.p., [1891], Graff 2182
New York Public Library, Archives and Manuscripts Division
　Century Company Papers, Series II, MssColl 504
Old Dominion University Libraries, Special Collections and University Archives,
　　　Patricia W. and J. Douglas Perry Library, Norfolk, VA
　Robert Morton Hughes Papers, General Joseph E. Johnston Collection
Peabody Institute Library Archives, Peabody, MA
　George Peabody Death and Burial Scrapbook
　H.M.S. Monarch Logbook
　Peabody Funeral Correspondence Scrapbook
Phillips Library, Peabody Essex Museum, Rowley, MA
　George Peabody Papers, Mss 181
Transylvania University Special Collections and Archives, Lexington, KY
　J. Winston Coleman Papers
University of Kentucky Libraries Special Collections, Lexington, KY
　J. Winston Coleman Kentuckiana Collection
Virginia Historical Society, Richmond, VA
　Harriett (Cary) Christian Scrapbook
　Hobson Family Papers
　Johns Family Papers
　Lee Family Papers
　Mary Custis Lee Papers
　United Confederate Veterans, Virginia Division, Lee Camp No. 1 Records
Virginia Military Institute Archives, Lexington, VA
　"Stonewall Jackson's Death and Funeral," Full Text Primary Resources, https://www.vmi
　　　.edu/archives/stonewall-jackson-resources/stonewall-jackson-death-and-funeral/
　William Nalle to Mrs. Thomas Botts Nalle, October 16, 1870, MS 0042,
　　　http://digitalcollections.vmi.edu/cdm/ref/collection/p15821coll11/id/1559
Virginia Museum of History and Culture
　Hannah Family Papers, Pro-Quest History Vault, https://congressional.proquest
　　　.com/histvault?q=002477-027-0152&accountid=7379
Washington and Lee University, Manuscript Collections, Lexington, VA
　Robert E. Lee Papers
　Robert E. Lee to W. I. Hawks, January 8, 1866, Lee-Jackson-Foundation Collection,
　　　https://repository.wlu.edu/handle/11021/20754

Book and Pamphlets

Addey, Markinfield. *Stonewall Jackson*. New York: C. T. Evans, 1863.
Anderson, Charles. *A Funeral Oration on the Character, Life, and Public Services of Henry Clay* . . . Cincinnati: Ben Franklin Office, 1852.
Anspach, F. R. *A Discourse Pronounced on Sabbath Evening, July 4, 1852 in the Lutheran Church of Hagerstown, on the Death of Henry Clay*. Hagerstown, MD: Mittag and Sneary, 1852.

Avirett, James B. *The Memoirs of General Turnery Ashby and His Compeers.* Baltimore: Shelby and Dulaney, 1867.

Baldwin, N. B. *A Discourse on Henry Clay . . .* New York: Holman and Gray, 1853.

Basler, Roy P., ed. *The Collected Works of Abraham Lincoln.* 8 vols. NJ: Rutgers University Press, 1953.

Besson and Son. "Spring & Summer Circular of the Philadelphia Mourning Store." Philadelphia: n.p., 1851.

Blassingame, John W. ed. *The Frederick Douglass Papers, Series One: Speeches, Debates, and Interviews.* 5 vols. New Haven, CT: Yale University Press, 1979–91.

Bradlee, Caleb D. *Death and the Resurrection, A Sermon . . .* Boston: John Wilson and Son, 1874.

Brooke, James V. *Eulogy on the Life and Services of Henry Clay Delivered . . . in Warrenton, Virginia, on Saturday, July 31st, 1852.* Baltimore: John Murphy and Co., 1852.

Brown, S. G. *A Eulogy on the Life and Character of Henry Clay, Delivered before the Students of Dartmouth College.* Boston: John Wilson and Son, 1852.

Burlingame, Michael, ed. *At Lincoln's Side: John Hay's Civil War Correspondence and Selected Writings.* Carbondale: Southern Illinois University Press, 2000.

———, ed. *Dispatches from Lincoln's White House: The Anonymous Civil War Journalism of Presidential Secretary William O. Stoddard.* Lincoln: University of Nebraska Press, 2002.

———, ed. *With Lincoln in the White House: Letters, Memoranda, and Other Writings of John G. Nicolay, 1860–1865.* Carbondale: Southern Illinois University Press, 2000.

Burlingame, Michael, and John R. Turner Ettlinger. *Inside Lincoln's White House: The Complete Civil War Diary of John Hay.* Carbondale: Southern Illinois University Press, 1997.

Burns, Jeremiah. *The Patriot's Offering, or, The Life, Services, and Military Career of the Noble Trio, Ellsworth, Lyon, and Baker.* New York: Baker and Godwin, 1862.

Butler, C. M. "Sermon, Delivered in the Senate Chamber, July 1, 1852, on the Occasion of the Funeral of Hon. Henry Clay." In *Monument to the Memory of Henry Clay,* ed. A. H. Carrier, 491–514. Cincinnati: W. A. Clarke, 1858.

———. "The Strong Staff Broken and the Beautiful Rod: A Sermon, Delivered in the Senate Chamber, July 1, 1852, on the Occasion of the Funeral of the Hon. Henry Clay." In *The Life and Speeches of the Hon. Henry Clay,* ed. Daniel Mallory. 1: 246–50. New York: A. S. Barnes and Co., 1857.

Capers, Gabriel. *Eulogy on the Life and Public Services of the Hon. Henry Clay, Delivered at Milton, Florida on the 16th of August, 1852.* Mobile: Dad, Thompson and Co., 1852.

Carus, William, ed. *Memorials of the Right Reverend Charles Pettit McIlvaine.* New York: Thomas Whittaker, 1882.

Chadbourne, John S. *The Mortal and the Immortal: A Sermon Preached in St. James' Church, Baton Rouge . . .* New Orleans: Office of the Picayune, 1852.

Chaplin, Jeremiah, and Jane Dunbar Chaplin. *The Life of Charles Sumner.* Boston: D. Lothrop and Company, 1874.

Citizens of Louisville. *Robert E. Lee: In Memoriam: A Tribute Offered by the Citizens of Louisville.* Louisville: John P. Morton and Company, 1870.

Clay Monumental Association. *Articles for the Government of the National Clay Monumental Association.* New York: Van Norden and King, 1853.

———. *Ceremonies at the Laying of the Corner Stone of the National Monument, to Henry Clay, Near Lexington, KY.* Cincinnati: Cincinnati Gazette Company, 1857.

Coggeshall, William Turner. *Lincoln Memorial: The Journeys of Abraham Lincoln.* Columbus: Ohio State Journal, 1865.

Cole, Edward L. *Exercises Connected with the Unveiling of the Ellsworth Monument in Mechanicville, May 14, 1874.* Albany, NY: Joel Munsell, 1874.

Colton, Calvin. *The Last Seven Years of the Life of Henry Clay.* New York: A. S. Barnes and Co., 1856.

Cooke, John Esten. *A Life of Gen. Robert E. Lee.* New York: D. Appleton and Company, 1871.

———. *Stonewall Jackson: A Military Biography.* New York: Appleton and Co., 1876.

Cornell, William M., ed. *Charles Sumner, Memoir and Eulogies.* Boston: James H. Earle, 1874.

Correspondence Respecting the Visit of Her Majesty's Ship "Monarch" to the United States, Presented to Both Houses of Parliament by Command of Her Majesty. London: Harrison and Sons, 1870.

Crist, Lynda Lasswell, Mary Seaton Dix, and Kenneth H. Williams, eds. *Papers of Jefferson Davis.* 14 vols. Baton Rouge: Louisiana State University Press, 1971–2015.

Dabney, Robert Lewis. *The Life and Campaigns of Lieut.-Gen. Thomas J. Jackson.* New York: Blelock and Co., 1866.

Davis, Jefferson. *The Rise and Fall of the Confederate Government.* 2 vols. New York: D. Appleton and Co., 1881.

Douglas, Henry Kyd. *I Rode with Stonewall.* Chapel Hill: University of North Carolina Press, 1940.

Douglass, Frederick. "Eulogy for Charles Sumner: An Address Delivered in Washington, D.C., on March 16, 1874." In *The Frederick Douglass Papers*, edited by John W. Blassingame. Ser. 1, vol. 4, 397–401. New Haven, CT: Yale University Press, 1974.

Douglass, Helen. *In Memoriam: Frederick Douglass.* Philadelphia: J. C. Yorsten and Co., 1897.

Elliott, Robert B. *Oration of Hon. Robert B. Elliott, M.C. of South Carolina, Delivered in Faneuil Hall, April 14, 1874, under the Auspices of the Colored Citizens of Boston.* Boston: Published for the Committee of Arrangements by Charles L. Mitchell, 1874.

Ellsworth, Elmer. *The Zouave Drill . . . with a Biography of His Life.* Philadelphia: T. B. Peterson and Brothers, [1861].

"Ellsworth. Zouave Battle Cry." In *A Collection of Songs, Sung by J. M. Dunbar, the Blind Man.* New Hampshire: n.p., 1861.

Elsegood, Joseph L. *Death of Henry Clay: A Sermon Delivered, by Request, in Trinity Church, Easton . . .* Easton, PA: Davis, 1852.

Eulogies Delivered in the Senate and House of Representatives of the United States on the Life and Character of the Hon. John C. Calhoun . . . Hon. Henry Clay . . . and Hon. Daniel Webster . . . Vol. 2. Washington, DC: Foster and Cochran, 1853.

A Father's Talks with His Children about Three Great Characters. Lynchburg, VA: J. P. Bell, 1892.

Fisk & Raymond. *Fisk's Patent Metallic Burial Cases . . .* [New York]: E. O. Jenkins, 1853.

Foner, Philip S. *The Life and Writings of Frederick Douglass.* Vol. 2. New York: International Publishers, 1950.

Foote, Henry. *The Bountiful Return of Charity.* Boston: Barker, Cotter, and Co., 1869.

Foster, Ephraim H. *Funeral Oration . . . Delivered in the McKendree Church, Nashville, Tennessee on the Occasion of the Celebration of the Obsequies of Henry Clay, July 28th, 1852*. Nashville: W. F. Bang and Co., [1852].

Funeral Obsequies, October 15, 1870, Order of Procession. [Lexington, VA: n.p., 1870]. Library of Virginia.

Gregory, James M. *Frederick Douglass, The Orator*. 4th ed. Springfield, MA: Willey, 1895.

Hackett, Warren. *Reminiscences of the Geneva Tribunal*. New York: Houghton Mifflin, 1911.

Hanaford, Phebe A. *George Peabody*. Boston: B. B. Russell, 1870.

Heldrick, R. M. Music by S. L. Coe. "A Voice from Ellsworth!" Boston: n.p., 1861.

Hilliard, Henry W. "The Life and Character of Henry Clay." In *Monument to the Memory of Henry Clay*, ed. A. H. Carrier, 437–469. Cincinnati: W. A. Clarke, 1858.

History of the Confederated Memorial Associations of the South. New Orleans: Graham Press, 1904.

Holland, Frederic May. *Frederick Douglass: The Colored Orator*. Reprint, New York: Haskell House, 1969.

Hood, John Bell. *Advance and Retreat: Personal Experiences in the United States and Confederate States Armies*. New Orleans: G. T. Beauregard, 1879.

Howard, Oliver Otis. *The Autobiography of Oliver Otis Howard*. 2 vols. New York: Baker and Howard Company, 1908.

Hudson, A. L. "Ellsworth's Avengers!" Baltimore: Doyle, [1861].

———. "Ellsworth's Avengers!" New York: H. DeMarsan, [1861].

Hudson, A. Lora. "Ellsworth's Avengers, Song and Chorus." Boston: Oliver, Ditson, and Co., 1861.

In Memory of Col. Ellsworth. New York: H. De Marsan, 1861.

Jackson, Mary Anna. *Life and Letters of Gen. Thomas J. Jackson*. New York: Harper and Brothers, 1892.

———. *Memoirs of Stonewall Jackson by His Widow*. Louisville: Courier Journal Prentice Press, 1895.

Jenkins, Charles J. *Eulogy on the Life and Services of Henry Clay Delivered at the Request of the City Council, in Augusta, GA, Nov. 4, 1852*. Augusta: Steam Power Press of Chronicle and Sentinel, 1853.

Johnson, Bradley T. *Memoirs of the Life and Public Service of Joseph E. Johnston*. Baltimore: R. H. Woodward and Co., 1891.

Johnson, Samuel. *A Memorial of Charles Sumner*. Boston: A. Williams, and Co., 1874.

Jones, John Beauchamp. *A Rebel War Clerk's Diary at the Confederate States Capital*. 2 vols. Philadelphia: J. B. Lippincott, 1866.

Jones, Thomas. *Washington Family Relics, Speech of Hon. Thomas L. Jones of Kentucky in the House of Representatives, March 3, 1869*. Washington, DC: F. and J. Rives and Geo. A. Bailey, 1869.

Krauth, Charles. *Discourse on the Life and Character of Hon. Henry Clay, Delivered at the Request of the Citizens of Gettysburg*. Gettysburg, PA: H. C. Neinstedt, 1852.

Lakin, George A. *A Sermon on the Death of Henry Clay Preached in Trinity Church, Baltimore, on the 7th Sunday after Trinity, 1852*. Baltimore: A. P. Burt, 1852.

Lee, Susan Pendleton. *Memoirs of William Nelson Pendleton*. Philadelphia: J. B. Lippincott, 1893.

Lester, C. Edwards. *The Life and Public Service of Charles Sumner*. New York: United States Publishing Company, 1874.

The Life of James W. Jackson, the Alexandria Hero . . . Richmond: n.p., 1861.

Lincoln, Abraham. "Cooper Union Address." February 27, 1860. Abraham Lincoln Online. https://www.abrahamlincolnonline.org/lincoln/speeches/cooper.htm.

———. "Eulogy on Henry Clay." In *The Collected Works of Abraham Lincoln*, edited by Roy P. Basler, 2:121–32. New Brunswick, NJ: Rutgers University Press, 1953.

Lord, John C. *Our Strong Rods Broken and Withered*. Buffalo, NY: Jewett, Thomas and Co., 1852.

Lunt, George. *Threnody: On The Sailing of the Fleet from England to Convey the Remains of George Peabody to the United States*. Boston: [Boston Courier], 1869.

Magoon, Elias Lyman. *Living Orators in America*. New York: Baker and Scribner, 1849.

Maryland Historical Society. *In Memory of George Peabody*. Baltimore: J. Murphy, 1870.

McCabe, James Dabney. *The Life of Thomas J. Jackson, by an Ex-Cadet*. Richmond: J. E. Goode, 1864.

McCarthy, Carlton. *Walks about Richmond: A Story for Boys, and a Guide for Persons Visiting the City* . . . Richmond: McCarthy and Ellyson, 1870.

McGuire, Judith W. *Diary of a Southern Refugee during the War by a Lady of Virginia*. 2nd ed. New York: E. J. Hale and Son, 1867. Reprint, New York: Arno Press, 1972.

McKivigan, John R., ed. *The Frederick Douglass Papers*. Vol. 1. New Haven, CT: Yale University Press, 2009.

A Memoir of George Peabody, 1896, Proceedings of the General Assembly of South Carolina . . . [Charleston]: Lucas and Richardson, 1896.

Memorial Addresses on the Life and Character of Charles Sumner . . . Delivered in the Senate and the House of Representatives . . . Washington, DC: Government Printing Office, 1874.

A Memorial of Charles Sumner from the City of Boston. Boston: Printed by Order of the City Council, 1874.

Merrill, Walter M., ed. "William Lloyd Garrison and George Peabody." *Peabody Journal of Education* 70 (1994): 50–54.

M'Jilton, J. N. *God's Footsteps . . . Baltimore, July 4th, 1852, the Sunday Succeeding the Death of the Hon. Henry Clay*. Baltimore: G. W. Magers, 1852.

Moore, Bartholomew Figures. *An Address on the Life, Character and Public Services of Henry Clay*. Raleigh: Southern Weekly Post, 1853.

Morse, B. F. *An Address on the Life, Character and Public Services of Henry Clay, Delivered . . . at Weldon, North Carolina, upon Invitation*. Raleigh: Southern Weekly Post, 1853.

Nason, Elias. *The Life and Times of Charles Sumner*. Boston: B. B. Russell, 1874.

The New Testament of Our Lord and Savior Jesus Christ. New York: American Bible Society, 1861. Bibles Collection, American Antiquarian Society, Worcester, MA.

Otey, James H. *A Funeral Address upon the Occasion of the Death of Henry Clay; Delivered in Athens, Tennessee, July 3, 1852*. Athens: Sam P. Ivins, 1852.

Palmer, Beverly Wilson, ed. *The Selected Letters of Charles Sumner*. 2 vols. Boston: Northeastern University Press, 1990.

Peabody Institute . . . Third Annual Report of the Provost, June 2d, 1870. Baltimore: William K. Boyle, 1870.

Pickard, John B., ed. *The Letters of John Greenleaf Whittier*. Edited John B. Pickard. 3 vols. Cambridge, MA: Harvard University Press, 1975.

Pierce, Edward L. *Memoir and Letters of Charles Sumner*. 4 vols. Boston: Roberts Brothers, 1893.

Porter, Anthony Toomer. *In Memoriam. Gen. Joseph E. Johnston*. Charleston: Walker, Evans, and Coggswell Co., 1891.

Preston, Margaret Junkin. *The Life and Letters of Margaret Junkin Preston*. Edited by Elizabeth Preston Allan. New York: Houghton Mifflin, 1903.

Quintard, Charles T. "I Was Elected Chaplain." In *The Spirit Divided: Memoirs of Civil War Chaplains, the Confederates*, edited by John Wesley Brinsfield, 25–30. Macon, GA: Mercer University Press, 2006.

Rankin, J. E. *Frederick Douglass: Memorial Words Spoken at His Obsequies*. Washington, DC: Howard University, 1895.

———. "Frederick Douglass's Character and Career." In *Douglass in His Own Time*, ed. John Ernest, 168–75. Iowa City: University of Iowa Press, 2014.

Report of the Committee of Arrangements of the Common Council of New York, of the Obsequies in Memory of the Hon. Henry Clay. New York: McSpedon and Baker, 1852.

Richardson, R. H. *National Bereavements*. Chicago: S. C. Griggs and Co., 1852.

Robinson, Mary S. *Brother Soldiers*. New York: N. Tibbals, 1866.

Roosevelt, Theodore. "Address at Unveiling of Frederick Douglass Monument, at Rochester, June 10, 1899." In *State of New York, Public Papers of Theodore Roosevelt, Governor*, 332–35. Albany: Brandow Printing Company, 1899.

Russell, Thomas. *Remarks of Hon. Thomas Russell in Memory of Charles Sumner Made at the Commercial Club, Boston, March 21, 1874*. Boston: Printed for the Club, 1874.

Sargent, Epes. *The Life and Public Services of Henry Clay . . . Edited and Completed at Mr. Clay's Death by Horace Greeley*. Philadelphia: Porter and Coates, 1852.

Saunders, George. *Lincoln in the Bardo*. New York: Random House, 2017.

Schurz, Carl. *Eulogy on Charles Sumner Delivered by Carl Schurz before the City Government and Citizens of Boston . . .* Boston: Rockwell and Churchill, 1874.

Shea, John Gilmary. *The Fallen Brave, a Biographical Memorial of the American Officers Who Have Given Their Lives for the Preservation of the Union*. New York: Charles B. Richardson and Co., 1861.

Skinner, Henry Burchstead. *The Clay Memorial*. Boston: H. B. Skinner, 1852.

Smith, S. Lisle. *Eulogy upon the Life, Character, and Services of Henry Clay, Pronounced before the Common Council and Citizens of Chicago, July 20, 1852*. 2nd ed. Chicago: Daily Journal Office, 1852.

Southard, Samuel L. *Sermon on the Life and Death of Henry Clay, before the Young Men of Newark, N.J. Preached, at Their Request, in "The House of Prayer," July 25th, 1852*. Newark: Alfred H. Rogers, 1852.

St. Paul's Episcopal Church at Capitol Square, Richmond, VA. "A Walking Tour of St. Paul's." Brochure.

Sumner, Charles. *The Works of Charles Sumner*. 15 vols. Boston: Lee and Shepard, 1875–83.

Tator, Henry. *A Eulogy Commemorative of the Character of Hon. Henry Clay*. Albany, NY: Joel Munsell, 1852.

Thompson, John W. *An Authentic History of the Douglass Monument*. Rochester, NY: Rochester Herald Press, 1903.

Tilton, Theodore. "A Career Unique" from *Sonnets to the Memory of Frederick Douglass.*" In *Douglass in His Own Time*, edited by John Ernest, 183–89. Iowa City: University of Iowa Press, 2014.

Upfold, George. *A Funeral Discourse on the Occasion of the Decease of the Hon. Henry Clay*. Richmond: Holloway and Davis Palladium Print, 1852.

Walker, Timothy. *An Oration on the Life and Character of John Quincy Adams: Delivered before the Citizens of Cincinnati*. Cincinnati: Wright, Fisher, and Co., 1848.

Wallis, Severn Teackle. *Discourse on the Life and Character of George Peabody*. Baltimore: John Murphy and Co., 1870.

Warner, Charles Dudley. *Library of the World's Best Literature: A Biographical Dictionary*. Vol. 29. New York: R. S. Peale and J. A. Hill, 1898.

Washington, Booker T. *Frederick Douglass*. London: Hodder and Stoughton, 1905.

Waterman, Catharine H. *Flora's Lexicon*. Boston: Phillips, Sampson, and Company, 1852.

Wheeler, N. *The Phrenological Characters and Talents of Henry Clay, Daniel Webster, John Quincy Adams, William Henry Harrison, and Andrew Jackson, as Given by the Most Distinguished Phrenologists in the United States*. Boston: Dow and Jackson, 1845.

Wilson, James Grant, and John Fiske, eds. *Appleton's Cyclopaedia of American Biography*. Vol. 3. New York: D. Appleton and Co., 1887.

Winthrop, Robert C. *Eulogy Pronounced at the Funeral of George Peabody, at Peabody, Massachusetts, February 8, 1870*. 2nd ed. Boston: John Wilson and Son, 1870.

Government Documents

Contingent Expenses of the House of Representatives. H.R. Rep. No. 30-Misc. 4 (1848). U.S. Congressional Serial Set Database.

Contingent Expenses of the House of Representatives. H.R. Rep. No. 32-Misc. 6 (1852). U.S. Congressional Serial Set Database.

Funeral Expenses of William Henry Harrison, Late President of the United States. H.R. Rep. 27-55 (1841). U.S. Congressional Serial Set Database.

Report of the Secretary of the Senate of Expenditures from the Contingent Fund of the Senate. S. Doc. No. 30-Misc. 7 (1848). U.S. Congressional Serial Set Database.

Report of the Secretary of the Senate Showing the Payments Made from the Contingent Fund of the Senate for the Year Ending December 4, 1852. S. Doc. No. 32-Misc. 10 (1853). U.S. Congressional Serial Set Database.

Report of the Secretary of the Senate with a Statement of the Payments from the Contingent Fund of the Senate . . . S. Doc. No. 31-Misc. 7 (1851). U.S. Congressional Serial Set Database.

Periodicals

Aberdeen (SD) Daily News

Advocate of Peace (Boston, MA)

Alabama Journal (Montgomery, AL)

Albuquerque (NM) Morning Democrat

Alexandria Gazette

Alexandria Gazette and Virginia Advertiser

American (Baltimore, MD)

The American Missionary

Annals of Iowa

Arkansas Whig (Little Rock, AR)

Atchison (KS) Daily Champion

Atchison (KS) Daily Globe

Atlanta (GA) Constitution

Atlantic Democrat (Egg Harbor, NJ)

Atlantic Journal (May's Landing, NJ)
Atlantic Monthly
Baltimore Weekly Sun
Baltimore World
Bangor (ME) Daily Whig and Courier
Barre Gazette (Wilkes-Barre, PA)
Boston (MA) Daily Advertiser
Boston (MA) Daily Globe
Boston (MA) Evening Journal
Boston (MA) Herald
Boston (MA) Statesman and Weekly Post
Bourbon (Paris, KY) News
Brooklyn (NY) Eagle
Bryan (TX) Eagle
Budget (Troy, NY)
Buffalo Morning Express
Burlington (VT) Sentinel
Camden (TN) Chronicle
Camden (SC) Confederate
Cass County (MI) Republican
Century (New York, NY)
Charleston (SC) Courier
Charleston (SC) Mercury
Charleston (SC) Tri-Weekly Mercury
Charlotte (NC) Daily Observer
Chataquan (Jamestown, NY)
Chicago (IL) Daily Tribune
Chicago (IL) Republican
Chicago (IL) Tribune
Christian Intelligencer (New York, NY)
Christian Recorder (Philadelphia, PA)
Chronicle (Rochester, NY)
Cincinnati (OH) Commercial Tribune
Cincinnati (OH) Daily Commercial
Cleveland (OH) Gazette
Cleveland (OH) Plain Dealer
Columbus (GA) Daily Enquirer
Columbus (GA) Daily Enquirer-Sun
Commercial Appeal (Memphis, TN)
Confederate Veteran
Congregationalist and Boston (MA)
   Recorder
Congressional Globe
Constitution (Middletown, CT)
Daily Advertiser (Boston, MA)
Daily Advertiser (Newark, NJ)

Daily Advertiser (Portland, ME)
Daily Advertiser (Rochester, NY)
Daily Alabama Journal (Montgomery, AL)
Daily Arkansas Gazette (Little Rock, AK)
Daily Atlas (Boston, MA)
Daily Cincinnati Gazette
Daily Cleveland (OH) Herald
Daily Columbus (GA) Enquirer
Daily Commercial Register (Sandusky, OH)
Daily Constitution (Middletown, CT)
Daily Constitutionalist (Augusta, GA)
Daily Evening Bulletin (San Francisco, CA)
Daily Evening Traveller (Boston, MA)
Daily Gazette and Reporter (Trenton, NJ)
Daily Globe (Washington, DC)
Daily Inter Ocean (Chicago, IL)
Daily Journal (Wilmington, NC)
Daily Missouri Republican (St. Louis, MO)
Daily Morning News (Savannah, GA)
Daily National Intelligencer and
   Washington (DC) Express
Daily Ohio Statesman (Columbus, OH)
Daily (WA) Olympian
Daily Picayune (New Orleans, LA)
Daily Public Ledger (Maysville, KY)
Daily Register (Raleigh, NC)
Daily True Delta (New Orleans, LA)
Dallas Morning News
DeBow's Review
Democrat and Chronicle (Rochester, NY)
Detroit (MI) Free Press
Detroit (MI) Tribune
Dispatch (Philadelphia, PA)
Dispatch (Pittsburgh, PA)
Dubuque (IA) Daily Times
Duluth (MN) Tribune
Emporia (KS) Daily Gazette
Evening Star (Washington, DC)
Farmer's Cabinet (Amherst, NH)
Fayetteville (AK) Observer
Flake's Weekly Galveston (TX) Bulletin
Floridian and Journal (Tallahassee, FL)
Frankfort (KY) Commonwealth
Frank Leslie's Illustrated Newspaper
   (New York, NY)
Frederick Douglass' Paper (Rochester, NY)

Freedom's Champion (Atchison, KS)
Freeman (Indianapolis, IN)
Friend (Honolulu, HI)
Fun
Galveston (TX) Daily News
Gazette (Worcester, MA)
Gentleman's Journal (London)
Georgia Telegraph (Macon)
Georgia Weekly Telegraph (Macon, GA)
Georgia Weekly Telegraph and Georgia
    Journal & Messenger (Macon, GA)
Gleason's Pictorial Drawing Room
    Companion (Boston, MA)
Goodhue Volunteer (Red Wing, MN)
Grand Forks (ND) Daily Herald
Greencastle (IN) Democrat
Guardian
Harper's Weekly
Hartford (CT) Daily Courant
Hawaiian Gazette (Honolulu, HI)
Herald (Chicago, IL)
Hinds County (Mississippi) Gazette
Huntsville (AL) Gazette
Idaho Daily Statesman (Boise, ID)
Idaho Statesman (Boise, ID)
Illinois Daily Journal (Springfield, IL)
Illinois State Journal (Springfield, IL)
Independent (New York, NY)
Independent Democrat (Concord, NH)
Indiana Farmer (Indianapolis, IN)
Indianapolis (IN) Sentinel
Inter-Ocean (Chicago, IL)
Iowa State Register (Des Moines, IA)
Jamestown (NY) Journal
Journal of Education of Upper Canada
Kansas City (MO) Star
Kentucky New Era
Kentucky Whig (Mt. Sterling, KY)
Knickerbocker Monthly
Knoxville (TN) Journal
Lancaster (SC) Ledger
Leavenworth (KS) Daily Times
Leslie's Weekly (New York, NY)
Lexington (KY) Herald Leader
Lexington (VA) Gazette

Liberator (Boston, MA)
Literary World (New York, NY)
Little Rock (AK) Daily Republican
Los Angeles (CA) Herald
Los Angeles (CA) Times
Louisville Daily Times
Louisville Evening Bulletin
Lowell (MA) Daily Citizen and News
Lynchburg Virginian
Macon (GA) Daily Telegraph
Macon (GA) Telegraph
Macon (GA) Weekly Telegraph
Mail (Lowell, MA)
Maine Farmer (Augusta, ME)
McClure's Magazine
Milwaukee (WI) Daily Journal
Milwaukee (WI) Daily Sentinel
Milwaukee (WI) Sentinel
Minneapolis (MN) Tribune
Mississippi Palladium (Holly Springs, MS)
Missouri Republican (St. Louis, MO)
Morning News (Savannah, GA)
Morning (Portland) Oregonian
Mountaineer (Greenville, SC)
Nashville (TN) Daily Union
Nassau Literary Magazine
Natchez (MS) Weekly Courier
The Nation
National Era (Washington, DC)
National Police Gazette (New York, NY)
New-England Historical and Genealogical
    Register (Boston, MA)
New Hampshire Patriot (Concord, NH)
New Hampshire Patriot and State Gazette
    (Concord)
New Hampshire Sentinel (Keene, NH)
New-Orleans (LA) Commercial Bulletin
New Orleans (LA) Picayune
New York Age
New York Daily Times
New York Evangelist
New York Examiner
New York Herald
New York Illustrated News
New York Independent

New York Observer
New York Observer and Chronicle
New York Times
New York Tribune
New York Weekly Herald
New York Weekly Tribune
New York World
Newark (NJ) Daily Advertiser
Newark (OH) Advocate
News (Chicago, IL)
News (Saginaw, MI)
News-Tribune (Duluth, MN)
North American (Philadelphia, PA)
North American and United States Gazette
  (Philadelphia, PA)
North American Review (Boston, MA)
Observer (Lancaster, PA)
Omaha (NE) World Herald
Open Court
Patriot (Harrisburg, PA)
Peabody (MA) Press
Pennsylvania Grit (Williamsport, PA)
Philadelphia (PA) Inquirer
Pittsfield (MA) Sun
Placer (CA) Times and Transcript
Post (Rochester, NY)
Post Express (Rochester, NY)
Post Intelligencer (Seattle, WA)
Press (New York, NY)
Press (Philadelphia, PA)
Providence (RI) Journal
Provincial Freeman (Toronto)
Public Opinion
Punch
Raleigh (NC) News and Observer
Redbook
Register (Mobile, AL)
Richmond (VA) Daily Dispatch
Richmond (VA) Daily Whig
Richmond (VA) Dispatch
Richmond (VA) Enquirer
Richmond (VA) Examiner
Richmond (VA) Planet
Ripley (OH) Bee
Rochester (NY) Chronicle

Rochester (NY) Daily Advertiser
Rochester (NY) Democrat
Rocky Mountain News (Denver, CO)
Sacramento (CA) Daily Union
Salem (MA) Gazette
Salt Lake (UT) Semi-Weekly Tribune
Salt Lake (UT) Weekly Tribune
San Francisco Bulletin
San Francisco Evening Bulletin
Saturday Evening Post
Scotio Gazette (Chillicothe, OH)
Selma (AL) Daily Reporter
Semi-Weekly Interior Journal
  (Stanford, KY)
Semi-Weekly Messenger (Wilmington, NC)
Sheffield and Rotheram (UK) Independent
Sioux City (IA) Daily Journal
Southern Bivouac (Louisville, KY)
Southern Historical Papers
Southern Review (Baltimore, MD)
Spirit of Jefferson (Charlestown, WV)
Spirit of the Times (New York, NY)
Springfield (IL) Daily Republican
Star (Washington, DC)
State (Columbia, SC)
State Gazette (Trenton, NJ)
St. Louis (MO) Globe-Democrat
St. Paul (MN) Daily News
Sun (Baltimore, MD)
Sunday Morning Republican
  (St. Louis, MO)
Times (London)
Times Picayune (New Orleans, LA)
Topeka (KS) Weekly Capital
Torchlight (Providence, RI)
Trenton (NJ) State Gazette
Tri-Weekly Commercial (Wilmington, NC)
Tri-Weekly Maysville (KY) Eagle
Union and Advertiser (Rochester, NY)
Vanity Fair
Vermont Chronicle (Bellows Falls, VT)
Vermont Watchman (Montpelier, VT)
Vermont Watchman and State Journal
  (Montpelier, VT)
Volksblatt (Cincinnati, OH)

Washington (DC) Post
Washingtonian
Weekly Champion and Press (Atchison, KS)
Weekly Crescent (New Orleans, LA)
Weekly Herald (New York, NY)
Weekly (Macon) Georgia Telegraph
Weekly (Prescott) Arizona Miner
Weekly Raleigh (NC) Register
Weekly (San Francisco) Alta California

Weekly Sentinel and Wisconsin Farm
    Journal (Milwaukee, WI)
Wheeling (WV) Register
Wilkes-Barre (PA) Times
Wilmington (NC) Journal
Wisconsin Patriot (Madison, WI)
Wisconsin State Register
    (Portage. WI)
Worcester (MA) Daily Spy

Other Primary Sources

"The Clay Statue. A Model of a Man. Designed by the Goddess of Liberty. New York: J. F. Magee, [1850]," American Political Prints, 1766–1876, Catalog of the Collection in the Library of Congress. Harpweek. Accessed February 20, 2015. http://loc.harpweek .com/default.asp.

Currier and Ives. "Death of Col. Ellsworth after Hauling Down the Rebel Flag." 1861. Lithograph. Library of Congress, Washington, DC. https://www.loc.gov/resource /pga.08555.

1850 Census Data. "Historical, Demographic, Economic, and Social Data, 1790–1970." Inter-University Consortium for Social and Political Research. Accessed February 1, 2010. http://www.icpsr.umich.edu/icpsrweb/ICPSR/studies/00003.

Haines, Michael R. "District of Columbia Population by Race, Sex, Age . . ." Table Aa2868-2964. Historical Statistics of the United States Millennial Edition Online. https://hsus -cambridge-org.grinnell.idm.oclc.org/HSUSWeb/search/searchTable.do?id=Aa2868 -2964.

"July 4th '76-'61." N.p.: n.p., [1861]. Archive of Americana. https://www.readex.com /content/archive-americana.

Library Company of Philadelphia. "Marcus Aurelius Root." Catching a Shadow: Daguerreotypes in Philadelphia, 1839–1860. Accessed February 13, 2015. http://www .librarycompany.org/%5C/catchingashadow/section5/index.htm.

Morgan, Matt. "Charles Sumner." Frank Leslie's Illustrated Newspaper, March 28, 1874.

Nast, Thomas, "Let Us Clasp Hands across the Bloody Chasm." Harper's Weekly, September 21, 1872.

———. "Let Us Have Complete Restoration, While You Are About It." Harper's Weekly, December 28, 1872, 1021.

Taylor, Richard. "Stonewall Jackson and the Valley Campaign." North American Review 126 (Mar.–Apr. 1878): 238–261.

Wallis, John Joseph. "Table Ea636-643—Federal Government Expenditure, by Major Function: 1789–1970." Historical Statistics of the United States Millennial Edition Online. Accessed February 16, 2017. https://hsus-cambridge-org.grinnell.idm.oclc.org /HSUSWeb/search/searchTable.do?id=Ea636-643.

Waud, Alfred R. "Funeral Service over Col. Ellsworth at the White House East Room." 1861. Pencil on paper, 26.9 × 38.2 cm. Library of Congress Prints and Photographs Division, Washington, DC. Accessed March 1, 2011. https://www.loc .gov/item/2004660356/.

Secondary Sources

Books

Adams, Peter. *The Bowery Boys: Street Corner Radicals and the Politics of Rebellion.* Westport, CT: Praeger, 2005.

Alexander, Bevin. *Lost Victories: The Military Genius of Stonewall Jackson.* New York: Henry Holt, 2004.

Ames, Kenneth L. *Death in the Dining Room, and Other Tales of Victorian Culture.* Philadelphia: Temple University Press, 1992.

Anbinder, Tyler. *Five Points.* New York: Free Press, 2001.

Anderson, Benedict. *Imagined Communities.* New ed. New York: Verso, 2006.

Anderson, Eric. *Race and Politics in North Carolina, 1872–1901.* Baton Rouge: Louisiana State University Press, 1981.

Anderson, Paul Christopher. *Blood Image: Turner Ashby in the Civil War and the Southern Mind.* Baton Rouge: Louisiana State University Press, 2002.

Andreason, Byron C., and Guy C. Fraker. *Looking for Lincoln in Illinois.* Carbondale: Southern Illinois University Press, 2015.

Andrews, J. Cutler. *The North Reports the Civil War.* Pittsburgh: University of Pittsburgh Press, 1955.

Andrews, William L. *To Tell a Free Story.* Urbana: University of Illinois Press, 1986.

Apple, Lindsey. *The Family Legacy of Henry Clay: In the Shadow of a Kentucky Patriarch.* Lexington: University Press of Kentucky, 2011.

Applegate, Debby. *The Most Famous Man in America: The Biography of Henry Ward Beecher.* New York: Doubleday, 2006.

Archer, J. Clark, et al., eds. *Historical Atlas of U.S. Presidential Elections: 1788–2004.* Washington, DC: CQ Press, 2006.

Ash, Stephen V. *Rebel Richmond: Life and Death in the Confederate Capital.* Chapel Hill: University of North Carolina Press, 2019.

———. *When the Yankees Came: Conflict and Chaos in the Occupied South, 1861–1865.* Chapel Hill: University of North Carolina Press, 1995.

Baker, H. Robert. *The Rescue of Joshua Glover: A Fugitive Slave, the Constitution, and the Coming of the Civil War.* Athens: Ohio University Press, 2006.

Baltzell, E. Digby. *Puritan Boston and Quaker Philadelphia.* New York: Free Press, 1979.

Baptist, Edward. *The Half Has Never Been Told: Slavery and the Making of American Capitalism.* New York: Basic Books, 2014.

Bauer, K. Jack. *Zachary Taylor: Soldier, Planter, Statesman of the Old Southwest.* Baton Rouge: Louisiana State University Press, 1985.

Baxter, Maurice G. *Henry Clay and the American System.* Lexington: University Press of Kentucky, 1995.

Benson, T. Lloyd. *The Caning of Senator Sumner.* Belmont, CA: Thomson/Wadsworth, 2004.

Berlin, Ira, Steven F. Miller, Joseph P. Reidy, and Leslie S. Rowland, eds. *The Wartime Genesis of Free Labor: The Upper South.* Ser. I, vol. 2, *Freedom: A Documentary History of Emancipation, 1861–1867.* Cambridge: Cambridge University Press, 1993.

Berman, Myron. *Richmond's Jewry, 1769–1976.* Charlottesville: University Press of Virginia, 1979.

Binnington, Ian. *Confederate Visions: Nationalism, Symbolism, and the Imagined South in the Civil War*. Charlottesville: University of Virginia Press, 2013.

Blair, William. *Cities of the Dead*. Chapel Hill: University of North Carolina Press, 2004.

Blight, David. *American Oracle: The Civil War in the Civil Rights Era*. Cambridge, MA: Belknap Press of Harvard University Press, 2003.

———. *Frederick Douglass: Prophet of Freedom*. New York: Simon and Schuster, 2018.

———. *Frederick Douglass's Civil War: Keeping Faith in Jubilee*. Baton Rouge: Louisiana State University Press, 1989.

———. *Race and Reunion: The Civil War in American Memory*. Cambridge, MA: Belknap Press of Harvard University Press, 2001.

Blue, Frederick J. *Charles Sumner and the Conscience of the North*. Arlington Heights, IL: Harlan Davidson, 1994.

Bonner, Robert E. *Colors and Blood: Flag Passions of the Confederate South*. Princeton, NJ: Princeton University Press, 2002.

Bordewich, Fergus M. *America's Great Debate: Henry Clay, Stephen A. Douglas, and the Compromise That Preserved the Union*. New York: Simon and Schuster, 2012.

Bostwick, Douglas W. *Memorializing Robert E. Lee: The Story of Lee Chapel*. Charleston: Jogglingboard Press, 2005.

Boyd, Stephen R. *Patriotic Envelopes of the Civil War: The Iconography of Union and Confederate Covers*. Baton Rouge: Louisiana State University Press, 2010.

Bradley, Mark L. *This Astounding Close: The Road to Bennett Place*. Chapel Hill: University of North Carolina Press, 2000.

Brands, H. W. *The Reckless Decade, America in the 1890s*. Reprint, Chicago: University of Chicago Press, 2002.

Briggs, John Channing. *Lincoln's Speeches Reconsidered*. Baltimore: Johns Hopkins University Press, 2005.

Brown, Thomas J. *Civil War Canon: Sites of Confederate Memory in South Carolina*. Chapel Hill: University of North Carolina Press, 2015.

———. *Civil War Monuments and the Militarization of America*. Chapel Hill: University of North Carolina Press, 2019.

———. *Politics and Statesmanship: Essays on the American Whig Party*. New York: Columbia University Press, 1985.

Brundage, Fitzhugh. *The Southern Past: A Clash of Race and Memory*. Cambridge, MA: Harvard University Press, 2005.

Bullock, Stephen C. *Tea Sets and Tyranny: The Politics of Politeness in Early America*. Philadelphia: University of Pennsylvania Press, 2016.

Burke, Peter. *Eyewitnessing: The Uses of Images as Historical Evidence*. Ithaca, NY: Cornell University Press, 2001.

Burlingame, Michael. *Abraham Lincoln: A Life*. 2 vols. Baltimore: Johns Hopkins University Press, 2008.

Burrows, Edward G., and Mike Wallace. *Gotham: A History of New York City to 1898*. New York: Oxford University Press, 1999.

Cashin, Joan E. *First Lady of the Confederacy: Varina Davis's Civil War*. Cambridge, MA: Harvard University Press, 2006.

Censer, Jane Turner. *The Reconstruction of White Southern Womanhood, 1865–1895*. Baton Rouge: Louisiana State University Press, 2003.

Chambers, Lenoir. *Stonewall Jackson.* 2 vols. New York: William Morrow, 1959.

Chernow, Ron. *Titan: The Life of John D. Rockefeller, Sr.* New York: Random House, 1998.

Chittum, Charles H. *The Story of Finding the Coffin in Which Gen. Robert E. Lee Was Afterward Buried.* Lexington, VA: Library of Virginia, 1928.

Clark, Charles E. *Maine: A Bicentennial History.* New York: W. W. Norton, 1977.

Clark, Kathleen Ann. *Defining Moments: African American Commemoration and Political Culture in the South, 1863–1913.* Chapel Hill: University of North Carolina Press, 2005.

Clarke, Frances M. *War Stories: Suffering and Sacrifice in the Civil War North.* Chicago: University of Chicago Press, 2011.

Clavin, Matthew. *Toussaint Louverture and the American Civil War.* Philadelphia: University of Pennsylvania Press, 2010.

Clinton, Catherine. *Civil War Stories.* Athens: University of Georgia Press, 1998.

Clinton, Catherine, and Nina Silber, eds. *Battle Scars: Gender and Sexuality in the American Civil War.* New York: Oxford University Press, 2006.

Cobb, James C. *Away Down South: A History of Southern Identity.* New York: Oxford University Press, 2005.

Colaiaco, James. *Frederick Douglass and the Fourth of July.* New York: Palgrave Macmillan, 2006.

Coleman, J. Winston. *Last Days, Death and Funeral of Henry Clay.* Lexington, KY: Winburn Press, 1951.

Collins, Donald E. *The Death and Resurrection of Jefferson Davis.* New York: Rowman and Littlefield, 2005.

Connelly, Thomas L. *The Marble Man: Robert E. Lee and His Image in American Society.* New York: Alfred A. Knopf, 1977.

Connelly, Thomas L., and Barbara L. Bellows. *God and General Longstreet: The Lost Cause and the Southern Mind.* Baton Rouge: Louisiana State University Press, 1982.

Conniff, Richard. *House of Lost Worlds: Dinosaurs, Dynasties, and the Story of Life on Earth.* New Haven, NY: Yale University Press, 2016.

Cook, Adrian. *The Alabama Claims: American Politics and Anglo-American Relation, 1866–1872.* Ithaca, NY: Cornell University Press, 1975.

Cook, Robert J. *Civil War Memories.* Baltimore: Johns Hopkins University Press, 2017.

Cormack, Margaret, ed. *Sacrificing the Self: Perspectives on Martyrdom and Religion.* New York: Oxford University Press, 2002.

Coski, John M. *The Confederate Battle Flag: America's Most Embattled Emblem.* Cambridge, MA: Harvard University Press, 2005.

Costello, Matthew R. *The Property of the Nation: George Washington's Tomb, Mount Vernon, and the Memory of the First President.* Lawrence: University Press of Kansas, 2019.

Cothran, James R., and Erika Danylchak. *Grave Landscapes: The Nineteenth-Century Rural Cemetery Movement.* Columbia: University of South Carolina Press, 2018.

Cox, Karen L. *Dixie's Daughters: The United Daughters of the Confederacy and the Preservation of Confederate Culture.* Gainesville: University Press of Florida, 2003.

———. *No Common Ground: Confederate Monuments and the Ongoing Fight for Racial Justice.* Chapel Hill: University of North Carolina Press, 2021.

Craughwell, Thomas J. *Stealing Lincoln's Body.* Cambridge, MA: Belknap Press of Harvard University Press, 2007.

Crouthamel, James L. *Bennett's New York Herald and the Rise of the Popular Press.* Syracuse, NY: Syracuse University Press, 1989.

Curl, James Stevens. *A Celebration of Death.* New York: Charles Scribner's Sons, 1980.

Cushman, Stephen. *Belligerent Muse.* Chapel Hill: University of North Carolina Press, 2014.

Dearing, Mary R. *Veterans in Politics: The Story of the G.A.R.* Reprint, Westport, CT: Greenwood Press, 1974.

De Meissner, Sophie Radford. *Old Naval Days: Sketches from the Life of Rear Admiral William Radford, U.S.N.* New York: Henry Holt, 1920.

Dirck, Brian R. *The Black Heavens: Abraham Lincoln and Death.* Carbondale: Southern Illinois University Press, 2019.

Domby, Adam H. *The False Cause: Fraud, Fabrication, and White Supremacy in Confederate Memory.* Charlottesville: University of Virginia Press, 2020.

Donald, David Herbert. *Charles Sumner and the Coming of the Civil War.* New York: Alfred A. Knopf, 1960.

———. *Charles Sumner and the Rights of Man.* New York: Alfred A. Knopf, 1970.

Downs, Gregory P. *After Appomattox: Military Occupation and the End of War.* Cambridge, MA: Harvard University Press, 2015.

Du Bois, Eugene E. *The City of Frederick Douglass: Rochester's African-American People and Places.* Rochester, NY: Landmark Society of Western New York, 1994.

Dyer, Brainerd. *Zachary Taylor.* Baton Rouge: Louisiana State University Press, 1946.

Edmonds, Helen. *The Negro and Fusion Politics in North Carolina, 1894–1901.* Chapel Hill: University of North Carolina Press, 1951.

Elliott, Sam D. *John C. Brown of Tennessee: Rebel, Redeemer, and Railroader.* Knoxville: University of Tennessee Press, 2017.

Ernest, John, ed. *Douglass in His Own Time.* Iowa City: University of Iowa Press, 2014.

Evans, Michael. *The Death of Kings: Royal Deaths in Medieval England.* New York: Hambledon Continuum, 2007.

Fahs, Alice. *The Imagined Civil War: Popular Literature in the North and South, 1861–1865.* Chapel Hill: University of North Carolina Press, 2001.

Fahs, Alice, and Joan Waugh, eds. *The Memory of the Civil War in American Culture.* Chapel Hill: University of North Carolina Press, 2004.

Farwell, Byron. *Stonewall: A Biography of General Thomas J. Jackson.* New York: W. W. Norton, 1992.

Faust, Drew Gilpin. *The Creation of Confederate Nationalism: Ideology and Identity in the Civil War South.* Baton Rouge: Louisiana State University Press, 1988.

———. *Mothers of Invention: Women of the Slaveholding South in the American Civil War.* Chapel Hill: University of North Carolina Press, 1996.

———. *This Republic of Suffering: Death and the American Civil War.* New York: Alfred A. Knopf, 2008.

Fellman, Michael. *Citizen Sherman: A Life of William Tecumseh Sherman.* New York: Random House, 1995.

Fermer, Douglas. *James Gordon Bennett and the New York Herald.* New York: St. Martin's Press, 1986.

Fields, Barbara Jeanne. *Slavery and Freedom on the Middle Ground.* New Haven, CT: Yale University Press, 1985.

Fishwick, Marshall W. *Lee after the War*. Westport, CT: Greenwood Press, 1973.

Flood, Charles Bracelen. *Lee: The Last Years*. Boston: Houghton Mifflin, 1981.

Foner, Eric. *Forever Free: The Story of Emancipation and Reconstruction*. New York: Alfred A. Knopf, 2005.

———. *Reconstruction*. New York: Harper and Row, 1988.

Foote, Lorien. *The Gentlemen and the Roughs: Violence, Honor, and Manhood in the Union Army*. New York: New York University Press, 2010.

Foreman, Amanda. *A World on Fire*. New York: Allen Lane, 2010.

Foster, Gaines M. *Ghosts of the Confederacy: Defeat, the Lost Cause, and the Emergence of the New South, 1865–1913*. New York: Oxford University Press, 1987.

Fought, Lee. *Women in the World of Frederick Douglass*. New York: Oxford University Press, 2017.

Fox, Richard Wightman. *Lincoln's Body: A Cultural History*. New York: W. W. Norton, 2015.

Frederickson, George M. *The Black Image in the White Mind: The Debate on Afro-American Character and Destiny, 1817–1914*. Middletown, CT: Wesleyan University Press, 1971.

Freeman, Douglas Southall. *R. E. Lee: A Biography*. 4 vols. New York: Charles Scribner's Sons, 1934–35.

Fuller, Howard J. *Clad in Iron: The American Civil War and the Challenge of British Naval Power*. Annapolis, MD: Naval Institute Press, 2008.

Ezekiel, Tobias, and Gaston Lichtenstein. *The History of the Jews of Richmond from 1769 to 1917*. Richmond: Herbert T. Ezekiel, 1917.

Gallagher, Gary W. *Becoming Confederates: Paths to a New National Loyalty*. Athens: University of Georgia Press, 2013.

———. *Lee and His Army in Confederate History*. Chapel Hill: University of North Carolina Press, 2001.

———. *Lee and His Generals in War and Memory*. Baton Rouge: Louisiana State University Press, 1998.

Gannon, Barbara A. *Americans Remember Their Civil War*. Denver: Praeger, 2017.

———. *The Won Cause: Black and White Comradeship in the Grand Army of the Republic*. Chapel Hill: University of North Carolina Press, 2011.

Garlick, Harry. *The Final Curtain: State Funerals and the Theatre of Power*. Amsterdam: Rodopi, 1999.

Geary, Patrick. *Living with the Dead in the Middle Ages*. Ithaca, NY: Cornell University Press, 1994.

Georgi, Karen. *Critical Shift: Rereading Jarves, Cook, Stillman, and the Narratives of Nineteenth-Century American Art*. University Park: Penn State University Press, 2013.

Giguere, Joy M. *Characteristically American: Memorial Architecture, National Identity, and the Egyptian Revival*. Knoxville: University of Tennessee Press, 2014.

Gillis, John R. *Commemorations: The Politics of National Identity*. Princeton, NJ: Princeton University Press, 1994.

Gobel, David, and Daves Rossell, eds. *Commemoration in America*. Charlottesville: University of Virginia Press, 2013.

Goldfield, David. *Still Fighting the Civil War: The American South and Southern History*. Baton Rouge: Louisiana State University Press, 2002.

Goodheart, Adam. *1861: The Civil War Awakening*. New York: Alfred A. Knopf, 2011.

Goody, Jack. *The Culture of Flowers*. New York: Cambridge University Press, 1993.

Gordon, Bruce, and Peter Marshall, eds. *The Place of the Dead: Death and Remembrance in Late Medieval and Early Modern Europe*. New York: Cambridge University Press, 2000.

Goulka, Jeremiah, ed. *The Grand Old Man of Maine: Selected Letters of Joshua Lawrence Chamberlain, 1865–1914*. Chapel Hill: University of North Carolina Press, 2004.

Govan, Gilbert E., and James W. Livingood. *A Different Valor: The Story of General Joseph E. Johnston, C.S.A.* New York: Bobbs-Merrill, 1956.

Greiman, Jennifer. *Democracy's Spectacle: Sovereignty and Public Life in Antebellum American Writing*. New York: Fordham University Press, 2010.

Gwynne, S. C. *Rebel Yell: The Violence, Passion, and Redemption of Stonewall Jackson*. New York: Scribner, 2014.

Halbwachs, Maurice. *On Collective Memory*. Edited by Lewis A. Coser. Chicago: University of Chicago Press, 1992.

Hamilton, Holman. *Prologue to Conflict: The Crisis and Compromise of 1850*. Reprint, Lexington: University Press of Kentucky, 2008.

———. *Zachary Taylor: Soldier in the White House*. Vol. 2. New York: Bobbs-Merrill, 1951.

Harlow, Luke E. *Religion, Race, and the Making of Confederate Kentucky, 1830–1880*. New York: Cambridge University Press, 2014.

Harris, M. Keith. *Across the Bloody Chasm: The Culture of Commemoration among Civil War Veterans*. Baton Rouge: Louisiana State University Press, 2014.

Harsh, Joseph L. *Confederate Tide Rising: Robert E. Lee and the Making of Confederate Strategy, 1861–1862*. Kent, OH: Kent State University Press, 2013.

Heidler, David S., and Jeanne T. Heidler. *Henry Clay: The Essential American*. New York: Random House, 2010.

Hendler, Glenn. *Public Sentiments: Structures of Feeling in Nineteenth-Century American Literature*. Chapel Hill: University of North Carolina Press, 2001.

Hertz, Robert. *Death and the Right Hand*. Translated by Rodney Needham and Claudia Needham. London: Cohen and West, 1960.

Hettle, Wallace. *Inventing Stonewall Jackson: A Civil War Hero in History and Memory*. Baton Rouge: Louisiana State University Press, 2011.

Hewitt, Nancy. *Women's Activism and Social Change: Rochester, New York, 1822–1872*. Ithaca, NY: Cornell University Press, 1984.

Hidy, Muriel. *George Peabody: Merchant and Financier, 1829–1854*. Rev. ed. New York: Arno Press, 1978.

Hindle, Brooke. *Emulation and Invention*. New York: W. W. Norton, 1983.

Hobsbawm, Eric, and Terence Ranger, eds. *The Invention of Tradition*. Cambridge: Cambridge University Press, 1992.

Hodes, Martha. *Mourning Lincoln*. New Haven, CT: Yale University Press, 2015.

Hodges, Graham Russell. *New York City Cartmen, 1667–1850*. New York: New York University Press, 1986.

Hoffer, Williamjames Hull. *The Caning of Charles Sumner: Honor, Idealism, and the Origins of the Civil War*. Baltimore: Johns Hopkins University Press, 2010.

Holloway, Karla F. C. *Passed On: African American Mourning Stories*. Durham, NC: Duke University Press, 2002.

Holt, Michael F. *The Political Crisis of the 1850s*. New York: John Wiley, 1978.

————. *The Rise and Fall of the American Whig Party.* New York: Oxford University Press, 1999.

Holzer, Harold. *Lincoln: President-Elect.* New York: Simon and Schuster, 2008.

Huntington, Richard. *Celebrations of Death.* New York: Cambridge University Press, 1979.

Ingraham, Charles. *Elmer E. Ellsworth and the Zouaves of '61.* Chicago: University of Chicago Press, 1925.

Isenberg, Nancy, and Andrew Burstein, eds. *Mortal Remains: Death in Early America.* Philadelphia: University of Pennsylvania Press, 2003.

Jackson, John P., Jr., and Nadine M. Weidman. *Race, Racism, and Science: Social Impact and Interaction.* Denver: ABC-CLIO, 2004.

Jackson, Maurice, and Jacqueline Bacon, eds. *African Americans and the Haitian Revolution.* New York: Routledge, 2010.

Janney, Caroline E. *Burying the Dead but Not the Past: Ladies' Memorial Associations and the Lost Cause.* Chapel Hill: University of North Carolina Press, 2008.

————. *Remembering the Civil War: Reunion and the Limits of Reconciliation.* Chapel Hill: University of North Carolina Press, 2013.

John, Arthur. *The Best Years of the Century.* Urbana: University of Illinois Press, 1981.

Johnson, Paul A. *A Shopkeeper's Millennium: Society and Revivals in Rochester, New York, 1815–1837.* New York: Hill and Wang, 1978.

Kachun, Mitch. *Festivals of Freedom: Memory and Meaning in African American Emancipation Celebrations, 1808–1915.* Amherst: University of Massachusetts Press, 2003.

Kahler, Gerald E. *The Long Farewell: Americans Mourn the Death of George Washington.* Charlottesville: University of Virginia Press, 2008.

Kammen, Michael. *Digging Up the Dead: A History of Notable American Reburials.* Chicago: University of Chicago Press, 2010.

————. *Mystic Chords of Memory: The Transformation of Tradition in American Culture.* New York: Alfred A. Knopf, 1991.

Kasson, John F. *Rudeness and Civility: Manners in Nineteenth-Century America.* New York: Hill and Wang, 1990.

Kaufman, Will. *The Civil War in American Culture.* Edinburgh: Edinburgh University Press, 2006.

Kelsey, Marie Ellen. *Ulysses S. Grant: A Bibliography.* Westport, CT: Praeger, 2005.

Ken, Jeremiah. *Christian Mummification: An Interpretive History of the Preservation of Saints, Martyrs, and Others.* Jefferson, MO: McFarlane, 2012.

Kendrick, Stephen. *The Lively Place: Mount Auburn, America's First Garden Cemetery, and Its Revolutionary and Literary Residents.* Boston: Beacon Press, 2016.

Kennedy, John F., Jr. *Profiles in Courage.* New York: Harper's, 1956.

Klein, Norman. *The History of Forgetting.* London: Verso, 1997.

Kleinberg, Ariad. *Flesh Made Word: Saints' Stories and the Western Imagination.* Cambridge, MA: Harvard University Press, 2008.

Korda, Michael. *Clouds of Glory: The Life and Legend of Robert E. Lee.* New York: HarperCollins, 2014.

Koslofsky, Craig. *The Reformation of the Dead.* New York: St. Martin's Press, 1999.

Koudounaris, Paul. *Heavenly Bodies: Cult Treasures and Spectacular Saints from the Catacombs.* London: Thames and Hudson, 2013.

Kramer, Lloyd S. *Lafayette in Two Worlds*. Chapel Hill: University of North Carolina Press, 1996.

Krick, Robert K. *The Smoothbore Volley That Doomed the Confederacy*. Baton Rouge: Louisiana State University Press, 2002.

Laderman, Gary. *The Sacred Remains: American Attitudes toward Death, 1799–1883*. New Haven, CT: Yale University Press, 1996.

Landis, Michael. *Northern Men with Southern Loyalties: The Democratic Party and the Sectional Crisis*. Ithaca, NY: Cornell University Press, 2014.

Laqueur, Thomas. *The Work of the Dead: A Cultural History of Mortal Remains*. Princeton: Princeton University Press, 2016.

Lash, Jeffrey. *Destroyer of the Iron Horse: General Joseph E. Johnston and Confederate Rail Transport, 1861–1865*. Kent, OH: Kent State University Press, 1991.

Lawson, Melinda. *Patriot Fires*. Lawrence: University Press of Kansas, 2002.

LeBeau, Bryan F. *Currier and Ives: America Imagined*. Washington, DC: Smithsonian Institution Press, 2001.

Lee, Heath Hardage. *Winnie Davis: Daughter of the Lost Cause*. Lincoln, NE: Potomac Books, 2014.

Leepson, Marc. *Flag: An American Biography*. New York: Thomas Dunne Books/ St. Martin's Press, 2005.

Lehuu, Isabelle. *Carnival on the Page: Popular Print Media in Antebellum America*. Chapel Hill: University of North Carolina Press, 2000.

Lepore, Jill. *The Mansion of Happiness*. New York: Alfred A. Knopf, 2012.

Levine, Robert S. *Martin Delaney, Frederick Douglass, and the Politics of Representative Identity*. Chapel Hill: University of North Carolina Press, 1997.

Lewis, Charlene M. Boyer. *Ladies and Gentlemen on Display: Planter Society at the Virginia Springs, 1790–1860*. Charlottesville: University of Virginia Press, 2001.

Lewis, Lloyd. *Sherman: Fighting Prophet*. New York: Harcourt, Brace, 1932.

Linden, Blanche M. G. *Silent City on a Hill: Picturesque Landscapes of Memory and Boston's Mount Auburn Cemetery*. Boston: University of Massachusetts Press, 2007.

Lively, Matthew W. *Calamity at Chancellorsville: The Wounding and Death of Confederate General Stonewall Jackson*. El Dorado Hill, CA: Savas Beatie, 2013.

Logan, Frenise A. *The Negro in North Carolina: 1876–1894*. Chapel Hill: University of North Carolina Press, 1964.

Long, Renata Eley. *In the Shadow of the Alabama*. Annapolis, MD: Naval Institute Press, 2015.

Love, Eric T. *Race over Empire: Racism and U.S. Imperialism, 1865–1900*. Chapel Hill: University of North Carolina Press, 2004.

Lubet, Steven. *Fugitive Justice: Runaways, Rescuers, and Slavery on Trial*. Cambridge, MA: Harvard University Press, 2010.

Madaus, Howard Michael, and Richard H. Zeitlin. *The Flags of the Iron Brigade*. Madison: Wisconsin Veterans Museum, 1997.

Maltz, Earl M. *Fugitive Slave on Trial: The Anthony Burns Case and Abolitionist Outrage*. Lawrence: University Press of Kansas, 2010.

Mancoff, Debra N. *Flora Symbolica: Flowers in Pre-Raphaelite Art*. New York: Prestel, 2003.

Marshall, Anne E. *Creating a Confederate Kentucky: The Lost Cause and Civil War Memory in a Border State*. Chapel Hill: University of North Carolina Press, 2010.

Marszalek, John F. *Sherman: A Soldier's Passion for Order*. New York: Free Press, 1993.

Martinez, Jaime Amanda. *Virginia at War, 1865*. Lexington: University Press of Kentucky, 2010.

Masur, Kate. *An Example for All the Land*. Chapel Hill: University of North Carolina Press, 2010.

Mathisen, Erik. *The Loyal Republic: Traitors, Slaves, and the Remaking of Citizenship in Civil War America*. Chapel Hill: University of North Carolina Press, 2018.

Mayes, Edward, ed. *Lucius Q. C. Lamar, His Life and Speeches*. Nashville: Publishing House of the Methodist Episcopal Church, South, 1896.

McClain, Charles. *In Search of Equality: The Chinese Struggle against Discrimination in Nineteenth-Century America*. Berkeley: University of California Press, 1994.

McConnell, Stuart. *Glorious Contentment: The Grand Army of the Republic, 1865–1900*. Chapel Hill: University of North Carolina Press, 1992.

McCurry, Stephanie. *Confederate Reckoning*. Cambridge, MA: Harvard University Press, 2010.

McFeely, William S. *Frederick Douglass*. New York: W. W. Norton, 1991.

McIvor, David. *Mourning in America: Race and the Politics of Loss*. Ithaca, NY: Cornell University Press, 2016.

McKay, Ernest. *Henry Wilson: Practical Radical*. Port Washington, NY: Kennikat Press, 1971.

McKelvey, Blake. *Rochester on the Genesee: The Growth of a City*. 2nd ed. Syracuse, NY: Syracuse University Press, 1993.

McKenna, James T. *The Four Assassins of Ellsworth, Lincoln, Garfield, Harrison*. Creston, IA: Gazette Print, 1894.

McPherson, James M. *For Cause and Comrades: Why Men Fought in the Civil War*. New York: Oxford University Press, 1987.

———. *This Mighty Scourge: Perspectives on the American Civil War*. New York: Oxford University Press, 2007.

Meier, Kathryn Shively. *Nature's Civil War: Common Soldiers and the Environment in 1862 Virginia*. Chapel Hill: University of North Carolina Press, 2013.

Meredith, Roy. *The Face of Robert E. Lee in Life and Legend*. Rev. ed. New York: Fairfax Press, 1981.

Meyer, Richard E., ed. *Cemeteries and Gravemarkers: Voices of American Culture*. Ann Arbor: UMI Research Press, 1989.

Meyer-Fong, Toby. *What Remains: Coming to Terms with Civil War in 19th Century China*. Stanford, CA: Stanford University Press, 2013.

Miller, Brian Craig. *Empty Sleeves: Amputation in the Civil War South*. Athens: University of Georgia Press, 2015.

———. *John Bell Hood and the Fight for Civil War Memory*. Knoxville: University of Tennessee Press, 2010.

Mitchell, Mary H. *Hollywood Cemetery: The History of a Southern Shrine*. Richmond: Library of Virginia, 1999.

Mitchell, Reid. *Civil War Soldiers*. New York: Penguin Books, 1988.

Moats, Sandra M. *Celebrating the Republic: Presidential Ceremony and Popular Sovereignty, from Washington to Monroe.* DeKalb: Northern Illinois University Press, 2010.

Morris, James McGrath. *Pulitzer: A Life in Politics, Print, and Power.* New York: HarperCollins, 2010.

Moses, Wilson Jeremiah. *Creative Conflict in African American Thought.* New York: Cambridge University Press, 2004.

Muller, John. *Frederick Douglass in Washington, D.C., The Lion of Anacostia.* Charleston: History Press, 2012.

Nash, Steven E. *Reconstruction's Ragged Edge.* Chapel Hill: University of North Carolina Press, 2016.

Neely, Mark E., Jr. *The Boundaries of American Political Culture in the Civil War Era.* Chapel Hill: University of North Carolina Press, 2005.

Neely, Mark, Jr., and Harold Holzer. *The Union Image: Popular Prints of the Civil War North.* Chapel Hill: University of North Carolina Press, 2000.

Neff, John R. *Honoring the Civil War Dead: Commemoration and the Problem of Reconciliation.* Lawrence: University Press of Kansas, 2005.

Nelson, Megan Kate. *Ruin Nation: Destruction and the American Civil War.* Athens: University of Georgia Press, 2012.

Netherton, Nan, et al. *Fairfax County Virginia: A History.* Fairfax: Fairfax Board of Supervisors, 1978.

Nevins, Alan. *Hamilton Fish: The Inner History of the Grant Administration.* New York: Dodd, Mead, 1936.

Newman, Simon P. *Parades and the Politics of the Street: Festive Culture in the Early American Republic.* Philadelphia: University of Pennsylvania Press, 1997.

Newton, Stephen H. *Joseph E. Johnston and the Defense of Richmond.* Lawrence: University Press of Kansas, 1998.

Nicolay, Helen. *Lincoln's Secretary: A Biography of John G. Nicolay.* New York: Longmans, Green, 1949.

Nolan, Alan T. *Lee Considered: General Robert E. Lee and Civil War History.* Chapel Hill: University of North Carolina Press, 1991.

Nora, Pierre. *Realms of Memory.* Edited by Lawrence D. Kritzman. 3 vols. New York: Columbia University Press, 1998.

Nord, David Paul. *Communities of Journalism: A History of American Newspapers and Their Readers.* Chicago: University of Illinois Press, 2001.

Norrell, Robert J. *Up from History: The Life of Booker T. Washington.* Cambridge, MA: Belknap Press of Harvard University Press, 2009.

Oakes, James. *The Radical and the Republican.* New York: W. W. Norton, 2007.

O'Keefe, Rose. *Frederick and Anna Douglass in Rochester, New York.* Charleston: History Press, 2013.

Oriard, Michael. *Reading Football: How the Popular Press Created an American Spectacle.* Chapel Hill: University of North Carolina Press, 1993.

Parish, Peter J. *The North and the Nation in the Era of the Civil War.* Edited by Adam I. P. Smith and Susan-Mary Grant. New York: Fordham University Press, 2003.

Parker, Franklin. *George Peabody: A Biography.* Rev. ed. Nashville: Vanderbilt University Press, 1995.

Patterson, Orlando. *The Ordeal of Integration.* Washington, DC: Civitas, 1997.

Perry, Mark. *Conceived in Liberty: Joshua Chamberlain, William Oates, and the American Civil War*. New York: Viking Press, 1997.

Peter, Robert. *History of Fayette County, Kentucky*. Chicago: O. L. Baskin, 1882.

Peterson, Merrill. *Lincoln in American Memory*. New York: Oxford University Press, 1994.

Piston, William Garrett. *Lee's Tarnished Lieutenant: James Longstreet and His Place in Southern History*. Athens: University of Georgia Press, 1987.

Porter, Roy. *Flesh in the Age of Reason*. New York: W. W. Norton, 2004.

Potter, David M. *The Impending Crisis: America before the Civil War, 1848–1861*. Edited by Don E. Fehrenbacher. Reprint, New York: Harper Perennial, 2011.

Power, John Carroll. *Abraham Lincoln: His Life, Public Services, Death, and Great Funeral Cortege*. Chicago: H. W. Roker, 1889.

Preston, Dickson J. *Young Frederick Douglass, The Maryland Years*. Baltimore: Johns Hopkins University Press, 1980.

Puckle, Bertram S. *Funeral Customs: Their Origin and Development*. London: T. Werner Laurie, 1926.

Purcell, Sarah J. *Sealed with Blood: War, Sacrifice, and Memory in Revolutionary America*. Philadelphia: University of Pennsylvania Press, 2002.

Rable, George. *The Confederate Republic*. Chapel Hill: University of North Carolina Press, 1994.

Rachleff, Peter J. *Black Labor in the South: Richmond Virginia, 1865–1890*. Philadelphia: Temple University Press, 1984.

Randall, Ruth Painter. *Colonel Elmer Ellsworth: A Biography of Lincoln's Friend and First Hero of the Civil War*. Boston: Little, Brown, 1960.

Ray, Frederic E. *"Our Special Artist": Alfred R. Waud's Civil War*. Mechanicsburg, PA: Stackpole Books, 1994.

Reeves, John. *The Lost Indictment of Robert E. Lee: The Forgotten Case against an American Icon*. New York: Rowman and Littlefield, 2018.

Reis, João José. *Death Is a Festival: Funeral Rites and Rebellion in Nineteenth-Century Brazil*. Chapel Hill: University of North Carolina Press, 1991.

Remini, Robert V. *Henry Clay, Statesman for the Union*. New York: W. W. Norton, 1991.

Ring, Natalie J. *The Problem South: Region, Empire, and the Liberal State, 1880–1930*. Athens: University of Georgia Press, 2012.

Robertson, James I., Jr. *Stonewall Jackson: The Man, the Soldier, the Legend*. New York: Macmillan, 1997.

Robinson, Michael D. *A Union Indivisible: Secession and the Politics of Slavery in the Border South*. Chapel Hill: University of North Carolina Press, 2017.

Rosenzweig, Roy A., and David Thelen. *The Presence of the Past: Popular Uses of History in American Life*. New York: Columbia University Press, 1998.

Ross, Michael A. *The Great New Orleans Kidnapping Case*. New York: Oxford University Press, 2015.

Rotundo, E. Anthony. *American Manhood*. New York: Basic Books, 1993.

Rubin, Anne Sarah. *A Shattered Nation*. Chapel Hill: University of North Carolina Press, 2005.

Sanborn, Margaret. *Robert E. Lee: The Complete Man*. New York: J. B. Lippincott, 1967.

Sánchez-Eppler, Karen. *Touching Liberty: Abolition, Feminism, and the Politics of the Body*. Berkeley: University of California Press, 1993.

Savage, Kirk. *Standing Soldiers, Kneeling Slaves: Race, War, and Monument in Nineteenth-Century America*. Princeton, NJ: Princeton University Press, 1997.

Schantz, Mark. *Awaiting the Heavenly Country*. Ithaca, NY: Cornell University Press, 2008.

Schechter, Patricia A. *Ida B. Wells-Barnett and American Reform, 1880–1930*. Chapel Hill: University of North Carolina Press, 2001.

Schurz, Carl. *Life of Henry Clay*. 2 vols., 3rd ed. New York: Houghton Mifflin, 1887.

Schwartz, Barry. *Abraham Lincoln and the Forge of National Memory*. Chicago: University of Chicago Press, 2000.

Schwartz, Margaret. *Dead Matter: The Meanings of Iconic Corpses*. Minneapolis: University of Minnesota Press, 2015.

Seeman, Erik R. *Death in the New World: Cross-Cultural Encounters, 1492–1800*. Philadelphia: University of Pennsylvania Press, 2010.

———. *The Huron-Wendat Feast of the Dead*. Baltimore: Johns Hopkins University Press, 2011.

Sexton, Jay. *Debtor Diplomacy: Finance and American Foreign Relations in the Civil War Era, 1837–1873*. New York: Oxford University Press, 2005.

Shackel, Paul A. *Memory in Black and White: Race, Commemoration, and the Post-bellum Landscape*. New York: AltaMira Press, 2003.

Shamir, Milette, and Jennifer Travis, eds. *Boys Don't Cry? Rethinking Narratives of Masculinity and Emotion in the U.S.* New York: Columbia University Press, 2002.

Sharp, Lesley A. *Bodies, Commodities, and Biotechnologies*. New York: Columbia University Press, 2007.

Shea, William L., and Terrence J. Winschel. *Vicksburg Is the Key: The Struggle for the Mississippi River*. Lincoln: University of Nebraska Bison Books, 2005.

Sheehan-Dean, Aaron. *Why Confederates Fought: Family and Nation in Civil War Virginia*. Chapel Hill: University of North Carolina Press, 2007.

Silber, Nina. *Gender and the Sectional Conflict*. Chapel Hill: University of North Carolina Press, 2008.

———. *The Romance of Reunion: Northerners and the South, 1865–1900*. Chapel Hill: University of North Carolina Press, 1997.

———. *This War Ain't Over: Fighting the Civil War in New Deal America*. Chapel Hill: University of North Carolina Press, 2008.

Sinnema, Peter W. *The Wake of Wellington: Englishness in 1852*. Athens: Ohio University Press, 2006.

Slap, Andrew. *The Doom of Reconstruction: The Liberal Republicans in the Civil War Era*. New York: Fordham University Press, 2007.

Smith, Diane Monroe. *Fanny and Joshua*. Hanover, NH: University Press of New England, 2013.

Smith, Elbert B. *The Presidencies of Zachary Taylor and Millard Fillmore*. Lawrence: University Press of Kansas, 1988.

Smith, Jeffrey. *The Rural Cemetery Movement*. Lanham, MD: Lexington Books, 2017.

Somkin, Fred. *Unquiet Eagle: Memory and Desire in the Idea of American Freedom, 1815–1860*. Ithaca, NY: Cornell University Press, 1967.

Spann, Edward K. *The New Metropolis: New York City, 1840–1857*. New York: Columbia University Press, 1981.

Standaert, Nicolas. *The Interweaving of Rituals: Funerals in the Cultural Exchange between China and Europe*. Seattle: University of Washington Press, 2008.

Stowell, Daniel W. *Rebuilding Zion: The Religious Reconstruction of the South, 1863–1877*. New York: Oxford University Press, 1998.

Sundquist, Eric J., ed. *Frederick Douglass: New Literary and Historical Essays*. New York: Cambridge University Press, 1990.

Swanburg, W. A. *Pulitzer*. New York: Charles Scribner's Sons, 1967.

Sweeney, Fionnghuala. *Frederick Douglass and the Atlantic World*. Liverpool: Liverpool University Press, 2007.

Symonds, Craig L. *Joseph E. Johnston: A Civil War Biography*. New York: W. W. Norton, 1992.

Takagi, Midori. *"Rearing Wolves to Our Own Destruction": Slavery in Richmond, Virginia, 1782–1865*. Charlottesville: University Press of Virginia, 1999.

Tapley, Harriet Silvester. *Chronicles of Danvers (Old Salem Village) Massachusetts, 1632–1923*. Danvers, MA: Danvers Historical Society, 1923.

Taylor, Anne-Marie. *Young Charles Sumner and the Legacy of the American Enlightenment, 1811–1851*. Amherst: University of Massachusetts Press, 2001.

Tenneriello, Susan. *Spectacle Culture and American Identity, 1815–1940*. New York: Palgrave Macmillan, 2013.

Thelen, David. *Memory and American History*. Bloomington: Indiana University Press, 1990.

Thomas, Emory M. *Robert E. Lee, A Biography*. New York: W. W. Norton, 1995.

Transactions of the Illinois State Historical Society for the Year 1908, Ninth Annual Meeting. Springfield: Illinois State Historical Library, 1908.

Travers, Len. *Celebrating the Fourth: Independence Day and the Rites of Nationalism in the Early Republic*. Amherst: University of Massachusetts Press, 1997.

Tripp, C. A. *The Intimate World of Abraham Lincoln*. New York: Free Press, 2005.

Truesdell, Winifred Porter. *Catalog Raisonné of the Portraits of Col. Elmer E. Ellsworth*. Champlain, NY: Print Connoisseur, 1927.

Trulock, Alice Rains. *In the Hands of Providence: Joshua L. Chamberlain and the American Civil War*. Chapel Hill: University of North Carolina Press, 1992.

Upchurch, Thomas A. *Legislating Racism: The Billion Dollar Congress and the Birth of Jim Crow*. Kentucky: University Press of Kentucky, 2004.

Vandiver, Frank E. *Mighty Stonewall*. New York: McGraw-Hill, 1957.

Varon, Elizabeth. *Disunion! The Coming of the American Civil War, 1789–1859*. Chapel Hill: University of North Carolina Press, 2008.

———. *We Mean to Be Counted: White Women and Politics in Antebellum Virginia*. Chapel Hill: University of North Carolina Press, 1998.

Venet, Wendy Hamand. *Gone but Not Forgotten: Atlantans Commemorate the Civil War*. Athens: University of Georgia Press, 2020.

Verdery, Katherine. *The Political Lives of Dead Bodies: Reburial and Postsocialist Change*. New York: Columbia University Press, 1999.

Waldstreicher, David. *In the Midst of Perpetual Fetes: The Making of American Nationalism, 1776–1820*. Chapel Hill: University of North Carolina Press, 1997.

Wall, Joseph Frazier. *Andrew Carnegie*. Pittsburgh: University of Pittsburgh Press, 1989.

Wallace-Sanders, Kimberly. *Mammy: A Century of Race, Gender, and Southern Memory.* Ann Arbor: University of Michigan Press, 2008.

Watson, Harry L. *Liberty and Power: The Politics of Jacksonian America.* Rev. ed. New York: Hill and Wang, 2006.

Waugh, Joan. *U.S. Grant: American Hero, American Myth.* Chapel Hill: University of North Carolina Press, 2009.

West, Michael Rudolph. *The Education of Booker T. Washington.* New York: Columbia University Press, 2006.

Williams, Robert C. *Horace Greeley: Champion of American Freedom.* New York: New York University Press, 2006.

Wilson, Charles Reagan. *Baptized in Blood: The Religion of the Lost Cause, 1865–1920.* Reprint, Athens: University of Georgia Press, 2009.

Wood, Amy Louise. *Lynching and Spectacle: Witnessing Racial Violence in America, 1890–1940.* Chapel Hill: University of North Carolina Press, 2009.

Woods, Michael. *Emotional and Sectional Conflict in the Antebellum United States.* New York: Cambridge University Press, 2014.

Wright, John D. *Lexington: Heart of the Bluegrass.* Lexington, KY: Lexington-Fayette County Historical Commission, 1982.

Yalom, Marilyn. *The American Resting Place.* New York: Houghton Mifflin, 2008.

Yung, Judy, Gordon H. Chang, and H. Mark Lai. *Chinese American Voices: From the Gold Rush to the Present.* Berkeley: University of California Press, 2008.

Zboray, Ronald J., and Mary Saracino Zboray. *Voices without Votes: Women and Politics in Antebellum New England.* Hanover: University of New Hampshire Press, 2010.

Zeller, Paul G. *The Second Vermont Volunteer Infantry Regiment, 1861–1865.* Jefferson, NC: McFarland, 2002.

Articles and Papers

Angell, Stephen W. "A Black Minister Befriends the 'Unquestioned Father of Civil Rights': Henry McNeal Turner, Charles Sumner, and the African American Quest for Freedom." *Georgia Historical Quarterly* 85 (Spring 2001): 27–58.

Aptheker, Herbert. "DuBois on Douglass: 1895." *Journal of Negro History* 49 (1964): 264–68.

Argo, Brenda S. "Madame Octavia Levert's Tribute to Henry Clay." *Louisiana Studies* 12 (1973): 631–38.

Armour, Robert A., and Carol J. Williams. "Image Making and Advertising in the Funeral Industry." *Journal of Popular Culture* 14 (1981): 701–10.

Ayers, Edward L. "Not Forgotten: Remembering Appomattox." *Southern Cultures* 21 (Winter 2015): 7–12.

Baker, Andrew C. "American Hero, Confederate Idol: Consul General Fitzhugh Lee and the Limits of Sectional Reconciliation." *Virginia Magazine of History and Biography* 127 (2019): 42–68.

Barnhart, Terry A. "Apostles of the Lost Cause: The Albert Taylor Bledsoe–Alexander Stephens Controversy." *Georgia Historical Quarterly* 96 (2012): 371–412.

Becker, J. W. "The Lincoln Funeral Train." *Journal of the Illinois State Historical Society* 9 (October 1916): 315–19.

Bellanta, Melissa. "His Two Mates around Him Were Crying: Masculine Sentimentality in Late-Victorian Culture." *Journal of Victorian Culture* 20 (2015): 471–90.

Bernasconi, Robert. "'Our Duty to Conserve': W. E. B. DuBois's Philosophy of History in Context." *South Atlantic Quarterly* 108 (2009): 519–40.

Bishir, Catherine W. "Memorial Observances." *Southern Cultures* 15 (Summer 2009): 61–85.

———. "'A Strong Force of Ladies': Women, Politics, and Confederate Memorial Associations in Nineteenth-Century Raleigh." In *Monuments to the Lost Cause: Women, Art, and the Landscapes of Southern Memory*, edited by Cynthia Mills and Pamela H. Simpson, 3–26. Knoxville: University of Tennessee Press, 2003.

Blight, David W. "For Something beyond the Battlefield: Frederick Douglass and the Struggle for the Memory of the Civil War." In *Beyond the Battlefield: Race, Memory, and the American Civil War*, 93–119. Amherst: University of Massachusetts Press, 2002.

———. "'What Will Peace among the Whites Bring?': Reunion and Race in the Struggle over the Memory of the Civil War in American Culture." *Massachusetts Review* 34 (1993): 393–410.

Bohland, Jon D. "Look Away, Look Away, Look Away to Lexington: Struggles over Neo-Confederate Nationalism, Memory, and Masculinity in a Small Virginia Town." *Southeastern Geographer* 53 (Fall 2013): 267–95.

Brantley, Daniel. "Black Diplomacy and Frederick Douglass' Caribbean Experiences, 1871 and 1889–1891: The Untold Story." *Phylon* 45 (1984): 197–209.

Brooke, John. "To Be 'Read by the Whole People': Press, Party, and Public Sphere in the United States, 1789–1840." *Proceedings of the American Antiquarian Society* 110 (2000): 41–118.

Brown, Thomas J. "Civil War Remembrance as Reconstruction." In *Reconstructions: New Perspectives on the Postbellum United States*, edited by Thomas J. Brown, 206–36. New York: Oxford University Press, 2006.

———. "The Monumental Legacy of Calhoun." In *The Memory of the Civil War in American Culture*, edited by Alice Fahs and Joan Waugh, 130–56. Chapel Hill: University of North Carolina Press, 2004.

Brundage, Fitzhugh. "Women's Hand and Heart and Deathless Love: White Women and the Commemorative Impulse in the New South." In *Monuments to the Lost Cause: Women, Art, and the Landscapes of Southern Memory*, edited by Cynthia Mills and Pamela H. Simpson, 64–82. Knoxville: University of Tennessee Press, 2003.

Burkhardt, Patrick. "The Lost Cause Ideology and Civil War Memory at the Civil War Semicentennial: A Look at the Confederate Monument in St. Louis." *The Confluence* 2 (Spring/Summer 2011): 16–25.

Burstein, Andrew. "Immortalizing the Founding Fathers: The Excesses of Public Eulogy." In *Mortal Remains: Death in Early America*, edited by Nancy Isenberg and Andrew Burstein, 91–107. Philadelphia: University of Pennsylvania Press, 2003.

Butsch, Richard. "Bowery B'hoys and Matinee Ladies: The Re-gendering of Nineteenth-Century American Theater Audiences." *American Quarterly* 46 (1994): 374–405.

Caric, Ric N. "From Ordered Buckets to Honored Felons: Fire Companies and Cultural Transformations in Philadelphia, 1785–1850." *Pennsylvania History* 72 (2005): 117–58.

Carmichael, Peter S. "'Oh for the Presence and Inspiration of Old Jack': A Lost Cause Plea for Stonewall Jackson at Gettysburg." *Civil War History* 41 (1995): 161–67.

———. "So Far from God and So Close to Stonewall Jackson: The Execution of Three

Shenandoah Valley Soldiers." *Virginia Magazine of History and Biography* 111 (2003): 33–66.

Caron, Timothy Paul. "'How Changeable Are the Events of the War': National Reconciliation in the Century Magazine's Battles and Leaders of the Civil War." *American Periodicals* 16 (2006): 151–71.

Cashin, Joan E. "Hungry People in the Wartime South: Civilians, Armies, and the Food Supply." In *Weirding the War: Stories from the Civil War's Ragged Edges*, edited by Stephen Berry, 160–75. Athens: University of Georgia Press, 2011.

Chapman, Mary, and Glenn Handler. "Annals of Blubbering: Presidential Tears from George Washington to George Bush." In *Sentimental Men: Masculinity and Politics of Affect in American Culture*, edited by Mary Chapman and Glenn Handler, 1–16. Berkeley: University of California Press, 1999.

Chesson, Michael B. "Harlots or Heroines? A New Look at the Richmond Bread Riot." *Virginia Magazine of History and Biography* 92 (April 1984): 131–75.

Clinton, Catherine. "'Public Women' and Sexual Politics during the American Civil War." In *The Struggle for Equality*, edited by Orville Vernon Burton, Jerald Podair, and Jennifer L. Weber, 119–34. Charlottesville: University of Virginia Press, 2011.

Cook, Cita. "The Lost Cause Legend about Winnie Davis: 'The Daughter of the Confederacy.'" In *The Human Tradition in the New South*, edited by James C. Klotter, 1–17. New York: Rowman and Littlefield, 2005.

———. "Women's Role in the Transformation of Winnie Davis into the Daughter of the Confederacy." In *Women in the South across Four Centuries*, edited by Thomas H. Appleton Jr. and Angela Boswell, 144–60. Columbia: University of Missouri Press, 2003.

Deacon, Andrea. "Navigating 'The Storm, the Whirlwind, and the Earthquake': Re-assessing Frederick Douglass, the Orator." *Rocky Mountain Review of Language and Literature* 57 (2003): 65–83.

DiGirolamo, Vincent. "Newsboy Funerals: Tales of Sorrow and Solidarity in Urban America." *Journal of Social History* 36 (2002): 5–30.

Downs, Alan. "'The Responsibility Is Great': Joseph E. Johnston and the War in Virginia." In *Civil War Generals in Defeat*, edited by Steven E. Woodworth, 29–70. Lawrence: University Press of Kansas, 1999.

Drake, Amy. "The Funerals of Winnie Davis and Varina Davis, the Daughter and First Lady of the Confederacy." Mentored Advanced Project Research Paper, Grinnell College, August 10, 2007.

Dytch, Meredith M. "'Remember Ellsworth!': Chicago's First Hero of the American Civil War." *Chicago History* 11 (1982): 15–27.

Eastman, Joel W. "Maine Fortifications: The Civil War and Beyond." In *Maine: The Pine Tree State from Prehistory to the Present*, edited by Richard W. Judd, Edwin A. Churchill, and Joel W. Eastman, 366–67. Orono: University of Maine Press, 1995.

Fahs, Alice. "The Feminized Civil War: Gender, Northern Popular Literature, and the Memory of the War, 1861–1900." *Journal of American History* 85 (1999): 1461–94.

———. "The Market Value of Memory: Popular War Histories and the Northern Literary Marketplace, 1861–1868." *Book History and Print Culture* 1 (1998): 107–39.

Fariello, M. Anna. "Personalizing the Political: The Davis Family Circle in Richmond's Hollywood Cemetery." In *Monuments to the Lost Cause: Women, Art, and the*

Landscapes of Southern Memory, edited by Cynthia Mills and Pamela H. Simpson, 116–32. Knoxville: University of Tennessee Press, 2003.

Faust, Drew Gilpin. "Equine Relics of the Civil War." *Southern Cultures* 6 (2000): 23–49.

Fellman, Michael. "Robert E. Lee: Postwar Southern Nationalist." *Civil War History* 46 (2000): 185–204.

Finkelman, Paul. "Manufacturing Martyrdom: The Antislavery Response to John Brown's Raid." In *His Soul Goes Marching On: Responses to John Brown and the Harpers Ferry Raid*, edited by Paul Finkelman, 41–66. Charlottesville: University Press of Virginia, 1995.

Fishkin, Shelly Fisher, and Carla L. Peterson. "We Hold These Truths to Be Self-Evident: The Rhetoric of Frederick Douglass's Journalism." In *Frederick Douglass: New Literary and Historical Essays*, edited by Eric J. Sundquist, 166–88. New York: Cambridge University Press, 1990.

Foxman, Ellen F., et al. "Temperature-Dependent Innate Defense against the Common Cold Virus Limits Viral Replication at Warm Temperature in Mouse Airway Cells." *Proceedings of the National Academy of Sciences of the United States of America* 112 (January 20, 2015): 827–32.

Gallagher, Gary W. "Jubal A. Early, the Lost Cause, and Civil War History: A Persistent Legacy." In *Lee and His Generals in War and Memory*, 199–226. Baton Rouge: Louisiana State University Press, 1998.

———. "The Making of a Hero and the Persistence of a Legend: Stonewall Jackson during the Civil War and in Popular Memory." In *Lee and His Generals in War and Memory*, 101–17. Baton Rouge: Louisiana State University Press, 1998.

Gallman, J. Matthew. "Is the War Ended? Anna Dickinson and the Election of 1872." In *The Memory of the Civil War in American Culture*, edited by Alice Fahs and Joan Waugh, 154–79. Chapel Hill: University of North Carolina Press, 2004.

Garton, Stephen. "Scales of Suffering: Love, Death, and Victorian Masculinity." *Social History* 27 (November, 2010): 40–58.

Gesualdi, Maxine. "Man Tears and Masculinities: News Coverage of John Boehner's Tearful Episodes." *Journal of Communication Inquiry* 37 (2013): 304–21.

Gifford, James P. "The Celebrated World of Currier and Ives." *New York Historical Society Quarterly* 59 (1975): 348–65.

Gilmore, Russell S. "New York Target Companies: Informal Military Societies in a Nineteenth-Century Metropolis." *Military Collector and Historian* 35 (1983): 61–63.

Green, Fletcher M. "On Tour with President Andrew Jackson." *New England Quarterly* 36 (1963): 209–28.

Greenberg, Gerald S. "Ohioans vs. Georgians: The Galphin Claim, Zachary Taylor's Death, and the Congressional Adjournment Vote of 1850." *Georgia Historical Quarterly* 74 (1990): 575–98.

Griffen, Clyde. "Reconstructing Masculinity from the Evangelical Revival to the Waning of Progressivism." In *Meanings for Manhood: Constructions of Masculinity in Victorian America*, edited by Mark C. Carnes and Clyde Griffen, 183–204. Chicago: University of Chicago Press, 1990.

Gross, Jennifer L. "The United Daughters of the Confederacy, Confederate Widows, and the Lost Cause: 'We Must Not Forget or Neglect the Widows.'" In *Women on Their*

Own: Interdisciplinary Perspectives on Being Single, edited by Rudolph M. Bell and Virginia Yans, 180–200. New Brunswick, NJ: Rutgers University Press, 2008.

Grow, Matthew J. "The Shadow of the Civil War: A Historiography of Civil War Memory." *American Nineteenth Century History* 4 (2003): 77–103.

Hacker, J. David. "A Census-Based Count of the Civil War Dead." *Civil War History* 57 (2011): 307–48.

———. "Has the Demographic Impact of Civil War Deaths Been Exaggerated?" *Civil War History* 60 (2014): 453–58.

Hall, Melanie, and Erik Goldstein. "Writers, the Clergy, and the 'Diplomatisation of Culture': Sub-structures of Anglo-American Diplomacy, 1820–1914." In *On the Fringes of Diplomacy: Influences on British Foreign Policy, 1800–1945*, edited by John Fisher and Antony Best, 127–54. Surrey, UK: Ashgate, 2011.

Harris, W. C. "'In My Day It Used to Be·Called a Limp Wrist': Flip-Floppers, Nelly Boys, and Homophobic Rhetoric in the 2004 U.S. Presidential Campaign." *Journal of American Culture* 29 (2006): 278–95.

"Heroes." In *The U.S.-Mexican War: A Bi-national Reader*, edited by Christopher Conway, 158–160. Indianapolis, IN: Hackett, 2010.

Hettle, Wallace. "Mary Johnston and 'Stonewall' Jackson: A Virginia Feminist and the Politics of Historical Fiction." *Journal of Historical Biography* 3 (Spring 2008): 31–55.

Holmes, J. Wilfred. "Whittier and Sumner: A Political Friendship." *New England Quarterly* 30 (1957): 58–72.

Howard, June. "What Is Sentimentality?" *American Literary History* 11 (1999): 63–81.

Johnson, Abby Arthur, and Ronald M. Johnson. "Funeral Pageantry and National Unity: The Death and Burial of John Quincy Adams." *European Contributions to American Studies* 44 (2000): 144–51.

Johnson, Kenneth R. "The Peabody Fund: Its Role and Influence in Alabama." *Alabama Review* 27 (1974): 101–6.

Johnson, Lyman L. "Why Dead Bodies Talk: An Introduction." In *Body Politics: Death, Dismemberment, and Memory in Latin America*, edited by Lyman L. Johnson, 1–26. Albuquerque: University of New Mexico Press, 2004.

Jones, Archer. "The Vicksburg Campaign." *Journal of Mississippi History* 29 (1967): 12–27.

Jones, James Boyd, Jr. "Mose the Bowery B'hoy and the Nashville Volunteer Fire Department, 1849–1860." *Tennessee Historical Quarterly* 40 (Summer 1981): 170–81.

Jones, W. Burns, Jr. "The Marshall House Incident." *Northern Virginia Heritage* 10 (February 1988): 5–8.

Jumonville, Florence M. "The Wastebasket and the Grave: Funeralia in the South." *Southern Quarterly* 31 (1993): 98–118.

Kent, Christopher. "War Cartooned/Cartoon War: Matt Morgan and the American Civil War in *Fun* and *Frank Leslie's Illustrated Newspaper*." *Victorian Periodicals Review* 23 (Summer 2012): 153–81.

Kimmel, Michael S. "Masculinity as Homophobia: Fear, Shame, and Silence in the Construction of Gender Identity." In *Race, Class, and Gender in the United States: An Integrated Study*, edited by Paula S. Rothenberg, 86–88. 6th ed. New York: Worth Publishers, 2004.

Kinney, Martha E. "'If Vanquished I Am Still Victorious': Religious and Cultural Symbolism in Virginia's Confederate Memorial Day Celebrations, 1866–1930." *Virginia Magazine of History and Biography* 106 (1998): 237–66.

Klein, Stacey Jean. "Wielding the Pen: Margaret Preston, Confederate Nationalistic Literature, and the Expansion of a Woman's Place in the South." *Civil War History* 49 (2003): 221–34.

Krick, Robert K. "The Smoothbore Volley That Doomed the Confederacy." In *Chancellorsville: The Battle and Its Aftermath*, edited by Gary W. Gallagher, 107–42. Chapel Hill: University of North Carolina Press, 1996.

Laqueur, Thomas, and Lisa Cody. "Birth and Death under the Sign of Thomas Malthus." In *A Cultural History of the Human Body*, Vol. 5, *Death, Grief and Poverty in Britain, 1870–1914*, edited by Julie-Marie Strange, 5:53–56. New York: Cambridge University Press, 2005.

Lawton, Christopher. "Constructing the Cause, Bridging the Divide: Lee's Tomb at Washington College." *Southern Cultures* 15 (Summer 2009): 5–39.

Leepson, Marc. "The First Civil War Martyr: Elmer Ellsworth, Alexandria, and the American Flag." *Alexandria Chronicle*, Fall 2011, 1–4.

Levin, Kevin. "William Mahone, the Lost Cause, and Civil War History." *Virginia Magazine of History and Biography* 113 (2005): 378–412.

Levine, Robert S. "Frederick Douglass and Thomas Auld: Reconsidering the Reunion Narrative." *Journal of African American History* 99 (2014): 34–45.

"Lincoln Funeral Train Commemoration." *Military Trader*, April 2015, 8.

Linden-Ward, Blanche. "Strange but Genteel Pleasure Grounds: Tourist Uses of Nineteenth-Century Rural Cemeteries." In *Cemeteries and Gravemarkers: Voices of American Culture*, edited by Richard E. Meyer, 293–328. Logan: Utah State University Press, 1992.

Marler-Kennedy, Kara. "Immortelles: Literary, Botanical, and National Memories." *Romanticism and Victorianism on the Net: Materiality and Memory* 53 (2009). http://www.erudit.org/revue/ravon/2009/v/n53/029897ar.html.

McClure, Kevin R. "Frederick Douglass's Use of Comparison in His Fourth of July Oration: A Textual Criticism." *Western Journal of Communication* 64 (Fall 2000): 425–44.

Meslow, Scott. "An Icon Divided: Abraham Lincoln's Dual Popular-Culture Legacy." *The Atlantic*, June 22, 2012. https://www.theatlantic.com/entertainment/archive/2012/06/an -icon-divided-abraham-lincolns-dual-pop-culture-legacy/258828/.

Meyer, Donald Harvey. "Paul Carus and the Religion of Science." *American Quarterly* 14 (1962): 597–607.

Miller, Brian Craig. "Traumatized Manhood: Confederate Amputees in History, Memory, and Hollywood." In *The Civil War in Popular Culture: Memory and Meaning*, edited by Lawrence A. Kreiser Jr. and Randal Allred, 25–44. Lexington: University Press of Kentucky, 2014.

Mixon, Wayne. "The Shadow of Slavery: Frederick Douglass, the Savage South, and the Next Generation." In *Frederick Douglass: New Literary and Historical Essays*, edited by Eric J. Sundquist, 233–52. New York: Cambridge University Press, 1990.

Moore, Glenn. "A Civil War Feud: Jefferson Davis versus Joseph E. Johnston." *Proceedings and Papers of the Georgia Association of Historians* 14 (1993): 72–81.

Moran, Christopher S. "'The Star Spangled Banner in Triumph Shall Wave': The New York City Fire Department's Presentation Color Carried by Ellsworth's New York Zouaves, 1861." *Military Collector and Historian* 57 (Summer 2005): 58.

Morrison, Michael. "American Reaction to European Revolutions 1848–1852: Sectionalism, Memory, and the Revolutionary Heritage." *Civil War History* 49 (2003): 111–32.

Moses, Wilson J. "Where Honor Is Due: Frederick Douglass as Representative Black Man." *Prospects* 17 (October 1992): 177–89.

Myers, Cayce. "Southern Traitor or American Hero? The Representations of Robert E. Lee in the Northern Press from 1865 to 1870." *Journalism History* 41 (Winter 2016): 211–21.

Neely, Mark, Jr. "American Nationalism in the Image of Henry Clay: Abraham Lincoln's Eulogy on Henry Clay in Context." *Register of the Kentucky Historical Society* 73 (1975): 31–60.

———. "Apotheosis of a Ruffian: The Murder of Bill Pool and American Political Culture." In *New Directions in Mid-Nineteenth Century American Political History*, edited by Gary W. Gallagher and Rachel W. Shelden, 37–63. Charlottesville: University of Virginia Press, 2012.

Nolan, Alan T. "The Anatomy of the Myth." In *The Myth of the Lost Cause and Civil War History*, edited by Gary W. Gallagher and Alan T. Nolan, 11–34. Bloomington: Indiana University Press, 2000.

O'Brien, John. "Brady and Lee: 1866—The History of a Photographic Session." *Military Images* 7 (1986): 6–8.

O'Neill, Bonnie Carr. "Frederick Douglass: Celebrity, Privacy, and the Embodied Self." In *Literary Celebrity and Public Life in Nineteenth-Century United States*, 118–53. Athens: University of Georgia Press, 2017.

Paddon, Anna R., and Sally Turner. "African Americans and the World's Columbian Exposition." *Illinois Historical Journal* 88 (Spring 1995): 19–36.

Parker, Franklin. "The Funeral of George Peabody." *Essex Institute Historical Collections* 99 (1963): 67–87.

———. "George Peabody and Maryland." *Peabody Journal of Education* 37 (1959): 150–57.

———. "Robert E. Lee, George Peabody, and Sectional Reunion." *Peabody Journal of Education* 78 (2003): 91–94.

Parsons, Lynn Hudson. "The 'Splendid Pageant': Observations on the Death of John Quincy Adams." *New England Quarterly* 53 (1980): 464–5.

Paulus, Sarah Bischoff. "America's Long Eulogy for Compromise: Henry Clay and American Politics, 1854–1858." *Journal of the Civil War Era* 4 (2014): 28–52.

Phillips, Jason. "Taking Things Seriously: Death and Material Culture in Nineteenth-Century America." *Ohio Valley History* 20 (Winter 2020): 3–7.

Pluta, Anne C. "Presidential Politics on Tour: George Washington to Woodrow Wilson." *Congress and the Presidency* 41 (2014): 335–61.

Pryor, Elizabeth Brown. *Reading the Man: A Portrait of Robert E. Lee through His Private Letters*. New York: Penguin Books, 2008.

Purcell, Sarah. "All That Remains of Henry Clay: Political Funerals and the Tour of Henry Clay's Corpse." *Common-Place* 12 (April 2012). http://www.common-place.org/vol-12/no-03/purcell/.

———. "Henry Clay's Coffin: Material Culture and Politicized Mourning in 1852." *Ohio Valley History* 20 (Winter 2020): 33–45.

———. "Martyred Blood and Avenging Spirits: Revolutionary Martyrs and Heroes as Inspiration for the U.S. Civil War." In *Remembering the Revolution: Memory, History, and Nation-Making in the United States from the Revolution to the Civil War*, edited by W. Fitzhugh Brundage, Frances Clark, Claire Corbould, and Michael A. McDonnell, 280–93. Amherst: University of Massachusetts Press, 2013.

———. "Mourning Charles Sumner: The Flag Resolution and the Complications of Civil War Memory." In *Massachusetts and the Civil War: The Commonwealth and National Disunion*, edited by Matthew Mason, Katheryn P. Viens, and Conrad Edick Wright, 227–48. Boston: University of Massachusetts Press, 2015.

———. "Seeing Martyrdom: Elmer Ellsworth, James Jackson, and Revolutionary Martyrdom at the Onset of the U.S. Civil War." In *Visual Cultures—Transatlantic Perspectives*, edited by Volker Depkat, 51–67. Heidelberg: Universitätsverlag Winter, 2012.

Redfield, Marc. "Imagi-nation: The Imagined Community and the Aesthetics of Mourning." *Diacritics* 29 (1999): 58–83.

Renner, Richard Wilson. "Ye Kort Martial: A Tale of Chicago Politics, Theatre, Journalism and Militia." *Journal of the Illinois State Historical Society* 66 (1973): 376–86.

Rice, Joe M. "An Account of the Battle of Fredericksburg, 1863, Written by J. R. Williams." *North Louisiana Historical Association Journal* 17 (Winter 1986): 39–42.

Rice, Stephen P. "Picturing Bodies in the Nineteenth Century." In *A Cultural History of the Human Body in the Age of Empire*, edited by Michael Sappol and Stephen P. Rice, 5:213–35. New York: Berg/Oxford University Press, 2010.

Richenbacher, Wayne E. "The Demise of Stonewall Jackson: A Civil War Medical Case Study." *Journal of Military History* 79 (July 2015): 635–55.

Rollins, Brooke. "The Ethics of Epideictic Rhetoric: Addressing the Problem of Presence through Derrida's Funeral Orations." *Rhetoric Society Quarterly* 35 (2005): 5–23.

Ross, Michael A. "The Commemoration of Robert E. Lee's Death and the Obstruction of Reconstruction in New Orleans." *Civil War History* 51 (2005): 135–50.

Royster, Charles. "The Death of Stonewall." In *The Destructive War: William Tecumseh Sherman, Stonewall Jackson, and the Americans*, 193–231. New York: Alfred A. Knopf, 1991.

Rozear, Marvin P., et al. "R. E. Lee's Stroke." *Virginia Magazine of History and Biography* 98 (1990): 291–308.

Rozear, Marvin P., and Joseph C. Greenfield Jr. "'Let Us Cross over the River': The Final Illness of Stonewall Jackson." *Virginia Magazine of History and Biography* 103 (January 1995): 2, 29–46.

Russell, Mattie, ed. "Why Lamar Eulogized Sumner." *Journal of Southern History* 21 (1955): 374–78.

Samet, Elizabeth D. "Adding to My Book and My Coffin: The Unconditional *Memoirs* of Ulysses S. Grant." *PMLA* 115 (October: 2000): 1117–24.

Schaaf, Elizabeth. "George Peabody: His Life and Legacy, 1795–1869." *Maryland Historical Magazine* 90 (1995): 269–85.

Schmitz, Neil. "At the Stonewall Jackson Shrine." *Arizona Quarterly* 59 (Summer 2003): 5–34.

Sexton, Jay. "The Funded Loan and the *Alabama* Claims." *Diplomatic History* 27 (2003): 449–78.

Shutes, Milton H. "The Tears of Lincoln." *Pacific Historian* 14 (1970): 20–31.

Silber, Nina. "Colliding and Collaborating: Gender and Civil War Scholarship." In *Battle Scars: Gender and Sexuality in the American Civil War*, edited by Catherine Clinton and Nina Silber, 3–18. New York: Oxford University Press, 2006.

———. "Reunion and Reconciliation, Reviewed and Reconsidered." *Journal of American History* 103 (2016): 59–83.

Sinha, Manisha. "The Caning of Charles Sumner: Slavery, Race, and Ideology in the Age of the Civil War." *Journal of the Early Republic* 23 (Summer 2003): 233–62.

Soboul, Albert. "Religious Feeling and Popular Cults during the French Revolution: 'Patriot Saints' and Martyrs for Liberty." In *Saints and Their Cults*, edited by Stephen Wilson, 217–32. New York: Cambridge University Press, 1983.

Steiner, Bernard C. "Severn Teackle Wallis: First Paper." *Sewanee Review* 15 (January 1907): 58–74.

———. "Severn Teackle Wallis: Second Paper." *Sewanee Review* 15 (April 1907): 129–47.

Stow, Simon. "Agonistic Homegoing: Frederick Douglass, Joseph Lowery, and the Democratic Value of African American Public Mourning." *American Political Science Review* 104 (November 2010): 681–89.

Stowell, Daniel W. "Stonewall Jackson and the Providence of God." In *Religion and the American Civil War*, edited by Randall M. Miller, Harry S. Stout, and Charles Reagan Wilson, 187–207. New York: Oxford University Press, 1998.

Tharp, Brent W. "'Preserving Their Form and Features': The Commodification of Coffins in the American Understanding of Death." In *Commodifying Everything: Relationships of the Market*, edited by Susan Strasser, 119–42. New York: Routledge, 2003.

Thompson, Jerry. "When General Albert Sidney Johnston Came Home to Texas: Reconstruction Politics and the Reburial of a Hero." *Southwestern Historical Quarterly* 103 (2000): 452–78.

Travis, Jennifer. "Soldier's Heart: The Vocabulary of Injury and the American Civil War." In *Wounded Hearts: Masculinity, Law, and Literature in American Culture*, 23–50. Chapel Hill: University of North Carolina Press, 2005.

Vandiver, Frank E. "Introduction." In Joseph Johnston, *Narrative of Military Operations*, vii–xxxi. Reprint, Bloomington: Indiana University Press, 1959.

Vaughn, William P. "Partners in Segregation: Barnas Sears and the Peabody Fund." *Civil War History* 10 (1964): 260–74.

Welch, Allen Howard. "George Peabody's Funeral: A Tarnished Homecoming." *Essex Institute Historical Collections* 109 (1973): 116–37.

Wert, Jeffry D. "James Longstreet and the Lost Cause." In *The Myth of the Lost Cause and Civil War History*, edited by Gary W. Gallagher and Alan T. Nolan, 127–46. Bloomington: Indiana University Press, 2000.

Whitridge, Arnold. "The Alabama, 1862–64." *History Today* 5 (1955): 174–85.

Williams, Clay. "Lost Chance to Save Vicksburg." *Journal of Mississippi History* 60 (1998): 5–19.

Wilson, Charles Reagan. "The Death of Southern Heroes: Historic Funerals of the South." *Southern Cultures* 1 (Fall 1994): 3–22.

———. "Foreword." In *Vale of Tears: New Essays on Religion and Reconstruction*, edited by Edward J. Blum and W. Scott Poole, vii–x. Macon, GA: Mercer University Press, 2005.

———. "The Southern Funeral Director: Managing Death in the New South." *Georgia Historical Quarterly* 67 (1983): 49–69.

Winter, William C. "The Zouaves Take St. Louis." *Gateway Heritage* 19 (Spring 1999): 20–29.

Winterer, Caroline. "From Royal to Republican: The Classical Image in Early America." *Journal of American History* 91 (2005): 1264–90.

Wolcott, Oliver H., and Wayne C. Temple. "Col. Ellsworth Patriotic Stationery." *Lincoln Herald* 6 (1959): 136–40.

Wyatt-Brown, Bertram. "The Civil Rights Act of 1875." *Western Political Quarterly* 18 (December 1965): 769–70.

Wynes, Charles E. "John Stephens Durham, Black Philadelphian: At Home and Abroad." *Pennsylvania Magazine of History and Biography* 106 (October 1982): 527–37.

Zafar, Rafia. "Franklinian Douglass: The Afro-American as Representative Man." In *Frederick Douglass: New Literary and Historical Essays*, edited by Eric J. Sundquist, 99–117. New York: Cambridge University Press, 1990.

Theses and Dissertations

Farrell, James Joseph. "The Dying of Death: The Meaning and Management of Death in America, 1830–1920." PhD diss., University of Illinois, Urbana-Champaign, 1980.

Flood, Karen Pomeroy. "Contemplating Corpses: The Dead Body in American Culture, 1870–1920." PhD diss., Harvard University, 2001.

Johnson, Christopher Leevy. "Undertakings: The Politics of African-American Funeral Directing." PhD diss., University of South Carolina, 2004.

Tharp, Brent. "Preserving Their Form and Features: The Role of Coffins in the American Understanding of Death." PhD diss., College of William and Mary, 1996.

Websites

Architect of the Capitol, "Lying in State or in Honor." Accessed January 24, 2021. https://www.aoc.gov/nations-stage/lying-state-honor.

Edvinsson, Rodney. "Historical Currency Converter." Accessed November 2, 2016. http://www.historicalstatistics.org/Currencyconverter.html.

Green, Hilary. *Confederate Monument Removal, 2015–2020: A Mapping Project*. Accessed January 6, 2021. https://hgreen.people.ua.edu/csa-monument-mapping-project.html.

MeasuringWorth Foundation. *Measuring Worth*. Accessed February 21, 2010. http://www.measuringworth.com/ppowerus/.

Senate Historical Office and House of Representatives Historical Office. *Biographical Directory of the United States Congress*. Accessed March 10, 2016. http://bioguide.congress.gov/biosearch/biosearch.asp.

Index

Abbey, Charles E., 59
abolitionists, 20, 67, 114, 187; and Clay's funeral, 38–43; and Peabody, 97, 100. *See also* Douglass, Frederick; Sumner, Charles
Adams, Charles Wesley, 135
Adams, John Quincy, 16, 21, 27, 74, 228n22, 229n42
Adams, Julius, 30
Advance and Retreat (Hood), 162
African Americans: "Afro-American" as term for mixed race, 202; Clay's funeral and mourning, 39, 43; Douglass as symbol for, 182–83, 219; enslaved people displaced in Virginia, 77; former enslaved people, lack of rights, 109; and invasion of Alexandria, 64; Lee's funeral and mourning, 132; memory and eulogies for Sumner, 153–58, *154*; and racial uplift narrative, 178, 182–84, 194–99; in Richmond, 136; and Sumner's Civil Rights Bill, 140, 144–45, 153; Sumner's funeral and mourning, 1–2; Sumner's insistence on rights for, 142–43. *See also* Douglass, Frederick
Alabama, CSS (warship), 96, 106–7, 109, 253n51
Alexandria, Virginia, 45, 47–53, *51*, 62–65, 223; Confederate veterans' monument, 165
Allen, Kenneth, 148
American Colonization Society, 39
American Missionary magazine, 177
American Revolution/Revolutionary War, 6, 12, 58, 119–20
Annals of the War (McClure), 163
antebellum era, 29–30, 72, 190;
Anthony, Susan B., 187, 188

anticolonization activists, 41
anxiety, political, 7–8; and Clay's funeral and mourning, 4, 12–13, 17, 33–34; and Jackson's death, 84–85; military, 75
Argus newspaper (Portland, Maine), 130
Arlington House (Lee estate, Virginia), 126, 133
Army of Northern Virginia, 81, 119–20, 138
Army Register bill (flag bill), 140–41, 143–47, 150–53
Arthur, Chester, 169
Arthur, Prince, 113
Ashby, Turner, 74
Ashland (Clay's estate), 26, 39, 42–43
Asing, Norman, 40
Associated Press, 1–2, 132
Atlanta Compromise, 196
Atlanta Constitution, 128, 132, 203, 215
Atlantic Democrat, 58
Atlantic Monthly, 54, 66–67
Auld, B. F., 187
Auld, Thomas, 187
Australia, 59
Ayers, Edward, 119

Baltimore, Maryland, 22, 23, *51*, 95–96; Bloodtubs gang, 70, 72; Peabody Institute, 95, 99
Baltimore Confederate Society, 173
Baltimore Weekly Sun, 23
Baltimore World, 196
Bangor Daily Whig and Courier, 131
Banks, Louis Albert, 200
Banneker, Benjamin, 202
"Battles and Leaders" series *(Century Magazine)*, 162–63
Baxter, John, 126
Baylor, George, 128

Beauregard, P. G. T., 135
Bellanta, Melissa, 59
Benjamin, Judah P., 82
Benjamin Franklin (U.S. mail boat), 11–12, 16, 24
Benner, Henry, 32
Bigler, John, 40
Binnington, Ian, 84
Bishir, Catherine, 209
Black, William R., 119
Black Lives Matter movement, 221, 224
Blight, David, 4, 93, 128, 133; on Douglass, 157, 182, 277n49; print culture, view of, 162; white memory, view of, 64, 94, 97, 218
"Bloody Sunday" voting rights march, 221
Blue-Gray reunions, 167
Bonner, Robert E., 81
Boston, Massachusetts: Faneuil Hall, 146, 155; Peabody's funeral and mourning, 104, 107–8, 118; Sumner's funeral and mourning, 142, 146, 148–49, 152–56
Boston City Council, 146
Boston Daily Advertiser, 129–30
Boston Free Soil newspaper, 40
Boston Globe, 209
Boston Statesman and Weekly Post, 149
Boston Traveller, 118
Boutwell, George, 129
Bradford, Augustus W., 116–17
Bradlee, Caleb, 148
Bragg, Braxton, 160
Breckinridge, John C., 126
British-American relations, 95–97, 101–13; *Alabama* controversy, 106–7; naval competition, 104–11, *105*; Peabody Trust, 99–100
Brooklyn Eagle, 200
Brooks, Preston, 142, 147
Brown, Elijah S., 63
Brown, George William, 101, 260n182
Brown, John, 48, 67, 120
Brown, John C., 128
Brown, S. G., 19–20
Brown, Thomas J., 6
Brownell, Francis E., 45, 48–50, 52, 62, 70–71, *71*; Currier and Ives engraving of, 55, *56*

Buckner, Simon, 168
Bunker Hill, Battle of, 58
Burlingame, Michael, 60
Burnet, William, 125–26
Burns, Ken, 171
Butler, Benjamin, 106, 115
Butler, Clement Moore, 14, 21

Caleb Cushing (federal revenue ship), 109
Calhoun, John C., 16
California, 39–40
California State Fair, 33
Cameron, Simon, 47–48
Canada, 106
Capitol Rotunda, lying in state at: Clay, 21, 33; Douglass, motion to allow, 184–85; Lewis, 185, 221, 222; Sumner, 1–2, 145–46. *See also* lying in state
cartoons, political, 1, *2, 19,* 19–20, 144, 209
Cashin, Joan, 216
Censer, Jane Turner, 207
Centennial Exposition (Philadelphia, 1876), 158, 166
Century Magazine, 162–63
Chamberlain, Joshua, 109–12
Chandler, Thomas Coleman, 76
Charleston Courier, 27, 86, 131
Charleston Mercury, 20
Chesapeake and Ohio Railroad, 137
Chicago Daily Tribune, 147–48, 169
Chicago Republican, 130
Chicago Tribune: on Jackson, 88–89; on Peabody, 105, 107; on Sumner's flag bill, 151–52; "Winnie Davis" poem, 215, 216
Chinese immigrants, 39–40
Christian Recorder, 34
Cincinnati Daily Gazette, 11
civic culture, 28, 36, 216, 230n50
civic identity, 8, 29–30, 98, 174; African American, 184, 193; and cities, 122–24, 128, 135–39, 174; Confederate, 98, 121, 127–29, 133–39, 174, 216; rituals of, 7–8, 23–24, 29, 35–36, 108, 154, 177. *See also* national identities
civic organizations, 134
Civil Rights Bill (Sumner), 140, 144–45, 153

Civil War: beginning of, 53; casualties, 85; Ellsworth's funeral as cause of increased conflict, 49–50; mobilization, 53, 55–65, 57, 73, 93–94; naval clashes, 109; population displacement, 77, 79. *See also* memory

Civil War battles and campaigns: Antietam, 120; Appomattox Courthouse, 121; Bull Run, First Battle of, 60, 75, 160; Bull Run, Second Battle of, 75; Chancellorsville, 75–76, 79, 90, 120; Fair Oaks (Seven Pines), 160; Gettysburg, 90, 109, 111, 120, 222; Jackson, Mississippi, 160; Lee's invasion of Maryland, 75, 120; Second Manassas, 83; Seven Days Campaign, 120, 160; Seven Days' Campaign, 75; surrender at Appomattox Court House, 121, 125, 161; Valley campaign (1862), 75; Vicksburg, Mississippi, 160, 169

Civil War memory. *See* memory, Civil War

"clanking chain" trope, 41

"clasp hands" metaphor, 149, 249n3, 266n55

class, changing ideals of, 30–31

Clay, Clement Claiborne, 150

Clay, Henry: as architect of economic development, 17–18, 21; Ashland estate, 26, 39, 42–43; colonizationist views of, 42; as Great Compromiser/Pacificator, 12–14, 18, 34; oratorical skills, 19–20; photography and portraits of, *19,* 19–20, 32; physical being, attention paid to, 18–20, *19,* 22; political career, 17–18; political cartoons of, *19,* 19–20; as presidential candidate, 17, 19; as slaveholder, 17, 38

Clay, Henry, funeral and mourning of, 7, 8, 11–44, 74, 218, 222; abolitionist response to, 38–43; anxieties about union during mourning of, 4, 12–13, 17, 33–34; body of, 18–21; body on board *Benjamin Franklin,* 11–12, 16, 24; coffin, 11, 22–23, 231n67; costs of, 27–28; Currier and Ives engraving, *15*; and death of national compromise, 43–44; Douglass's view of, 42, 182; imagined community, real community, national identity, 26–29; and Independence Day celebrations, 24, 41; material culture of, 29–33; monuments to, 44, 236–37n178; and politics, 33–38; and public grief, 14–18; racial solidarity message in funeral commemorations, 39–40; tour of body, 14, 21–26, *22, 25,* 229n42; unity through, 8, 13, 23, 27, 31, 33–34, 39, 43; Whig Party's memorialization of, 35

Clay, Henry, Jr., 30

Clay, James, 26, 43

Clay, Lucretia, 23

Clay, Thomas, 23

Clay Festival Association, 24, 35, 234n118

"The Clay Statue. A Model of a Man. Designed by the Goddess of Liberty," *19, 20*

Cleveland, Grover, 168

Cleveland Plain Dealer, 40, 41

colonizationists, 39, 41–42

The Colored Orator (Holland), 201–2

Colston, Raleigh, 77

Columbia, allegorical figure of, *1, 2*

Commercial Advertiser, 115

commercialization of funerals and mourning, 11, 30, 32–33, 54, 233n89

Commerell, John Edmund, 108, 110

community: imagined, 6, 26–29, 134; real, 28–29

Compromise of 1850, 13–14, 17, 18, 33, 37; and California statehood, 40; Douglass's denunciation of, 42–43

Confederacy, 46, 48; identity, 98, 121, 127–29, 133–39, 174, 216; occupied areas, 87; public confidence, cracks in, 80; tears and future of, 84–87. *See also* Confederate armies; Confederate flag; Confederate nationalism; Davis, Varina Anne "Winnie," funeral and mourning of; Jackson, James William; Jackson, Thomas J. "Stonewall"; Johnston, Joseph E.; Lee, Robert E.; Lost Cause, Civil War

Confederate armies: Army of Northern Virginia, 81, 119–20, 138; Army of the Tennessee, 160; Department of Northern Virginia, 160

Confederate flag, 223, 224; and Ellsworth's death, 48–49, 52–55, 57, 61–63, 66; and Robert E. Lee's grave, 223; "Stainless Banner," 81; and Stonewall Jackson's death, 76, 81, 83; and Winnie Davis's death, 214, 216

Confederate Memorial Day, 91–93

Confederate Memorial Literary Society, 174, 212

Confederate Museum ("Confederate White House"), 212, 214

Confederate nationalism, 8, 46; home defense, 66–67, 81; and James Jackson's death, 61–65; in postwar context, 92–93; and Thomas "Stonewall" Jackson's death, 73–75, 80–81, 84, 87; and Thomas "Stonewall" Jackson's grave, 90–93. *See also* Lost Cause

Confederate Veteran magazine, 181, 210

Confederate "White House," 180, 212

Congress: and Clay's funeral and mourning, 27, 32, 44; and Douglass's funeral and mourning, 184–85; House of Representatives, 106; Johnston in, 161, 166; and Peabody, 100, 105; and Sumner's bills, 140, 143–44, 157; and Sumner's funeral and mourning, 145–46

consolation literature, 29

Cook, Adrian, 106

Cook, Cita, 210

Cook, Clarence, 33

Cooke, John Esten, 131, 247n207

Cooper, James, 44

Cooper Union (New York), 125, 132

Courier Journal (Louisville), 150

COVID-19 pandemic, 221

Craft, Ellen, 33

Craft, William, 33

Crews, William H., 204–5

Crittenden, John J., 44

Croffut, W. A., 162

Crystal Palace Exhibition (London, 1851), 101

Cummings, Elijah, 185

Currie, Katie Cabell, 214

Currier and Ives engravings, *15, 55, 56, 91*

Curtis, George William, 58–59, 151

Custis, George Washington Parke, 120

Dabney, Robert Lewis, 90

Daily Alabama Journal, 20

Daily Atlas (Boston), 31

Daily Evening Bulletin (San Francisco), 130

Daily Picayune, 34

Daily Whig (Richmond), 61

Davis, Jefferson, 7, 62, 79, 211; executive mansion museum, 174; funeral, 167; and Jackson's funeral, 81; Johnston, dispute with, 158, 160–62, 169; Lee as closest adviser to, 119; and Lee's memorial, 129; monument to, 224; *The Rise and Fall of the Confederate Government,* 162

Davis, Varina (wife of Jefferson Davis), 180, 210, 214, 216

Davis, Varina Anne "Winnie," funeral and mourning of, 4, 9, 178–80, 209–20, 283n163; "Angel of Grief" monument to, 216, *217,* 218, 224; contradictory elements in, 211, 219; "Daughter of the Confederacy," 180, 210–11, 216, 218; funeral route, 209–10, 212t, *213,* 218; gendered nature of, 211–12; and reconciliation, 180–81, 209–11, 214–19

death, culture of, 7, 30, 32

DeBow's Review, 70

Declaration of Independence, 42

Decoration Day, 93, 165

Democrat and Chronicle (Rochester), 206

Democratic-Republicans, western, 17

Democrats, 14, 17, 235n137; 1898 campaign, 207; Clay's funeral and mourning, 33–38, 43; clubs, 36; Douglass's funeral and mourning, 178, 183, 190, 202–7, 209; Ellsworth funeral and mourning, 58; Jackson's funeral and mourning, 89; Johnston as, 161, 166; Johnston's funeral and mourning, 161, 166, 169; Lee's funeral and mourning, 126–28, 130–31, 136; and Missouri Compromise, 33–34; Peabody's funeral and mourning, 96–97, 109–10; Sumner's funeral and mourning, 141–42, 147, 149–50

flags, 267n64; Confederate, 45, 48–50, 52–55, 57, 61–63, 66, 76, 81, 83, 158, 214, 216, 223–24; at half-staff, 52, 80, 102, 104, 129, 136, 173, 190, 212; potential divisiveness of, 152–53; Sumner's Army Register bill, 140–41, 143–47, 150–53; U.S., 129, 215, 216; on Winnie Davis's casket, 180–81. *See also* Confederate flag

floral arrangements, 31–32, 82–83, 172, 186

Floyd, George, 221–22

Foote, Henry S., 18, 107–8

forgetting, 9; African American views of, 154–55, 157; and Douglass's memorialization, 183–84; and Johnston's funeral, 159–60, 170; and Sumner, 140–44, 147, 149–51, 154–55. *See also* memory, Civil War; reunification

forgiveness: Confederate/Southern, 9, 101, 117, 149–50, 152–53; national, 97, 101, 117–18, 125, 128, 156–58, 214

Forney, John W., 88

Fort Sumter, South Carolina, 53

founders, Douglass's denunciation of, 42

Fourteenth Amendment, 109, 161

Francis Skiddy (steamboat), 52

Frankfort Commonwealth, 25–26

Frank Leslie's Illustrated Newspaper, 1, 2, 52, 108–9, 117, *154*

Freedman's Savings Bank, 183

Freedmen's Bureau, 142

Free Soil Party, 34, 40, 142

French Algerian military costume, 47

Freylinghuysen, Theodore, 34

Fugitive Slave Act (1850), 13, 33, 42, 115, 142

funerals and mourning: bridge between antebellum and Civil War era, 6, 12; bridge between Civil War era and twenty-first century, 221–24; commercialization of, 7, 30, 32–33, 70, 233n89; and Confederate present, 84; and contested meanings, 5–6, 8, 13, 64, 93–94, 180–82, 187, 195–96; floral arrangements, 31–32, 82, 83, 172, 186; forms of, 14–17; as impartial, 35; malleability of, 211, 219; military importance of, 73; modern forms of, 8, 16, 30–32; partisan, 7, 33–38, 43–44;

66, 130, 147, 176; personal and familial grief, 85–86; presidential, 7–8, 12, 16–18, 74–75, 136, 188, 190; private grief, 74, 132–35; scale of, 8, 30; technological advancement, role in, 16–17; traditional purposes of, 147; as "universal," 1, 3, 8, 13, 24, 33–34; viewing of body, importance of, *2*, 16, 21, 23, 26, 49, 52, 54, 82–83, 110, 112, *154*, 229n47. *See also* national unity; tears; *specific funerals and mourning*

Fusion Party, 204–7

Gannett, William Channing, 191–92

Gannon, Barbara, 97

Garrison, William Lloyd, 114–16, 142

General Order No. 61 (Confederate), 73, 77

gentility, 30–31

Giles, William Branch, 116

Gladstone, William, 103, 107

Gobineau, Joseph-Arthur de, 200

"good death," 20–21

Goodwin, S. A., 174

Gordon, John B., 127, 164, 180, 211

Gorman, Arthur, 184–85

Grand Army of the Republic (GAR): and Douglass's funeral, 188; and Johnston, 158, 166–67; and Sumner, 143–44; and Winnie Davis's funeral, 209–11, 219

Granite Club, 36

Grant, Julia, 216

Grant, Ulysses S., 1, 104, 120–21, 160; and *Alabama* controversy, 106; funeral and mourning of, 7–8, 167–68, 176, 188, 190; and Santo Domingo, 152, 183; Sumner's opposition to, 143, 145, 152

Greeley, Horace, 32, 96, 129, 143, 147, 149, 235n137, 249n3

Greenhalge, Frederic, 200–201

Green Mount Cemetery (Baltimore), 171, 172–73

Grimké, Francis, 198

Guthrie, James, 36

Gwynne, S. C., 74

Hacker, J. David, 6

Haentjens, Clément, 186

Haiti, 183, 186–87, 193
Hall, Newman, 102
Hampton, Wade, 127–28
Hannah, Samuel Baldwin, 83
Harmony Grove cemetery (Peabody, Massachusetts), 95, 112
Harpers Ferry, 48
Harper's Weekly, 52, 58–59, 88, 108–9, 144
Harrison, Benjamin, 161
Harrison, William Henry, 27
Hart, W. H. H., 196
Hartford Daily Courant, 63
Hawks, Wells, 128
Hay, John, 54, 66–67, 70, 72
Heard, Josephine D. H., 196
Henry, Patrick, 160
Herald (Boston), 203
Herald (Columbus, Georgia), 205
Herald (New York), 67
Herndon, William, 47
Hettle, Wallace, 90
Hill, A. P., 76
Hilliard, Henry W., 43
Holland, F. M., 280n111
Holland, Frederic May, 201–2
Hollywood Cemetery (Richmond, Virginia), 91, 137–38, 159, 174; Winnie Davis buried at, 180, 212, 214, 216, 224
Hollywood Memorial Association, 91, 137–38, 174, 212
Holmes, Thomas, 54
home, defense of, 66–67, 81
Hood, John Bell, 160, 162, 245n152
Hooker, Joseph, 76
House, Edward H., 62
Howard, Oliver Otis, 171, 172
Howard University, 183, 186, 196
Hunt, Henry Jackson, 169
Hutchinson, John, 188
Hutchinson Family Singers, 188

iconography, 31
identity. *See* civic identity; Lost Cause; national identities; Union Cause
Illinois State Journal, 55
Illustrated News (New York), 49–50, 50

illustrated news weeklies, 52, 110. See also *Frank Leslie's Illustrated Newspaper*; *Harper's Weekly*
imagined community, 6, 13, 26–29, 134
imagined reconstitution of nation, 3–6, 8–9, 64, 98, 141, 176, 178, 181, 183
Imboden, John D., 125
immortelle (flower), 31–32, 172
Independence Day, 24, 41
Independent (New York), 67–68, 114–15
Indiana State Fair, 32–33
Inter-Ocean (Chicago), 1, 148

Jackson, Andrew, 27, 28, 75
Jackson, Eleanor Junkin, 75, 84
Jackson, James William, 45, 48–49; Currier and Ives engraving of, 55, *56*; funeral and mourning of, 49, 52–53, 61–67, 81; as hero, 65–66; as hero and traitor, 59–61; as martyr, 49, 52, 53, 61–67, 243n120; as secessionist, 61–62
Jackson, Mary Anna Morrison, 75, 76, 80, 82–83, 133
Jackson, Thomas J. "Stonewall": career of, 75–76; death of, 72, 75–77; mythology of, 73–74, 84; religiosity of, 75, 76, 81, 84, 88
Jackson, Thomas J. "Stonewall," funeral and mourning of, 8, 44, 46–47, 72–93, 218; as Confederate martyr, 46, 76–77, 90; constraints on arrangements, 77–80; grave of as Confederate memorial, 90–93, *91*; in Lexington, 75–77, *78*, 83–85, 90–92, 123; military consequences of death, 73–75; and mobilization, 73, 84–87; monuments to, 165, 223, 224; and Richmond, 77–86, *78*, 90–91; tears shed and sense of resolve, 85–86; tour of body, *78*, 80–85; Union response to death of, 88–90
Janney, Caroline, 97, 138, 164
Jenifer, J. G., 187
Johnson, Andrew, 101, 121, 142
Johnson, Bradley T., 172
Johnson, Reverdy, 128
Johnston, Albert Sidney, 261n186
Johnston, George, 171

Massachusetts: and Army Register bill, 140–41, 143–47, 150–53; Grand Army of the Republic (GAR), 143–44
Massachusetts Historical Society, 148–49
Masur, Kate, 186
material culture, 3, 29–33, 57, 59, 77; coffins, 11, 231n67; floral arrangements, 31–32, 82–83, 172, 186; hearses, 30–31. *See also* flags; monuments; *specific cemeteries*
Mayo, Joseph, 79
McCabe, James Dabney, 87
McCarthy, Carlton, 136
McClellan, George B., 89, 120, 160, 168
McClure, Alexander K., 163
McGuire, Judith W., 79–80, 84
McIvor, David, 5
McKinney, Philip W., 172
McLane, James L., 174
McLane, Robert, 171
McNeilly, James Hugh, 214
McPherson, James, 58
Meier, Kathryn Shively, 85
memorabilia, 29, 32, 57, 59. *See also* relics
Memorial Day, 92–93, 159, 165
memory, Civil War: African American, 153–58, *154*; emancipationist, 3, 9, 178, 193, 196, 250n7; as guide to present-day action, 197–98; imagined reconstitution of nation, 3–6, 8–9, 58, 64, 98, 141, 176, 178, 181, 183; lack of control over, 9, 122, 141–42, 164, 170, 173–76; military, 46, 134, 140–41, 151, 157; and mobilization, 53, 55–65, *56*, *57*, 73, 93–94; national identity as a product of Civil War, 98; political vs. military, 142–43, 157; presidential, 188; and print culture, 161–62, 174–75; pro-Democratic political strategy, 205; racialized, 181; reconciliationist, 4, 9, 43, 98, 118, 128, 150–51, 162, 164, 167, 170, 178; rival themes of, 4–5, 8; and sacrifice, 53, 93–94, 118, 218; silencing of, 9, 250n7; and Southern civic identity, 135–36; Sumner's move against, 140–41; transatlantic, 101, 108–13, *111*; triumphalist, 38; visual, 55; white supremacist, 4, 9, 178, 181–82, 199–204, 219–20; women's role

in, 60, 133, 211–12. *See also* forgetting; Lost Cause
Memphis Commercial, 202
Metropolitan African Methodist Episcopal (AME) church (Washington, D. C.), 177, 186, 187–88, 224
Mexican-American War, 30, 33, 120, 160; Buena Vista, Battle of, 30
Miantonomoh, USS, 110
military memory, 46, 134, 140–41, 151, 157
Miller, Brian Craig, 118
Miller, Elvira Sydnor, 181
Minkins, Shadrach, 33
Minneapolis Tribune, 202
Monarch, HMS (warship), 95, 104–13, *105*
Monroe, James, 27, 28, 91
monuments, 3; to African American Civil War soldiers and sailors, 192; to Clay, 44; Confederate, 44, 136–37, 159, 165–66, 207–9, *208,* 223; dedications, 165; to Douglass, 177, 192–95, *194,* 199, 223–24; to emancipation, 193; to Jackson, 165, 223, 224; to Jefferson Davis, 224; to Lee, 122, *123,* 138–39, 165–66; to Peabody, 95, 112; to Robert Gould Shaw, 155; to Shaw, 155; to Washington, 81, 95; to Winnie Davis ("Angel of Grief"), 216, *217,* 218, 224
Morgan, John Hunt, 44
Morgan, John T., 127
Morgan, J. S., 99
Morgan, Matt, 1, *2*
Morning Sentinel (Milwaukee), 59–60
Mother Emanuel AME Church (Charleston, South Carolina), 223
Mount Hope Cemetery (Rochester, New York), 177, 190, 192, 223
mourning culture, 30–32, 59, 97. *See also* funerals and mourning
Murray, George Washington, 184, 187

Narrative of Military Operations Directed during the Late War between the States (Johnston), 158, 161–62
Nassau Literary Magazine, 88
Nast, Thomas, 144

Wells, Ida B., 183, 193, 195

Westminster Abbey, 102–4, *103*

"What, to the Slave, Is the Fourth of July?" (Douglass), 41–42

Wheeler, Joseph, 173

Wheeler, Samuel W., 41

Whigs, 11, 13–14; Clay as presidential candidate, 19; Clay's funeral and mourning, 28, 32–38, 41, 43–44, 234n118; and commercialism, 32–33; Ellsworth's funeral and mourning, 66, 70; fracturing of, 17, 33; James Jackson's funeral and mourning, 61, 65–66; Lee's funeral and mourning, 131, 136–37; and Missouri Compromise, 33–34; state conventions, 35; Sumner as, 142

White, Hugh, 83

White, William S., 83

white supremacy, 4–5, 9, 80–81, 178, 181–82, 199–204, 219–20; in twenty-first century, 222–24

Whitman, Walt, 69

Whittier, John Greenleaf, 144, 147

Whittington, Henry B., 52–53

Wickham, W. H., 51–52

Wickham, Williams Carter, 137

Williams, Ralph, 222

Wilson, Henry, 45

Winthrop, Robert C., 100, 110–11, 114, 118, 148–49

women: Ladies' Memorial Associations, 91–93, 133, 137–38, 174, 207, 212; memory, role in, 60, 133, 211–12; mythic protection of Southern, 132; and revenge, 60–61; and Richmond bread riot, 79, 80. *See also* Davis, Varina Anne "Winnie," funeral and mourning of

Woods, Michael E., 61

World's Columbian Exposition (1893), 183

Wright, A. R., 127

Zolnay, George Julian, 216

Zouaves. *See* Eleventh New York (Ellsworth's Fire Zouaves)